THE PUEBLO INDIAN REVOLT OF 1696

D0078084

THE PUEBLO INDIAN REVOLT OF 1696 AND THE FRANCISCAN MISSIONS IN NEW MEXICO

Letters of the Missionaries and Related Documents

Translated, Edited, and with an Introduction by

J. MANUEL ESPINOSA

UNIVERSITY OF OKLAHOMA PRESS : NORMAN AND LONDON

BY J. MANUEL ESPINOSA

Spanish Folk Tales from New Mexico (New York, 1937, 1977)

First Expedition of Vargas into New Mexico, 1692 (trans.) (Albuquerque, 1940)

Crusaders of the Rio Grande (Chicago, 1942)

The Folklore of Spain in the American Southwest: Traditional Spanish Folk Literature in Northern New Mexico and Southern Colorado (ed.) (Norman, 1985)

The Pueblo Indian Revolt of 1696 and the Franciscan Missions in New Mexico: Letters of the Missionaries and Related Documents (trans. and ed.) (Norman, 1988)

Library of Congress Cataloging-in-Publication Data

The Pueblo Indian revolt of 1696 and the Franciscan missions in New
    Mexico : letters of the missionaries and related documents/
    translated, edited, and with an introduction by J. Manuel Espinosa.
    —1st ed.
        p.   cm.
    Bibliography: p.
    Includes index.
    ISBN 0–8061–2139–4 (cloth)
    1. Pueblo Revolt, 1860—Sources.   2. Pueblo Indians—History—
Sources.   3. Franciscans—Missions—History—17th Century—Sources.
4. New Mexico—History—To 1848—Sources.   5. Indians of North
America—New Mexico—History—Sources.   6. Pueblo Indians—Missions.
7. Indians of North America—New Mexico—Missions.   I. Espinosa, J.
Manuel (José Manuel), 1909–
E99.P9P86   1988
978.9'02—dc19   88-10022
ISBN: 0–8061–2365–6 (pbk.)

The paper in this book meets the guidelines for permanence and durability of the Committee on Production Guidelines for Book Longevity of the Council on Library Resources, Inc.

To
Betty, Joe, Ray, John, and Tom

CONTENTS

Preface   *Page*   xv

Historical Introduction   3

Letters and Documents   59

PART ONE

Governor Vargas's Expedition of 1692 to Reconquer New Mexico: Repossession of the Missions by the Franciscans

1. Governor Vargas grants repossession of religious authority at Santa Fe to the Franciscans, Santa Fe, September 14, 1692   63

2. Governor Vargas grants repossession of religious authority over the missions of Acoma, Zuñi, and Moqui to the Franciscans, site of Doñana, December 18, 1692   66

PART TWO

The Reconquest and Resettlement of New Mexico, 1693–94: Pueblo Indian Resistance Delays the Reestablishment of the Missions

3. Letter of Fray Salvador de San Antonio to Governor Vargas, encampment at the foot of the mountains near Santa Fe, December 18, 1693   71

4. *Auto* of Governor Vargas, military camp outside Santa Fe, December 18, 1693   72

5. Governor Vargas's journal, military camp outside Santa Fe, December 27, 1693   73

6. Petition of Fray Salvador de San Antonio to Governor Vargas, Santa Fe, March 20, 1694   74

7. *Auto* of Governor Vargas, Santa Fe, March 20, 1694   79

8. Petition of Fray Salvador de San Antonio to Governor Vargas, Santa Fe, March 24, 1694   80

9. *Auto* of Governor Vargas, Santa Fe, March 31, 1694   81

10. Statement of the missionaries of the custody of New Mexico indicating their readiness to take up residence among the pacified Tewa and Tano Indians, Santa Fe, September 22, 1694   86

PART THREE

Reestablishment of the Franciscan Missions, 1694–95

11. Extracts from Governor Vargas's journal on the reestablishment

of the missions, September 18–October 7 and November 1–
December 21, 1694   91

12. *Carta patente* of Fray Francisco de Vargas to each of the missionaries, Santa Fe, December 20, 1694   113

13. Letter of Fray José Diez, Tesuque, December 22, 1694   115

14. Letter of Fray Antonio Carbonel (Carboneli), Cochití, December
26, 1694   117

15. Letter of Fray Gerónimo Prieto, San Juan, December 26, 1694   118

16. Letter of Fray Francisco Corbera, San Ildefonso, December 27,
1694   121

17. Letter of Fray Miguel de Trizio, Santo Domingo, December 27,
1694   128

18. Letter of Fray Juan Alpuente, Zia and Santa Ana, December 28,
1694   129

19. Letter of Fray Diego Zeinos, Pecos, December 28, 1694   132

20. Letter of Fray Juan Antonio del Corral, San Felipe, December
30, 1694   133

21. Letter of Fray José García Marín, Santa Clara, December 31,
1694   135

22. Letter of Fray Juan Muñoz de Castro, Santa Fe, January 4, 1695   142

23. Governor Vargas to the viceroy, letter of transmission, Santa Fe,
January 10, 1695   146

PART FOUR

Warnings by the Franciscan Missionaries to Governor Vargas of Secret Plans by
Pueblo Indian Leaders for a General Revolt, December 13–20, 1695

24. Opinion of the *definitorio* of the Franciscan community, Santa Fe,
December 13, 1695   155

25. *Carta patente* of Fray Francisco de Vargas, Santa Fe, December
18, 1695   156

26. Replies of the missionaries to the *carta patente* of Fray Francisco de
Vargas, December 20, 1695   158

27. Letter of Fray Francisco Corbera, San Ildefonso, December 20,
1695   158

PART FIVE

Repeated Warnings and Pleas to Governor Vargas for Military Protection of
the Missions, March 7–April 21, 1696

28. Petition of Fray Francisco de Vargas and the *definitorio* to Governor Vargas, Santa Fe, March 7, 1697   163

29. *Auto* of Governor Vargas, Santa Fe, March 8, 1696   165
30. *Carta patente* of Fray Francisco de Vargas, Santa Fe, March 9, 1696   168
31. Letter of Fray José Arbizu, San Cristóbal, March 9, 1696   170
32. Letter of Fray Juan de Zavaleta, Santa Fe, March 9, 1696   172
33. Letter of Fray Juan Alpuente, Pecos, March 9, 1696   172
34. Letter of Fray Alfonso Jiménez de Cisneros, Cochití, March 9, 1696   173
35. Letter of Fray Blas Navarro, Picurís, March 9, 1696   173
36. Letter of Fray José García Marín, Santa Clara, March 9, 1696   174
37. Letter of Fray José Diez, Tesuque, March 9, 1696   174
38. Note of Fray Diego de Ramírez, Bernalillo [ca. March 9, 1696]   176
39. Letter of Fray Diego de Chavarría, Taos, March 9, 1696   176
40. Letter of Fray José Arbizu, San Cristóbal, March 10, 1696   177
41. Letter of Fray Gerónimo Prieto, San Juan, March 10, 1696   179
42. Letter of Fray Francisco Corbera, San Ildefonso, March 10, 1696   181
43. Letter of Fray Antonio Carbonel, Nambé, March 10, 1696   183
44. Letter of Fray Pedro de Matha, Zia, March 10, 1696   183
45. Letter of Fray Francisco de Jesús María Casañas, San Diego del Monte de Jémez [ca. March 10, 1696]   183
46. Letter of Fray Miguel Trizio, San Juan de los Jémez, March 11, 1696   184
47. Petition of Fray Francisco de Vargas to Governor Vargas, Santa Fe, March 13, 1696   184
48. *Auto* of Governor Vargas, Santa Fe, March 15, 1696   186
49. *Carta patente* of Fray Francisco de Vargas to all the missionaries, Santa Fe, March 16, 1696   190
50. *Carta patente* of Fray Francisco de Vargas to the missionaries of the Jémez and Keres pueblos, Santa Fe, March 16, 1696   192
51. Letter of Fray Juan de Zavaleta, Santa Fe, March 16, 1696   195
52. Letter of Fray Diego de Chavarría, Santa Fe, March 16, 1696   195
53. Letter of Fray Blas Navarro, Santa Fe, March 16, 1696   196
54. Letter of Fray José Diez, Santa Fe, March 16, 1696   196
55. Letter of Fray Juan Alpuente, Santa Fe, March 16, 1696   197
56. Letter of Fray Antonio Carbonel [Santa Cruz], March 21, 1696   197
57. Letter of Fray Miguel Trizio, Bernalillo, March 18, 1696   198
58. Letter of Fray Alfonso Jiménez de Cisneros, Bernalillo, March 18, 1696   198
59. Letter of Fray Pedro de Matha, Bernalillo, March 19, 1696   199
60. Letter of Fray Francisco de Jesús María Casañas [Bernalillo, ca. March 19, 1696]   200

61. Letter of Fray José Arbizu, Santa Cruz, March 17, 1696   200
62. Letter of Fray José García Marín, Santa Cruz, March 18, 1696   201
63. Letter of Fray Francisco Corbera, Santa Cruz, March 18, 1696   202
64. Letter of Fray Gerónimo Prieto [Santa Cruz, ca. March 18, 1696]   202
65. Decision of the *definitorio,* Santa Fe, March 22, 1696   203
66. Petition of Fray Francisco de Vargas and the *definitorio* to Gover-
    nor Vargas, Santa Fe, March 22, 1696   204
67. *Auto* of Governor Vargas, Santa Fe, March 22, 1696   208
68. *Carta patente* of Fray Francisco de Vargas, Santa Fe, March 26,
    1696   213
69. Letter of Fray José Diez, San Diego de Tesuque, March 29, 1696   216
70. Letter of Fray Antonio Carbonel, Nambé, March 31, 1696   219
71. Letter of Fray José Arbizu, Santa Fe, April 2, 1696   223
72. Letter of Fray Gerónimo Prieto, Santa Cruz, April 2, 1696   224
73. Letter of Fray José García Marín, Santa Cruz, April 2, 1696   224
74. Letter of Fray Miguel Trizio, Bernalillo, April 17, 1696   225
75. Letter of Fray Pedro de Matha, Zia, April 17, 1696   227
76. Letter of Fray Francisco de Jesús María Casañas, Bernalillo, April
    18, 1696   228
77. Letter of Fray José Arbizu, Santa Cruz, April 18, 1696   230
78. Letter of Fray Alfonso Jiménez de Cisneros, Cochití, April 21,
    1696   232
79. Letter of Fray Francisco de Vargas to the father commissary gen-
    eral, Santa Ana, May 17, 1696   234

PART SIX

The Pueblo Indian Revolt of 1696

80. Letter of Fray Alfonso Jiménez de Cisneros to Governor Vargas,
    San Felipe, June 4, 1696   239
81. Letter of Governor Vargas to Fray Francisco de Vargas, Santa Fe,
    June 9, 1696   239
82. Letter of Bartolomé de Ojeda, Indian governor of the pueblo of
    Santa Ana, to Fray Francisco de Vargas, Santa Ana [June 10,
    1696]   240
83. Viceregal order to Fray Francisco de Vargas, Mexico City, July 4,
    1696   241
84. *Carta patente* of the commissary general to the missionaries in
    New Mexico, Querétaro, July 19, 1696   242
85. Letter of Fray Francisco de Vargas to the commissary general,
    Santa Fe, July 21, 1696   243

86. Letter of Fray Francisco de Vargas to the father guardian at El
    Paso, Santa Fe, July 21, 1696   246
87. Letter of Fray Francisco de Vargas to the provincial, Santa Fe,
    July 21, 1696   249
88. Governor Vargas to the viceroy, letter of transmission of *autos* and
    reports, June–July, Santa Fe, July 31, 1696   257

PART SEVEN

The Restoration and Expansion of the Franciscan Missions Following the Suppression of the Pueblo Revolt, 1696–97

89. Letter of Fray Francisco de Vargas to Governor Vargas, Santa Fe,
    November 23, 1696   283
90. *Auto* of Governor Vargas, Santa Fe, November 23, 1696   284
91. Letter of Fray Francisco de Vargas to the viceroy, Santa Fe, No-
    vember 28, 1696   289
92. List of missionaries needed in New Mexico, accompaniment to
    Fray Francisco de Vargas's letter to the viceroy, Santa Fe, Novem-
    ber 28, 1696   291
93. Letter of Governor Vargas to the viceroy, Santa Fe, November
    28, 1696   292
94. Order of the viceroy to the commissary general, to send eight
    additional missionaries to New Mexico, Mexico City, April 3,
    1697   294
Bibliography   297
Index   307

ILLUSTRATIONS

Canyon scene, northern New Mexico   12
The church at San Ildefonso Pueblo, 1899   18
Sculpture of Saint Francis   26
The church at Santo Domingo Pueblo, 1899   35
The church at Cochití Pueblo, 1906   38
The church at Santa Ana Pueblo, 1899   45
The church at Zuñi Pueblo, 1879   52
Pueblo Indian man, 1902   56

MAP

Missions and Towns in Northern New Mexico in 1695   6

PREFACE

THE Franciscan letters and related documents published in this volume in English for the first time describe in detail the critical Pueblo Indian revolt of 1696 in New Mexico as related by the missionaries at the pueblo missions where they lived side-by-side with their Indian charges: the prelude to the revolt, the warnings by the missionaries of impending revolt, the bloody revolt, its suppression, and the subsequent reestablishment of the missions. The quelling of the Pueblo Indian revolt of 1696 by the Spaniards and their Indian allies was a crucial turning point in the history of the region.

New Mexico had been founded and settled as a Spanish colony in 1598, and the early decades of the seventeenth century witnessed a period of phenomenal success by the Franciscan missionaries sent there. Toward the middle of the century, however, oppressive treatment of the Indians by unscrupulous Spanish governors, compounded by economic hardships, weakened respect for all Spanish authority and led to constant hostile acts and plotting by rebellious Pueblo Indian leaders. In 1680 a secretly planned and well-executed general Pueblo Indian revolt took place, and the Spaniards who survived the bloody massacre fled southward to El Paso del Río del Norte. For twelve years the Indians held New Mexico as their own, and virtually every vestige of Spanish religious worship (with the dramatic exception at Zuñi, referred to below) was systematically destroyed. In 1692, Governor Diego de Vargas led a military expedition into New Mexico that met virtually no resistance, convincing him that he could return and reconquer the region for Spain. The following year he returned with a small but well-equipped army, a band of Franciscan missionaries, and over one thousand colonists, and after a bloody battle at Santa Fe the region appeared to be restored to Spanish rule. But hostile Pueblo Indian leaders, recalling their decisive victory in 1680, plotted secretly and awaited another opportunity. In the spring of 1696 they believed that the opportunity was at hand. The revolt erupted on June 4 of that year with the murder of five Franciscan missionaries and more than a score of residents at the missions. This time the rebellion lacked unified leadership, reflecting the factional differences that had developed among the key Pueblo Indian leaders since their successful revolt of 1680, and after a bloody six months' war of attrition, peace was restored, the Indians returned to their abandoned pueblos from the mesas and mountains to which they had withdrawn, and the missions were gradually reestablished.

The documents translated in this volume illustrate dramatically the difficult role of the Franciscan missionaries, as preachers of the Gospel of Christ, frontline emissaries of peace, and brave frontiersmen, in the conduct of

Spanish-Indian relations in New Mexico in the colonial period. The conflict between the teachings of the Franciscan missionaries and those of the Pueblo Indian medicine men, the feared and respected protectors and custodians of the secrets of their ancient worship of the gods of the powers of nature, whose teachings were ever present in the hearts and minds of the Indians, is vividly illustrated in these letters of the Franciscan missionaries. This struggle for the minds and souls of the Pueblo Indian people was a powerful underlying force in shaping the destiny of this isolated frontier outpost on Spanish North America's vast and precarious "rim of Christendom." The documents describe the tireless efforts of the missionaries at their missions and the real hardships they suffered, providing a candid, first-hand view of their successes and failures in converting the Pueblo Indians to the Christian way of life, and of the New Mexican scene in general as they viewed it during those years. In addition, the documents show the importance of the missions as peace-keeping defensive outposts and of the role of the missionaries as the agents of peaceful diplomacy for the civil authorities.

The remodeled adobe Franciscan mission churches of New Mexico as seen today, originally built by the missionaries and the Christianized mission Indians, evoke a serene and pastoral era of romance, for the old mission churches were and are, in their simple beauty, a wondrous expression of Spain's Christian spirit of that era and of the zeal and dedication of the missionaries. Eleanor B. Adams aptly reminds us, however, of the human side of the story, so vividly portrayed in the documents translated in the following pages, when she writes, "Those who have leafed through the thousands of dusty folios preserved in the archives and libraries of Spain and Mexico cannot feel that romantic idealization of a very human history is either necessary or advisable." There is, indeed, a tendency on the part of many popular writers to minimize the daily perils and struggles for survival on this remote and hostile frontier as it existed some three hundred years ago—conditions "which often brought out the worst in men, and could also inspire the loftiest and most unselfish efforts." [1]

Of the more than ninety documents in English translation included in this volume, over 75 percent deal specifically with the Pueblo Indian revolt of 1696 and the events surrounding it. They reveal for the first time in print, as recorded in the original documents themselves, the stark realities of those perilous and dramatic days when the future of New Mexico hung in the balance and when its history might have been quite different had the rebel Pueblo Indian chieftains and medicine men won the day. They include the letters of Fray Francisco de Vargas, the custodian, to his missionary companions; the letters

---

1 Eleanor B. Adams, *Bishop Tamarón's Visitation of New Mexico, 1760*, 22–23.

of the missionaries written to him in reply; the exchange of correspondence, and clash in views, between Fray Francisco de Vargas and the governor, Don Diégo de Vargas; reports and correspondence to and from superior authorities in Mexico City and Querétaro; and other closely related documents.

To place the story of the Pueblo Indian revolt of 1696 in perspective within the reconquest period, I have included translations of selected documents for the years immediately preceding and following the revolt. Those for the year 1692 record the reestablishment of jurisdiction over the abandoned Pueblo missions by the three Franciscan chaplains who accompanied Governor Vargas on his first expedition to reconquer New Mexico, which met no Pueblo Indian resistance, in the summer and fall of that year. Those for 1693–94 relate to Vargas's colonizing expedition in the fall of 1693, which met resistance at Santa Fe, and the discouraging wait by the missionaries to be assigned to their designated missions; the victory by the Spaniards; and the eventual assignment of the missionaries to some of the missions ten months later in the fall of 1694. The documents for the last six months of 1696 and for 1697 include the custodian's letters and reports to superiors in New Spain describing the tragic results of the revolt for the missions, the orders and decrees sent by them in reply granting assistance to the missions, and correspondence of Governor Vargas to the viceroy on the subject.

The bulk of the translations have been made from photostatic facsimiles of the original documents in the Biblioteca Nacional de México, Mexico City, and the Archivo General de Indias, Seville, Spain. The Franciscan documents in the Biblioteca Nacional are remnants of the archive of the Convento Grande de San Francisco de México. The photostats I used are those preserved in the Manuscripts Division of the Library of Congress, Washington, D.C. Those from Mexico were made for the Library of Congress under the direction of France V. Scholes, and those from Spain were made under the direction of Roscoe R. Hill and Lansing B. Bloom. A few of the translations are from Vargas's original journals preserved in the Spanish Archives of New Mexico, Santa Fe, New Mexico; from sections of Vargas's journals which found their way to the Huntington Library, San Marino, California, as a part of the Ritch Collection; from transcripts of sections of Vargas's journal from the Archivo General de la Nación, Mexico City, and in the Bolton Collection of the Bancroft Library, Berkeley, California; from photostats of contemporary copies of Vargas's journals from the Archivo General de Indias in the Manuscripts Division of the Library of Congress; and from photostats of documents from the Archives of the Archdiocese of Santa Fe, Albuquerque, New Mexico.

The original Franciscan letters and reports for the period preserved in the Biblioteca Nacional de México were translated by me from photostats of the original letters and reports written and signed in the handwriting of the

Franciscan friars who wrote them in New Mexico. In view of the idiosyncracies of their penmanship, spelling, abbreviations, flourishes, and individual style, the textual reading of these letters was itself a fascinating adventure. Available contemporary handwritten copies of some of the originals, written for official purposes in New Spain, also preserved in the Biblioteca Nacional, were useful to me in filling in a few damaged spots in the original documents.

In translating the documents, for which I alone assume responsibility, I have attempted to establish a degree of consistency and clarity. When proper names appear, sometimes in a variety of alternate spellings, I have used wherever possible the accepted modern spelling. Abbreviations which would be awkward or unclear in translation are spelled out in full in the English translation. Since the documents have very little or no punctuation at all in most cases, I felt justified in bringing some order out of chaos while attempting to retain the flavor of the original writings. Spanish words common in English usage, such as cabildo, plaza, patio, presidio, sierra, mesa, tortilla, and the like, have been retained without change or explanation.

In the development of this study I wish to acknowledge my indebtedness to Dr. Herbert E. Bolton, the inspiring pioneer of Spanish Borderlands studies, who introduced me, when I was one of his graduate students at the University of California, Berkeley, to the rich mine of original documents on the Vargas period in New Mexico history that he had uncovered in Mexican archives, documents that no American historian had previously investigated, and which he encouraged me to explore. I also wish to express special appreciation to Dr. France V. Scholes, on the faculty of the University of New Mexico at the time, who assisted me in my study of Franciscan documents relating to seventeenth-century New Mexico from the archives of Mexico, a subject on which his knowledge was unequaled. Others who were helpful include Dr. Ignacio Rubio Mañé of the Archivo General, Mexico City; Dr. John L. Kessell, University of New Mexico; and members of the staffs of the Manuscripts Division, Library of Congress, Washington, D.C.; the Coronado Collection, University of New Mexico Library, Albuquerque; the Ayer Collection, Newberry Library, Chicago; the Rich Collection, Huntington Library, San Marino; and the State Records Center and Archives, Santa Fe.

J. MANUEL ESPINOSA

Washington, D.C.

THE PUEBLO INDIAN REVOLT OF 1696

Rarely does one see them {the Pueblo Indians} traveling, one or two by themselves, even though the journey might be a long one, when they are not singing all the way about the happy or sad events of war and peace and other things that happened to their elders which they enjoyed when they were free, from which it is clear that their desire to return to their former freedom is ever present.

—Juan de Villagutierre y Sotomayor, *relator* of the Council of the Indies, Madrid, Spain, "Historia de la conquista, Pérdida y restauración de . . . la Nueva México . . . ," MS written about 1703.

HISTORICAL INTRODUCTION

THE Pueblo Indian revolt in New Mexico in 1696 was the last serious effort by the Pueblo Indian medicine men and war chiefs, and their embattled warriors, to drive out the Spaniards. The Spanish victory was the final stage in securing the reconquest and the permanence of the Spanish settlements in northern New Mexico. It was also the ending of an era and the beginning of another. In the eighteenth century the Franciscan missions were no longer at the center of Indian policy. In a new era of secularism, frontier defense focused more on new policies for dealing with the destructive inroads of the outlying tribes of Apaches, Navajos, Utes, and Comanches.

Isolated from the urban influences of the large cultural centers far to the south, the Hispanic people managed to survive in a barren and impoverished land that provided a meager existence. They developed a remarkable degree of self-sufficiency and remained in many respects close to the spirit of sixteenth- and seventeenth-century Spain. Those centuries were Spain's Golden Age of civilization—in art, literature, architecture, science, and the humanities. It was an era in which Catholic religious unity, in thought and action, pervaded Hispanic society at all levels. The Spanish crown and the Catholic church were all-powerful in Spain. These influences and forces of unity dominated the cultural and political direction of Spain's empire in America for over two centuries and were reflected on the most remote frontiers of settlement.

In New Mexico, from the beginning and throughout nearly the entire colonial period, the missionaries were all Franciscan friars. They found a large number of Indian nations whose people resided in permanent villages, or pueblos, which became the nuclei of Franciscan Indian missions, in the midst of which the Spanish settlements were planted. But the task of the missionaries to Christianize the natives, which was their primary goal, was never finished, because the Pueblo Indians were strongly wedded to their religious beliefs, based on the mysterious powers of nature, which dominated every aspect of their lives. Although outwardly they appeared to accept the Christian teachings of the Spanish missionaries, inwardly they clung to the religion of their ancestors, influenced by their medicine men, the chosen protectors of their ancient beliefs and rites. The key protagonists in this clash of civilizations, therefore, were the Pueblo Indian priests and "sorcerers," the zealous protectors of their religion, supported by loyal war chiefs and warriors, and the Franciscan missionaries, who preached the gospel of Christ, protected by Spanish arms.

To understand the reasons for the Pueblo Indian revolt of 1696, which was preceded by the more devastating one of 1680, it is necessary to recognize the

3

basic clash of religious beliefs that occurred with the zealous efforts of the missionaries to stamp out the old Indian religious practices—"idolatry," "witchcraft," "the work of the devil." Other factors—subjection to Spanish government rule, economic exploitation, the meager resources of the land for
subsistence, the severe droughts and starving times, and the bad example of
some of the Spanish civil authorities—compounded the problem and led to
distrust, suspicion, and conflict. The Pueblo Indian leaders blamed the Spaniards and the new religion they brought with them for the severe droughts and
bitter winters that visited the region, which appeared to them to be more frequent than usual in the last half of the seventeenth century. Governor Diego de
Vargas, in recording one of his harangues directed to a band of Pueblo Indian
rebels in 1694, wrote: "They answered with a thousand blasphemies . . .
among the diabolical reasons they gave, one was that their god, the devil, provided them with food and enabled them to have an abundance of corn." [1]

The Discovery and Conquest of New Mexico

New Mexico was discovered by Spaniards more or less by accident fewer than
twenty years after the conquest of Mexico by Hernán Cortéz, and in his genera-
tion. In 1528 an expedition of five ships, following an unsuccessful voyage
from the West Indies to Florida, was shipwrecked on the coast of the Gulf of
Mexico. Four bedraggled survivors, led by Alvar Núñez Cabeza de Vaca, wan-
dered for eight years through what is now Texas and the southern fringe of
New Mexico and Arizona. In 1536 they reached the northern frontier of New
Spain and were escorted to Mexico City to report their experiences. To quote
Herbert E. Bolton, "These four castaways were the real great European pio-
neers of the great Southwest. First to see New Mexico and Arizona, they fur-
nished the immediate cause of the discovery and conquest of the Pueblo
Indians." [2]

In Mexico City, Cabeza de Vaca reported that he had met Indians who told
him there were cities in the north inhabited by thousands of Indians who had
great wealth and lived in large, many-storied houses—"another Mexico." The
viceroy followed up on this information, and in 1539 Fray Marcos de Niza was
chosen to lead a small exploratory expedition into New Mexico. The information he brought back kept the illusion alive that there were fabulous cities of
great wealth in the Pueblo Indian country. In 1540 the viceroy dispatched to
the region a full-scale expedition led by Francisco Vásquez de Coronado. Five

---

1. Vargas's journal, March 8, 1694, AGN, *Historia*, tomo 39. See Bibliography for list of abbreviations
used in the notes.
2. Herbert E. Bolton, *Coronado, Knight of Pueblos and Plains*, 10.

Franciscan missionaries accompanied the expedition. After establishing his base in the center of the Pueblo Indian country, Coronado and his men traveled great distances into the surrounding area, but none of the reported fabulous cities and great wealth were found. After two years of fruitless effort the *conquistador* and his followers returned to New Spain. Although the purpose of the expedition was not accomplished, in the course of their explorations Coronado and his companion were the first Europeans to traverse the vast area between Kansas and northern Arizona.[3]

It was forty years before the next expedition into New Mexico was organized. As the frontier of New Spain advanced northward, interest renewed in the Pueblo Indian country. Meanwhile, in view of the oppressive characteristics of the old-style military conquests of the early *conquistadores* in America, and after the passage of several decrees, the Royal Ordinances of 1573 defined more precisely the policies to be followed in making new discoveries and settlements in Indian lands, with emphasis on peaceful conquest. The definitive ordinances of 1573 do not use the word *conquest,* using instead the word *pacification.* These new conditions of exploration and settlement prevailed thereafter as the letter of the law, at least, and tempered the plans of greedy adventurers. So it was that Fray Agustín Rodríguez, a Franciscan lay brother, in 1581 obtained the viceroy's permission to investigate New Mexico. He was accompanied by Francisco Sánchez Chamuscado, a small group of soldiers and Indian servants, and two other friars. For almost a whole year much of the area that had been explored by Coronado was retraced. The return of the expedition, with the news of finding a large number of pueblos with a high degree of civilization, created a sensation in Mexico. Antonio de Espejo also led a small expedition in the fall of 1582 and returned home ten months later with promising reports.

The reports of the Rodríguez-Chamuscado expedition led the Spanish crown and the Council of the Indies to issue a royal *cédula* on April 19, 1583, authorizing the pacification and colonization of New Mexico. It was decreed that arrangements must be made at no cost to the crown and in conformity with the laws of 1573, which were now to receive a major test, since the conquest of New Mexico was the first great venture of this nature attempted under the code.[4] The delays in selecting a leader for the colonizing expedition inspired two illegal expeditions to the Pueblo country in 1590 and 1593, both unsuccessful. Finally, Don Juan de Oñate was selected. An international objective that influenced the timing of the enterprise was to establish a defensive

---

3. Bolton, *Coronado*, 68, 69, 352.
4. George P. Hammond and Agapito Rey, *Don Juan de Oñate, Colonizer of New Mexico, 1595–1628*, I, 4.

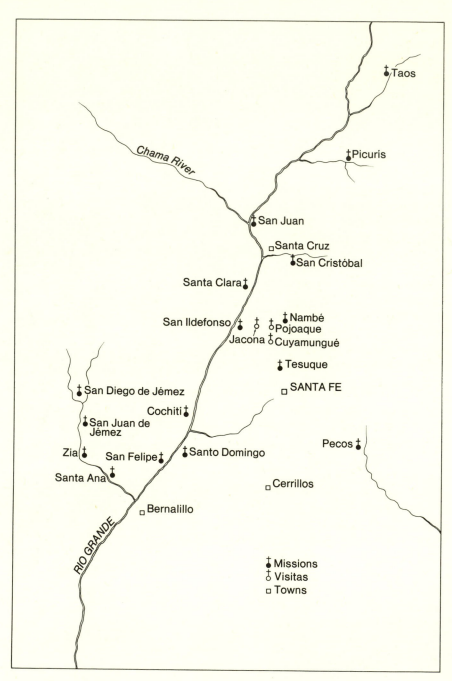

Map of missions and towns in northern New Mexico, 1695.

outpost to protect northern New Spain from encroachments by envious European rivals.[5]

The Oñate expedition was successful in establishing a permanent colony in what was already known as the center of the populous Pueblo Indian country. In perspective, Oñate's contribution to the history of North America was his establishment of a permanent European colony in this distant corner of the Spanish Empire, a new center for the exploration of the region, and his opening of a challenging new opportunity for the conversion of many thousands of Indians to Christianity.

Oñate set out from Mexico on January 26, 1598, with a caravan of 129 soldier-colonists, many of whom took their families, eighty-three wagons and carts drawn by mules and oxen, hundreds of horses, and some seven thousand head of cattle, sheep, and goats driven on foot. Ten Franciscan missionaries accompanied the expedition. On reaching the Pueblo Indian country, Oñate was received in apparent friendship by the Indians, and at a number of the pueblos he and the Franciscan father commissary staged great ceremonies where Indian chiefs swore allegiance as subjects of the Spanish crown and the Catholic church and became citizens of the Spanish Empire. On July 11, Oñate founded the first Spanish capital in New Mexico on the east bank of the Río Grande and named it San Juan de los Caballeros. Later the camp was moved to nearby Yunque, which was named San Gabriel, on the left bank of the Chama where it flows into the Río Grande. San Gabriel remained the capital of New Mexico until Governor Pedro de Peralta, Oñate's successor, founded Santa Fe in 1610.[6]

The colonists saw little or no evidence of real wealth in New Mexico, and there was much dissatisfaction. The unrest continued for a decade, as Oñate and his lieutenants neglected the colony while absent on exploratory expeditions for months at a time.[7]

In the course of Oñate's explorations a tragic incident occurred at Acoma in early December, 1598. A group of Spanish soldiers stopped there to seek food supplies. As the Spaniards approached the steep cliffs of the pueblo, Juan Zaldívar and twelve of his men were attacked by surprise and killed. This bloody disaster was a serious blow to Spanish authority. A general meeting was called by the governor to make plans for the punishment of Acoma. It was Oñate's first test of the meaning of peaceful conquest and "just war" under the Royal Ordinances of 1573. There were different interpretations in defining a "just war," and in seventeenth-century New Mexico some military governors ignored the laws. Later, in the days of Governor Vargas, the Franciscan mis-

5. *Ibid.*, I, 16–34.
6. *Ibid.*, I, 14, 17, 337–62.
7. *Ibid.*, I, 24–26, 30–31; II, 746–60, 1010–33.

sionaries generally supported his wars against rebel and apostate Indians as "just wars."[8] In reviewing the case against Acoma, it was considered that Spanish law could be applied since the pueblo had sworn obedience and vassalage to the Spanish crown, and the people were therefore royal subjects. The friars were consulted for their opinions, and the commissary and his colleagues outlined the requirements for a just war. Punishment of transgressors of the law and the preservation of peace were defined as justification for war, and Oñate made arrangements for a punitive expedition to Acoma. An army of seventy soldiers left for the pueblo on January 12, 1599. They were met by Indians ready for battle. The customary offer of peace was spurned, and after two days of bitter fighting, Acoma was captured. The pueblo was burned and laid waste, and seventy or eighty men and five hundred women and children were captured. The rest escaped or were killed. The Acomas were charged for the killing of Spaniards and for having failed to submit peacefully, and the captives were questioned, formally tried, and cruelly punished.[9]

This drastic action quieted the Indians. At least no similar major acts of rebellion occurred for many decades thereafter. But the bitter memory was not easily forgotten by the Acomas, and they and Indian leaders at other pueblos continued to resent the demands of Oñate and his officers for food and blankets.

It was clear to Oñate that he needed reinforcements and food supplies to hold the province. He was successful in his appeal for help from the viceroy, and additional colonists and supplies were sent to New Mexico, but it was not sufficient to prevent the colony from enduring great hardships, and many of the Spaniards were completely disillusioned. Some proposed the abandonment

8. There were different interpretations of the ordinances and other related laws governing Indian relations in the colonial period, and up until the 1670s some arbitrary and irresponsible governors ignored or paid only lip service to them. In the 1690s, under the governorship of Diego de Vargas, the Franciscan missionaries were generally in agreement with him in his waging of "just wars" against defiant and apostate Indians who engaged in open rebellion against "the two majesties," church and state. Fray Isidro Félix de Espinosa, a veteran of the Texas missions and historian of the Missionary College of Santa Cruz de Querétaro, in his *Crónica*, written in 1748, after referring to authorities, including the illustrious Montenegro, presents a realistic appraisal of the type of situation that existed in New Mexico in the years covered by the documents translated below. He writes: "All of these agree that, in the missions that were established by evangelization without armed protection, the missionaries lost their lives at the hands of the infidels or were forced to flee, and on the contrary, those who had good results and made progress were those who undertook to preach the gospel to them with sufficient escort and military protection to restrain the audacity of the barbarians. It is one thing to make war on them to convert them, which was never in anyone's mind; it is another thing to have arms in readiness for the defense and protection of the missions, to assure the goal of winning souls." The subject of this paragraph is well analyzed in detail in Lino Gómez Canedo, *Evangelización y conquista, experiencia franciscana en hispanoamerica*, 69–86.

9. Hammond and Rey, *Oñate*, I, 19–22, 428–79. A dramatic first-hand account of the battle at Acoma may be found in the *Historia de Nueva México*, written in balladlike form by Captain Gaspár Pérez de Villagrá, a participant in the battle, and published in Alcalá, Spain, in 1610. See the English translation by Gilberto Espinosa, *History of New Mexico by Gaspár Pérez de Villagrá, Alcalá, 1619*, 185–276.

of the province, and the viceroy and the king and his council seriously considered withdrawal. Meanwhile, Oñate persisted in his efforts to convince the viceroy to maintain the colony.[10]

As conditions worsened in New Mexico, Fray Lázaro Ximénez was sent to Mexico to explain in greater detail the critical situation and to plead for help. He returned to New Mexico early in 1608 with instructions to maintain the colony and await further advice from the viceroy. Then a veritable miracle occurred. In December, 1608, Fray Lázaro returned to Mexico City with the report that seven thousand natives had been baptized and that many others were ready for baptism. This favorable news, reinforced by other documents, was forwarded by the viceroy to the king. In 1609, King Philip III accepted the solution that New Mexico should be maintained as a missionary field at royal expense.[11] The permanent Spanish occupation of New Mexico was assured. "The religious motive was one of the chief factors—if not the deciding factor—which impelled the Spaniards to the course which they followed in New Mexico, at least to the end of the seventeenth century."[12] Throughout the century, from 1609 onwards, New Mexico became primarily a mission area.

Civil Authority and Society in New Mexico

From the time of its discovery, the province of New Mexico formed a part of the viceroyalty of New Spain.[13] Oñate's desire was to be independent of supervisory authority by the viceroy and to be subject directly to the king and the Council of the Indies in Spain, but he failed in his effort. Under his successors full responsibility for the government of New Mexico was assumed by the viceregal authorities of New Spain. Governors of the province were appointed by the viceroy, who exercised general supervision over military and civil administration. The audiencia in Mexico City became the court of appeal, and it advised the viceroy on all matters of high policy concerning the province. In financial matters the viceroy and the officials of the royal treasury in Mexico City had control. The measure of control which the viceregal authorities were able to maintain over local administration in New Mexico varied from time to time, but at best it was ineffective because of distance, delays in communica-

---

10. Hammond and Rey, *Oñate*, I, 30–31; II, 701–39, 980–83, 1036–38.

11. *Ibid.*, I, 32–34; II, 1104–1105.

12. Lansing B. Bloom, "Spain's Investment in New Mexico under the Hapsburgs," *The Americas*, I (1944): 9–10.

13. For an excellent review of civil authority and society in seventeenth-century New Mexico, see France V. Scholes, "Civil Government and Society in New Mexico in the Seventeenth Century," *New Mexico Historical Review*, X (1935): 71–111. See also Marc Simmons, *Spanish Government in New Mexico, passim*, and Oakah L. Jones, Jr., *Los Paisanos, Spanish Settlers on the Northern Frontier of New Spain*, 100, 129–32, and 136–65, *passim*.

tion and action, and cases in which arbitrary and self-seeking provincial governors were mere favorites of the viceroy or adventurers.

When Pedro de Peralta was appointed governor to succeed Oñate in 1609–10, administration of the province was thenceforth based on general colonial legislation and policy. Peralta and his successors had the usual rank and titles of governor and captain general. The governor and captain general held virtually absolute authority in civil and military matters, and his official term of office was for three years. It was his function to promote the general advancement of the province, to secure the administration of justice, to defend the province, to protect the missions, and to protect the settled Pueblo Indians from abuse and exploitation. His powers were wide enough to permit an honest and energetic leader to maintain discipline and justice, or to make it possible for a self-seeking official to become a local tyrant. On all important matters he was expected to consult with the leaders of the clergy and the cabildo, the municipal government of the Villa of Santa Fe, the capital of the province.

The local military establishment was small and loosely organized, for before 1680 there was no regular presidio or paid garrison. The military force was composed of a group of professional soldier-citizens who received no regular salary from the crown but were granted *encomiendas* that enabled them to obtain revenue through stock raising, farming, and various forms of exploitation of Indian labor. The number of the *encomendero*-soldiers was set at thirty-five. In times of crisis, all able-bodied civilians were subject to military service.

The governor and captain general was assisted in administering the province by the secretary of government and war, who was an active adviser as well as the notary who attested to all the official documents issued in the governor's name; his appointed local authorities and administrators of rural jurisdictions, called *alcaldías;* and the cabildo at Santa Fe. There were six to eight *alcaldías,* each under an *alcalde mayor.* The functions of the *alcaldes mayores* were of considerable importance, since they came into direct day-to-day contact with the Indian pueblos, the missions, and the *estancias* of the non-Indian population and were responsible directly to the governor for their actions. From about 1660 onward it was customary to divide the province into two major administrative districts known as the Río Arriba and the Río Abajo—the upper and lower portions of the Río Grande valley and the neighboring districts. It appears that the major reason for this division was the need for more adequate defense in the lower area, where Apache raiders were especially active. The governor personally administered the Río Arriba, and his lieutenant governor took charge of the Río Abajo.

The cabildo consisted of four *regidores,* or councilmen, elected annually by the citizens, and two *alcaldes ordinarios,* or magistrates, elected by the councilmen; they were assisted by an *alguacil,* or bailiff, and a notary elected by them. All elections were subject to the confirmation of the governor. The cabildo had authority to make local ordinances, subject to the governor's approval, and had criminal jurisdiction in certain local matters. Also, the cabildo had an influence that extended beyond the limits of the capital. It was the spokesman of the entire community both in pleas to the governor and in petitions to the viceroy and the king. Moreover, the governor was instructed to seek its advice on all matters of importance, so that it became a sort of advisory council for the entire province. In general, the cabildo represented the soldier-citizens, the dominant class in the community. It was the only form of democratic self-government in the province.

The colonists were always outnumbered by the native Indian population by approximately thirty to one in the area of Spanish settlement, which was concentrated within a radius of roughly fifty to eighty miles north and south of Santa Fe along the Río Grande valley and a similar distance to the east and west. The total population of the colony was about 750 by 1630 and increased to about 2,900 in 1680.[14] As the number of Spaniards and mestizos slowly increased, especially during the second half of the century, small hamlets were formed and more farmlands were occupied where water, labor, and land were available. The more important rural areas were the valleys north and south of Santa Fe along and beyond the Río Grande valley in the heart of the Pueblo Indian country. Before 1680 the population of the colony was a homogeneous, inbred group, as there was little to attract new colonists, since the agricultural resources were limited, trade was by barter, and minerals, except for salt, some lead, and a few minor ores, were not being exploited. The province was first and foremost a Franciscan mission field, and the Spanish population was there mostly to sustain and defend the missions.

Among the colonists, those of predominantly Spanish blood dominated the patterns of social life and customs. In the beginning there was clearly a considerable number of Spanish-born citizens, with a handful of non-Spanish Europeans. By 1680 most of the population had been born in the province itself. Over the years, blood mixture was inevitable in an isolated community which lived as neighbors among sedentary Indians who outnumbered them and on whom they were dependent economically. Moreover, many of the first colonists were themselves mestizos. The colonists, therefore, although a homogeneous group, were made up of Spanish-born Spaniards, American-born Spaniards, mestizos, and a variety of ethnic mixtures. The servants, muleteers, farm and ranch hands, and menial workers were mestizos, New Mexican and Mexican Indians, Negroes, mulattos, and a mixture of these in varying de-

14. Jones, *Los Paisanos,* 110, 129.

Canyon scene, Northern New Mexico. *Photograph courtesy of the Prints and Photographs Division, Library of Congress, Washington, D.C.*

grees of racial predominance. There was a high proportion of lower-class elements and even some fugitives from justice.

With the existence of a large proportion of persons of mixed blood, some obtained prominence who were referred to as *mulato pardo, pardo, mestizo-amulatado,* or *mulato,* including captains in the Spanish military forces and at least one *alcalde mayor.* From the mid-seventeenth century on there were Pueblo Indian leaders who were mestizos, mulattos, *coyotes* (mixture of Indian and mestizo), and *lobos* (mixture of Negro and Indian) and there were *ladinos* among them who were quite proficient in speaking, reading, and writing in the Spanish language. There were some local admixtures across the whole spectrum. In general, however, social distinctions were simpler than those in New Spain. Certainly no difference was made between Spaniards and creoles, and the position of the mestizo in New Mexico was apparently better than in the more densely settled areas of New Spain.

But despite the easy and free intermingling of classes, there was clearly a well-defined local aristocracy based on family, royal service, and worldly possessions. The aristocrats' wealth was greater than that of families of lesser social standing, the best lands were theirs, they had greater opportunities to engage in trade, and they received the best *encomiendas.* They were the true professional servants of the crown, the small standing military force ready to provide military escort for the missionaries and to be at the beck and call of the governor in leading forays against troublesome Indians. In the main they attempted to keep their blood pure, but against heavy odds.

It must be kept in mind that New Mexico was a raw frontier outpost, and life in general was characterized by roughness and a lack of luxury and refinement. Among the mass of the colonists, folk life represented all of the virtues and vices of impoverished villagers anywhere in the western world in the seventeenth century, with the added trying obstacles and conditions of family life on a frontier. The common folk were predominantly illiterate, and there were no local schools for their education. Most of them lived and died in the province, with rare opportunities for contact with the outside world—especially for the women, whose experience was limited to their neighborhood, nearby farms and hamlets, and hearsay about the surrounding frontiers. The population of Santa Fe in the seventeenth century was probably never more than a few hundred. The residents represented a cross-section of all classes of society in the colony.

The friars were the one really learned class in the community, and in private conversations with them and in the sermons they preached the people heard the best standards of speech in the province. A friar was usually a welcome visitor in the home, for he, like the governor, had seen other lands. Some of them brought the solace of medical skill and knowledge. Actually, the libraries of some of the governors and Franciscan convents, though relatively small, contained a remarkably broad cross-section of well-known contemporary and traditional Spanish histories, literary works, devotional writings, and works of a politico-moralistic character, along with the supply of breviaries, choral books, and prayer books periodically sent up to the missions.[15]

The fundamental problems of political and religious experience were essentially the same in Santa Fe as in less isolated and more cultured centers. Heresy was just as great a sin there as in Mexico City—greater, perhaps, because the influence of unorthodoxy might be more immediate. Likewise, the basic problems of the proper relations between church and state presented themselves in this struggling community with the same persistence. In 1626 the authority of the dread Inquisition was established there.

Franciscan Administrative Organization

Since the Spanish government after 1609 was committed to support New Mexico as a mission field, it was clear thenceforward that the administrators of the missionary work, the Franciscan order, the sole ecclesiastical authorities in the province, would play a dominant role parallel to that of the civil authorities.[16] The first superior of the Franciscans who entered New Mexico with Oñate had the title of commissary. In 1616 the Franciscan missions of New Mexico were raised to the status of *custodia*, custody, and the Franciscan superior of the missionaries was named *custodio*, or custodian. The official title of the custody thenceforward was the Custody of the Conversion of Saint Paul of New Mexico.[17]

The first Franciscan missionaries in New Spain had arrived from Spain in 1523 and 1524. Other religious orders followed. Eventually the Franciscans were to become the sole group chosen for the advance into New Mexico. The Franciscan missionaries increased in number in New Spain, and in 1535 they were organized as the Province of the Holy Gospel (*Santo Evangelio*), with headquarters in Mexico City. As the northern frontier of New Spain advanced, additional Franciscan provinces and custodies were established. By the third

---

15. See Eleanor B. Adams and France V. Scholes. "Books in New Mexico, 1598–1680," *New Mexico Historical Review*, XVII (1942): 1–45. See also Eleanor B. Adams, "Two Colonial New Mexico Libraries, 1704, 1776," *ibid.*, XIX (1944): 135–67, and J. Manuel Espinosa, ed., and trans., *First Expedition of Vargas into New Mexico, 1692*, 202–203.

16. The best secondary authorities on this subject are France V. Scholes, "Problems in the Early Ecclesiastical History of New Mexico," *New Mexico Historical Review*, VII (1932): 32–74, and Michael A. McCloskey, O.F.M., *The Formative Years of the Missionary College of Santa Cruz de Querétaro, 1683–1733*. See also the introduction to Adams, *Bishop Tamarón's Visitation*, 1–33.

17. Oñate had written in his journal in early August, 1598: "The Indians in their chapel venerate Saint Paul on the feast day of his conversion, and thus Saint Paul is considered as the patron saint of all New Mexico. . . . Thus these provinces are called the *conversión evangélica*, and they have the conversion of Saint Paul as their emblem." Hammond and Rey, *Oñate*, I, 323.

decade of the seventeenth century New Mexico was well established as a custody of the Province of the Holy Gospel of New Spain. Most of the missionaries to New Mexico were recruited from Spanish-born volunteers from Spain, and until the end of the seventeenth century nearly all of them were born and educated in Spain.

The basic unit of Franciscan administration was the convent, where a group of friars lived under the guidance of a guardian. Over the entire order, comprising all of the provinces, was the minister general, elected by the general chapter. To assist in the administration of Franciscan affairs in the Spanish overseas colonies, a Spanish commissary general for the Indies was appointed to reside in Madrid and to have supervision over all the Franciscan provinces in the Spanish Indies, subject to the minister general of the order. Within America two lesser commissaries general were appointed, one for New Spain and one for Peru.

The Franciscan custody did not have the status of a full-fledged province. It was, generally, a semi-independent administrative area, autonomous and self-governing in local affairs but still subject to the general control of the province of which it formed a part. The custody had its own chapter and its own committee of *definidores* elected by the custodian, the local prelate of the group. In the New World new custodies came into existence along with the expansion of Franciscan enterprise. One by one, most of the custodies in New Spain reached provincial status. The only two that were established subject to the general supervision of the Province of the Holy Gospel and that did not attain full provincial status were the custodies of Tampico and New Mexico. The custody of New Mexico remained under the control of the Province of the Holy Gospel, and the election of the custodian always remained in the hands of the authorities of the province.

In 1616 when the jurisdiction was raised to a custody, the first prelate appointed with the title of custodian of New Mexico was Fray Estévan de Perea. In 1626, when Fray Alonso de Benavides became custodian, he was appointed, in addition, commissary of the Holy Office of the Inquisition for the province. Such wide authority gave the custodian great influence, so that, except for the civil governor of the province, he was the most powerful personage in New Mexico, and in some cases he was in reality more influential than the governor. The custodian in New Mexico was chief and leader of all the friars, directed their activities, and represented them, with the advice of his *definidores* in important matters, in all their relations with the local civil authorities. He represented, in relation to the custody, the same authority that the provincials enjoyed in their provinces. He was the prelate of the entire community, civil and ecclesiastical, for no bishop exercised active authority in New Mexico before the eighteenth century. Therefore, he enjoyed quasi-episcopal authority, as granted by papal bulls. To him the Spanish residents of the colony paid tithes. He was ecclesiastical "judge ordinary" for the entire province.[18]

In the second half of the seventeenth century the Franciscan provinces in the northern part of New Spain were not greatly understaffed, yet they needed more missionaries if they were to advance much farther. To help meet this need it was proposed to set up missionary training colleges in New Spain, an idea pursued in New Spain and Spain by a friar of the Franciscan province of Michoacán, Fray Antonio Llinás. In October, 1681, the Council of the Indies, through the minister general and the commissary general of the Indies, authorized Father Llinás to gather twenty-four religious from the Spanish Franciscan provinces and to lead them into the country of pagan Indians in New Spain. The band was gathered in early March, 1682, and the site of the missionary college was determined to be the Convent of Santa Cruz de Querétaro. Royal authorization for the project of the Missionary College of Santa Cruz de Querétaro was granted by a *cédula* of April 18, 1682, and another *cédula* of the same date instructed the Casa de Contratación to provide Father Llinás and the friars of his party with their necessities and with passage to the Indies. The viceroy of New Spain and all ecclesiastical and civil officials of the viceroyalty were ordered to do everything possible to aid in the enterprise. After various shifts in personnel, at least twenty-seven friars were in the band that departed from Cádiz on March 4, 1683. At the end of May the missionaries were safe at Vera Cruz. By the fall of 1683 the group was established at the convent in Querétaro. By that time seven additional volunteers joined the group from the Franciscan province of New Spain. The convent had never been intended to house more than fifteen friars, but there were now more than thirty in the crowded quarters there.

The immediate superior of the missionary college was the Franciscan commissary general of New Spain. The college was under the jurisdiction of a guardian, whose powers over his subjects were much akin to those of a minister provincial in his province. The guardian or, in his absence, his vicar dispatched missionaries both for preaching among the faithful and for missions among the pagans. Missionaries in established missions remained subject to the guardian. As soon as the bishops decided to place the diocesan clergy in charge of any of these missions, the college missionaries were required to surrender them without question. At no time were the missionaries of the college permitted to receive canonical title to any parish, but if the bishops permitted, they might found friaries in the larger towns. These might be staffed with

18. See France V. Scholes, *Troublous Times in New Mexico, 1659–1670;* and France V. Scholes and Lansing B. Bloom, "Friar Personnel and Mission Chronology, 1598–1629," *New Mexico Historical Review,* XIX (1944): 319–36, and XX (1945): 58–82.

other friars, for the college missionaries must always push ahead into new pagan country. Whenever they went into pagan country, the missionaries entered under the leadership of the commissary or custodian of the missions.[19]

The history of the College of Santa Cruz de Querétaro from 1683 to 1697 divides into two periods. In the first period, between 1683 and 1690, the emphasis in the college work was on missions among the faithful in Spanish communities, with only incidental attention to missions among the pagans. But in the early 1680s the college made an attempt to obtain an assignment to a definite field of labor among pagan Indians. This occurred when the remnant of Spaniards and loyal Indians was forced to return to El Paso and remain there following the Pueblo revolt of 1680 in New Mexico. At that time the college made its request, as the Franciscans had gathered the loyal Indians in a few missions in the El Paso district. The Franciscan commissary general refused the services of the Querétaro friars because he was concerned that they should confine themselves to their successful work among the faithful. In fact, from 1686 to the early 1690s requests for missionaries to preach missions among the faithful constantly increased to such a degree that there was scarcely present at the college the minimum number of friars required to sustain monastic routine. Thenceforward, however, the missionary college of Querétaro became an important element in the administrative history of the missions of New Mexico. There volunteer friars were given instructions in the techniques of missionary work, in the laws of church and state regarding that work, and, when possible, in the dialects of the tribes they would encounter, a task that did not have much success in the case of New Mexico because of the difficult Indian languages encountered there.

The Franciscan Missions, 1610–80

One of the first problems of missionaries on new frontiers was to gather the nations into villages, where they could be more easily instructed and organized into stable communities receptive to European patterns of government and society. In New Mexico tens of thousands of sedentary Pueblo Indians "with souls to save" were already congregated in their pueblos, removing a major initial obstacle. The surrounding nomadic and warlike tribes remained a challenge; efforts to convert some of them were for the most part fruitless.

When Governor Peralta arrived in New Mexico in 1610, he was accompanied by nine missionaries. At about that time, Santo Domingo became the Franciscan headquarters, where the father commissary, later elevated to the title of custodian, usually resided. Missionary activity was at a minimum

19. McCloskey, *Formative Years,* 37.

The church at San Ildefonso Pueblo, 1899. *Photograph courtesy of the National Anthropological Archives, the Smithsonian Institution, Washington, D.C.*

when Oñate's government came to a close, at which time there were apparently only three friars left in New Mexico.[20] In 1611 eight new friars were sent to New Mexico. As a result of the increased number of friars during the years from 1610 to 1616, there was a marked expansion of the missionary program. By 1616 there were ten mission centers with friars and convents: Santa Fe and the pueblos of San Ildefonso, Nambé, Galisteo, San Lázaro, Santo Domingo, Zia, Sandía, Isleta, and Chililí. In addition, there were *visitas,* or missions, where religious services were performed periodically by resident friars from neighboring convents, at the pueblos of San Juan, Cochití, San Felipe, and Santa Ana. The missionaries were ministering to approximately ten thousand Christianized Indians. In 1616 a new group of seven friars arrived in New Mexico. That year, Fray Estévan de Perea, who had arrived in 1610, was named the local prelate with the title of custodian. He served in that capacity until 1621. The decision by the Franciscan authorities in Mexico City to give the New Mexican missions the status of a custody within the Province of the

20. Scholes and Bloom, "Friar Personnel and Mission Chronology, 1598–1629," 326–27. For the names of all the friars and the founding dates and early history of the missions of New Mexico, see the texts and notes in Scholes and Bloom and the notes in Frederick W. Hodge, George P. Hammond, and Agapito Rey, *Fray Alonso de Benavides' Revised Memorial of 1634,* and in Peter P. Forrestal, C.S.C., and Cyprian Lynch, O.F.M., *Benavides' Memorial of 1630.*

Holy Gospel was inspired in part by the progress that had been achieved since 1610. In 1621, as a result of reports sent by the custodian Perea the previous year, six friars went to New Mexico with the supply caravans of that year. When Fray Alonso de Benavides arrived as custodian in 1625 with mission supplies, he was accompanied by eleven other friars.

During the nine years from the beginning of 1617 to the end of 1625, the Franciscans, with substantial increases in personnel, carried forward the work already started among the Tewas, Tanos, Keres, and Río Grande and Manzano Tiwas, and the mission field was expanded to include Pecos, Picurís, Taos, the Jémez pueblos, and the Tompiro pueblo of Abo. There were setbacks especially at the frontier missions at Jémez, Picurís, and Taos, where native opposition was considerable. But from 1626 to the end of 1629 additional missions were established in the Tewa, Manzano Tiwa, and Tompiro areas; work was resumed at Picurís and Taos; and the mission of San Diego del Monte de Jémez was reestablished during Benavides's prelacy after a revolt of the Jémez in 1623 that could not be subdued at that time. At the end of Benavides's term as custodian, in 1629, there were two convents in the Jémez area at San José de Jémez and San Diego del Monte de Jémez. In 1632 a missionary suffered martyrdom in the vicinity of the Jémez pueblos, and in the 1630s San José apparently was abandoned and San Diego became the center of missionary activity among the Jémez until the general Pueblo revolt of 1680.

In the spring of 1629, Perea, reelected as custodian, returned to New Mexico with a large mission supply caravan and a group of thirty additional friars. At the close of the year there were forty-six friars serving at about thirty-five missions and *visitas* and ministering to some thirty-five thousand Christianized Indians. The period from 1610 to the mid-1630s has been aptly referred to as the golden age of the Franciscan missions in New Mexico. Perhaps there would have been more convents and churches had it not been for the devastating raids on some of the pueblos by hostile Apache tribes, the abandonment of others because of crop failures and consequent starving times, and the toll of epidemics of smallpox and *cocoliztli* or *tabardillo,* described as "severe and continuous fever."[21]

New Mexico's two outstanding churchmen during this period of great mission expansion and development were Fray Estévan de Perea and Fray Alonso

21. In 1629, Fray Gerónimo de Zárate Salmerón stated that "there have been baptized 34,650 souls." In 1638, Fray Juan de Prada wrote, "The people that may be counted today in these settlements will total forty thousand or a little less." Benavides states in his *Memorial of 1630* and revised *Memorial of 1634* that "more than five hundred thousand souls of barbarous Indians have been converted to our holy Catholic faith." This is obviously an exaggeration, unless he was referring to all of northern New Spain and all the tribes to the north, west, and east of New Mexico that he hoped would someday be converted. See Forrestal and Lynch, *Benavides' Memorial of 1630,* 5, 5n.11, 73; and Hodge, Hammond, and Rey, *Fray Alonso de Benavides' Revised Memorial of 1634,* 98, 224n.3.

de Benavides. Scholes considers Perea the more important of the two. Perea labored in New Mexico from 1610 until his death there in 1638, whereas Benavides was in New Mexico less than four years. Perea wrote a report on the missions and mission founding during the remarkable year 1629 which included a dramatic account of his efforts to establish permanent missions at Acoma, Zuñi, and the Hopi pueblos. In 1629 he was establishing his tenth and last church and convent at Santa Clara. His short *Verdadera relación,* published in Seville in 1632,[22] gives a glimpse of developments in which Benavides himself had not participated, although they were contemporary with the last months of his service. At the court of Philip IV, among his petitions Perea urged that the Indians of his custody be free from the obligations of paying tribute and of being obliged to render personal service, a request that was granted by the king in 1635. Scholes describes Perea's contribution in the following laudatory terms: "Perea was one of the great figures in the history of the Church in New Mexico. For some thirty years, except for the brief period from 1626 to 1629, he was the dominant figure in the religious life of the province. . . . His long years of service, and his paramount influence give him a pre-eminent position in New Mexican history, a position greater than that of Benavides. Perea, more than any other friar, deserves the honor of being called the Father of the New Mexican Church."[23]

Fray Alonso de Benavides has long enjoyed the greatest reputation of any Franciscan who served in the New Mexico missions because of the phenomenal success of his *Memorial,* printed in Spain in 1630 and again in revised form in 1634. He accomplished much for the New Mexico missions, and he impressed the authorities in New Spain and Spain with his glowing reports on the progress of the missions.

The best description of the daily life led by the friars and their Pueblo Indian converts at the missions in New Mexico about 1630 is found in Benavides's reports to the royal court and to his Franciscan superiors in Spain. Since Benavides's reports were written to convince the crown of the need for much greater help for the missions, his glowing accounts of the idyllic Catholic religious life of the Indians at the missions must be read with this in mind. Nevertheless, the basic facts he presents on mission life appear to be accurate in substance.

Each mission, established at a convenient site off the central square of a well-populated Indian pueblo, had its church, convent or missionary headquarters, and workshops. The church, where religious services were held and where in-

22. Lansing B. Bloom, "Fray Estévan de Perea's Relación," *New Mexico Historical Review,* VIII (1933): 211–35.

23. Scholes, "Problems in the Early Ecclesiastical History of New Mexico," 67.

struction in Christian doctrine was given, was usually well built.[24] The exterior of the fortresslike adobe mission churches was quite plain, plastered with mud that blended more or less with the sandy earth from which it came, in contrast to the often sumptuous and ornate interior. The interior walls were always well painted. In the more ornate churches, the ceiling *vigas,* or beams, were carved and painted with interlaced flower designs in bright colors. The neighboring mountains provided a variety of trees for use in construction. The wood was hewed and shaped by skilled Indian carpenters and craftsmen trained by the friars. "In this way," wrote Benavides, "there have been erected more than fifty churches."[25] The main altars, side altars, and walls of the churches were adorned with religious paintings, some with gilded frames, and painted wooden figures of Christ on the Cross, scenes from the Passion, the Blessed Virgin, and favored saints. Some of the statues and paintings were of fine workmanship from Mexico City or Spain, others were the work of lesser trained artists from New Spain, and a few were made by local artists inspired more by zeal than by talent. Choirs, accompanied by instrumental and organ music performed by mission Indians well trained by the friars, gave a special indigenous note to the solemnity of the celebration of mass. The religious ornaments, sacred vessels, vestments, fine altar cloths, and the like, provided to the missionaries by means of the mission supply caravans from New Spain, were additions that enabled them to celebrate religious services with the splendor and ceremony of Spain's Catholic church tradition.[26]

At each mission the natives were taught reading and writing in Spanish, religious music, and the ways of Christian life. Christian doctrine was given the first place, but the friars realized the importance of teaching the Indians to be useful citizens in the manner of western European society and set up workshops where the new Christians were taught all the trades and useful occupations, such as tailoring, shoemaking, carpentry, smithery, and the rest.

The methods of indoctrination followed a common pattern. In the beginning a few elements were stressed, such as veneration of the Cross and the Blessed Virgin, respect for the missionaries, the teaching of basic Catholic prayers stated as a profession of faith in the fundamental beliefs of the Catholic religion, instruction concerning the sacraments, and regular attendance at mass and other religious services conducted by the friars. Admission to the sacraments of the church—baptism, communion, penance, and matrimony—

24. George Kubler, *The Religious Architecture of New Mexico,* 7–9, 29–30.

25. *Benavides' Memorial of 1630,* 36. The extensive editorial notes of Hodge, Hammond, and Rey, in their edition of *Benavides' Revised Memorial of 1634,* contain a mine of information on the history of the early pueblo and mission sites in New Mexico.

26. For example, see the inventories published in Hodge, Hammond, and Rey, *Benavides' Revised Memorial of 1634,* Appendix IV, 109–24, and in Bloom, "Perea's *Relación,*" 219–21.

was granted as soon as the Indians received sufficient instruction. Benavides wrote:

> Once the Indians have received holy baptism, they become so domestic that they live with great propriety. Hardly do they hear the bell calling to mass before they hasten to the church with all the cleanliness and neatness they can. Before mass, they pray together as a group, with all devotion, the entire Christian doctrine in their own tongue. They attend mass and hear the sermon with great reverence. They are very scrupulous not to miss, on Saturdays, the mass of Our Lady, whom they venerate highly. . . .[27] The boys and girls repair to catechism every morning and afternoon and are very careful not to be absent. The chanters, who take alternate weeks in the chapels, sing in the church every day at the hour of Prime, High Mass, and Vespers, and they are very punctual. All of them go to confession in their own language and prepare for this sacrament by examining their sins, bringing them indicated on knotted strings. . . .[28]
>
> During Lent they all come with much humility to the processions, which are held on Monday, Wednesday, and Friday. On these days of meeting with the friars, they perform penances in the churches. During Holy Week they flagellate themselves in most solemn processions.[29]

Most of the convents had only one friar each, and he ministered to four, six, or more neighboring pueblos. More than twenty Indians, devoted to the service of the church, lived with him in the convent. They took turns as porters, sacristans, cooks, bell ringers, gardeners, refectioners, and in other tasks. The Indian sacristans at each mission were responsible for the maintenance of the church and convent and for overseeing certain church activities. Benavides noted, "They perform their duties with as much circumspection and care as if they were friars." To support the poor of each pueblo, the mission Indians were required to sow some grain and raise some cattle and sheep for this purpose, because, said Benavides, "If he left it to their discretion, they would not do anything." Through these required labors they provided the meat and wool not only to feed and clothe the poor but also to pay the various workmen who built the churches and to supplement the needs of the friar himself. Benavides emphasized that in all of these tasks, "All the wheels of the clock must be kept in good order by the friar, without neglecting any detail, otherwise all would be lost."[30]

The economic life of the province was based on agriculture and stock raising, along with a primitive commerce. It was at the missions and ranches of

27. *Revised Memorial of 1634*, 99.
28. *Memorial of 1630*, 36.
29. *Revised Memorial of 1634*, 100.
30. *Ibid.*, 101, 102.

the Spaniards that the Pueblo Indians, as laborers, learned the principles of breeding and herding livestock. Large herds of cattle and sheep were owned by the Franciscan custody, and those assigned to each mission shared the pueblo range, tended by Pueblo herdsmen and shepherds. The friars always defended the extent of their use of lands both for cultivation and for range on the grounds that all their essential food had to be raised on the spot, that they shared it with their Indian charges when necessary, that in case of famine they frequently fed large numbers of Indians and Spaniards from their reserves of food and livestock, and that only by breeding and exporting livestock could they obtain funds necessary for the purchase of those ecclesiastical articles, vestments, and other church furnishings not supplied by direct subvention from the royal treasury.

Stock raising introduced a new phase of economic life, for the horse, the mule, the ox, the domesticated sheep for food and wool, and the pig were introduced by the Spaniards. Chickens (*gallinas de Castilla*) were also introduced by them, but only on a limited scale, and were used by the Spaniards among other luxury food items brought in from New Spain. In the cultivation of the land, the most important crops were mostly the traditional Indian staples such as corn, beans, chili, and, in certain areas, cotton. Although new cereals and fruits were introduced by the Spaniards, they never took the place of the native staples. Wheat never took the place of corn, and the new fruits that were introduced were found mostly in the convent orchards and vineyards. Probably the most important contribution of the Spanish conquest to the cultivation of the soil, rather than the introduction of new foodstuffs, was the introduction of the iron-edged plow and other iron-bladed tilling instruments along with beasts of burden.

In extolling the successful conversion of the tens of thousands of Pueblo Indians, Benavides wrote:

> Today they are so well instructed in everything, especially in what pertains to the Faith and Christianity, that it is wonderful to consider that ever since they began to be baptized less than twenty years ago, and particularly during the last eight years when the harvest of souls has been most abundant, they have given the impression of having been Christian for a hundred years. . . . This land, where formerly there was nothing but estufas of idolatry, today is entirely covered with very sumptuous and beautiful churches which the friars have erected.[31]

To facilitate religious indoctrination, groups of smaller Indian pueblos were sometimes consolidated into larger and more conveniently located units, one

---

31. *Memorial of 1630*, 65. These quotes are an example of how Benavides in his account idealized the reality of the mission scene he described, as noted earlier.

of the factors for the fluctuation in the number of pueblos from 1610 to 1680, along with famine, pestilence, and abandonment of some of the earlier pueblos because of devastating Apache attacks.

From the mid-1630s on there was a definite slowing down of the mission program. Efforts by the missionaries to win to Christianity peacefully the recalcitrant frontier pueblos of the west (Acoma, Zuñi, and the Hopi pueblos); Jémez, across the Río Grande from the heart of the pueblo country; Picurís to the east; and the independent-spirited pueblo of Taos, relatively isolated to the north, met constant resistance. And there were ominous signs of rebellion among Indian war captains and medicine men at Isleta, Alameda, San Felipe, and Cochití as well, not to mention the surrounding Apache groups. One of the most important factors in emboldening Indian medicine men and war captains to stir up latent forces of rebellion was the persistent strife between the local Spanish civil authorities and the clergy, which rocked the province especially from the 1630s to the 1670s. Although the missionaries saw the dangers this conflict posed by its bad example for the Indians, it went on unabated. Most of the difficulty stemmed from the firm and persistent stand taken by the missionaries against the evil practices of a succession of corrupt governors.

As a result of the quarrels between the governors and the clergy in the 1630s and 1640s, the missions received a definite setback. The Indians of Taos killed their friar and destroyed their church, and the father guardian of Jémez also lost his life. The Taos church was not rebuilt for many years. Although there was apparently no break in the continuity of the Jémez mission, the natives of the pueblo became restless, and their leaders were implicated in abortive plots for rebellion between 1644 and 1653. Moreover, many of the churches were without resident priests because the roster of friars serving in the province always fell short of the number needed. In 1631, the viceroy had entered into an agreement with the Franciscan order with regard to the number of friars to be supported by the royal treasury, the amount of supplies to be furnished each triennium, the number and cost of wagons, and related matters. This agreement fixed a maximum quota of sixty-six friars to administer the missions, but in 1656 the number actively in service was forty-six, and the full quota was never reached.[32]

Pueblo Indian medicine men, who were unwilling to give up their traditional influence, backed by many of the Pueblo Indian chiefs and warriors, were always a threat to the authority of the friars at the missions by stirring up trouble among peaceful mission converts. Some of the most troublesome ones were a small group of renegades of racial mixture, including mistreated mulattos and Negroes, originally from New Spain, who had gone to New Mexico

32. Scholes, *Troublous Times in New Mexico*, 10.

from areas north of Mexico City in the hope of escaping from a life doomed to lowly servitude and who had taken up residence with the Indians. The friars, despite these and other obstacles, zealously tried to put an end to the practice of native religious ceremonials, what they viewed as idol worship, and to impose rigid monogamy on a people whose code of marital and sexual relationships was quite flexible. To maintain mission discipline the friars resorted to physical punishment for such offenses as persistent failure to attend religious services, sexual immorality, idolatry, and participation in certain native ceremonial dances. Whipping was commonly used as an instrument of discipline in such cases, as in criminal justice among the Spaniards themselves and in western society in general in that era. Scholes refers to an extreme case at one of the Hopi pueblos in the 1650s in which the friar, on his own initiative and without consent from his superiors, punished an Indian so severely for acts of idolatry that the Indian died. Several Hopi captains complained to the father custodian, who, after investigation, confined the accused friar to a convent and temporarily deprived him of the right to say mass and perform other ecclesiastical functions. Another case was that of a Hopi Indian of that same period who was guilty of impersonating the father guardian during his absence from the pueblo. He summoned the Indians to the church, where he put on the friar's vestments, took the incense burner and censed the altar, chanted the *Salve,* and then sprinkled holy water. For this offense, and because he was charged for grave sexual immorality as well, the offender was taken to the convent in Santa Fe, where the prelate sentenced him to a period of service in the convent, where he could be instructed in the faith. He proved incorrigible, however, and committed several robberies, and finally Governor Juan Manso condemned him to receiving two hundred lashes while being paraded through the public streets on pack animals, after which he was sold at public auction to purge him of his sins and as an example to others. Isolated incidents such as these were examples of the ever-present traumatic clash of the Pueblo Indian system and its enforced adherence to the new faith and social standards. There were evidences of more widespread calamities to come because of this clash of cultures.

No discussion of the Franciscan missions of New Mexico is complete without reference to the mission supply service, upon which the missions relied for their very existence. Both the friars and the governors made use of the mission supply caravan and its military escort for the transportation of their goods and for protection of the trail herds. The mission supply caravan was sent every three years, although on some occasions a longer interval elapsed. Religious articles, including fine religious art, for the missions constituted a major part of the supplies carried in the caravans, as the friars wished to make sure that religious services at the mission churches should be conducted with appropri-

Saint Francis, as portrayed
by a seventeenth-century
sculptor of Spain or New
Spain. Santa Cruz Church,
Santa Cruz, New Mex-
ico, 1931. *Photograph by
J. Manuel Espinosa.*

ate solemnity and dignity. The caravans also included farm implements and
tools of iron, food and spices, necessary household articles, clothing and clothing materials, medicine and drugs, and other supplies needed for the daily
labors of the missionaries. Included also were supplies for the civil authorities
and the colonists. The detailed inventories of the articles that reached New

Mexico in the wagons of the mission supply caravans from New Spain, and especially the lists of furnishings for the churches, the altar silver, candlesticks and fine silk and linen for the altar, and richly brocaded vestments for the performance of religious services on special days of the religious calendar, are indeed impressive. These inventories present an important aspect of the religious scene in New Mexico, both at the missions and in Santa Fe.[33]

The position of the father procurator general of the mission supply service was of great importance and responsibility, as it was his task to carry out the many details of organizing the large mission caravan. This involved the purchase of supplies for the friars and the organization of a wagon train, consisting, at the peak period of the 1650s, of more than thirty-five wagons, several hundred mules, cattle, and other livestock, with the necessary majordomos, drivers, and servants. As Scholes has stated: "It is impossible to overemphasize the services of the mission caravans in the history of New Mexico. .. . . They were the most important bond of union between New Spain and the faraway frontier settlements in New Mexico. Throughout the seventeenth century New Mexico was little more than a mission province, and the successful expansion of the mission field was based on the steady, sure service of supply which the Crown provided."[34]

Conflict Between the Civil Authorities and the Church, 1610−80

The period from 1610 to 1680, with very few exceptions, was one of almost endless confrontation between the governors of New Mexico and the local ecclesiastical authorities.[35] Some of the governors were self-seeking adventurers of the worst sort and used every means to exploit the Indians for personal benefit. Arrogant and unprincipled, the more notorious ones ruled like Oriental potentates and lied to gain influence at court. One of them, Governor Diego Dionisio de Peñalosa, in the end was tried by the Inquisition, expelled from the empire by the king, and in exile posed at European courts as a Spanish prince and betrayed his country.

33. See the inventories published in Hodge, Hammond, and Rey, *Benavides' Memorial of 1634*, Appendix IV, 109−24, and Bloom, "Perea's *Relación*," 219−21. Contemporary documents contain numerous specific references to religious art introduced into New Mexico from Spain and New Spain in the seventeenth century, for the churches and for household devotion, along with that which was brought in by individual colonists. No one as yet has made a systematic study of the extensive religious art that graced New Mexican churches and homes of the colonists in New Mexico in that century, which had such a great religious influence on the people.

34. France V. Scholes, "The Supply Service of the New Mexico Missions in the Seventeenth Century, Part III," *New Mexico Historical Review*, V (1930): 403.

35. This subject is necessarily based on the unsurpassed research and studies of France V. Scholes, especially his *Church and State in New Mexico, 1610−1650* and *Troublous Times in New Mexico, 1659−1670*. Unless otherwise indicated, the information in the paragraphs that immediately follow are drawn largely from these two studies, first published in issues of the *New Mexico Historical Review*.

Despite the letter of Spain's humane Indian laws, instead of protecting the native royal subject, some governors enslaved unconverted and apostate captives, and even Christianized Indians, who were required to perform a variety of extensive services for the governors' own personal profit. Some of the governors' like-minded soldier-*encomendero* leaders lived near the missions where they could encroach on the supply of Indian labor near at hand. Exploitation of the Indians by the civil authorities was a constant source of controversy between the local civil and ecclesiastical authorities.

The obligation of the governors to cooperate in the missionary program was stated in numerous royal orders and decrees. They failed miserably in these obligations. Thus the conflict between church and state persisted with such rancor that it is not surprising that even some of their most loyal Indian followers lost respect for their new masters, both friars and soldiers, and came to suspect and react violently against Spanish authority in general. The lesser officials, members of the cabildo of Santa Fe and the *alcaldes mayores* of the rural districts, were often mere instruments of their unscrupulous superiors.

At the same time, the laws gave the church authority over the Indians in ordinary ecclesiastical courts but reserved cases of "sorcerers" (*hechizeros*) to civil justice. This often caused misunderstanding. The economic resources of the missions, the power of ecclesiastical censure, including the authority of the Inquisition, brought more than one provincial governor to ruin. Ecclesiastical authority was concentrated to a remarkable degree, as the Franciscans were the sole representatives of the church in New Mexico. These were fundamental reasons why the conflicting issues of church and state were so significant a factor during this period.

The history of church and state relations in New Mexico before 1680 falls into three periods. The first extended from 1610 to 1650, during which friction between the custodian of the Franciscan missionaries and the governor and his lieutenants became progressively worse. During this period the Inquisition played a relatively minor role. The second period, from 1659 to 1664, witnessed the rule of two of the province's most unscrupulous and unworthy characters to hold the office of governor. Under these circumstances the Inquisition, whose commissary was the custodian and prelate, was a significant instrument of ecclesiastical policy. In the third period, from 1670 to 1680, increased economic hardships resulting from a series of damaging droughts, and a growing boldness on the part of the Apaches in raids on the properties of the Spaniards and on the settled Indian pueblos where the missions were located, added to the political instability of the government. The whole fabric of the Spanish colony was increasingly endangered by hostile elements among the Pueblo Indians, egged on by influential war captains and "sorcerers," who secretly planned rebellion.

Since the Spanish settlements and the mission pueblos were scattered over a relatively wide area, the danger was much greater than the governors in Santa Fe fully realized. Exploitation of the Indians by the governor and the group of soldier-*encomenderos,* slave raids by them in the guise of defensive action (raids illegal by royal decrees ignored by them), and drastic punishment of Indian "offenders" added fuel to the fire. The permanence of the missions depended on the growth of a sizeable Spanish colony, but the colony could not be maintained without the labor of Indians, and it was perhaps inevitable that the civil authorities, soldiers, and colonists should yield to the temptation to exploit the Indians.

As Scholes has summarized the irreconcilable controversies between local Spanish civil and ecclesiastical authorities between 1618 and 1678:

> Almost every general issue that could possibly cause irritation was presented in some form: the issue of ecclesiastical privilege and immunity; the exercise of ecclesiastical jurisdiction and the validity of ecclesiastical censures; the relative power of Church and State; questions of orthodoxy; the problem of Indian labor; control and direction of the missions and of the religious and social life of the natives; the exploitation of the Indians; the enslavement of the unconverted tribes.[36]

It is no wonder that some of the Franciscan prelates showed excessive zeal in defending their legal and moral rights in their basic objective of winning the souls of the natives, protecting the religious spirit of the colony, and carrying out what they considered their most important duty, the defense and protection of the missions.

A few examples will illustrate the chaotic politics at the highest levels of authority that were a major factor leading to the revolt in 1680. Governor Juan de Eulate (1618–25) had open contempt for the church and its ministers. He is said to have boasted on one occasion that he would send the custodian to Mexico as prisoner if the latter excommunicated him. He denied military escort for friars who wished to convert and indoctrinate frontier pueblos and even hindered the building and repairing of churches and convents by maltreating and insulting Spaniards who helped in this work and discouraging the Indians in their part of the work. He informed the Indians of Taos Pueblo that they need not obey or serve the friars in any respect, except that they should go to mass when the friars called them. Most important of all to the friars, Eulate refused to support the church in the campaign of the friars to do away with idol worship, Indian ceremonial dances, and concubinage among the Indians. His objective was to win over the Indians to exploit them. He permitted slave raids among the unconverted heathen tribes, as a result of which some Indians were

---

36. Scholes, "Church and State in New Mexico, 1610–1650," *New Mexico Historical Review,* XI (1936): 150.

sent to New Spain to be sold as slaves, orphans in converted pueblos were seized to be used as house servants, and the Indians were exploited in many other ways.

The complaints of the friars finally convinced the Holy Office in Mexico City that an agent, or commissary, should be appointed for New Mexico with full authority to investigate all cases of heresy, error, and ecclesiastical offenses over which the Inquisition had jurisdiction. Thus the powers of prelate and ecclesiastical judge ordinary were combined with those of the Holy Office in 1626, and no doubt it was expected that this union of authority would enable the church effectively to combat the numerous errors and heresies said to be current in New Mexico and to defend the missions against the hostility of the civil authorities.

Governor Felipe Sotelo Osorio (1625–29) was charged by the Inquisition for heretical and blasphemous statements in public, including ridicule of the missionaries and the celebration of the mass, and for immorality. Although he seldom attended mass, on one occasion he entered mass late, and after the ceremony, with the scandalized citizenry assembled in the churchyard, he upbraided some of the soldiers for not rising when he entered. One soldier tried to explain by saying that he could not rise during the Sanctus. The governor is reported to have replied angrily: "I swore to Christ the other day that you people must rise even if they are elevating the Host." He is also reported to have made fun of excommunication by saying that if he were excommunicated he would force absolution within two hours.[37]

In the charged atmosphere of constant quarreling between the civil and ecclesiastical authorities three missionaries were added to the roll of Franciscan martyrs. The quarrel between Governor Luis de Rosas (1637–41) and the clergy emboldened the Indians of Taos to kill their friar and to destroy their church, and the guardian of Jémez also lost his life. Indian leaders at the Jémez missions were implicated in abortive plots for rebellion from the mid-1640s to the early 1650s. The Jémez Pueblos, in league with the Apaches, killed a Spaniard, and several of the leaders were hanged, others whipped, and some given terms of servitude. And there was a more general conspiracy involving Indians of Isleta, Alameda, San Felipe, Cochití, and Jémez, along with several Apache groups. The movement failed, and nine of the conspirators were hanged. These were sounding rods for the explosion of 1680, but they were little heeded as such by the Spanish governors.

During the governorship of Juan Manso (1656–59) there apparently was a

37. Scholes, "The First Decade of the Inquisition in New Mexico," *New Mexico Historical Review*, X (1935): 203–204.

lull in the conflict between the civil and ecclesiastical authorities in the province, but the old issues once more became acute during the evil administrations of Governor Bernardo López de Mendizábal (1659–61) and his successor, Governor Diego Dionisio de Peñalosa (1661–64). During these years the authority of the Inquisition was brought into play with notable success as a weapon in defense of the church. The story of Inquisition activity in New Mexico during the Mendizábal-Peñalosa period proved how effective this weapon could be at a time of crisis. But the Inquisitors finally realized that the Holy Office had become too closely identified with ordinary ecclesiastical jurisdiction in the province and that its authority had been used for purposes beyond its true function. In order to prevent loss of prestige and respect for the tribunal, it became necessary to clarify the position of the local representatives with regard to the long-standing civil-ecclesiastical controversies. Thus a policy of nonintervention was adopted after 1665. The separation of the offices of custodian of the missions and commissary of the Holy Office in 1668 was directed toward this end. This removed one source of friction, and the Inquisitors deserve credit for their clear-sighted and impartial attitude toward local affairs at this critical period. Another factor was the commendable character of the custodians and governors who administered local affairs during those years. The prelates of the 1670s concentrated more on missionary administration than dispute. However, the unhappy events of the Mendizábal-Peñalosa period left deep scars that were never entirely obliterated. The reconciliation of opposing interests that was achieved on the eve of the Pueblo revolt in 1680 was probably largely a result of urgent necessity.

For several years, 1667 to 1672, droughts and resulting crop failures caused widespread suffering, and it was necessary for the friars and colonists to pool their food supplies. The Apache raids increased in frequency and violence, and the punitive expeditions against them achieved only temporary success. Famine and the Apache attacks finally forced abandonment of the pueblos of the Manzano Tiwas and the Tompiros. Various abortive local conspiracies were incited by Pueblo medicine men and war chiefs, and toward the end of the 1670s rebellious Indians grew bold enough to raid the Villa of Santa Fe. Governor Juan Francisco de Treviño (1675–77), like Governor Manso, worked in close harmony with the missionaries. During his administration energetic measures were taken to combat the open resurgence of the Pueblo religion, and the severe punishment of native medicine men was an added irritation in inciting the general Pueblo Indian conspiracy of 1680.

The most unfortunate result of the years of conflict between the civil authorities and the church was the demoralizing effect it had on the Indians and the opportunity it presented for rebellious plotting by Pueblo Indians and increas-

ing boldness on the part of the Apache tribes. Seventy years of local controversy between the Spanish civil and ecclesiastical authorities had made the
province a house divided against itself, and reconciliations brought about in
the 1670s came too late to nullify the cumulative effect.

When the procurator-general of the mission supply caravan, Fray Francisco
de Ayeta, arrived in New Mexico in 1675 with mission supplies, he found the
missions in desperate straits. It was decided, therefore, that on his return to
Mexico City he advise the viceroy concerning the situation. The appeal was not
for the missions but for the strengthening of the military defense of the province, without which all of New Mexico and the missionary enterprise might go
down in ruin. Ayeta asked for fifty additional soldiers for the garrison, full
equipment for them, one thousand horses, and other supplementary equipment. For the transport of the soldiers the Franciscans offered twenty-five wagons. The request was granted, and in 1677, Ayeta conducted the supplies and
reinforcements to New Mexico. At about the same time Governor Antonio de
Otermín was appointed governor.

Father Ayeta was back in Mexico City the following year preparing for the
next mission supply service. In 1680 he departed for New Mexico with the
added reinforcements and supplies, and in August he arrived at the Río
Grande, where he was informed that a successful general revolt of the Pueblo
Indians had taken place and that the Spaniards had been forced to flee to El
Paso. Ayeta immediately placed all the mission supplies at the disposal of
Otermín and the Spanish colonists who had been able to escape.[38] Throughout
the winter of 1680–81, Father Ayeta played a leading part in the resettlement
of the fugitives in the El Paso district and in the plans to reconquer the province in 1681. Efforts at reconquest were made by Otermín, followed by those
of three of his successors, but they all failed.[39] New Mexico was temporarily
lost.

The Pueblo Indian Revolt of 1680

Popé, the leader of the Pueblo revolt of 1680, was a notorious enemy of the
Spaniards from the Tewa pueblo of San Juan. In the time of Governor Treviño
he was arrested with some forty other Tewas accused of various killings and acts
of idolatry and witchcraft. Three were hanged, one hanged himself, and the
others were whipped and condemned to servitude. Popé fled to Taos, the
northernmost of the pueblos, where he remained in hiding, filled with hate

38. Scholes, "The Supply Service of the New Mexico Missions, Part III," 400–402.
39. See especially Charles W. Hackett, "Otermín's Attempts to Reconquer New Mexico, 1681–1682,"
Old Santa Fe, III (1916): 44–84, 103–32; and "The Causes for the Failure of Otermín's Attempt to Reconquer New Mexico, 1681–1682," in *The Pacific Ocean in History,* ed. H. Morse Stephens and Herbert E.
Bolton, 439–51.

and vowing vengeance. For years he had the secret intention of plotting a general revolt to drive out the Spaniards and the missionaries. In the summer of 1680, from his hiding place in Taos, he laid out his plans to a few loyal medicine men and war captains. Aware of previous failures, they used every means to secure secrecy. The plan as it eventually was carried out was to strike the Spaniards by surprise with one decisive blow, either to destroy them or to drive them out.[40]

At that time there were approximately twenty-nine hundred Spanish people in New Mexico, living chiefly along the Río Grande and its tributaries in the region between Isleta and Taos. There were thirty-three Franciscans distributed throughout the province, ministering to twenty-five thousand Christian Pueblo Indians, including Acoma, Zuñi, the Hopi pueblos far to the west and Taos in the relatively distant north. The Pueblo Indian war chiefs had under their command approximately six thousand warriors, some of them now expert horsemen riding horses acquired from the Spaniards. Popé's plan was to unite the warriors of the various pueblos and Apache tribes and to attack by surprise the vastly outnumbered Spanish garrison at Santa Fe and the weakly guarded Spanish settlements and missions. Every three years the mission supply caravan arrived at Santa Fe from New Spain to replenish Spanish supplies, but this year it was late, and the rebel Pueblo leaders timed their blow to take advantage of the situation. The revolt was boldly and brilliantly conceived.

Cleverly shrouding himself in mystery in the secrecy of the kiva (*estufa*) at Taos, Popé issued orders to his loyal confederates throughout the province, all pledged to secrecy. He claimed that in the kiva at Taos the god Poheyemo appeared to him in person from the underworld and in personal conversation with him appointed him his *teniente*, or representative, ordering him to kill all the Spaniards and missionaries, destroy every vestige of their Christian religion, and return the Indians to the freedom of the past; and telling him that anyone who did not obey his orders would be summarily killed. The word was spread that the "representative" of Poheyemo was very tall and black, with frightful eyes that were large and yellow. The stratagem was to leave it unclear whether or not Popé was Poheyemo's chosen representative or the earthly embodiment of Poheyemo himself. To add to the wonder of his supernatural powers, Popé stated that there had appeared before him inside the kiva at Taos "three devils in the form of Indians, most horrifying in appearance, shooting flames of fire from all the senses and extremities of their bodies, named Caudi [Caidi], Tilimi [Tilim, Tilimpin] and Tleume [Thewme]," who instructed him on the specific manner in which he should carry out the revolt. The justi-

---

40. Charles W. Hackett is the authority on the Pueblo Revolt of 1680. See especially Charles W. Hackett and Charmion O. Shelby, *Revolt of the Pueblo Indians of New Mexico, and Otermín's Attempted Reconquest, 1680–1682.*

fication for revolt given by Popé and his confederates was clearly stated: to rid themselves of the heavy tribute demanded from them by the governor and the soldier-*encomenderos*, an extreme burden in these particular years of drought and starving, and to rid themselves of the missionaries who were forcing on them a new religion while the ancient native one was being suppressed. The religious conflict was clearly a major factor, and the revolt was led by Popé and other vengeful war captains and warriors inspired by a small number of medicine men and elders who were ready to protect their power and authority at any cost. It was not a popular mass movement. Among Popé's principal companions in coordinating the general revolt were the following war chiefs: El Jaca, of Taos; Don Luis Tupatú, of Picurís; Alonso Catiti, of Santo Domingo; Luis Cuniju, of Jémez; the Tanos' spokesman Antonio Bolsas; Cristóbal Yope of San Lázaro; the Keres leader Antonio Malacate, and several other influential medicine men and war chiefs.[41]

The date set for the outbreak was August 11. But the plot was discovered on the ninth, and so the general revolt was advanced to the morning of August 10. Governor Otermín was unaware of the seriousness of the revolt until the twelfth, and it was not until the thirteenth that it was decided to call into Santa Fe the settlers and missionaries from the surrounding area. Meanwhile, in the outlying areas the Spaniards and missionaries were taken completely off their guard and massacred. On August 15 the Indians laid siege to Santa Fe. The first onslaught was made by some five hundred warriors, soon followed by larger reinforcements arriving from every direction, swelling their ranks to over three thousand combatants against scarcely two hundred armed Span-

---

41. All the contemporary testimony points to Popé as the instigator and leader of the revolt. (See Hackett's publications in the Bibliography, below.) Fray Angélico Chávez has presented the theory that the ancestors of the leader, a mulatto named Domingo Naranjo living among the Indians, were Negro slaves in New Spain who had intermarried with Mexican Indians and who entered New Mexico in Oñate's day. He concludes that the description of Poheyemo's "representative" as an alleged tall black person fits that of Naranjo, most of whose relatives hated their Spanish superiors. (Fray Angélico Chávez, "Pohe-yemo's Representative and the Pueblo Revolt of 1680," *New Mexico Historical Review*, 42 (1962): 85–126.) It is, of course, well known that some of the principal leaders in Pueblo Indian uprisings in New Mexico in the second half of the seventeenth century were mulattoes, *coyotes*, and *mestizos* with a predominant Indian strain who lived as Indians in some of the pueblos with Indian women. In the realm of surmises, regarding the message from the secrecy of the kiva in Taos, to awe the people, that three beings appeared before Popé shooting flames of fire from their extremities and instructing him how to destroy the Spaniards, it might also be added that the hallucination of seeing flames shooting out of one's body is known to occur to peyote eaters. It is also of record that among Negroes and mulattoes who entered New Mexico in menial positions, demonology, brought from Africa, was practiced, and some of them, as well as Mexican Indians, were known to use the hallucinatory peyote mushroom. (France V. Scholes, "The First Decade of the Inquisition in New Mexico," 208–20.) Hence, a variety of undocumented theoretical factors could be deduced. New Mexican scholars of Indian descent have advanced the view that the revolt was a popular, nativist revolution for freedom and liberty in the modern sense of these terms. Their observations are important in evaluating the forces at work in the revolt. (See the writings of Jack D. Forbes, Alfonso Ortiz, and Joe S. Sando.)

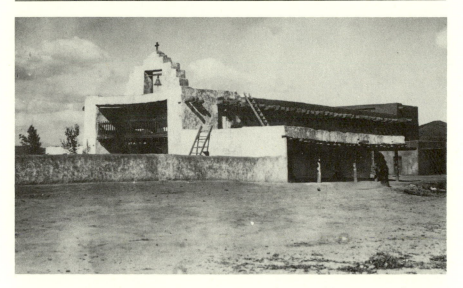

The church at Santo Domingo Pueblo, 1899. *Photograph courtesy of the National Anthropological Archives, the Smithsonian Institution, Washington, D.C.*

iards. The siege of Santa Fe lasted nine days and ended with the flight of the surviving colonists southward to the El Paso district. Twenty-one Franciscan missionaries and 380 colonists were killed.

At the missions the missionaries were subjected to the most barbarous and depraved treatment before they were murdered. At Jémez, when the *alcalde mayor* and the guardian of the mission fled, Fray Juan de Jesús remained in his convent cell. That night a group of Jémez rebels entered the cell and took Fray Juan to the cemetery, where they lit many candles, stripped him naked, mounted him on a pig, and beat him cruelly as they ridiculed him and led him about the cemetery. Then they took him off the pig, made him get down on all fours, and took turns mounting his back and whipping him. Fray Juan suffered all of this with only the words, "Do with me as you wish, for this joy of yours will not last more than ten years, after which you will consume each other in wars." This angered the tormenters, and they killed him with war clubs and threw his body in the rear of the pueblo.

When the Acomas heard that the missionaries were being killed, they seized Fray Lucas Maldonado and Fray Juan de Val, along with an old Christian mestiza. All three were stripped naked and tied together with a rope, the old Indian woman between the two friars. They were then led about the pueblo while their captors beat them. They were then taken to the entrance of the convent, where they were stoned to death, lanced, and thrown into a deep pit nearby.

At the moment of the uprising Fray Agustín de Santa María was on his way from the Hopi pueblos and was waylaid near Zuñi by some Zuñis and Acomas. Upon seeing them, he dismounted and knelt on the ground with his hands clasped, looking to the heavens, saying nothing, and there he was beaten to death with war clubs and pierced with lances, and his body was left on the side of the road. At the Moqui pueblos, Fray José de Espeleta (Oraibi), Fray José Trujillo (Xongopavi) and Fray José de Figueroa (Aguatuvi) were shot, despite the pleading of an Indian who had been raised by Father Espeleta.[42] The other Franciscan missionaries who lost their lives were killed with similar brutality, all on August 10, 1680.[43]

During the years 1680 to 1692 the Pueblo Indians held their land as its undisputed rulers. The houses of the Spanish settlers were robbed of household goods and burned, and the horses and livestock left behind were appropriated. The churches were burned and destroyed, strippd of their sacred vessels, imagery, and ornaments, and in every way foully desecrated. Some churches were converted into barns. The official Spanish archives at Santa Fe were piled up in the public square and burned. All men, women, and children were ordered to remove from their necks crosses and rosaries and to destroy or burn them. The name of Christ, the Virgin Mary, and the saints were not to be invoked. Those who had contracted Christian marriages were ordered to cast off their wives and marry others at their pleasure. No one should use the Castilian language or show any sign of love for the missionaries. An old witchdoctor, Pedro Naranjo, was sent with instructions from Popé to the various pueblos to revive the performance in public of the religious dances and practices that the missionaries had suppressed. Then Popé made a general tour of inspection accompanied by the Taos leader El Jaca; the former governor of Picurís, Luis Tupatú; the Keres leader, Alonso Catiti; and other lieutenants. Church ornaments of value or attraction were distributed among them. At Santa Ana a large feast was prepared with food from the kitchens of the missionaries and the Spanish governor and served on a long table in the manner of the Spaniards. Popé sat at the head, and Catiti at the other end, and the other leaders were seated around. Popé and

42. Fray Silvestre Vélez de Escalante, "Extracto de Noticias . . ." [1778], Ms., AGN, *Historia,* tomo 2. Escalante's report on the above events and on the events that transpired in New Mexico between 1680 and 1689, summarized below, including the testimony given at El Paso by the Pueblo Indian leader Bartolomé de Ojeda, captured at the time of Governor Cruzate's attack on Zia in 1689, are based on his examination of the documents he found in the government archives in Santa Fe (see also note 1 to document 82, below, on Ojeda).

43. The complete list of the missionaries with their names and the missions where they were killed may be found in Hackett and Shelby, *Revolt of the Pueblo Indians,* I: 109–11.

Catiti were brought holy chalices, and they both used them to toast curses to the Spaniards and the Christian religion. Popé, raising his chalice, and as though addressing the father custodian, addressed Catiti, saying, "To your health, reverend father." Catiti replied, "The same to you, your excellency the governor."[44]

Otermín, who believed the cause was hopeless and who displayed weak leadership, led an expedition to reconquer New Mexico in 1681–82. He re-occupied Isleta pueblo, where he received the submission of the entire population, numbering 511 persons, but failed in all efforts farther north. He managed to sack and burn ten abandoned pueblos south of Cochití and then returned to El Paso. Pedro Reneros de Posada, governor of New Mexico from 1686 to 1689, made an expedition as far north as Zia in 1688, sacked Santa Ana, and only succeeded in capturing a few horses and sheep. Domingo Jironza Petriz de Cruzate, governor from 1683 to 1686 and again from 1689 to 1691, attained greater initial success than his predecessors in his expedition of 1689, but also failed. He destroyed Zia in a bloody battle, where the rebels defended themselves with great valor, some preferring to die in the flames of their burning houses rather than give up. Many of the natives were killed in the struggle, including four rebel leaders who were captured and shot in the pueblo square, and seventy others were taken as captives to El Paso. A pretentious expedition was proposed by the frontier Captain Toribio de la Huerta in 1689, and a second expedition by Cruzate in 1690, neither of which materialized.

With the loss of the upper Río Grande region, El Paso assumed real importance as an outpost of frontier defense. The temporary settlement of the fugitives from New Mexico in the El Paso district placed a heavy burden on the struggling community. Some of the fugitives fled southward to Parral and other localities in northern New Spain. For the accommodation of the Indian allies who had withdrawn with the Spaniards, the villages of Senecú, Socorro, and Isleta were established in the vicinity of El Paso. The previously discussed plan of establishing a presidio at El Paso now became a reality. In 1683 a garrison of fifty soldiers was stationed there. The El Paso district became the temporary capital of New Mexico and the headquarters for the cabildo of Santa Fe. At this most critical period in the early history of New Mexico, El Paso became the haven of the New Mexican exiles, the safeguard of the frontier settlements of New Vizcaya, and the base of operations from which the lost province was eventually to be reconquered by Spanish arms.

In New Mexico, meanwhile, the Pueblo Indians, who for twelve years were again the sole rulers of their land, split into warring factions among them-

44. Escalante, "Extracto de Noticias."

The church at Cochití Pueblo, 1906. *Photograph courtesy of the Prints and Photographs Division, Library of Congress, Washington, D.C.*

selves. The Keres of Zia, Santa Ana, San Felipe, Cochití, and Santo Domingo, with the Jémez, Taos, and Pecos, fought against the Tewas, Tanos, and Picurís, and deposed Popé, rising against his despotic rule and the heavy tribute he demanded of them on his frequent tours. In his place they elected Don Luis Tupatú, who governed the Tewas and Tanos until 1688, when Popé was again reelected. After Popé's death, Tupatú was again elected. Catiti, the leader of the Keres, died during this time, and thereafter the Keres ruled their pueblos independently. The natives of Acoma were divided, some remaining on the Rock, others moving away, both groups at war with each other. The Zuñis and Hopis were also at war. The Apaches were at peace with some of the pueblos and hostile to others. The Utes, since the revolt, were at war with all of the pueblos, especially those of Taos, Picurís, the Tewas, and Jémez.[45] Thus, the unity forged for a brief inspired moment in the fall of 1680 lasted only a short time. The Pueblo leaders lost their great opportunity to consolidate their strength to withstand further Spanish invasion.

45. Escalante, "Extracto de Noticias."

The Reconquest and Recolonization of New Mexico

The historic Spanish reconquest and resettlement of New Mexico was achieved under the leadership of Governor Diego de Vargas Zapata Luján Ponce de León. Vargas belonged to one of Spain's most prominent and prestigious noble families. He served in various official positions on the northern frontier of New Spain for over a decade before his appointment as governor and captain general of New Mexico on June 18, 1688. He took possession of the government at El Paso on February 22, 1691, and planned to reconquer the province immediately and at his own expense. Economic problems in the El Paso region, and participation in campaigns against hostile Indians in New Vizcaya, Sonora, and Sinaloa occupied his attention until the end of the year, when the viceroy was then able to direct his attention to the reconquest of New Mexico.

Vargas planned two entries into the north: first, a preliminary visit to the revolted province to learn the state of affairs there, to reduce and conquer the apostate rebels by force of arms if necessary, and to verify the reports of quicksilver mines in the elusive Sierra Azul. This was to be followed by a carefully organized colonizing expedition whereby the former Spanish settlements and missions in New Mexico would be reestablished.[46]

The preliminary military expedition into New Mexico in 1692 was a complete success, although the small force came very near to being annihilated at Santa Fe, at Jémez, and at the Moqui pueblos. There the Spaniards were outnumbered ten to one by enemy warriors, who were at first eager to engage in battle. But in each case Vargas's bold diplomacy and the exhortations of the missionaries saved the day. Vargas estimated that during the course of his expedition he had traveled more than six hundred leagues. In public ceremonies, through Fray Francisco Corbera, president of the chaplains who accompanied him, Vargas granted religious administrative authority over the region to the Franciscans.[47] In the four-month campaign twenty-three pueblos of ten Indian nations were restored to Spain's empire in America without the wasting of a single ounce of powder or the unsheathing of a sword and without costing the royal treasury a single *maravedí*. Not even a drop of enemy blood was shed, except in conflicts with the hostile Apaches. Seventy-four persons in captivity were set free, among them a number of Spanish women and children, and 2,214 Indians, mostly children, were baptized. Everywhere, despite the ruins

46. See especially J. Manuel Espinosa, *Crusaders of the Río Grande: The Story of Don Diego de Vargas and the Reconquest and Refounding of New Mexico;* and Espinosa, *First Expedition of Vargas*. This section is based largely on these two works. The latter is a translation of Vargas's complete campaign journal of his first expedition and related documents, and the former is a comprehensive history of the reconquest and recolonization of New Mexico.

47. See documents 1 and 2, below.

of destroyed churches, convents, and homes, the Spanish language was still alive among many of the Pueblo Indians.

A remarkable evidence of the culture that emanated from each former mission center may be gleaned from the books and religious articles recovered at Zuñi, which Indians had kept in hiding there since the revolt of 1680. Vargas records in his journal that the Indian governor and his captains asked him to climb up to a room on the second floor, off the flat roof of one of the dwellings, where he was shown an altar with two large candles burning, and when some pieces of vestments were removed, a large number of religious articles and books were revealed. In accepting these articles Vargas told the Indians that he was taking them with him so that the father custodian at El Paso del Río del Norte might again consecrate them. He left two large bells that were among the articles found, stating that upon his return with the priest who should be designted to reestablish the mission at Zuñi, he would bring back the other articles for the church and the convent which he had ordered them to build. Vargas noted in his journal:

> With these arguments they remained very happy and satisfied, and they invited me to go and partake of the food they had prepared for me, which I did, accompanied by the reverend missionary fathers. We all marvelled at having experienced the said action on the part of the said Indians, which had not been experienced in any of the other pueblos or the *villa* of the said kingdom, for everywhere else they said that the religious articles had been lost or destroyed, or that they had been carried off by the Apaches.[48]

New Mexico's submission was as yet a formality, as no Spaniards had remained in the north. But the way had been prepared, and the final phase of the reconquest of New Mexico was at hand. Vargas returned to El Paso and immediately began preparations for the colonizing expedition which would seal the victory for Spain.

When the glad tidings of the successful campaign and the impending restoration of the whole region of New Mexico were received in Mexico City, the occasion was one for great rejoicing. The viceroy officially thanked the governor of New Mexico for his services, and promised everything necessary for the permanent preservation of that which had been regained. By viceregal decree Vargas was now granted the right to solicit colonists and enlist one hundred soldiers for the establishment of a presidio at Santa Fe, wherever and in whatever manner might be most convenient. The viceroy agreed to send a number of volunteer families from Mexico City. Since the five settlements of the El Paso district had a total of only 112 households to draw upon, all of them in a

---

48. The complete listing of the books and religious articles found at Zuñi is presented in Espinosa, *First Expedition of Vargas*, 201–203.

miserable economic state, Vargas traveled great distances throughout New Vizcaya and New Galicia recruiting additional soldiers and colonists.

For the reestablishment of the missions, friars were immediately made available at El Paso, and more were promised. The commissary general of New Spain issued a circular letter requesting volunteers from other parts of New Spain. Eight friars of the College of Santa Cruz de Querétaro were accepted from those who volunteered in answer to the letter. They were Miguel Trizio, José Diez, José García Marín, Gerónimo Prieto, Antonio Baamonde, Blas Navarro, Domingo de Jesús María, and Francisco de Jesús María Casañas. They were among the eighteen friars who left El Paso with Governor Vargas and the colonizing expedition destined for New Mexico.[49]

Finally, the expedition was ready: it consisted of one hundred soldiers, seventy families, eighteen Franciscan friars, and a number of Indian allies. The expedition was accompanied by nine hundred head of livestock, more than two thousand horses, and one thousand mules. Prominent among the leaders and colonists were former residents of New Mexico. The main body of the expedition set out for Santa Fe on October 4, 1693, amid great pomp and ceremony. All those who were able traveled on horseback; the other colonists crowded into twelve mule- and horse-drawn wagons that had been outfitted at Parral. Six wagons and eighty mules were employed in the transportation of the supplies, and three cannon were carried in three small carriages. On October 13, Vargas and the cabildo took final leave of El Paso, escorted by two squads of "leather-jackets," one to guard the royal banner and the other to guard the horses.

When the expedition entered the pueblo country, it learned that the natives, despite their promises of 1692, were again in rebellion against the Spaniards and were ready to resist them. Only Pecos, Santa Ana, Zia, and San Felipe remained loyal. As the expedition advanced toward Santa Fe, the faithful Indian governor of Pecos, Juan de Ye, hastened to warn Vargas that the Tewas, Tanos, Picurís, Taos, Jémez, Acomas, and Moquis were prepared for battle.

---

49. See documents 3–10, below, for complete listings of this missionary group. The ready availability of missionaries was in part the result of a series of independent international developments that occurred on the distant gulf coast of Texas between 1682 and 1693, where, to forestall a French threat to occupy the region under La Salle and claim it for France, an attempt was made by Spain to establish Franciscan missions which eventually was unsuccessful. The missionary resources built up for that effort turned, at a most opportune moment, to the advantage of the missions of New Mexico. With missionaries from the College of Santa Cruz de Querétaro, Fray Damian Massanet had founded several missions in Texas between 1690 and 1693, but the missionaries and soldiers were beset by floods, drought, disease, and insurmountable Indian hostility, and the attempt to found missions in Texas came to an end. Meanwhile, Fray Pedro Sitjar had been sent to Spain to gather more missionaries for the college, and he returned to New Spain in 1692 with twenty-eight religious. These men were barely settled in Querétaro when the commissary of New Spain sent out the circular letter asking for volunteers to reestablish the missions of New Mexico. See McCloskey, *Formative Years*, 62–70.

Undaunted, Vargas climbed the steep mountain trail of La Bajada and entered into the valley of Santa Fe.[50]

Without fear, Vargas proceeded directly to Santa Fe and peacefully entered the plaza, where the natives awaited without weapons, quiet and composed. Vargas addressed the Indians, who were polite but not enthusiastic, and to avoid a rupture between the Indians and the soldiers, the Spaniards pitched camp just outside the city. Thus far, by keeping the uncertain natives divided in loyalty, and with the support of several influential Indian chieftains, Vargas appeared to have the advantage in a war of nerves.

With rumors rife that the Tewas and Tanos at Santa Fe had merely feigned obedience in order to cloak their treacherous plans, Vargas calmly made plans for the refounding of the missions and for the distribution of the missionaries at Santa Fe and eleven other pueblos.[51] The loyal Juan de Ye feared the consequences and offered to get reinforcements from his pueblo of Pecos. Because of these circumstances the custodian presented Vargas with a petition, signed by him and all the other missionaries, pleading against the distribution of the missionaries at that time. He regarded such an act as dangerous and injudicious and urged that the warnings of the ever-faithful Juan de Ye be heeded. Vargas responded courteously but reserved the decision to his own judgment.[52]

For two weeks the Spaniards camped outside the gates of the walled city of Santa Fe, virtually without shelter, while twenty-two of their number died of exposure and were buried under the winter snow. Vargas finally decided to call a general council of war, composed of all of the leading Spanish citizens, the missionaries, and the military officers. The gathering was held in his tent, and their petitions and complaints were registered and opinions expressed. On a motion of the cabildo, this gathering took officially the form of a *cabildo abierto,* or open town meeting. It was unanimously agreed that the Tanos be obliged to return to their former pueblo of Galisteo and that the villa be reoccupied by the Spaniards, by force if necessary. The missionaries repeated that the time was not auspicious to distribute the missionaries as Vargas had planned.[53] These meetings could be clearly observed by the Indians, who knew full well what the colonists were demanding, and they were ready for resistance.[54]

At four o'clock in the morning of the next day, Vargas was aroused from

50. Before entering the hostile valley of Santa Fe, a small band of colonists fled to El Paso. Espinosa, *Crusaders,* 145–46.

51. Vargas's journal, December 17, 1693, AGN, *Historia,* tomo 38, and AGI, *Guadalajara,* legajo 140.

52. See documents 3 and 4, below.

53. Vargas's journal, December 24, 26–27, 1693. AGI, *Guadalajara,* legajo 140, and document 5, below.

54. The paragraphs that follow, describing the days preceding the battle of Santa Fe and the victorious outcome for the Spaniards, are based on Vargas's journal and related documents in AGI, *Guadalajara,* legajo 140, summarized in Espinosa, *Crusaders,* 151–62.

sleep by a messenger from the villa sent by a Spanish spy, who had wrapped himself in his cloak and in the darkness had mingled with the Indian throng in the patio, listening to the harangue of their governor, the gist of which was: "Arise, massacre the Spaniards!" Upon receiving this information in the early morning of December 28, Vargas immediately sounded the alarm. The governor of Pecos was sent to his pueblo for reinforcements, and there was no delay in sending for the Spanish families and soldiers living inside the villa. Some left all their belongings behind. As one of the Spaniards escaped with his wife and children, they were met by a storm of darts, clods, and stone hatchets thrown from the walls, accompanied by hideous and vengeful threats. A squadron sent to examine the stronghold found its wall tops already lined with warriors. When these saw the approaching soldiers, they raised blood-curdling shouts interspersed with repellent blasphemy and accompanied by a barrage of stones and other missiles. Indians had arrived from the surrounding area apparently to aid the rebels, but they did not enter the fray.

For better protection Vargas quickly transferred his camp to a flat, open meadow directly in front of, and an arquebus shot distant from, the stronghold. Then, with the cabildo and most of the soldiers, Vargas rode to the gateway of the villa. On the wall above the doorway stood the rebel war captains and the most valiant warriors, among them Antonio Bolsas. Remembering his tactics of the previous year, Vargas patiently harangued the rebels from below, and Bolsas finally said that he would deliberate with the people and give an answer in the evening. Vargas returned to his tent, but received no answer.

At about seven o'clock the next morning, December 29, 140 Pecos Indian allies came to the aid of Vargas. He again sallied forth to parley with the rebels, but they were defiant. The army was again formed, and Vargas boldly marched to the villa. But he had scarcely started to move forward when the Indians cried out to the Spaniards that the whole countryside was against them, including every Apache camp, as far west as the Moqui pueblos, and that they would kill everyone except the missionaries, whom they would enslave. These boasts were followed by a storm of darts, arrows, stones, and other heavy objects. "Santiago! Santiago! Death to these rebels!" cried out Vargas to his men, and the battle was on.

By the morning of December 30, Santa Fe was won by the Spaniards, and as a sign of victory the royal banner was placed upon the walls and a cross was placed over the main entrance. The Indians were asked to come out to obtain pardon, and most of the women and children complied, accompanied by the rebel Bolsas. Later in the day fifty-four others, men, women, and children, were driven out of hiding and delivered to the guards. Large supplies of beans, maize, grain, and seed were confiscated and distributed to the Spanish families. Vargas then ordered the colonists to take their lodging in the ample quarters of the vanquished.

The fifty-four rebels first taken out of hiding that day, fifteen found later, and Antonio Bolsas, one of the leading spirits of the uprising, were executed at the rear of the stronghold on the following charges: having stoned and destroyed a cross placed in the center of the square, broken a statue of the Virgin Mary, and committed treason against God and the royal crown. Those who had surrendered of their own free will, about four hundred of both sexes, were distributed among the soldiers and settlers in servitude for a period of ten years. After the ten-year period, if sufficiently instructed in Christian doctrine and citizenship, they might return to a pueblo of their choosing. As a result of the battle, eighty-one rebels perished: seventy by execution, nine in battle, and two by suicide. Of the Spaniards, only one had died in battle. The Spaniards now had a solid foothold in New Mexico. The victory was a crucial turning point in the history of the region.[55]

As the year 1694 opened, the Spanish colonists were safely established within the walls of Santa Fe. But for the time being it was like being stranded on a barren island, for all the surrounding tribes were hostile. Among twenty-odd pueblos, only four, namely, Pecos and the Keres of Santa Ana, Zia, and San Felipe, remained faithful to their promises of 1692. The natives of nearly all the other pueblos withdrew to mesa tops and the rims of hidden canyons. Those of Santo Domingo and Jémez were on the mesas near their respective pueblos, the other Keres on the mesa of La Cieneguilla de Cochití, and most of the Tanos and Tewas on the mesa of San Ildefonso, with others in nearby canyons. The Picurís and Taos remained in their more distant pueblos.

Obviously Vargas's great task was to break down a deep feeling of suspicion and distrust on the part of the natives, who feared punishment for the crimes of 1680. Furthermore, the Spaniards were not only conquerors but also zealous crusaders for the Catholic faith, and most of the older Indian leaders were determined to retain their ancient way of life, which the Spaniards aimed to stamp out. The year was characterized by constant warfare that prevented the colonists from planting their fields. Consequently, they still depended on what they were able to seize from the granaries of the enemy and what little was sent up from Mexico. Vargas, with the aid of the missionaries, spent months pleading with the natives to submit peacefully, and only after all such efforts failed did he embark upon a bloody and protracted military offensive.

In late March of 1694 the custodian Fray Salvador de San Antonio, in an exchange of correspondence with Governor Vargas, reviewed the course of

55. *Ibid.*

The church at Santa Ana Pueblo, 1899. *Photograph courtesy of the National Anthropological Archives, the Smithsonian Institution, Washington, D.C.*

events to date and urged Vargas to delay his campaign against the hostile surrounding pueblos, reminding him of the dangers to the unprotected friars and colonists while he was away campaigning, and calling attention to the precarious food supply. Vargas was courteous in his replies but reserved action to his own judgment.[56]

On April 17 the mesa of La Cieneguilla de Cochití was taken by assault with the aid of loyal Indian allies. The natives were forced to submit, and considerable grain and livestock were captured. Toward the end of June, Father Francisco Farfán arrived at Santa Fe with a colony of approximately sixty-six families, totaling 230 persons, from Mexico. This meant more reinforcements, but it also meant additional mouths to feed. Faced with the grim necessity of obtaining provisions at all costs, Vargas decided to embark immediately upon a campaign to crush the rebellious natives of Jémez and Santo Domingo, but since the Río Grande was running dangerously high, the campaign was temporarily postponed. In view of this delay and the pressing need of feeding the colony, Vargas decided upon a trip to the abandoned Tano and Tewa pueblos, and from there to Picurís, to obtain maize. This mission having proved fruitless, he proceeded to Taos. The natives, upon learning of the approach of the Spaniards, fled hastily into the nearby mountains, and large stores of grain left at the pueblo were easy prey. The grain reached Santa Fe without mishap.

The delayed campaign againt the Jémez and their Santo Domingo confederates was now carried out. On July 24 the well-fortified rock of Jémez was carried by assault after a short and bloody battle. The "miraculous" victory resulted in the capture of great quantities of much-needed grain. With addi-

56. See documents 6–9, below.

tional Indian allies, Vargas now marched to the mesa of San Ildefonso. On September 8 the harried natives atop the mesa laid down their arms and sued for peace. All New Mexico, except Picurís and Taos in the north and Acoma, Zuñi, and the Moqui pueblos in the far west, was now reconquered for Spain.

The victorious campaigns of 1694 were soon followed by the spread of settlement and of Spanish institutions. Missions were refounded, political jurisdictions (*alcaldías*) were reestablished, the Indian pueblos were rebuilt and reoccupied, and local Indian governments were again set up in them. These governments were on the Spanish model, the local Pueblo Indian officials, freely elected by their own people, being formally installed in office by the Spanish authorities. In Santa Fe natives from the surrounding pueblos were again trading their produce with the settlers and mingling as friends.

The missionaries were now convinced that peace was secure, and on September 22, 1694, they informed Vargas that they were ready to be assigned to missions at the pacified pueblos to the extent that their numbers permitted.[57] Between September 24 and December 21, 1694, Vargas, accompanied by the vice-custodian Fray Muñoz de Castro and the assigned missionaries, visited a number of the pueblos, where in formal ceremonies the rights and duties of the local Indian authorities were outlined and the loyalty of the Indian leaders was affirmed, and where the missionaries assigned were left to assume their ministries. Assignments to other pueblos would be made on the expected arrival of additional missionaries from El Paso.[58]

On December 20, 1694, the recently appointed custodian, Fray Francisco de Vargas, now established at Santa Fe, sent a letter to the missionaries at the various missions thus far established requesting reports on the status of their missions, their accomplishments to date, and proposals for the future. The replies were prompt, detailed, and informative, and most of them were quite candid in their appraisals. The letters to their custodian present a vivid picture of the primitive conditions at the Pueblo Indian missions, the process of organizing the newly reestablished missions, and the religious efforts being made by the friars. They also present thoughtful comments on the character and qualities of their Indian charges. In general the reports were optimistic in tenor, although they agreed that progress in evangelizing the adult Indians was slow and uncertain.[59]

As the year 1695 opened, New Mexico appeared to be at last laying the foundations of self-sufficiency and permanency. Eleven Indian missions had

---

57. See document 10, below.

58. See document 11, below. This document, or series of documents, describes in detail the ceremonies at the various pueblos visited. In December, 1694, Vargas freed a number of Indians who had been held captive following the battle at Santa Fe.

59. See documents 12–22, below.

been reestablished in the region surrounding Santa Fe, and the only important pueblos still without a mission or *visita* were Picurís and Taos, both of which were soon to have resident missionaries.[60] Ranches and farm sites were surveyed and occupied in the Santa Cruz Valley and along the Río Grande southwest of Santa Fe. On April 22, 1695, the sixty-six families recently brought up from Mexico were settled at the Villa Nueva de Santa Cruz, thus founding New Mexico's second most important settlement. On May 9, forty-four additional families arrived from Mexico and were settled in the environs of Santa Fe. They brought with them horses, mules, and additional livestock. Soon much-needed farm implements arrived from Mexico. Although New Mexico was still a financial burden upon the government at Mexico City, the future looked bright. Before the end of the year another Spanish settlement was established at Bernalillo, on the Río Grande some forty-five miles south of Santa Fe.

The Pueblo Indian Revolt of 1696

Now that the missionaries were distributed and the military force was somewhat scattered, some of the hostile native governors, war chiefs, and medicine men began to plot another general revolt and massacre like that of 1680, and for similar motives. As the severe winter of 1695–96 set in, the economic hardships of the Spanish settlers were increasingly evident to the Indians, and this put confidence in the hearts of those who had lost little of their hatred for the Spaniards. Some of the friars suspected that such a plot was afoot as early as July, 1695, through rumors they heard and suspicious activity they observed at the various Indian pueblos.[61]

By early December it became increasingly clear to the missionaries that Pueblo Indian leaders were plotting a general revolt, and they notified their custodian. Their reports were so alarming that the custodian convoked a meeting of the *definitorio* of the Franciscan community at Santa Fe to review the situation. The prospect of withdrawing all the missionaries to Santa Fe to assure their safety was seriously discussed. On December 13, after long deliberation, a letter was written to Governor Vargas requesting that he send soldiers to the various pueblos to observe for themselves the seriousness of the situation.[62] Since Vargas did not wish to arouse the suspicion of Indian leaders about his motives for such action, he made no immediate military moves.

On December 18 the custodian Fray Francisco de Vargas decided that it was time to obtain a further appraisal of the situation from the friars at their various

---

60. See document 23, below. This document, a letter from Governor Vargas to the viceroy, summarizes the status of affairs in New Mexico as the year 1695 opened.

61. See document 88, below.

62. See document 24, below.

missions, and he addressed a letter to them to convene at Zia in the event that a general revolt should take place, advising them that he had assurances from the governor that he would send a well-armed military escort to protect the missionaries and that the soldiers would remain there until Christmas if nothing happened in the interim. Father Francisco Corbera, at San Ildefonso, wrote to the custodian, "The uprising will take place, sooner or later." Meanwhile, nothing new happened, and it appeared that the rebellion expected at that time by the missionaries had miscarried because of its discovery and the precautionary measures taken.[63] The months that followed were treacherous ones for the missionaries, and their religious activities at the missions were becoming completely ineffectual because of increasing hostile acts by their Indian charges. Widespread rumors of an impending revolt continued.

In early March 1696, the fears of the missionaries for their safety became so alarming that the custodian pleaded with Governor Vargas to station an adequate guard of soldiers at each mission. The governor promised to send soldiers to those missions that deemed military protection absolutely necessary, and the custodian promptly sent letters to the missionaries requesting their recommendations.[64] In their replies the missionaries described the desperate situation in which they found themselves. They referred to evidence that meetings were being held by rebel leaders to perfect plans for a general revolt at the opportune moment, which might occur at any time. Father Prieto, writing from San Juan, indicated that a well-planned uprising had been set for March, with Zuñi, Acoma, and the Moquis joining with the rebel pueblos, but that it had miscarried when discovered by the missionaries. Fray José Arbizu, writing from San Cristóbal, stated that most of the natives of the pueblo had already withdrawn with their belongings to the mountains of Chimayó, at the approaches to which they had built horse traps. Some of the missionaries asked for guards of from six to twelve soldiers; others left the decision to the governor. The mission establishments were in a state of chaos.[65]

On March 13 the custodian sent another petition to the governor, reporting on the replies of the missionaries to his previous letter and pleading for the military protection requested. Governor Vargas, in his reply of March 15, made it clear to the custodian that he had a total of only one hundred soldiers at his disposal, the complement of the presidio at Santa Fe, and of them sixty were needed to guard the horses; of the remaining forty, ten were employed in guarding the gates to the city, twenty-six were being sent with beasts of burden to El Paso to bring aid in livestock and food supplies, and the four others were his top-level associates, the lieutenant governor, the captain of the pre-

---

63. See documents 25–27, below.
64. See documents 28–30, below.
65. See documents 31–47, below.

sidio, the *alférez,* and the *ayudante.* Nevertheless, on the basis of his appraisal he promised to provide four soldiers each for San Juan, San Ildefonso, Taos, Picurís, and each of the Jémez pueblos. The governor assured the custodian that he would continue his vigilance in constantly reconnoitering and scouting the area. Meanwhile, since the missionaries believed that a revolt was imminent, all of them had withdrawn to the protection of Santa Fe, Bernalillo, and Santa Cruz.

Although Governor Vargas admitted to the gravity of the situation, he firmly believed that he could dissuade a sufficient number of Indian leaders from participating in a general revolt, and he continued to refer to the fears of the missionaries as based on rumors and presumptions. He, too, was closely observing the movements of the Indians and had frequent meetings with their leaders. He used the stratagem of explaining to them that the stationing of soldiers at several of the pueblos was for their own protection as well as that of the Spaniards against raids by Apaches and other hostile surrounding tribes. Thus, Vargas believed that by discreet arguments he would not needlessly offend friendly Indian leaders and at the same time would allay the suspicions of leaders whose loyalty was suspect.[66]

Informing the missionaries of the governor's decisions, the custodian requested that each of them report his final resolutions so that the custodian could present them to the governor. The tenor of the replies from the missionaries was that under the circumstances they could not in conscience return to their missions without walking knowingly into the jaws of death, which would be sheer folly and could hardly be considered martyrdom in defense of the faith, for which they were prepared. The custodian sadly presented the information to Governor Vargas, stating that he could not force the missionaries to return to their missions, nor could he impede any of them from returning if they were willing to do so at the risk of their lives. He stated that the rebellious Indians feared only the rigor of Spanish arms. Vargas replied that there was little more that he could do beyond his ongoing efforts.[67]

Since the governor had made his position clear, the custodian, in informing the missionaries of the outcome of his pleas, asked them again for their opinions and advice. In their written replies, dated from March 29 to April 21, some of them of considerable length, the friars repeated in more desperate language the views that they had already expressed many times, and some were caustic in response to the governor's continued comment that their fears were based on "rumors and suppositions." They referred to repeated insults heaped upon them by the Indians during religious services; the profaning of religious articles and statues; the theft of large numbers of livestock, sheep, and horses

66. See documents 48–49, below.
67. See documents 50–67, below.

from the mission establishments; the inability to maintain any discipline among their charges and the disruption of all religious aspects of mission life; the abandonment or semiabandonment of the missions by the natives; and the false story persistently circulated by representatives of rebel Indians that the Spaniards were planning to kill all the rebel and apostate Indians at the opportune time, thus inciting and arousing fear in the minds of the otherwise peaceful Indian populace.[68] Resigned to whatever might befall them, a few of the missionaries quietly returned to their missions. Most of the salvageable religious articles of the missions had already been removed to Santa Fe and Santa Cruz.

Toward the end of March, Governor Vargas reported to the viceroy on the discouraging developments of recent months. The plea that clung to every word of his letter was for more colonists and much needed food and other supplies. He estimated that there were 276 families in the upper Río Grande country, and he repeated that the colony would continue to be in grave danger until there were at least 500 families settled there, along with the presidio of one hundred soldiers. Then and then only, he stated, could New Mexico offer security and self-sufficiency to the settlers and success to the missionaries.[69] Seven weeks later, on May 17, the father custodian wrote a short letter to the Franciscan commissary general stating that Fray José Diez was on his way to Mexico to report verbally on the critical status of the missions, and indicating that the subject was not discussed in the letter because it might conflict with what Governor Vargas might be reporting to the viceroy.[70]

Finally, the event predicted by the missionaries took place. On June 4, 1696, news of widespread acts of open rebellion began to pour into Santa Fe from every side. That day the Indians brutally murdered five missionaries and twenty-one Spaniards, burned and desecrated mission churches and convents and abandoned their pueblos, and the rebel leaders took their people to nearby mesa tops and mountains. The missionaries who lost their lives were Fray Francisco Corbera, Fray José Arbizu, Fray Antonio Carbonel, Fray Francisco de Jesús María, and Fray Antonio Moreno.[71] The general revolt had been planned with poor coordination, but the prospects for what might immediately follow were fearful to contemplate. Only the loyal leaders at Pecos, Tesuque, San Felipe, Santa Ana, and Zia, and the warriors who followed them, remained faithful to the Spaniards.

During the evening of that fateful day Vargas received four communications

---

68. See documents 68–78, below.

69. Vargas to the viceroy, Santa Fe, March 28, 1696. AGI, *Guadalajara,* legajo 141; Espinosa, *Crusaders,* 238–39.

70. See document 79, below.

71. The cruel manner in which these friars met their deaths is described in documents 87 and 88, below.

reporting these events. The first was from Fray Alfonso Jiménez de Cisneros, of Cochití, writing from San Felipe, reporting that after mass the entire population of Cochití had withdrawn to a nearby mesa with all the cattle, sheep, and horses of the mission, whereupon he fled on foot to San Felipe.[72] There he joined Fernando de Chávez, the *alcalde mayor* of Bernalillo, who was there with the residents of that village. The other letters to the governor were from Chávez and Roque Madrid, the *alcalde mayor* of Santa Cruz, and the loyal Indian governor of Tesuque, who requested immediate military aid. Because of the many warnings from the missionaries and the resulting precautionary steps already taken by the governor, he was not taken completely by surprise.

Governor Vargas acted swiftly. Among other steps, he wrote to the custodian on June 9 telling him to withdraw immediately all of the remaining missionaries to the safety of Santa Fe.[73] A similar message was sent to Roque Madrid at Santa Cruz to call in all the missionaries in the vicinity who might still be at their posts. The *alcalde mayor* at Pecos was ordered to gather one hundred friendly Indian warriors and, with the two missionaries there, hasten to Santa Fe. Military squadrons were sent out to defend all the places to which he had directed the Spanish settlers to be withdrawn for safety, and scouting parties scoured the area for information on rebel movements. Bartolomé de Ojeda, the loyal Indian governor of Santa Ana, kept Vargas posted on developments and reported that he had definite information that the Jémez had been joined by hostile Acomas and were awaiting Moqui, Zuñi, and Ute confederates before attacking. On June 11 he reported that this conspiracy had apparently broken up, for there were fresh tracks leading toward Acoma.[74] During the ensuing weeks of campaigning, Vargas and his principal military leaders were constantly in the saddle. Much was learned of the location of the secret rebel hiding places by spies and through the grilling of captured rebels.

Scraps of evidence pointed to Lucas Naranjo of Cochití as one of those primarily responsible for the continuing warfare, and to the location where he was in hiding with a large force of warriors. From his temporary headquarters at Santa Cruz, on July 23, Vargas led a well-organized army to find Naranjo, and after crossing the Río Grande near the pueblo of San Juan, the force reached the rebel leader's well-guarded mountain stronghold. Naranjo and his warriors were quietly waiting among the rocks overlooking a dark forested canyon through which the Spaniards had to pass, where he planned to entrap and annihilate them. During the perilous attack, Naranjo was observed making a determined effort to kill Fray Juan Alpuente, the chaplain of the expedition. An arrow struck the chaplain in the leg, but he was unscathed thanks to the pro-

---

72. See document 80, below.
73. See document 81, below.
74. See Ojeda's letter to Vargas, document 82, below.

The church at Zuñi Pueblo, 1879. *Photograph courtesy of the National Anthropological Archives, the Smithsonian Institution, Washington, D.C.*

tection of his leather boots. Naranjo now became the special target of the Spaniards, and within moments a soldier appeared holding aloft Naranjo's severed head. Shortly afterward, the hostile Indians fled and victory was won. Vargas and his men returned to Santa Fe to celebrate the victory, and his Indian allies returned to their pueblos. The Pecos were given Naranjo's head, at their request, to carry back to their pueblo as a trophy of victory. For the Spaniards the victory was a crucial turning point in the war.[75]

After two months of constant military campaigning, the war to subdue the rebellion was half won. Of the five most powerful enemy groups—the Jémez and their confederates, Acoma and the western pueblos, Naranjo and his following, Picurís, and the concentration at Taos—two had been effectively broken up. The victory over the Jémez was decisive, and it impressed their confederates from Acoma, Zuñi, and the Moqui pueblos, who were no longer a serious factor in the revolt. Naranjo, the guiding spirit of a large group in the Cochití Mountains, was dead. The economic pressure on the Indians was dev-

75. See document 88, below.

astating, as the fields could not be cultivated and the Spaniards carried off large quantities of corn and other supplies after each battle. The Spaniards had only to hold on a few more months, for the hardships that were being suffered by the Indians, many of whom were roaming like beasts in the mountains and canyons, starving and homeless, could not possibly be endured in the coming winter months. Lack of cooperation among the rebel leaders, in fact enmity between some of them, intensified by the suffering of the Indian populace that followed them about in constant fear, was working strongly in Vargas's favor. Only the western and the northern and northeastern pueblo areas remained to be visited by Vargas to assure that remaining pockets of resistance were under his control.

On July 31, 1696, Vargas sent a detailed report to the viceroy notifying him for the first time of the Pueblo Indian revolt and the existing state of the rebellion at that date. The report was accompanied by a copy of his day-to-day journal since his last report, which had been sent on March 28 past, and letters to the viceroy dated July 30 and August 1. The large package of mail also included correspondence to be delivered at El Paso and Parral. The report of July 31 presented a detailed record of the general Indian revolt from the events of June 4 through the crucial victory of the Spaniards on July 23.[76] In his letter of July 30, Vargas repeated his request for more colonists. He requested immediate replacements for the fifty-eight soldiers and male settlers who had died in the wars of the reconquest and in epidemics. He also included an extensive inventory of immediate needs such as food supplies, clothing, oxen, livestock, mules, arms, and maize necessary to feed the colony until the next harvest, stating that grain that he could capture by force of arms from the enemy would supply the colony for only three or four months.[77]

Since the authorities in Mexico City were usually dealing with the needs of distant New Mexico on the basis of information three to four months old, the length of time for mail to travel from one point to the other, action on urgent messages was usually too late to be of immediate help. A month after the revolt of June 4, both civil and religious authorities in Mexico were sending instructions to Governor Vargas and the father custodian based on the situation in New Mexico as it existed several months before the outbreak of the general revolt. Thus, much of the advice given to the governor and the custodian on July 4, 1696, was off the mark.[78]

By July 19, the Franciscan commissary general in Mexico had learned of the

76. See document 88, below. In this important document Vargas places in broader perspective the important Franciscan documents of the period but vainly emphasizes his own achievements while making only passing reference to the important role of the missionaries through their repeated advance warnings of the impending revolt and their many contributions during the course of the rebellion in the period reported.

77. See Espinosa, *Crusaders*, 268–69.

78. See document 83, below, and Espinosa, *Crusaders*, 263.

revolt in New Mexico and the martyrdom of five of the missionaries, and he wrote a letter of condolence addressed to all of the missionaries there, praising the martyrs for giving up their lives for the greater glory of God and exhorting the others to persist in their efforts.[79] On July 21 the custodian wrote to the commissary general notifying him of the Indian revolt, the tragic deaths of five of the missionaries, and the deplorable status of the missions.[80] That same day he addressed to the father guardian at El Paso an interesting personal letter in the nature of a defense of his actions relative to the revolt, with criticism of Vargas's policies. In it he noted: "I cannot write . . . at length about all that which has happened. The omissions of the lord governor in reporting on this revolt are many."[81]

A letter from Fray Francisco de Vargas to the father provincial, Clemente de Ledesma, dated July 21, 1696, was his most detailed and comprehensive report to any of his superiors in Mexico on the revolt of June 4 and the current status of the custody and missions of New Mexico. The letter, along with other papers, was carried in person by Fray Juan de Alpuente, as the custodian did not wish to entrust the messages to a civilian messenger who might permit his letters and the accompanying papers to fall into the hands of Governor Vargas, "or that they be hidden, or that anyone obscure the truth which is so clear and evident."[82]

Meanwhile, the last skirmishes of the warfare in New Mexico were being fought. In August, Vargas led an expedition to Acoma. There he attempted to lure the Acomas down from their mesa so that he could fight them more to his advantage. But none descended, and after three days the siege was lifted and he returned to Santa Fe. Vargas was now ready for an expedition to Picurís and Taos. With Santa Cruz as temporary headquarters, this campaign began in early September. At Taos, Vargas succeeded in attaining the peaceful submission of the Indian leaders and the return of the people from the nearby mountain canyons to their pueblo. Early in October, Vargas then proceeded to Picurís. Picurís was found abandoned. The Spaniards pursued the fugitives, accompanied by a number of Apaches, Tewas, and Tanos, who were headed for the buffalo plains. On October 26 the Spaniards caught up with the rebels on the slopes of a ravine, where the Indians made a desperate attempt to escape. Some eighty men, women, and children were captured. Don Lorenzo, the governor of Picurís, and some others had escaped eastward with the Apaches, where they were made slaves of the Cuartelejo Apaches in what is now western Kansas. The captives were taken by Vargas and his party to Santa Fe, where

79. See document 84, below.
80. See document 85, below.
81. See document 86, below.
82. See document 87, below.

they were distributed among the soldiers and citizens who had participated in the campaign, to be held hostage until the Picurís should return to their pueblo. The last serious obstacle to the restoration of peace and order in New Mexico had been crushed.[83]

Following the Picurís campaign, more groups of frightened natives gradually emerged from their mesa and mountain retreats, and a number of the rebel Indian leaders voluntarily submitted. Some of the most recalcitrant rebel leaders were tracked down with the aid of Indian allies and executed. By the end of November all the Indians in the districts surrounding Santa Fe, Santa Cruz, and Bernalillo were at peace. Vargas was awaiting peaceful gestures from some of the Tanos, the Jémez, Santa Clara, Pojoaque, and Acoma and the western pueblos, but they were no longer a danger. During the long months of war a large number of the dispersed Indians took up residence among the Apaches and in the western pueblos, and others had joined the Navajos. Thus, as the pueblos were reoccupied, their populations were more sparse than before the revolt. Otherwise, by the end of 1696 the submission of the Pueblo Indians to Spanish authority was complete. New Mexico could now turn to peaceful pursuits, the most important of which were economic reconstruction and reestablishment of the missions. Basic agricultural pursuits had been abandoned during the war, and the missions, with several rare exceptions, were in a shambles and without adequate supplies for their reestablishment.[84]

The custodian, Fray Francisco de Vargas, who only a few months earlier had virtually given up hope, now, with peace restored and the Indians returning to their pueblos, viewed the future with renewed hope and optimism. On November 23 he wrote to Governor Vargas in a conciliatory and friendly tone, requesting a reply attesting to his merits and services and those of the other missionaries during the period of Indian warfare. The governor replied in detail with fulsome praise of the valuable contributions of the custodian and his missionaries in the course of the long months of the rebellion and paid special tribute to the five Franciscan martyrs.[85] Five days later the custodian wrote to the viceroy recounting the sad situation of the missions but emphasizing the hopeful prospects for the future. He requested, after consultation with the governor, that a complement of twenty missionaries be assigned to the New Mexico missions, fifteen for the northern missions and five for the El Paso area. A listing of their proposed distribution accompanied the letter.[86]

A letter to the viceroy from Governor Vargas, in full accord with that of the custodian, accompanied the mail to Mexico City. The governor closed his

83. Espinosa, *Crusaders*, 272–83.
84. *Ibid.*, 296–97.
85. See documents 89–90, below.
86. See documents 91–92, below. The total was twenty-one including the father procurator general.

Pueblo Indian Man, 1902. *Photograph courtesy of the Prints and Photographs Division, Library of Congress, Washington, D.C.*

letter with a strong statement that the missionaries who should come should not do so with the illusion that guards would be provided for the protection of their lives; he did not want them to be making petitions for guards to be stationed at the missions, but they could rely on his vigilance.[87] Several months later the authorities in Mexico approved the sending of additional missionaries to provide the complement requested by the governor and the custodian.[88] The New Mexico communities still were to have many a "starving time" to overcome, but welcome aid continued to be provided by the authorities in Mexico. The Pueblo Indian revolt of 1696 was the last stand of the Pueblo Indian medicine men and war chiefs to throw off the yoke of Spanish rule.[89]

Considering the success that he achieved in reconquering and recolonizing New Mexico, Governor Vargas stands out as one of the great figures in the colonial history of Spanish North America. The records also show the important contribution to the success of the enterprise by the bold and capable Spanish military leaders with whom Vargas surrounded himself, the military support of loyal Pueblo Indian leaders and their warriors, and the courageous cooperation of the Franciscan missionaries under their able leader, the custodian Fray Francisco de Vargas. The custodian's diplomacy contributed greatly to the successful repacification of New Mexico. Fray Francisco de Vargas must be recognized as one of the notable churchmen of New Mexican colonial history. The common goals of the governor and the custodian, expressed in their

87. See document 93, below.
88. See document 94, below.
89. In 1696, Governor Vargas's five-year appointment as governor expired. Although he had early appealed for reappointment, Don Pedro Rodríguez Cubero had already obtained the governorship for a term of five years and took office at Santa Fe in July, 1697. Rodríguez Cubero was able to arouse the colonists and cabildo almost unanimously against Vargas, and after his thirty days' *residencia* Vargas was imprisoned at Santa Fe for nearly three years. At the Spanish court across the Atlantic, ignorant of these local developments, the king approved the reappointment of Vargas to the governorship to succeed Rodríguez Cubero, giving him the honorary title of "Pacificator" and granting him the title of Marqués de la Nava de Barcinas. It was not until the spring of 1700 that the authorities in Madrid learned that Vargas had been held a prisoner in Santa Fe since October 2, 1697. After his release, in the summer of 1700, he was fully exonerated, and in the winter of 1703 he returned to his old post as governor of New Mexico. Before his arrival, Rodríguez Cubero had fled in cowardly fashion, and the cabildo promptly humiliated itself by retracting all the charges which it had preferred against Vargas. (Espinosa, *Crusaders,* 307–56.) Vargas was soon campaigning. In the following spring, however, while pursuing a band of troublesome Apaches in the Sandía Mountains, he was stricken by a severe fever. The chaplain of the expedition urged him to return to Bernalillo immediately, but he replied that there was no better way to die, if this were to be his fate, than in the service of God and king. However, his illness worsened, and after much pleading by his companions he was carried to Bernalillo on the shoulders of faithful Indian allies, where he was given medical treatment. On April 5, after making his last confession several times, he requested that he be clothed in the habit of the Third Order of Saint Francis. (Letter from Juan Páez Hurtado to Ignacio López de Zárate, Santa Fe, April 20, 1704, Archives of the Marqués de la Nava de Barcinas, Madrid, courtesy of John L. Kessell.) On April 7 he drew up his last will and testament. Governor Vargas died at Bernalillo on April 8, 1704, and his body was taken to Santa Fe for burial. (Espinosa, *Crusaders,* 358–62.)

candid, realistic, sometimes acerbic, but mutually respected, exchanges of views, represented a basic harmony between church and state during the crucial period, confirmed by the documents translated below, that was in marked contrast with the bitter conflicts between the two authorities that had characterized the troublous years in the province before 1680. That earlier conflict contributed to the Pueblo revolt of 1680 and the expulsion of the Spaniards. The advance warnings of the Franciscans apprising Governor Vargas of the plans of rebel Indian leaders to carry out the general revolt in 1696 removed the element of surprise that had accompanied the successful revolt of 1680, and they were a factor that contributed to the victory of the Spaniards.

It would be many years before the New Mexico frontier would be free from the dangers of outlying, wandering Indian tribes: Navajos, Utes, and Apaches. Nevertheless, with the suppression of the Pueblo Indian revolt of 1696 and the pacification of the pueblos, the permanency of the European settlements in northern New Mexico was assured.

During the century that followed, the Spanish-speaking population of New Mexico grew at a remarkable rate. In 1697, according to contemporary estimates of the cabildo, the population of the colony totaled some 1,500 persons, including approximately 96 New Mexican Spanish families, totaling 404 persons; 17 families of Mexicans of the group that had been residing at Santa Fe before 1680 and who had returned from El Paso in 1693, totaling 71 persons; 124 families of residents from Zacatecas and Sombrerete, including twenty-five orphans, totaling 449 persons; and 83 persons listed as bachelors, orphans, single women, and other individuals of mixed blood.[90] This did not include the higher officials and their families and the Franciscan missionaries.

By 1776 the population of New Mexico, exclusive of the El Paso district, identified as Spanish and persons of mixed blood reached approximately 9,742. By 1790 the Hispanic population of northern New Mexico was over 15,000. The most populous centers were Santa Fe, Santa Cruz, and Albuquerque. The total population of the region, including Indians, was approximately 25,709. The Hispanic residents of northern New Mexico by then far outnumbered their Pueblo Indian neighbors.[91] This distant corner of the old Spanish Empire, now a part of the United States, the oldest continuous Hispanic community in the American Southwest, remains to this day a community that is nearly half Spanish in language and cultural background.

90. The cabildo of Santa Fe to the King, December 28, 1698. AGI, *Guadalajara*, leg. 142.
91. The above census estimates are based on Jones, *Los Paisanos*, 110–34, and Alicia V. Tjarks, "Demographic, Ethnic and Occupational Structure of New Mexico," *The Americas* 35 (1978): 45–88.

THE PUEBLO INDIAN REVOLT OF 1696

Letters of the Franciscan Missionaries
and Related Documents

PART ONE

Governor Vargas's Expedition of 1692 to Reconquer New Mexico: Repossession of the Missions by the Franciscans

1. GOVERNOR VARGAS GRANTS REPOSSESSION OF RELIGIOUS AUTHORITY AT SANTA FE TO THE FRANCISCANS, SANTA FE, SEPTEMBER 14, 1692[1]

SEPTEMBER 14, the year 1692. Possession of the place for the church, its temple and convent, and other things connected with it and pertinent thereto granted by Don Diego de Vargas Zapata Luján Ponce de León, governor and captain general of this kingdom and provinces of New Mexico and castellan of its fortress and presidio for His Majesty, in the Villa of Santa Fe,[2] capital of the kingdom of New Mexico, which has just been reduced and conquered anew on the said day, month, and year, *ut supra*.

On the 14th of the month of September of 1692. Governor and captain general. Fray Francisco Corbera, of the regular observation of our seraphic father Saint Francis, who is an apostolic missionary in the Custody of the Conversion of Saint Paul of New Mexico and president of the fathers who are serving as chaplains of the royal army, Fray Miguel Muñis de Luna and Fray Cristóbal Alonso Barroso. I state that as it was the will of God our Lord, by virtue of His holy Passion and by the intercession of the Virgin Mary, our patroness and protectress, that yesterday, the thirteenth of September, we had the good fortune of winning the peaceful submission of the rebel Indians of the Villa of Santa Fe and also of those of the surrounding pueblos who have come to offer peace; and since my seraphic religion was the one that administered to them before their revolt; and since today, the fourteenth, Your Lordship took possession of the said Villa and capital of this kingdom for the king, our lord Don Carlos the Second, may God keep him; and since Your Lordship is such a Catholic and loyal vassal of His Majesty: that you fulfill his wish by granting us possession of the church and convent or of a place for us, since the one that was there previously has been demolished. Therefore, I beg and request that Your Lordship grant it to me in writing so that it will be of permanent record that my sacred religion will have use of the said church and convent, which is the property and possession of the church of His Holiness and the convent of His Majesty. For these reasons I ask this of Your Lordship in the name of my sacred religion. I ask this with justification and in the manner deemed appropriate.

1. BNM, leg. 4, doc. 1. See Bibliography for list of abbreviations.
2. Two towns in New Mexico carried the designation villa in the seventeenth century: the capital at Santa Fe (founded in 1610) and Santa Cruz (founded in 1695), about twenty-five miles north of Santa Fe. With the reconquest of New Mexico by Governor Vargas, the villa of Santa Fe again became the capital and the seat of the cabildo, or town council, for the royal province. Santa Fe is generally referred to in the documents as "la Villa" and Santa Cruz as "la Villa Nueva."

And in order that this, my petition, may be of record, I signed it on the four-teenth day of September, the year sixteen hundred ninety-two.

Fray Francisco Corbera

Presentation. In the Villa of Santa Fe, capital of this kingdom of New Mex-ico, on the fourteenth day of the month of September of the year sixteen hun-dred ninety-two. Before me, Don Diego de Vargas Zapata Luján Ponce de León, governor and captain general of this said kingdom and castellan of its fortress and presidio for His Majesty, the reverend father preacher, apostolic missionary, chaplain of this army, and president of those who accompany him, Fray Francisco Corbera, presented the petition, brought forward and seen by me, said governor and captain general. I state that I am prompt to deliver to you the entire complement which in justice you have requested in it, and that it be of record, I signed along with my secretary of government and war.

Don Diego de Vargas Zapata Luján Ponce de León. Before me, Don Alfonso Rael de Aguilar, secretary of government and war.

Possession. And immediately following, I, said governor and captain gen-eral, being in the patio of the walled pueblo of this said Villa of Santa Fe, held by the natives of the Tewa and Tano nations which I have just reduced to obe-dience to the divine and human majesties, and having thus in his royal name again reclaimed, revalidated, and promulgated his sole and royal possession, as is applicable to him as the absolute and sovereign monarch of this kingdom and domain, and having also, in recognition of said possession, ordered the royal *alférez* of the company of the presidio to raise the standard, acclaiming as king and lord of this said kingdom the one who is in absolute authority, the king, our lord Carlos the Second, saying Viva! which was also repeated by me, the said governor and captain general, the said reverend father apostolic minis-ters and missionaries and the loyal vassals and soldiers of His Majesty who have followed me on this undertaking, expedition, reduction, and conquest for our holy faith, and the natives were absolved of their apostasy today, the said day, in the said patio, by the said reverend fathers in my presence and with my as-sistance, and the said ceremony having been completed, the aforesaid reverend father Fray Francisco Corbera requested possession, as recorded in his request, with the assistance of the persons who were present. Whereupon, in the name of His Majesty I grant, ratify, corroborate, pronounce, and declare in due form and in solemnity the said need and designate the location that he may wish to select, carrying out the royal wishes of the king, our lord, may God keep him, and so order, in keeping with my promise in response to his royal zeal to propa-gate and establish our holy faith, the return of the site and place for rebuilding the holy temple and church for the administration of the holy sacraments and the convent and the adjoining property related thereto. To all of which, with his authority to speak in the name of the said administration, as it pertained to, belongs to, and has been under his sacred religion since the first conquest of this said kingdom, I grant royal possession as well as corporal and civil *velquasi* so that as a legitimate right he shall apprehend and enjoy it without any prejudice, because the spoliation and revolt of the said natives were why the religious lost the said right, which in the name of His Majesty they have enjoyed and enjoy and which they maintain in the populated missions at this time in the land and provinces of this kingdom.

And taking over the said possession in the said patio, the said reverend father, in accordance with the ceremonies of our Roman Catholic Mother Church, as well as with the sign of the holy cross, celebrated the rendering of salt water for the exorcism and absolution of the said apostasy. At the same time, he prepared a record book to list in it the children and other persons who now live and have lived during the said past twelve years in this kingdom and who have given birth and raised the children who are now found here. And he assumed the said possession in his own name and in the name of his sacred religion as I, said governor and captain general, took him by the hand and kissed his holy habit, thanking him for all of the aforesaid and acknowledging the said possession referred to.

And so that his petition and all else be of record, I gave him this said original signed by me, by the captain of the presidio, by the *alférez,* by the *sargente mayor,* Don Fernando de Chávez, by the captain Antonio Jorge, and by José Gallegos, and it is sealed with my name and is on plain paper, as stamped paper is not available in these parts. And it was signed also by my secretary of government and war on said day, month, and year, *ut supra.*

Don Diego de Vargas Zapata Luján Ponce de León; Roque Madrid; Juan de Dios Lucero de Godoy; Don Fernando de Chávez; Antonio Jorge; José Gallegos. Before me, Don Alfonso Rael de Aguilar, secretary of government and war.

Certification. I certify, as secretary of this holy custody, that it is faithfully copied from the original which remains in the archive of the aforesaid custody, which was copied by order and mandate of the reverend father Fray Salvador de San Antonio, preacher and present custodian and ordinary ecclesiastical judge of this said Custody of the Conversion of Saint Paul of New Mexico. And that it be of record that it is the truth, I signed this at the Convent of Our Lady of Guadalupe of El Paso del Río del Norte on the twenty-seventh day of the month of December, the year sixteen hundred ninety-two.

Fray Juan Alvarez, secretary

2. GOVERNOR VARGAS GRANTS REPOSSESSION OF RELIGIOUS AUTHORITY OVER THE MISSIONS OF ACOMA, ZUÑI, AND MOQUI TO THE FRANCISCANS, SITE OF DOÑANA, DECEMBER 18, 1692[1]

DECEMBER 18, the year 1692. By virtue of the petition presented by the reverend father missionary Fray Francisco Corbera, president of the chaplains who accompanied the aforesaid with the army of the conquest of the kingdom of New Mexico, who at the villa and capital of Santa Fe was granted possession of both the parish of said natives and the administration of the holy sacraments to them, having proceeded to reduce the rock [*peñol*] of Acoma and the provinces of Zuñi and Moqui, he was granted possession there in like manner, the ceremony being repeated in the same manner as before by act of the lord governor and captain general of this said kingdom and provinces of New Mexico and castellan of its forces and presidio for His Majesty.

On the 18th of December of the year 1692, the following was presented. Lord governor and captain general. Fray Francisco Corbera, of the regular observation of our seraphic father Saint Francis, preacher missionary of the Conversion of Saint Paul of New Mexico. I state that our Lord God having been served by Your Lordship's said successful reduction not only of the kingdom of New Mexico but also of the provinces of Zuñi and Moqui and of the rock of Acoma, and by your having granted to me the possession, in the name of my sacred religion, which I requested of Your Lordship over the kingdom of New Mexico, which Your Lordship carried out in the Villa of Santa Fe, its capital, and since it is apparent that Zuñi and Moqui are indeed distinct provinces, I request and beseech that Your Lordship deign to grant me possession of the said provinces under the same circumstances as in the previous case. I request that justice be granted as you may see fit. And that it be of record, I signed at this place of the camp [*ranchería*] on the eighteenth of December of sixteen hundred ninety-two.

Presentation. At this place and site of the uninhabited camp of the heathen *Indios gentiles mansos* and the place of Doñana, today, Thursday, the eighteenth of the month of December, the year sixteen hundred ninety-two, the reverend father missionary Fray Francisco Corbera, president of the chaplains who have assisted in the new conquest and reduction for our holy faith and for the royal crown which I have just completed with regard to the entire kingdom of New Mexico, the rock of Acoma, and the provinces of Zuñi and Moqui, presented the petition on my way back from those provinces. Before me, Don Diego de

1. BNM, leg. 4, doc. 2.

Vargas Zapata Luján Ponce de León, governor and captain general of said kingdom and castellan of its forces and presidio for His Majesty.

Auto. And seen by me, the said governor and captain general, and in accordance with the same terms of possession, which, by virtue of the said petition, I granted to him verbally and in my power in the Villa of Santa Fe, the capital, which it was of the said kingdom of New Mexico, for the administration of the holy sacraments, which belongs to his holy religion, repeating the said clauses and in their same tenor and form I grant it to him in the name of His Majesty so that he may apprehend it in behalf of his said sacred religion, royally and corporally *velquasi,* with regard to the rock of Acoma, which is inhabited by the Keres nation, and likewise the rock of Zuñi on the large mesa where the natives of the pueblos of the said province of Zuñi reside, and likewise those of the province of Moqui, with its pueblos of Aguatuvi, Gualpi, Moxonabi, and Jongopavi, in all of which the aforesaid reverend father president Fray Francisco Corbera, accompanied by the reverend father missionary Fray Cristóbal Alonso Barroso, as a sign of said possession gave absolution to the said natives of said nations of the rocks [*peñoles*] and provinces from their sin of apostasy and also baptized the infants, children, and youths who had been born and the other persons who had not been baptized since they rose in revolt against our holy faith and the royal crown.

And it is also of record that on the said rock of the province of Zuñi, as a sign of said possession, the reverend father president celebrated for them the holy sacrifice of the mass on a feast day and Sunday. And likewise, they said mass for me at the encampment and parade ground which I established at the pueblo of Aguatuvi, of the province of Moqui, and thus the said natives received them as ministers as they had served since the beginning, when this land was originally won by the said religious of our father Saint Francis. Also, they answered the questions that were asked by the religious, who were their ministers of said sacred religion. At Zuñi the natives delivered to the religious the books, as recorded in the *autos* of said campaign, war, and conquest carried out on my expedition to the rock and province of Zuñi, which is a part of the large mesa on which all of its natives live. Most of the said books had the marks of use by the religious who had owned the said books.

And therefore it shall be of permanent record that to the said seraphic and sacred religion of our father Saint Francis belong the said pastorate and administration of the holy sacraments, as regards the said nations and provinces of Zuñi, Moqui, and the rock of Acoma, expressed by the public functions which as a sign of said possession were performed in them by the aforesaid reverend father in charge, assisted by his aforesaid companion, and to no other religious order that may wish to be brought at any time, even if it might come to said parts, as could occur, with one of its members serving as the chaplain of some armed military camp of His Majesty, for those under my charge entered previously and have come for the said purpose of the said conquest, and the said reverend fathers have raised their mere right, since at present they are in legitimate possession, administering the said holy sacraments in the district of El Paso del Río del Norte, which is a part of this kingdom of New Mexico.

And so that the said possession may be of record, I signed with the military leaders. It was also signed by the aforesaid reverend father Fray Francisco Corbera. The witnesses were Captain Juan García de Noriega, *alguacil mayor* of the illustrious cabildo, who resides in the town of El Paso del Río del Norte, and the campaign captain Juan de Dios Lucero de Godoy, with the assistance of my secretary of government and war.

Don Diego de Vargas Zapata Luján Ponce de León; Fray Francisco Corbera; Juan García de Noriega; Martín de Alday, Juan de Dios Lucero, Antonio Pérez. Before me, Don Alfonso Rael de Aguilar, secretary of government and war.

I certify, as secretary of this holy custody, that it is faithfully and legally copied from the original, which remains in the archive of this holy Custody of the Conversion of Saint Paul of New Mexico. And that it be of record, I signed on the twenty-eighth day of the month of December, the year sixteen hundred ninety-two, at this convent of El Paso del Río del Norte.

Fray Juan Alvarez, secretary

PART TWO

The Reconquest and Resettlement of New Mexico, 1693–94:
Pueblo Indian Resistance Delays the Reestablishment
of the Missions

3. LETTER OF FRAY SALVADOR DE SAN ANTONIO TO GOVERNOR VARGAS, ENCAMPMENT AT THE FOOT OF THE MOUNTAINS NEAR SANTA FE, DECEMBER 18, 1693.[1]

LORD governor and captain general:

I, Fray Salvador de San Antonio, custodian and ecclesiastical judge of these provinces of New Mexico, by apostolic authority, with all of my community of apostolic missionaries, on this day of the present year at the foot of a mountainside about a mortar shot from the parade ground [*plaza de armas*] of the Villa of Santa Fe, appear before Your Lordship, first of all responding with humble compliance, promptness, and obedience in conformity with Your Lordship's request that the ministers designated on the day preceding the present date be in readiness to go to the missions indicated by Your Lordship, which are Villa of Santa Fe, Tesuque, Nambé, San Ildefonso, San Juan, San Lázaro, Picurís, Taos, Jémez, Zia, Pecos, and Cochití, with their *visitas*.[2] And shortly after the religious were named for the said missions, we received repeated rumors expressed by an Indian named Juan de Ye, governor of the Pecos, that the pueblos of the Tewas, Tanos, and Picurís, joined by the Apaches, are secretly planning to attack us as soon as the camp is divided and Your Lordship has left us. Moreover, we should fully trust the said Indian, for he was the one, at the time of the past revolt of the year '80, who warned Sergeant Major Francisco Gómez, now deceased, twenty days in advance, and as the time approached for carrying out the revolt, he repeated the warning eight days before it took place, and seeing that no one believed him, he told his minister, Father Fray Fernando de Velasco, "Father, the people are rising in rebellion, with the plan to kill all the Spaniards and religious; therefore, consider where you wish to go, and I will provide you with young men to lead you to safety," which in fact he did. We should believe the words of the said Indian, for he has always been faithful and truthful in all of his actions and in his behavior, and he has not separated himself from us for over a month. For this reason, and because of other actions that appear to be dangerous and contrary to our intentions which we see among the Indians of this land, I appear before Your Lordship with all of my religious to protest against the lack of safety, which Your Lordship has

1. HL-RC, 25; AGN, *Historia,* tomo 2, and BNM, leg. 3, doc. 1a: Fray Silvestre Vélez de Escalante, "Extracto de Noticias de lo acaecido en la Custodia de la Conversión de San Pablo de la Provincia de el Santo Evangelio de N.S.P.S. Francisco en el Nuevo Mégico, sacadas de los papeles que se guardan en el Archivo de Gobierno de la Villa de Santa Fé, empiezan desde el año de 1679." MS, 1778.

2. *Visita* was the designation for a Pueblo Indian mission, with its church or chapel, that did not have a resident missionary. There religious services were performed by the resident missionary of a nearby mission, from which he visited the *visita* under his charge by assignment from the custodian of the New Mexico missions.

promised us and which is referred to by the illustrious Montenegro,[3] so that the ministers of the gospel and other innocent vassals of His Majesty, who with such great pleasure have come to reside in this land and thereby achieve the royal wishes of the crown, may not perish. In view of this, and so that it be of permanent record that this protest has been made, we request that you provide us with an authenticated written reply indicating that which Your Lordship shall determine. Done at this said place, today, December 18, 1693.

Fray Salvador de San Antonio, custodian	Fray Juan Muñoz de Castro
	Fray Juan Daza
Fray Antonio de Sierra	Fray José Diez
Fray Juan de Zavaleta	Fray Antonio Carbonel
Fray Francisco de Jesús María	Fray Francisco Corbera
Fray Juan Alpuente	Fray Gerónimo Prieto
Fray Juan Antonio del Corral	Fray Antonio de Obregón
Fray Antonio Vahamonde	Fray Buenaventura de Contreras
Fray Domingo de Jesús María	Fray Diego Zeinos, secretary
Fray José Narváez Balverde	

4. *AUTO* OF GOVERNOR VARGAS, MILITARY CAMP OUTSIDE SANTA FE, DECEMBER 18, 1693 [1]

IN this parade ground, in view of the walled pueblo of the Villa of Santa Fe, which is occupied by the Tewa and Tano nations, the reverend father preacher Fray Diego Zeinos, secretary of the very reverend father custodian Fray Salvador de San Antonio, presented to me the petition contained on the preceding page in the name of the aforementioned contained in it, the very reverend father custodian Fray Salvador de San Antonio and the reverend father missionaries, whose signatures appear along with that of the said very reverend father and that of his said secretary.

And it has been examined by me, said governor and captain general, with the attention and consideration that its gravity merits, regarding concerns which are engaging my full attention. I am fully aware that it is my obligation to provide the help that is requested in the said reports in accomplishing my great obligation in the royal service. And the very reverend father custodian has carried out his obligation well, with his punctual arrival with this information, as also have, with equal resignation, the reverend father missionaries

3. Alonso de la Peña Rivas y Montenegro, *Itinerario para párrocos de indios,* Madrid, 1668, and later editions. Listed in the 1704 inventory of the library of Governor Vargas in Adams, "Two Colonial New Mexican Libraries, 1704, 1776," 150. Montenegro is also referred to in docs. 4 and 75.

1. HL:RC, 25.

mentioned and chosen with so much good judgment by his very reverend paternity. And their safety is very just and due, for by the authority of the illustrious Montenegro, cited, it is incumbent upon me, as my obligation, to provide the aforesaid attention and protection. And as I recognize those who treacherously gave feigned obedience, I will, on my part, carry out what is necessary, endeavoring to the best of my ability in the royal service and in that of God our Lord, and since it is His legitimate cause, I pray that He may give me the inspiration that I desire.

And that this said *auto* be of record, I signed, jointly with my secretary of government and war. Done at this military camp and place outside the said Villa of Santa Fe on the eighteenth day of the month of December, the year sixteen hundred and ninety-three. In addition, I ordered the secretary of government and war to give the testimony of the said petition and *auto* provided by me, as requested by the party. Done *ut supra*.

Don Diego de Vargas Zapata Luján Ponce de León. Before me, Alfonso Rael de Aguilar, secretary of government and war

5. GOVERNOR VARGAS'S JOURNAL, MILITARY CAMP OUTSIDE SANTA FE, DECEMBER 27, 1693 [1]

AND in this manner, those whose names are indicated having stated and presented their opinions to me, said governor and captain general, with the assistance of my secretary of government and war, at the said general meeting [*junta general*], I then turned to ask the very reverend fathers if they had anything to add. To this the said very reverend father replied that his intention and that of his other reverend father missionaries is different from that which is written and placed by me, said governor and captain general, at the head of these *autos* regarding the said meeting, and it is different from that of the said illustrious cabildo. For their declaration is directed only to the safety of the lives of the said religious, the reverend missionaries, who are ready and willing to go forth and carry out the purposes of their institute, which they have come to introduce anew, and to again establish Christianity to this said kingdom through the ministering of the holy sacraments and preaching of the holy gospel. And because of the said delay in initiating this work, they are very saddened, for they desire to be placed as soon as possible at the missions to which each of them has already been assigned.

And that it be of record, this was signed by the very reverend father custodian Fray Salvador de San Antonio, along with the other reverend father mis-

1. HL:RC, 25.

sionaries, jointly with me, said governor and captain general, and my secretary
of government and war.

Fray Salvador de San Antonio	Fray Francisco de Jesús María
Fray Antonio de Sierra	Fray José Diez
Fray Juan Daza	Fray Francisco Corbera
Fray Diego Zeinos	Fray Juan Antonio del Corral
Fray Antonio Carbonel	Fray Juan Alpuente
Fray Gerónimo Prieto	Fray Domingo de Jesús María
Fray Juan Muñoz de Castro	Fray Antonio de Obregón
Fray Juan de Zavaleta	

Don Diego de Vargas Zapata Luján Ponce de León
Before me, Alfonso Rael de Aguilar, secretary of government and war

6. PETITION OF FRAY SALVADOR DE SAN ANTONIO TO GOVERNOR VARGAS, SANTA FE, MARCH 20, 1694[1]

LORD Governor and captain general Don Diego de Vargas Zapata Luján
Ponce de León. I, Fray Salvador de San Antonio, father custodian and judge
ordinary and ecclesiastical of the Provinces and Custody of the Conversion of
Saint Paul of New Mexico, appear before Your Lordship as custodian of my
community and as ecclesiastical judge of this common society. And I state that
as Your Lordship knows, without any notice or representation other than a
proclamation or announcement by a public crier, which I heard from the win-
dow of my cell in the convent at El Paso, which Your Lordship ordered to be
announced on the twentieth of September of the past year, in this manner you
stated that on the fourth of October of that year the departure to this kingdom
would take place without fail.

In keeping with my profession and with the ardent desire I had to see the
ministers administering at their posts (along with other preparations), having
been assured protection and financial support by Your Lordship, I convened
fifteen religious fathers and one lay religious, ordering them to be ready on
October the second at the convent of El Paso for the said departure, and that on
the third we would all attend a high mass sung to the Holy Spirit, and a ser-
mon was preached by Father Fray Juan Daza with spiritual ferver in keeping
with the occasion, as Your Lordship knows.

The departure took place as planned, precisely on the day determined by
Your Lordship, Buenaventura de Contreras having provided you with ten of
the fourteen wagons, only ten of which were reserved for the eighteen reli-

1. AASF, 1694, No. 1, Reel 51, frames 140–48.

gious, including myself, for my household articles, and also all the rest, consisting of ornaments and jeweled articles for divine worship. And since we had had a terrible year of sickness and food shortage, as I addressed to Your Lordship through your lieutenant general, we left with little food, since we had no place from which to obtain it (although through the mercy of God and the assistance from Your Lordship it was not lacking to us), nor were we able to obtain from the four poor convents the necessary things to provide for the various administrative posts which Your Lordship placed under my charge, which were twelve, it may be noted: Villa of Santa Fe; Tesuque with its *visita* Cuyamungué; Nambé with its *visita* Pojoaque; San Ildefonso with its *visita* Jacona; San Juan with its *visita* Santa Clara; San Lázaro with its *visita* San Cristóbal; Picurís; Taos; Pecos; Cochití with its *visita* San Felipe; Zia with its *visita* Santa Ana; and the very large pueblo of Jémez. For which we only had eight chalices, eight communion tables, two crismatories, and one and a half iron forms to make hosts. All this I make known to Your Lordship, omitting other inconveniences for a multitude of reasons which I will mention to you when it is to the purpose.

Before reaching Sandía Your Lordship received a report with certain news that at the openings of the river, five leagues from this villa, the nations of the Tanos, Tewas, Picurís, and Apaches of the Colorado River and the Navajos had prepared a powerful ambuscade to kill and destroy all of us, an action and demonstration whereby the feigned peace of the previous year, which they offered Your Lordship, was proven. His Divine Majesty caused the said ambuscade to vanish because the Indian governor of Pecos, named Don Juan de Ye, did not cooperate in it, and he did not separate himself from us until the conclusion of this war, and he always told us that these people were not to be trusted, that we should not believe them, that they wished to fight, and that they had been preparing for this during the years that they had to themselves, of which Your Lordship is aware, for we saw it all carried out. I leave further discussion of these circumstances and events for their time.

We journeyed on to this villa, where we arrived on the sixteenth of December of said year. Although the residents came out to receive us, we saw in their countenances and in the snares that they had prepared in front of their gateway, where Your Lordship's fiscal was posted in the year of the conquest, on hanging crosses around their necks, in the case of a miserable dog and her children who were in a hovel at the entrance of this villa who did not deign to kneel with us at the litany and the prayers that we sang in the center of their patio, and in other actions which we all noticed, we knew and had confirmed that their peace was feigned and that their hearts were hostile. Such iniquities and other treacherous acts that they were forging I will indicate in my report, when God wills that it be made.

From the said villa Your Lordship led us to a hillock about two gunshots from it, where we remained, suffering to the extent that only God will ever know, until the night of the twenty-eighth, when these barbarians declared and proclaimed war against us, and at the cost of their lives and the capture of their wives and children we took shelter and found protection by taking over their own homes. The same day that we arrived at this villa, Your Lordship told me that afternoon that I should name the ministers and that he would go with them in person to their various administrations. And although I admired such inopportune speed, nonetheless on the next day, the seventeenth, I called them all and pointed out to them how I thought we should agree. This same day the voices were louder, especially that of the said Don Juan, that these people were not to be trusted and that what they were awaiting was for the lord governor to divide his forces so they could carry out their treachery, yet the religious were very prompt to obey and to proceed to carry out that for which they had come with so much joy and consolation. The next day, the eighteenth, I again called them to resolve scruples, and that they should not perish, like those of the year 'eighty, at the hands of the sacrilegious, and that I believed that Your Lordship and all of your camp would have perished. And I told them that I revoked all that had taken place the day before and gave them the motives for my doing so, and that I was proposing only what I could and should do and that they give me their views on the matter. And we all agreed that we should protest and make a counter statement to Your Lordship, which was done in writing, as is of record in Your Lordship's letters and mine. May it serve God that they be seen and heeded. The other things that we saw and experienced during the fourteen days while we were on the hillock Your Lordship was not ignorant of, nor the knowledge that while we slept these Judases watched us with the purpose of taking our lives. Thus it was, in the just judgment of God, that they all suffered on the thirtieth of December. The Tewas, their allies, besides having come to their assistance the day of the war, as we all saw, later declared war against us. Whether Your Lordship could or could not have gone out the next day to calm and quiet them or to punish them we shall see before the tribunal of God. What we see from here is that since the said action was not taken, they ascended and fortified themselves on a mesa near the pueblo of San Ildefonso, where Your Lordship went to visit them three times: the first time was ten days after winning this war. What Your Lordship could have done is not for me to ascertain. What I do know is that after many talks with them, a Spanish-speaking Indian told Your Lordship that to arrange for peace did not require much talking, that this could be arranged with the settlement of four points, and that therefore you should come to the villa and not spend the night at the pueblo of San Ildefonso. All of this Your Lordship carried out to see if you could reduce them to their pueblos. Since they did not come down nor come with their four points, Your Lordship again returned on the eighteenth; you went, you saw them better fortified, there was a messenger of no consequence, and Your Lordship returned. And it should be noted that in addition to the deference and courteous treatment Your Lordship extended to them on the said two occasions, some Indians were caught in the pueblo of Nambé, and Your Lordship had crosses placed on them, and with their *tlatoles* they were dispatched to the said mesa to tell them to come down. They paid no attention other than to show contempt for the crosses and rosaries, for two rosaries were found buried in a pot in the pueblo of Tesuque.

Finally, Your Lordship set out on the twenty-sixth of February of this year, 'ninety-four, determined to lay siege to them, and the said mesa was found to be so well fortified that in many battles with them it could not be won from them; rather, our men received much damage from them, even only from the stones they rolled down. If they received any damage from us we will not know until it is revealed by God. After twenty-one days of fighting, Your Lordship recognized the difficulties, and for other reasons which you may have had, you raised the siege on the day of the glorious patriarch Saint Joseph and returned to this villa, determined to proceed to Jémez, some twenty leagues from this villa, for they are the troublemakers on the other side.

Now, if Your Lordship was right or wrong in lifting the siege, we will soon detect whether or not it was an error, and may it be the wish of God and the Blessed Virgin that it not be at the price of grief and tears, for Your Lordship is well aware of the considerable damage that we have received from the said rebels. For besides the large amount of cattle and beasts that they have stolen, on the night of the fifteenth of February they sneaked in among the horses at an untimely hour of the night with gourds filled with stones and leather and sounded them to cause a stampede, and they ran off over two hundred beasts, among them eighty mules used for the wagons, the day you were to leave, in accordance with Your Lordship's signed order. Now, each time that Your Lordship has departed from this villa, you have left us almost alone without being able to do anything to defend from the enemy the little that has remained, as they have stolen so many beasts and so many cattle without our being able to prevent it. The next day, when Your Lordship left here for the mesa, ten Indians came and killed Juan de la Cruz and stole ten mules, and there was no way to pursue them, and we cannot bring back his corpse until another day. This same day they stole a number of cows, and also ten native boys ran away, and there was no way to pursue them. Therefore, if the strength of the place cannot defend us (may it be the will of God that it shall), there might be no memory of us, and if they are doing this while they are in a state of seige, what will they do next? Moreover, the mesa is about six or seven leagues from here, a region of good land which we could travel to with great difficulty if necessary.

From here to Jémez, such a great distance we would have to travel and in such a hostile neighborhood, what are we to do?

Now, to bring this letter to a close, I can only assume that at present, other than the Pecos and the three small pueblos of Zia, Santa Ana, and San Felipe, we no longer have any friends. For all of which it is necessary for me to propose, represent, and protest to your lordship that over three months ago, we, sixteen priests and two lay religious, arrived at this villa solely with the purpose of immediately taking on our administration by virtue of the kingdom being secure, conquered, quiet, and peaceful. This we do not see, nor is it recognizable, as is manifest, and our greatest hardship and disconsolateness is to find ourselves without hope of attaining it. For we see that no matter what we do, the Indians have not been willing to come down from the mesa or yield, only uttering blasphemies against God and his religion; that is why he wishes to punish them with his hand. The obscenities and other things that we are suffering, which are so contrary to the tranquility of our profession, are unmentionable, as will be seen in my report. The lack of food supplies is continual; the fields could be planted very easily, but it will not be easy to accomplish; the poor residents have lost all that they brought from El Paso, which they had acquired by their sweat and work for over thirteen years; of this I am aware, and I weep tearfully.

With all this that I see as self-evident, would that Your Lordship would repair this kingdom so that it can be populated and the religious may go out to fulfil their obligation and carry out the duties for which they came, for they are, and have been, eager to do so, as Your Lordship knows. What you are able to reply, I am not ignorant of, for I have listened to Your Lordship, to which I will reply only before the tribunal of God or that of His Majesty if the occasion should warrant it. Otherwise, I will only attempt to speak to my prelates so that they will know how we are conducting ourselves, punishing or rewarding us accordingly. For what I now am and represent, looking, as I should, at the gravity of a community and the preservation and safety of this flock of Christians so full of innocent people, I ask and beg of Your Lordship, and if necessary, I summon the help of God and His Majesty, may God save him, and of all this innocent flock, to either suspend the plan to go to Jémez, or to send a military leader, of which there are plenty who are competent, so that with the help of the Keres, for they are offering and even pleading and seeking permission, to attempt to restrain or reduce those miserable ones. It appears to me that the safest thing to do would be not to leave from here; because of not having conquered the mesa, we will be pursued by many dangers, be warned, Your Lordship. If Your Lordship must go to Jémez, I will follow you with all my community and wherever you might wish to go. But what is more certain is that I will object to Your Lordship, beseeching you with the authority of a community and the clamor of this Christian flock, which we both must be so much concerned with and attentive to, not to move from here until the arrival of the families that are awaited. Are they coming or are they not? If they come, Your Lordship will have more forces, but if they do not come, what will we do in that case? And if there were no more motive than this for the wagons not to leave, they would have to be held back officially, for is this kingdom to be repaired, or is it not? If it is, they will go with God's blessing. If it is not, Your Lordship will have the satisfaction of having what is available to take out the many children that are here. Besides the wagons, although they could leave through use of the mules that have remained, it would be necessary to waste two or three. Will the father procurator do this or not? It is enough that one fell apart in the incident at Doña Damiana because it was rotted. And finally, what Your Lordship has in hand is more important than the loss of all the wagons and carts of New Spain.

I hope that Your Lordship, in your greatness, nobility, and Christianity, will pay attention to my statements to provide what is most desirable to the benefit of both majesties. And I also ask and entreat Your Lordship to order your secretary of government and war to make a copy of this my petition and statement along with that which Your Lordship resolves and decides.

Fray Salvador de San Antonio

7. *AUTO* OF GOVERNOR VARGAS, SANTA FE, MARCH 20, 1694[1]

STATEMENT: In this Villa of Santa Fe, the fortress and capital of this kingdom of New Mexico, on the twentieth day of March of the year sixteen hundred ninety-four, at about six-thirty in the evening, the very reverend father custodian Fray Salvador de San Antonio, having come to greet me and to compliment me on the campaign, siege, and war I have engaged in with the rebel nations of the Tewas and their supporters of the pueblo and mesa of San Ildefonso, presented the petition contained on the preceding pages and on this said page. And as it has been seen by me, said governor and captain general, I refer in full to the legal truthfulness of the testimony of *autos* that I have had sent to His Most Excellent Lord Viceroy Conde de Galve and those that I have prepared in the prosecution of these events as well as that on the two expeditions: the first conquest of all of this said kingdom, at my own expense, and its rock of Acoma and the provinces of Zuñi and Moqui; the sending of *almagre* or

1. AASF, 1694, No. 1, Reel 51, frames 140–48.

vermilion earth, which is believed to be metal rich in fine quicksilver ore; and also the said testimony on the reconquest of this said villa and fortress on the said second expedition.

Therefore, by virtue of the testimony of the *autos* referred to, His Most Excellent Lordship the viceroy will make the decision and issue the orders that may be to his pleasure, since His Excellency has experience regarding the fickle nature even of the Indians raised and accustomed to living among Spaniards, as is evident from their insurrections in New Spain; in the cities of Querétaro, Celaya, Tlascala, and Mexico; and in the kingdom of Vizcaya and its province of Tarahumara. Thus, I only refer and defer to the said testimony of my *autos,* accompanied by the sorrow of still lacking the forces of the sixty-six and a half families, arms, munitions, and other military supplies, along with the aid which the said most excellent lordship, the viceroy Conde de Galve, is sending to this said kingdom to furnish and adorn the altars of the missions so that with their arrival the good results can be accomplished to calm and subdue the said rebels, which time and the strength of forces will demonstrate.

And with regard to my departure to Jémez, I reserve the decision to myself for the occasion that is most opportune. For I would do so now only when Father Fray Buenaventura de Contreras permits the departure of the wagons of this holy custody which are under his charge.

And in order that the said representation and the said petition be of record, along with what I, said governor and captain general, have replied, I order my secretary of government and war, regarding both it and the reply to it, to give the testimony to the said very reverend father custodian so that His Very Paternal Reverence may use it as he wishes. Thus I have determined and signed with my said secretary of government and war. Don Diego de Vargas Zapata Luján Ponce de León. Before me, Don Alfonso Rael de Aguilar, secretary of government and war.

8. PETITION OF FRAY SALVADOR DE SAN ANTONIO TO GOVERNOR VARGAS, SANTA FE, MARCH 24, 1694[1]

PETITION. Lord governor and captain general. Fray Salvador de San Antonio, custodian and ordinary ecclesiastical judge of the Provinces and Custody of the Conversion of Saint Paul of New Mexico. Inasmuch as it has come to my attention that Your Lordship wishes to provide the pueblos of El Paso, or the wagons with the families that are being brought by the father procurator general Fray Francisco Farfán, with corn supplies from this Villa of Santa Fe, for

1. AASF, 1694, No. 1, Reel 51, frames 140–48.

which Your Lordship has decided to dispatch a drove of beasts of burden as soon as possible, and since I am aware that the said corn supplies are so deteriorated in the amounts with which we found ourselves when we entered the said villa, which are scarcely enough to feed the people who are now here; and also considering that the next planting in the future is not only unlikely but almost morally impossible while there is no tranquility in the kingdom; and considering that it will not be just that this congregation of the faithful be deprived of the fruits which they now possess, having won them by force of arms and with manifest danger to their lives, therefore, to be of benefit to the two majesties and the preservation of this entire kingdom, I request and enteat Your Lordship to suspend the dispatch of the said corn supplies to the said pueblos, or of the wagons, until your lordship may be able to obtain the corn that you decide to bring from the pueblos, and after assembling it in a body, Your Lordship may examine it closely in person (and I offer my own services for said inspection) to determine the amount of *fanegas* that may be found at present and then make a list of all the people who are residing in this villa, finding out what each one consumes so that when the distribution is made, the amount necessary for the preservation of all of this kingdom may be reserved. And with regard to this, my petition, I request that Your Lordship send me a copy containing what you have decided so that at any time, and when suitable, I may confirm, in my capacity as ecclesiastical judge and, therefore, spiritual father of this republic, that I took the necessary measures for its useful preservation.

And with regard to the other petition, which I presented to Your Lordship in person on Saturday, the twentieth of this month of March of sixteen hundred ninety-four, I request that Your Lordship also provide me with a copy of what has been decided in regard to it. And if Your Lordship, because of the many activities that demand your attention, is unable to reply to the petition which I personally presented to you, I request that Your Lordship return the original with certification that you received it.

Done in this Villa of Santa Fe on the twenty-fourth day of the month of March, the year sixteen hundred ninety-four.

Fray Salvador de San Antonio, ecclesiastical judge. Before me, Fray Diego Zeinos, secretary and notary.

9. *AUTO* OF GOVERNOR VARGAS, SANTA FE, MARCH 31, 1694[1]

IN this Villa of Santa Fe on the twenty-fourth day of March, the year sixteen hundred ninety-four, the very reverend father lector and reverend missionary

1. AASF, 1694, No. 1, Reel 51, frames 140–48.

Fray Diego Zeinos, in the name of the very reverend father custodian Fray Salvador de San Antonio, ecclesiastical judge and custodian of this Custody of the Conversion of Saint Paul of New Mexico, presented to me the above petition contained on the preceding pages. Therefore, in response to what is mentioned therein, I refer entirely to the truth of my *autos,* letters, and reports which I have transmitted, the testimony of all of which I have transmitted and dispatched to His Excellency the viceroy, Conde de Galve, of all of the kingdom of New Spain. And His Magnificence, upon seeing what is truthfully stated in the said account regarding the state of affairs in this kingdom, will take whatever action he considers necessary. And future contingencies for changes have been foreseen in his *superior senado* and Royal Council of the Treasury and War by the honorable ministers who meet in said royal council, for it detained and withheld the alms which should have been received by the reverend father missionaries who returned to these missions on my first, royally favored, legal, and effective conquest, of which there can be no doubt or supposition, since it is infallible truth, as is manifest in the *autos* relating to it, its campaigns, events, orders, entries, and all relating to its political and military government, for which I myself gave mature consideration and decided upon, and also I accomplished the said conquest at my own expense.

Regarding the state of affairs and my report of it, although the conquest of Acoma and the provinces of Zuñi and Moqui has not been fully accomplished, Reverend Father Fray Joaquín de Hinojosa, who was then vice-custodian and president of the said custody at the pueblo of El Paso del Río del Norte, was obliged by the said news contained in the first mail which I dispatched to the said lord most excellent viceroy to ask him to increase and augment the number of ministers, since he was under the supposition that from the aforesaid report on the state of the conquest of this said kingdom, his three reverend father missionaries and preachers were there. Two of them were actually residing at said custody, one the reverend father preacher Fray Francisco Corbera, who came as president over the other two, and the other one remaining there being the reverend father preacher Fray Miguel Muñiz. The third one, Reverend Father Fray Cristóbal Barroso, left [for Spain] with the recent fleet [*flota*], and the said father on arriving in Mexico could not have failed to place himself at the feet of the said most excellent lord viceroy to tell His Magnificence of the faithfulness, benevolence, and friendship manifested by the said Indians of the pueblos, for only with the exception of the Jémez, Picurís, and Taos, all were completely reduced, submissive, and rendering vassalage to the king and to His Divine Majesty.

And as a result of this said report, the said reverend vice-custodian presented to the said most excellent lord viceroy the request for an increase in the number of said reverend religious, and it was expected that His Magnificence would then take the steps to endeavor again to establish our holy faith in this kingdom and that the reverend father Fray Cristóbal Barroso would then report all of this to his very reverend father superiors, as this was outside my legal jurisdiction. This was in time for Their Reverences to prevent the reverend father missionaries, who voluntarily and fervently offered to come to these parts, from withdrawing, ordering them to return to their provinces and, accordingly, for the most excellent lord viceroy not to provide the disbursement of funds for their travel or to delay making purchases and arrangements for the coming of the sixty-six and a half families, which His Magnificence provided for and decided should come on the tenth of September of sixteen hundred and ninety-three, leaving that day from Mexico under the leader named by His Excellency with the advice of the reverend father Fray Francisco Farfán, procurator general of this said custody, with the obligation to arrive within four months at El Paso del Río del Norte. The said father should have arrived there on the tenth of January, past, of this present year sixteen hundred ninety-four, bringing with him munitions and firearms. If the said families and the said war supplies had arrived accordingly, there is no doubt that the attitude of these nations would be quite different. I have no doubt that with divine favor I will succeed in getting them to recognize the power of the divine and human majesties.

And therefore, in view of the said glorious and triumphant conquest I achieved, the said reverend father president would not have to ask that he be given possession anew in behalf of his holy religion and of the said custody, as he would need only to recognize its firmness as a result of what has taken place with the submission and obedience of the said natives and nations, to whom the said reverend fathers their companions, administer and have administered the holy sacraments of baptism, marriage, and penance, saying numerous masses to them and explaining to them, through the tongue of the interpreter Pedro Hidalgo, the Christian doctrine through different talks. And proceeding to the Rock of Acoma and the province of Zuñi, they made the ascent with only two soldiers or residents to say mass to them, and on said rock and mesa they recovered from the natives the sacred vessels, monstrance, and statues of Christ our Redeemer, a missal, and books of the religious who died in the said province.

And finally, in all, having entered the said kingdom with His Majesty's arms and having reclaimed the said natives and nations and given them to understand that their only king, lord, and sovereign monarch is the king, our lordship, may God protect him, Lord Don Carlos the Second, king of the Spains and of this new world, and having restored anew to his royal possession this said kingdom, provinces, and Villa of Santa Fe, the capital and stronghold of New Mexico, and, likewise, having sent the *almagre,* or vermilion earth, for which I was so anxious to have the news that I hoped for regarding its quality. And this present coming had achieved successes, with greater difficulties and at great expense, that were not accomplished in the year 'eighty-one when the task was assigned in his royal name by decision and order of His Most Excellent Lordship the viceroy, who was the Count of Paredes, to his general of this said kingdom, who personally came to carry out this undertaking, General Antonio de Otermín, whose said lieutenant, with a troop of seventy selected from the said camp, was confronted by rebellious Indians in sight of the mesas that border on the pueblo of Cochití, the said general remaining with most of his said army, supplies, and convoy at the pueblo of La Alameda, only having accomplished the punishment of the said rebel, apostate enemy, who abandoned their pueblos, five of which were burned with their food supplies, with the loss of many of the horses and mules of the said army. He left this said kingdom with the natives of the Tiwa nation of the pueblo of Isleta, a distance of thirty leagues from this villa, beside the Camino Real, who are now located and exist as the pueblo of La Isleta del Paso del Río del Norte.

So one can measure and recognize the consequences of the advantages and boons of good fortune that God our Lord has deigned to give me. For His Majesty now finds himself with residents firmly implanted in this said kingdom, protected by this said stronghold, having shelter and home and grain to eat; and in this regard, as for me I exempted myself from special benefits, giving the order which is recorded in the said *autos* of the said illustrious cabildo, for I did not wish to make myself an exception or privilege myself by taking over the authority of reserving or separating anything for myself.

And notwithstanding my having inquired in El Paso if there was food there, it was not in the supposition that it might not be lacking for the said families, for through the courteous correspondence and confidence due to him in my dealings with the said reverend father procurator, Fray Francisco Farfán, I gave him advance notice by letter that the said district was completely without it and that he bring supplies from the valley of Parral and that I would pay for its cost, for the pestilence of the past year had left the said district completely without food supplies. And if the people of the vicinity had not left to come here, I would have been obliged to feed them, as most of them would have abandoned the region, leaving for elsewhere to seek recourse for themselves. Furthermore, for the maintenance of the soldiers of that presidio it was necessary for me to send them credit through a cash draft, not only for the value of food supplies they need, but also for that of the caravans for their transportation.

Therefore, with respect to the said proposal made by the very reverend father custodian that the said food supplies not leave this villa, I state that it is well considered and represents his great discretion and zeal and would have merit if I had not first attended to this by having carried from the pueblos of the said rebels who had risen against us two hundred ten loads of ears of corn recovered on four trips of five that have been carried out; with the coming of the additional residents, of even more concern in this regard, and in bringing a cargo of said food supplies, as is publicly and widely known, in deliberating thus, I had already revoked the idea before the presentation of this said letter. At the same time, I esteem and recognize the help and holy respect and reverence shown me, as is my respect for the authority of his person, with regard to his suggestion that a count should be made with regard to the consumption of the said food supplies. And my said order and decision for the support and assistance of food supplies for the journey of the said families will be of record in the campaign journal of which I refer.

And this and its presentation, as well as the previous writing, the said secretary of government and war will leave, each as it is, the two constituting my reply. And that it be of record, I signed, and the said secretary gave to the said very reverend father custodian the said testimony of said two writings, and that of this *auto* in this second one.

That it be of record, I decided thus and signed with the said secretary of government and war. Done, *ut supra*.

Don Diego de Vargas Zapata Luján Ponce de León. Before me, Alfonso Rael de Aguilar, secretary of government and war.

This copy is in accord with the original, which remains in the possession of His Lordship General Don Diego de Vargas Zapata Luján Ponce de León, governor and captain general of this kingdom of New Mexico, its new conqueror, restorer, reconqueror, and settler of it, and castellan of its forces and presidio for His Majesty, by whose order and command I, Captain Don Alfonso Rael de Aguilar, secretary of government and war of this said kingdom, copied it to the letter. It goes forward certain and true and corresponds with the original, and those present to see, correct, and revise it were Ayudante Antonio Valverde and Captain Lázaro de Mizquía, procurator general of this kingdom. Done in this Villa of Santa Fe on the thirty-first day of March, the year sixteen hundred ninety-four. In testimony whereof, I signed, and it goes on ordinary white paper, since paper with seal is not available in these parts. In testimony of its truth, I place my signature and customary rubric. Alfonso Rael de Aguilar, secretary of government and war.

This testimony concurs with the original, which rests in the archive of this holy Custody of the Conversion of Saint Paul of New Mexico, where I copied it verbatim. And I, as the secretary of the said custody, certify and attest that it corresponds with the said original. And that it be of permanent record, I gave the present testimony in this Villa of Santa Fe on the third day of April of this present year sixteen hundred ninety-four. Fray Diego Zeinos, secretary.

Since the very reverend father Salvador de San Antonio, custodian and judge ordinary and ecclesiastical of this holy custody, instructed that it would be more to his interest to see the original, I copied this one in place of the original, and this copy remained in the archive of this holy custody, to which I attest, Father Preacher Fray Juan Daza being present. Done, *ut supra*. Fray Diego Zeinos, secretary.

10. STATEMENT OF THE MISSIONARIES OF THE CUSTODY OF NEW MEXICO INDICATING THEIR READINESS TO TAKE UP RESIDENCE AMONG THE PACIFIED TEWA AND TANO INDIANS, SANTA FE, SEPTEMBER 22, 1694 [1]

WE, the religious missionaries who at the present moment reside in this Holy Custody of the Conversion of Saint Paul of New Mexico, ministering in this Villa of Santa Fe, say that since the reverend father Fray Juan Muñoz de Castro, preacher, commissary of the Holy Office, and vice-custodian of the said holy custody, has stated on this present day that the kingdom is at peace, thanks be to God, due to the successful establishment of peace with the Tewa and Tano Indians, who up to this time had shown themselves to be hostile and rebellious, and since we all are sufficiently convinced of the certainty, not only moral but also physical, that the said peace is true and secure, by reason of the previous and subsequent actions we have experienced on the part of the said already pacified natives, upon whose peace depended the entire security of the kingdom, and since His Paternal Reverence also has stated that some of the Pueblos of this said kingdom are requesting and clamoring for a priest to minister to them and teach them, the said father attending to the duties of his office and aiming to avoid any obstacle that might arise to prevent us, the religious of the said custody, from going to assume the various administrations, as designated by the mature judgment and accord of the very reverend Fray Salvador de San Antonio, former custodian (be it said) of the said holy custody, jointly we all have agreed that it was indeed our obligation to carry out the said designated ministries as regards both the obligation of our consciences and the credit to our seraphic order, even though we should be in danger of losing a thousand lives, which we would gladly give as well employed for these two highly justifiable aims as well as in the hope of thus being able to redeem them with the Precious Blood of our Redeemer. And thus, all of us, in unanimous agreement, fulfilling our duty of obedience, say that we are ready to assume the said ministries and that we see no objection whatever to being sent to serve in

1. BNM, leg. 3, doc. 6.

them by the said reverend father vice-custodian; indeed, we are of the opinion that a decision to the contrary might bring certain inconveniences that would be to the discredit of our seraphic order.

We so feel, declare, and sign, in this Villa of Santa Fe, on the twenty-second day of the month of September, the year sixteen hundred ninety-four.

Fray Antonio Carbonel	Fray Francisco Corbera
Fray Gerónimo Prieto	Fray Juan Alpuente
Fray José Diez	Fray Antonio de Obregón
Fray Francisco de Jesús María	Fray Diego Zeinos

PART THREE

Reestablishment of the Franciscan Missions, 1694–95

11. EXTRACTS FROM GOVERNOR VARGAS'S JOURNAL ON THE REESTABLISHMENT OF THE MISSIONS, SEPTEMBER 18–OCTOBER 7 AND NOVEMBER 1–DECEMBER 21, 1694 [1]

SAID governor and captain general sends Captain Francisco Lucero to the pueblo of the Pecos, since he knows their language, to notify the natives that they be ready for his visit to leave there the minister assigned to them.

On the said day, month, and year [September 18, 1694], I, said governor and captain general, since the said kingdom was already sufficiently at peace for the safety of the administering of the holy sacraments by the ministers who have been selected for this purpose, as well as to teach them [the natives] the Christian doctrine, had Captain Francisco Lucero de Godoy appear before me, and I requested him to go to the pueblo of the Pecos to notify them to be ready on the twenty-fourth of this month, to receive me, said governor and captain general, and the reverend father missionary who has been selected for them, and that all be prepared for the visit. And that it be of record, I signed this *auto* and measure with my secretary of government and war. Don Diego de Vargas Zapata Luján Ponce de León. Before me, Alfonso Rael de Aguilar, secretary of government and war.

The governor and captain general goes to visit the Pecos and Keres, taking with him the four reverend fathers who have been selected for their administration.

On the twenty-fourth of the present month of September of this year, I, said governor and captain general, left this Villa of Santa Fe with the four reverend fathers selected for the pueblos of the Pecos, Keres of San Felipe, Zia, and Jémez, accompanied by his reverence the vice-custodian and commissary of the Holy Office, who is the father preacher Fray Juan Muñoz de Castro. I also took with me the royal banner with a company of soldiers from this presidio, going out in festive spirit in consideration of a function of such importance. And that it be of record, I signed with my secretary of government and war. Don Diego de Vargas Zapata Luján Ponce de León. Before me, Alfonso Rael de Aguilar, secretary of government and war.

Letter. Lord governor and captain general. It will be most pleasing to me if this letter finds you in the good health which I hope you are enjoying. Today,

1. AGI, *Guadalajara*, leg. 140, doc. 5; AGN, *Historia*, tomo 39: 1695, transcripts in BC and copy of transcripts in LC.

all of our people give thanks to God our Lord for whatever you wish to order of us. I am sending to you your sons and our brothers, the said four captains, two of whom are from San Juan and two from Santo Domingo, who come humbly to place themselves at your feet to seek that in God's mercy you pardon them, who up to now have persevered in their folly. And thus, also, the governor of Santo Domingo begs in God's mercy that you pardon him also and that you not be under the impression that the people are fleeing, for now they all understand that there is a God and a king and that they are vassals of His Majesty and that you have come to protect us so that we might live in the tranquil and orderly manner in which we lived before this kingdom was lost, as will be seen in the future. For the said governors of these three pueblos of Santa Ana, San Felipe, and Zia and all of the captains of the three pueblos have told us that they have made peace with us and that our friendship will be eternal. And what they tell Your Lordship is true as regards both us and all of the Spaniards. And so that you may believe that they are acting in good faith, they bring, as witness to it and as their guide, this holy cross. And thus we, the said governors and captains of these three pueblos, ask you in God's mercy to pardon them and to deal with them in the friendly manner in which you treat us. And it is our only wish that God our Lord protect you many years for our well-being.

Your *compadre* and servant, who kisses your hands. And I ask that you send with the bearers a small amount of paper so that I may answer you and report to you regarding events here. Bartolomé de Ojeda.[2] Lord Governor and Captain General Don Diego de Vargas Zapata Luján Ponce de León. May God our Lord protect you many years at the Villa of Santa Fe. ✝ Hail Mary. Praise to the Blessed Sacrament.

Visit to the pueblo of the Pecos, leaving there its minister, *alcalde mayor,* and military captain.

In this pueblo of the Pecos, under the jurisdiction of the Villa of Santa Fe of this kingdom and provinces of New Mexico, on the twenty-fourth day of the month of September, the year sixteen hundred ninety-four. I, Don Diego de Vargas Zapata Luján Ponce de León, governor and captain general of this said kingdom and provinces of New Mexico, have come to this said pueblo on the visit which it was my duty to make, as ordered by His Majesty the king, may God protect him, as well as to bring back the reverend father preacher Fray Diego Zeinos, who has been selected as the minister missionary and apostolic guardian of the said natives, who again returns as the said minister to administer the holy sacraments and Christian doctrine and to preach the Holy Gospel. They promised to build their church so that divine worship may be cele-

2. BNM, leg. 3, doc. 6. See fn. 1, document 82, below.

brated with greater propriety, and at present they have preparations to build a chapel underway. This they have demonstrated with the lumber they have for the roof.

And I, said governor and captain general, instructing them at length, speaking and conferring with their cacique and governor as well as with the captains and elder Indians who are their leaders [*mandones*] and war captains, through the interpreters Captain Francisco Lucero de Godoy and Sergeant Juan Ruiz de Cáceres, they all answered in one voice, saying that they were pleased that I had come to make this visit and had brought for their minister the aforesaid reverend father preacher and that they had rebuilt for him his convent and residence, very spacious and appropriate. And I, said governor and captain general, having thanked them, and to give greater encouragement to the said old governor and his native people, told them that in order that they may live in an orderly political manner, recognizing their leader to govern them and administer justice among them, it was necessary for them to elect freely, meeting together as His Majesty the king, our lord, orders and directs them to do, and to present to me those elected from among those Indians best qualified and required to exercise the said offices and that I would present them with the rods of office and would receive in the name of His Majesty their oath, which they should make in recognition of the law of God our Lord and the holy cross, and which I, said governor and captain general, would confirm and approve so that he [the elected] would be and continue to serve as the head of the government of the said natives, and understanding my wishes, they assented and indicated that this was their true wish. And in fulfilment of the above, today, said day, at two o'clock in the afternoon they appeared before me bringing the rods and requested that I, said governor and captain general, present them to the said elected persons. They were: for governor of this said pueblo, Diego Marcos; for lieutenant governor, Augustín; for *alcaldes*, Pedro Pupo and Salvador Tunoque; for captain of war, Pedro Lucero Tuque; for *alcalde unfeto*, *alguacil*, Pedro Cristóbal Tundias; as fiscals, Antonio Quoaes, Pedro Coctze, Diego Ystico, and Augustín Gocho; and as captains of war, Juan Chiuta as chief war captain and Miguel Echos, Juan Ombire, Miguel Himuiro, Juan Diego, Diego Stayo, don Lorenzo de Ye, and Augustín Tafuno. And to all of the said I gave the said rods and canes. And they also asked me to name for them and leave as their *alcalde mayor* Sergeant Major Francisco de Anaya Almazán, who, being a highly merited person, I considered as a fit selection, and then I presented the cane to him as *alcalde mayor* and military captain of this said pueblo, taking his oath under allegiance to God our Lord and with the sign of the holy cross to carry out his office well and faithfully as a loyal vassal of His Majesty and to follow fully the instructions I should give him with regard to his said office.

And in this form I carried out these measures and completed the said visit and election. And I also asked them what male or female saint they wished to have as the titular patron of the said chapel, which is to be moved to the church which they are to rebuild and erect in the coming year, and they told me that their choice was Our Lady of the Angels of Porciúncula, which they already have as the titular patroness of the said pueblo. And that the said visit and election be of record, this was signed with me, said governor and captain general, by the said elected *alcalde mayor* and military captain, the captain of the presidio and sergeant major Antonio Jorge, the captain of artillery Francisco Lucero de Godoy, who served as interpreter, and my secretary of government and war. Done *ut supra*. Don Diego de Vargas Zapata Luján Ponce de León. Antonio Jorge. Francisco Lucero de Godoy. Before me, Alfonso Rael de Aguilar, secretary of government and war.

Visit to the pueblo of San Felipe, also leaving there its minister.

On the twenty-sixth of the present month of September, of this date and year, I, said governor and captain general, in continuing the said visits, proceeded to the said pueblo of San Felipe of the Keres nation, entering it to leave there their newly elected minister and teacher of Christian doctrine, who is the reverend father preacher and apostolic missionary Fray Antonio Carbonel. With the said people of this said plaza, I told all of them that I had come to visit them because the king, our lord, ordered me to do so and also to leave with them the aforesaid reverend father, who was with me, as their minister, whom they should obey and respect very much as such, attending punctually the instruction in Christian doctrine in the evening and in the morning and the divine services, as they were Christians. And they showed me that at present they have as a chapel a high *estufa* which is very spacious, which I permitted, since the said place was acceptable to the said father, telling them that in the coming year I, said governor and captain general, would give orders to provide a more suitable place. And also I ordered the said natives to elect, freely and voluntarily, a governor, *alcalde,* and other officials, and having done so, they brought before me those they had elected, bringing the rods and canes so that I might present them to them and receive their oath of allegiance under God our Lord and the sign of the holy cross in proper legal form. And with the interpreters present, I asked them to give me the names of the said governor, *alcaldes,* and others, which were given as follows: for governor, Gabriel de Velasco; for *alcaldes,* Francisco Graco and Martin Yaytigua; for fiscals, Baltasar Dierope, Juan Calabaza, Lázaro Caiquí, and Juan Murensse; and for captains of war, Andrés Caicochi, chief captain of war, and Sebastián Cayasero, Cristóbal Moche, Diego Situa, Juan Sebastian, José Yanatigua, Jacinto Conocono,

Gerónimo, and Augeme. And in the name of His Majesty I presented to all of the aforesaid the said rods and canes of office, promising them that I would help them in every way and would defend them against their enemies.

And that it be of record that I made said visit and that the aforesaid reverend father missionary Fray Antonio Carbonel was newly left as said minister and teacher of Christian doctrine in the said pueblo, and that as a sign of possession I had ordered the ringing of the bells and the singing three times of the "Glory Be to the Blessed Sacrament of the Altar," in which I, said governor and captain general, was joined by the said natives along with the soldiers, leaders, and officials, I signed along with my secretary of government and war. *Ut supra*. Don Diego de Vargas Zapata Luján Ponce de León. Before me, Alfonso Rael de Aguilar, secretary of government and war.

Visit to the pueblo of Santa Ana, the minister *doctrinero* [instructor in Christian doctrine] and reverend father preacher Fray Juan de Alpuente remaining in charge of administering the holy sacraments.

On the twenty-seventh day of this present month and year, I, said governor and captain general, entered this pueblo of Santa Ana of the Keres nation to make the visit that the king, our lord, has ordered me to make, and I found the natives gathered at its entrance to welcome me. And I dismounted along with the soldiers, as did likewise the father preacher Fray Juan de Alpuente, who newly remains in charge of the administration of the holy sacraments and instruction in Christian doctrine for the said natives, serving it as a *visita* of his said pueblo of Zia, where he has been selected as said minister *doctrinero*. And in sign of possession he knelt on his knees before the holy cross as I, said governor and captain general, also did, and as did the soldiers and the said natives. And they sang the "Hail to the Blessed Sacrament" three times with the said reverend father, and also it was ordered that the bell be rung as an act of possession.

And I went from that place and entered a room which they have prepared as a temporary chapel while they are building their church. And I told the said natives that it was the very reverend father, their minister, whom they should and must respect as such, and I ordered them to assist him and that it was their obligation as Christians to attend the instructions in Christian doctrine in the evening and in the morning and also to hear mass and participate in the divine services. And having arranged for the said natives to elect freely and voluntarily the best and wisest Indians of their said pueblo to serve as *alcaldes,* constable, fiscals, and captains of war, in the same number as they elected and named them before the Spaniards had left, they presented to me the following natives to exercise the said offices: First I, said governor and captain general, reelected as governor of this pueblo and chief captain of war of the said Keres Indians the one to whom I have given the title and patent and who is already in that office, Bartolomé de Ojeda by name; and for his lieutenant, Antonio Laivru Vina was elected; and as *alcalde,* Vicente Pochora; and as constable, Felipe Tachinaya; and as captains of war, Lorenzo Vsurugua, Pedro Puosta, José Chigigua, Antonio Tegua, Augustín Quisigua, and Antonio Texa; and for fiscals, Antonio Equiana, Luis Quiatto, and Lorenzo Nasga. To all of these I gave the rods and canes as symbols of their offices and received their oath of office, under obedience to God our Lord and with the sign of the holy cross, making clear to them their obligations in holding their said office and in having taken the oath for that purpose, to which they answered joyfully that they were ready to carry out their obligations as indicated. And that it be of record regarding the said visit, and what is referred to therein, I signed with my said secretary of government and war, on said day, *ut supra.* Don Diego de Vargas Zapata Luján Ponce de León. Before me, Alfonso Rael de Aguilar, secretary of government and war.

In the said pueblo we are met by the two captains who came to render the obedience of the Jémez of the mesa of San Juan and two others in their company of the Keres of Santo Domingo, who live on the said mesa and are their allies; they request pardon, and the governor and captain general concedes it to them, as referred to below.

At the said pueblo of Santa Ana on said day, I, governor and captain general, found that I was awaited there by four captains of the rebels who live on the mesa of San Juan of the Jémez, who separated from the pueblo of that name and went there in years past along with the Keres of the pueblo of Santo Domingo, and also two other captains representing the latter were awaiting me, having been informed of my arrival and visit. And when they saw me they welcomed me in humble submission and showed reverence and obedience to the divine and human majesties, saying that with the sign of the cross, which they carried for their protection, they sought pardon for themselves and their said people, who had sent them, so that I would respond to their plea; and thus they humbly requested the said pardon, promising that they would live as Christians and as vassals of His Majesty. And to assure them of their pardon, and telling them to inform their said native people likewise, I took the royal standard in my hand and assured them in the name of His Majesty and through the divine lady the Blessed Virgin of Remedies, represented on it, that I pardoned them and all of their people from the bottom of my heart. And afterwards I treated them kindly and as friends, and I gave to one of the captains a rosary that I was wearing around my neck, placing it around his neck and telling him that I was keeping the holy cross that he had brought in exchange for the rosary I had given to him as a sign and proof of his said pardon and that of his people and that with it and the holy cross that I had they could be assured of their pardon, and that their people should come down from the said mesa to the pueblo of Jémez to see me, as I was on my way there, God willing, to make my visit there and to leave there anew the father whom I was taking there. And they replied that they were departing immediately so that there would be sufficient time, as the mesa was quite a distance away, and that the said people would be there to see me, which they desired very much. And that it be of record, I have made this report and have signed it with my secretary of government and war. Don Diego de Vargas Zapata Luján Ponce de León. Before me, Alfonso Rael de Aguilar, secretary of government and war.

Visit to the pueblo of Zia, where the said governor and captain general left as its minister the said reverend father Fray Juan de Alpuente and which had as its titular patroness Our Lady of the Conception, to whom the natives are devoted.

On said day, the twenty-seventh of the present month of September of this date and year, I, said governor and captain general, in carrying out the said visit, entered this pueblo of Zia, which has as its titular patroness Our Lady of the Conception and whose natives are of the Keres nation. I arrived there at about five o'clock in the afternoon and found the natives waiting to welcome me outside of the said pueblo, the men separated from the women and children, and they all greeted me, saying in one voice, "Glory Be to the Blessed Sacrament." And after I arrived at the first small plaza at the entrance to the said pueblo, they showed me the residence that they had prepared for its minister *doctrinero,* referred to in today's visit to the pueblo of Santa Ana, who is newly elected for this said pueblo, the reverend father preacher Fray Juan Alpuente, who was at my side. I told the said assemblage gathered here, through the interpreter, that he was the father minister that I now brought to them and was placing there in the name of His Majesty so that he could administer to them the holy sacraments and teach them Christian doctrine, and that they should obey and respect him, responding punctually to all that he requested of them. And as a sign of possession the said minister and reverend father ordered that the bell be sounded, and falling to his knees, as I also did along with the said assemblage, before the holy cross which they had erected, he sang the "Praise Be to the Blessed Sacrament" three times. After this I went and entered his said residence, congratulating him and leaving him there.

And I told the said natives to elect, voluntarily, as the king our lord ordered of them, the Indians who were the wisest and most loyal to the royal crown to exercise the offices of *alcalde, topiles,* captains of the pueblo and of war, and fiscals for the holy church, and that the said governor whom they had elected when I entered the kingdom should be reelected along with his lieutenant, who was worthy and who had served His Majesty with loyalty. To this they replied that with the news of my coming on the said visit they had already held their meeting and had named those who should hold these positions. And therefore they presented them to me and gave me the rods and canes to present to them. And after they had taken the oath, I again gave the cane of governor of this said pueblo of Zia to its cacique, Don Cristóbal Cayquiro; to his lieutenant, Lorenzo Yaitigio; as *alcalde,* Cristóbal Otta; as constable, Nicolás Siute; as captain of the pueblo, Nicolás Zaa; as captains of war, Cristóbal Sibolo, Juan Luaca Punqueque, Cristóbal Delita, Juan Casquiro, Cristóbal Yustia, Alonso Zocoye, and Bartolo Saitu; and as fiscals, José Si, Antonio Mitia, Cristóbal Juscane, and Diego Istia. I presented to them the canes and rods in the name of His Majesty, and they took their oath, which I received from all of them in accordance with the law in the name of God and the sign of the cross, and through the interpreter I made clear to each of them the obligations of their office. And I emphasized to them that they should assist their minister and reverend father preacher in every way and build the church as soon as possible, as only the roof is lacking; at present they have prepared a temporary chapel. And that the said visit and that which took place may be of record, I signed this with my said secretary of government and war. Don Diego de Vargas Zapata Luján Ponce de León. Before me, Alfonso Rael de Aguilar, secretary of government and war.

Entry into the pueblo of Jémez.

On the twenty-eighth day of the present month of September of this date and year, I, said governor and captain general, entered this pueblo and mesa of the Jémez nation, which by force of arms I had reduced to submission and reconquered. And I found that its said natives had fulfilled their promise in every way, more so than I had expected, for which I gave infinite thanks to the divine lady and our protectress of the said reconquest. And since the said pueblo was dedicated to San Diego as its titular saint, I gave it the name of the said saint, naming the said mesa San Diego del Monte and Our Lady of Remedies. And proceeding with the said visit, I found the said natives gathered very attentively, both men and women. They had erected in the center of the plaza a beautiful cross on a pedestal and with steps leading up to it as an altar, in the form of a platform, all made of stone and lime. And there, with the assistance of the said interpreters, I told them that the purpose of my coming was to visit their said pueblo to ascertain the condition in which they found themselves in carrying out their obligations and as the king our lord, may God protect him, ordered me, for which reasons I also had brought them the father minister who was beside me, newly elected to assist them in administering the holy sacraments and to instruct them in Christian doctrine, whose name was the father preacher Fray Francisco de Jesús, and that they should always obey him in everything that he ordered and requested of them and that they should respect him very much.

And as a sign of possession the said reverend father ordered that the bell be sounded, and with all kneeling before the said holy cross, he invoked three times the "Glory Be to the Blessed Sacrament." And afterwards I went with the said father to the house that they had prepared for him and which was designated as his residence, which was very comfortable and large enough to house four religious, with all the necessities, with its offices and kitchens. And after the election of those who were to hold office, they presented themselves and I gave them the rods and canes of office and received their oath under God our Lord and the sign of the holy cross in the following manner: as governor, Alonso Juan Vilec; as lieutenant governor, Diego Efondo; as *alcalde,* Xuxu; as *alguacil,* Francisco Baaquioe; as captains of the pueblo, Antonio Auaa, Nicolás Delu, Antonio de Talu, and Miguel de Lena; as chief captain of war, Cristóbal Taneñe; as the other captains of war, Mateo Ganaa, Ignacio Pules, Diego Cuye, Lorenzo Epile, Alonso Consu, and Cristóbal Oraa Jenbolee; as chief fiscal, Nicolás Vastalee; and as other fiscals, Alonso Tontapee, Mateo Qui Equi, Mateo Astudee, and Francisco Bola. And for the pueblo of the said nation of the Keres Indians of Santo Domingo that had fled to the mesa of San Juan, their selected leaders took their oath with the sign of the cross in the following manner as captain of the pueblo, Mateo Hueache; as chief war captain, Estéban Soniti; as war captains, Estéban Oila and Mateo Tuleé; as chief fiscal, Cristóbal Tuyahuya; and as fiscals, Lorenzo Mano de Chile, Francisco Teeche, and Alonso Chalubo. And having instructed all of them in the obligations of their offices, they promised to carry them out fully, and I took leave of the reverend father after partaking of the food that was kindly prepared for us, and all the soldiers happily joined in the festivities in responding to their friendly gesture. I returned to the said pueblo of Zia. And that it be of record, I signed with my said secretary of government and war. Don Diego de Vargas Zapata Luján Ponce de León. Before me, Alfonso Rael de Aguilar, secretary of government and war.

The said governor and captain general arrives at the pueblo of Santo Domingo, and the Keres of Cochití come down there with their captain, El Zepe, and render obedience, agreeing to receive the Father and to build the church and convent.

On the thirtieth of the present month of September of the said date and year, being in the pueblo of Santo Domingo before returning to the Villa of Santa Fe, the captains of the Keres of Cochití with their governor, whom they call El Zepe, their leader whom they obey, arrived to render obedience. I received them in a very friendly manner, responding to the submission and affection with which they offered me the due obedience, demonstrating their intentions and promising that in every way as vassals of His Majesty and as Christians they would live in recognition of the two majesties and that they would welcome the father when he is taken to them, building his convent and church and giving him what was customarily given to their minister. I took leave of them, receiving the friendly treatment that they extended to me by responding in the same manner, and all were very pleased, as I was, in view of the courtesy and the desire that they expressed and which I acknowledged.

And that it be of record that on the said day, in the evening, I arrived at the said Villa of Santa Fe, finding that the natives of the neighboring pueblos were again there to trade and finding that both parties were happy and pleased in their dealings with one another, I made it of record and signed with my said secretary of government and war. Don Diego de Vargas Zapata Luján Ponce de León. Before me, Alfonso Rael de Aguilar, secretary of government.

Said governor and captain general sends notice to the pueblos of the Tewas to be ready there to welcome him and the minister who will be placed there and to prepare for his visit to them.

On October second of this present year and date, I, said governor and captain general, considering that the three reverend fathers who have been in this Villa of Santa Fe are ready to go to the missions of the pueblos of San Ildefonso, San Juan, and San Cristóbal, for which they have been selected, and since the said Indians have been subdued and can assure the safety of the said reverend ministers to enable them to proceed there to administer the holy sacraments and teach Christian doctrine, I ordered the sergent major and captain Antonio Jorge to have Sergeant Juan Ruiz accompany me as my interpreter on my visit to the said pueblos, and the others comprising the said nations, to apprise them of their obligations, and this action was taken. And that it be of record, I signed with my said secretary of government and war. Don Diego de Vargas Zapata Luján Ponce de León. Before me, Alfonso Rael de Aguilar, secretary of government and war.

Said governor and captain general leaves to visit the indicated pueblos of the Tewas and Tanos, taking with him the said ministers designated.

On the fifth day of the present month of October of this date and year, I, said governor and captain general, having made preparations for the three reverend father missionaries newly appointed for the three said pueblos, and with the reverend father vice-custodian, who is also commissary of the holy tribunal, Fray Juan Muñoz de Castro, ready to take them, I left this Villa of Santa Fe with the said fathers and the soldiers today, said day, at nine o'clock in the morning. I first went to the pueblo of Tesuque, which I visited, where the natives welcomed me with expressions of joy, having set up many arches. And in their plaza, with the said gathering of the people and with the assistance of the said reverend fathers, the "Glory Be" was sung three times, and I told them what their obligations were as Christians, which were to pray in the evening and in the morning before that holy cross until the arrival from the town of El Paso of the fathers who were now there, and that when they arrived their said prelate would designate the father to administer the holy sacraments to them and that I ordered them to have built and ready, so that he could do so, a chapel and house in which to live. To which they said that they would comply fully, and I replied that I would come in person to leave their said father with them.

And afterwards I explained to them the royal pleasure and manner in which they should elect the governing officials from the best Indians, and they had already elected their governor, who was Captain Domingo, and I freely left with them the power to elect the said officials, and they replied that they had already done so, as I had already told them to do so, and they had there the rods and canes so that I might present them to the ones elected: as governor, the said Domingo Romero; Domingo Romero [*sic*] as his lieutenant; as *alcalde*, Alonso Presnota; and as *alguacil*, Martín Juatito; as captains of war they left those they already had, and they reserved the election of fiscals until a father should be placed there as their minister. To those elected I presented the rods and canes and received their oath, which they made under God our Lord and the sign of the holy cross, indicating that they would perform their offices very well and that they would be loyal to His Majesty. After this I again repeated to them, through the interpreters, very minutely, all of that which it was their obligation to do, leaving them well instructed and aware of the requirements in performing their duties in the service of God and our lord the king. I took leave of them pleased to see the said people so docile and submissive as though the said war had not occurred. And that the above be of record, I signed with my said secretary of government and war. Don Diego de Vargas Zapata Luján

Ponce de León. Before me, Alfonso Rael de Aguilar, secretary of government and war.

The said governor and captain general goes to the pueblos of Cuyamungué and Pojoaque and carries out what is referred to below.

On the said day, month, and year, I went to the pueblos of Cuyamungué and Pojoaque, where I greeted all of the natives in the same friendly manner and engaged in the same activities as in the previously mentioned last visit, at the same time advising them in advance to make ready the church and the living quarters for the father minister to be chosen for them, indicating to them that a sufficient number of religious for all of the pueblos would soon be coming from the town of El Paso, where they were now stationed, and that I would bring them in person to the pueblos and that I was postponing, until that time, the election of the natives who would hold the positions of authority. I left them fully informed of these plans, and they replied that they were in accord. And that this said visit be of record, I signed with my said secretary of government and war. Don Diego de Vargas Zapata Luján Ponce de León. Before me, Alfonso Rael de Aguilar, secretary of government and war.

Visit to the pueblo of Jacona, which is under the charge of the minister who is assigned to the pueblo of San Ildefonso.

On said day, month, and year, I, said governor and captain general, entered this pueblo of Jacona, and its natives came out to welcome me with great courtesy. And after I and the reverend fathers had dismounted, the father selected for the pueblo of San Ildefonso, with this pueblo as his *visita,* with its administration under his charge, was introduced by me to the said natives. And I told them that in the name of His Majesty the king, our lord, may God protect him, I was placing and leaving him there and that they should obey him in every way and hold him in due respect and that they should build a chapel so that he could say mass for them and administer the holy sacraments and a house so he would have a place to live. And as a token of possession, the said religious, named Fray Francisco Corbera, directed them to fall to their knees and to sing the "Glory Be . . ." three times before the holy cross. And since some of the natives were in the cornfields, which were quite a distance away, they did not conduct the election of officials, postponing it until I visit the remaining pueblos to leave their father ministers with them. And as I took leave of them they agreed to carry out everything that they were ordered to do. And that it be of record, I signed with my said secretary of government and war. Don Diego de Vargas Zapata Luján Ponce de León. Before me, Alfonso Rael de Aguilar, secretary of government and war.

Visit to the pueblo of San Ildefonso, where the said governor and captain general left the reverend father Fray Francisco Corbera as minister.

On said day, month, and year, I, said governor and captain general, went to visit the pueblo of San Ildefonso to place the aforesaid newly appointed minister there. And having entered the pueblo, the aforesaid reverend father Fray Francisco Corbera took possession in the manner referred to previously, the Indians complying in every respect. For the present they had prepared a room for him, where I spent the night. They also conducted the election of the natives, naming the governing authorities and military officials as well as the fiscals of the holy church: José Ani; assistant fiscal, Matías Vide; captain of war, Matías Yandegua; and captains, Francisco Unpegue, Domingo Eyogue, and Matías Unxe. I presented the rods and canes of office to all of the electees in the name of His Majesty, and they took the required oath under God our Lord and the sign of the holy cross, swearing to perform their duties well and to carry out without fail the orders given to them. On the following day I took leave, leaving with them their newly designated reverend father minister, the aforesaid. And that the above be of record, I signed with my said secretary of government and war. Don Diego de Vargas Zapata Luján Ponce de León. Before me, Alfonso Rael de Aguilar, secretary of government and war.

Visit to the pueblo of Santa Clara, which is under the charge of the minister assigned to San Juan.

On the sixth day of the said month of October, of this date and year, I, said governor and captain general, went to this pueblo of Santa Clara. And I entered the plaza with its newly assigned minister, whom I came to place there temporarily until more religious arrive from among those available in the town of El Paso, for which reason the reverend father Fray Gerónimo Prieto is placed in charge of administering the holy sacrament there. He will carry out these duties from the pueblo of San Juan, where he is to be placed as minister *doctrinero* and guardian. And thus, in this manner I granted him the said possession, and I gave the said natives the same orders that I had given to the others referred to above. I also ordered the construction necessary at this time, and they showed me the living quarters they had prepared for the said father, which I entered and found to be very clean and capacious. And I told them to elect their officials, but they had already elected the Indians for this purpose, as follows: for chief war captain, Lucas Naranjo;[3] for governor, Blas Ozede; for lieutenant, Diego Catuna; for *alcalde,* Juan Yocteda; for constable, Francisco Vuei; for fiscal, Gerónimo Monguede; for war captain, Juan Chile; for cap-

3. Ibid. See fn. 2, document 88, below.

tains, Felipe Xupi and Estéban Tematende. I gave the electees the canes and rods of office in the name of His Majesty and took their required oath. I then left with the said minister to leave him at his principal pueblo, and the said natives remained very pleased to find themselves in tranquility and with their lives in safety. And that it be of record, I signed with my said secretary of government and war. Don Diego de Vargas Zapata Luján Ponce de León. Before me, Alfonso Rael de Aguilar, secretary of government and war.

Visit to the pueblo of San Juan, where I left Father Antonio Gerónimo Prieto.

On said day, month, and year, I, said governor and captain general, went with the said reverend father minister to his said pueblo of San Juan, where the natives came out to welcome me with the same submission and courtesies that I had received elsewhere. And entering the plaza in the manner referred to previously, I granted possession to the said guardian Fray Gerónimo Prieto. And also the said natives had a very good house prepared for him, and they promised that they would soon build a chapel. I then told them to elect the natives for their positions of authority, which they designated as follows: governor of the said pueblo, Miguel Xaede; lieutenant, Francisco Xucama; *alcalde,* Pedro Noaya; *alguacil,* Juan Jaquequi; chief fiscal, Francisco Xumatte; chief war captain, Juan Griego; and war captain, Francisco Cotu. I confirmed the election of the said officials in the name of His Majesty and received their oath in the required manner. And having left their said minister in charge, I took leave, leaving him pleased with the reception received from the said natives. And that it be of record, I signed with my said secretary of government and war. Don Diego de Vargas Zapata Luján Ponce de León. Before me, Alfonso Rael de Aguilar, secretary of government and war.

Visit to the pueblo of San Lázaro, where I left as their minister the reverend father Fray Antonio Obregón.

On said day, month, and year, I, said governor and captain general, went to this pueblo of San Lázaro, and the natives came out to meet me. And in the plaza, in the manner referred to on the other similar occasions, I pointed out and told them who the minister was whom I came to leave with them, both for them and for the natives of the pueblo of San Cristóbal, and that the name of their said minister and guardian *doctrinero* was the reverend father Fray Antonio Obregón and that they should carry out faithfully what he should ask them to do. And I granted possession to him in the manner indicated on the earlier occasions. And the said natives indicated the house they had prepared for him and promised to build him a chapel. Also they held their election in their customary manner and presented the following electees: for governor, Don Cristóbal Yope; for lieutenant, Cristóbal Xidee; for *alcalde,* Tomás Empoo; for *alguacil,* Francisco Ahee; for chief fiscal, Juan Machoa; for another fiscal, Miguel Senez; and for war captains, Sebastian Tzenepaya, Matias Manso, and Antonio Cajuei. And in the name of His Majesty I presented the canes and rods of office to the said and received their oath in the prescribed manner. They remained very submissive and ready to fulfill their obligations and to assist the father minister whom I left with them. And that it be of record, I signed with my said secretary of government and war. Don Diego de Vargas Zapata Luján Ponce de León. Before me, Alfonso Rael de Aguilar, secretary of government and war.

Said governor and captain general goes to the pueblo of San Cristóbal, and there he grants possession to the aforesaid minister at San Lázaro, the administration of the said pueblos remaining under his charge.

On the seventh day of the said month of this year, I, said governor and captain general, went to the pueblo of San Cristóbal, taking there its minister guardian and catechist the reverend father Fray Antonio de Obregón. And the said natives came out to meet me, as in the case of the other pueblos, and in their plaza I granted possession to the said reverend guardian, and in token of this he sang the "Praise Be . . . " three times, along with the said people. I charged them with the obligations required of them, also telling them that they should soon build a chapel and a house for the said father. And they all said that this would be fulfilled and demonstrated their submission and pleasure in being back in their said pueblo. And since some of those whom they elected for the said offices were in the corn fields, I left orders that at the end of the month, when they had completed their harvest, they should come to the Villa of Santa Fe, where I would present them with the canes and rods of office in the name of His Majesty in the prescribed manner as done in the other pueblos. And I took leave of them after leaving the said pueblo of San Lázaro under the care of the aforesaid reverend father guardian and minister. And that it be of record, I signed with my said secretary of government and war. Don Diego de Vargas Zapata Luján Ponce de León. Before me, Alfonso Rael de Aguilar, secretary of government and war.

Entry into the Villa of Santa Fe, after having made preparations for placing ministers in the pueblos that he will visit shortly, as he has done in those so indicated.

And then I immediately proceeded on my journey to the Villa of Santa Fe so as not to embarass the said natives with my presence any longer by interfering with their necessary labor in their cornfields, having passed through the pueblos which at present do not have settled missions since there are no fathers available for them. I left them with notice that they would arrive soon from El Paso del Río del Norte and that they should have their houses and convents ready for them. And I postponed the election of their fiscals until they were built, since they would be for the holy church, and [ordered] that those elected for the other offices should appear before me in the said Villa of Santa Fe at the end of this present month. They replied that they would do so, and I took leave of them, happy to see them subdued in their said pueblos and with the submissive obedience they displayed in welcoming me, acknowledging that they are vassals of His Majesty and Christians. I entered this villa at four o'clock in the afternoon. And that it be of record, I signed with my said secretary of government and war. Don Diego de Vargas Zapata Luján Ponce de León. Before me, Alfonso Rael de Aguilar, secretary of government and war.

Herewith the *autos* concerning the reconquest and the assignment of the father ministers in the pueblos of the Tewas and Tanos newly restored to the royal crown.

On the first of November of the year sixteen hundred ninety-four, the very reverend father Fray Francisco de Vargas entered the Villa of Santa Fe from the town of El Paso del Río del Norte, where he served as vice-custodian, newly elected following the resignation of the custodian, Father Fray Salvador de San Antonio, who left on the past Palm Sunday as stated in the *autos* that have been sent forward. The aforesaid Father Fray Francisco de Vargas entered, bringing with him the four missionary fathers who left El Paso with him for these parts during the time of the said war. And to confirm this arrival, I signed with my said secretary of government and war on said day. Don Diego de Vargas Zapata Luján Ponce de León. Before me, Alfonso Rael de Aguilar, secretary of government and war.

Said governor and captain general confers with the said reverend father vice-custodian with regard to the pueblos that do not have father ministers and decides to visit them in order to place in them the four father ministers he brought with him.

On the fifth day of the present month of November of this year, making ready for the visit with the aforesaid reverend father vice-custodian, Fray Francisco de Vargas, and cognizant of the fact that he had already been informed by the father commissary Fray Juan Muñoz de Castro, vice-custodian, who left the said Fray Salvador de San Antonio appointed in this kingdom, I, said governor and captain general, told him that it was now necessary to place father ministers in the two pueblos of Tesuque and Santa Clara, since they are those with the largest number of people, and also in the two pueblos of Santo Domingo and Cochití, already resettled by the Indians of the Keres nation, who have descended from the mesas to live in them. And thus the said reverend father vice-custodian Fray Francisco de Vargas selected as minister and catechist for the pueblo of Tesuque the father missionary Fray José Diez, who was serving as guardian in this villa, since he had conducted mass for them and had administered the holy sacraments to them. Thus, avoiding unnecessary difficulty, and since he had already advanced and won the goodwill of the Indians, the said selection was indeed wisely made. The same care and justification was shown in appointing in his place as guardian and pastor of this villa the said reverend father commissary of the Holy Office, Fray Juan Muñoz de Castro, and as his companion, Fray Antonio Moreno. And to attest to the said selections, I signed in this villa with my said secretary of government and war. Don Diego de Vargas Zapata Luján Ponce de León. Before me, Alfonso Rael de Aguilar, secretary of government and war.

Said governor and captain general departs with the said reverend father vice-custodian to the pueblos of the Tewas and Tanos, and they leave in possession the father missionaries selected for the pueblos of Tesuque and Santa Clara.

On the thirteenth day of the month of November of the year sixteen hundred ninety-four, I, said governor and captain general, left this said villa with the aforesaid reverend father vice-custodian, Fray Francisco de Vargas, for the pueblo of Tesuque with the major part of soldiers, their leaders and officers, and my secretary of government and war. And having arrived in view of the said pueblo, we found its people assembled with their Captain Domingo, they being of the Tewa nation, ready to receive me and the said reverend father vice-custodian, having decorated their chapel with arches and tree branches, and at its doorway, dressed for the said reception, stood its said appointed minister and catechist, Fray José Diez, who, having sung the customary prayers for the said reception and having removed his vestments, had come outside. And I took his hand and through an interpreter told the said natives that I gave him possession of the said chapel in the name of His Majesty, as its father minister who had been named and designated for them by the said reverend father vice-custodian, and that in proof of possession he had the said altar constructed and ordered that the bell of the said chapel be tolled. And in said plaza before the holy cross which had been erected there I ordered the said natives to sing the *alabado* three times, which I, said governor and captain general, did also, along with the soldiers, and I ordered them to assist and respect the father minister and obey everything he ordered of them, as I had done in the first pueblos as attested to in the said *autos*. And I passed on to the living quarters which they had designated and had ready for the said father and which is adequate. And the said Indians remained very pleased. This day I then went on to the pueblo of San Ildefonso to spend the night. In witness whereof, I signed with my said secretary of government and war. Don Diego de Vargas Zapata Luján Ponce de León. Before me, Alfonso Rael de Aguilar, secretary of government and war.

Entry into the pueblo of Santa Clara, where the said governor and captain general left Father Fray José García Marín.

On the fourteenth day of the present month and year I, said governor and captain general, left in this pueblo of Santa Clara, which I had entered with the aforesaid reverend father vice-custodian, Fray Francisco de Vargas, the father he had selected and designated as minister and catechist, Fray José García Marín, to whom I bestowed, in the same manner as in the others, in the name of His Majesty, possession of the chapel which they had built for him as well as the living quarters, and the natives were very pleased. And having told them through the interpreter, Juan Ruiz de Cáceres of their said obligation to him in the form referred to in the others, I passed on to visit and inspect, as determined by the aforesaid reverend vice-custodian, the other pueblos and missions established at San Juan and San Lázaro, where I observed with great pleasure the punctual assistance and obedience being given to their ministers and the great progress that had been made with the natives in teaching them the prayers and Christian doctrine. I, said governor and captain general, repeated to them what they were obliged to do and that they should rest assured that I would defend them from their enemies. And in testimony of the said visit and act of possession by the said ministers, I signed, along with my said secretary of government and war. Don Diego de Vargas Zapata Luján Ponce de León. Before me, Alfonso Rael de Aguilar, secretary of government and war.

Said governor departs for the pueblos of Cochití and Santo Domingo to make the said visit with the reverend father vice-custodian, leaving there the ministers referred to above.

On the twenty-seventh day of the month of November of this year, I, said governor and captain general, accompanied by the aforesaid reverend father vice-custodian and the said group of soldiers with their leaders and officers and my secretary of government and war, departed from this said villa to the pueblos of Cochití and Santo Domingo. And as we entered the said pueblo of Cochití, the natives, who by force of arms I had subdued at the mesa (as attested to in the said *autos* I sent on April twenty-seventh past of this year, war having broken out, and from which we emerged victorious, as recorded that day), were at the entrance of the said pueblo in full submission. They had set up many arches and had constructed their chapel and had prepared a house for the priest, the designated father minister missionary Fray Antonio Carbonel, who had moved from the pueblo of San Felipe, having been appointed and designated by the said reverend father vice-custodian, and who in the name of His Majesty was installed in the manner referred to previously. And the said natives demonstrated their full submission as his loyal vassals, and they gave food to the soldiers. And also I brought with me the canes and rods of office so that I could leave with them their officers of government, whom they elected, and which I gave to those elected. For this reason I spent the night in the said pueblo. I acknowledged the reestablishment of their pueblo government in this proper manner, and they requested that I free the people whom I had taken as prisoners the day of the battle and whom I had distributed as hostages among the people of this said villa, which I promised to do. In witness whereof, I signed with my said secretary of government and war. Don Diego de Vargas Zapata Luján Ponce de León. Before me, Alfonso Rael de Aguilar, secretary of government and war.

Said governor and captain general visits the pueblo of Santo Domingo.

On the twenty-eighth day of the present month of this year I, said governor and captain general, accompanied by the aforesaid father vice-custodian Fray Francisco de Vargas and by the said soldiers, proceeded to this pueblo of Santo Domingo in the same manner as referred to above. The natives were ready to receive me, with arches and all the rest, except for the chapel, which was to be located some distance from the mesa they had descended from, and therefore with the little time they have had, they have only been able to repair most of the houses of the said pueblo as well as to prepare the residence for the minister catechist. And having designated the location for the chapel, I passed to the center of the said plaza, where I found that they had erected a holy cross. And before it, on their knees, the said father and the said people, in proof of possession, sang three times the "Praise Be to the Blessed Sacrament," and through the said interpreter I gave them to understand the obligations that were required of them and that the said father Fray Miguel Trizio, who was left with them, was the one whom they should look to as their minister and whom they should assist in every way, and they answered that they would obey him in every way. And they asked that I accept their officials, whom they had already designated, which I did, and they presented the elected officials, to whom I gave the said rods and canes. And since I had no reason to continue on to the other pueblos, since the reverend father vice-custodian had no more ministers to provide other than reverend father Fray Antonio del Corral, who was to replace Father Carbonel, whom he had removed from the pueblo of San Felipe, since he was already acquainted with the said Indians of the pueblo of Cochití and its population was much larger. And thus I took leave of the said father and returned to this said villa with the said soldiers, sending my lieutenant with a squadron of ten soldiers to go on in the company of the said reverend father vice-custodian in his said visit to the other populated missions of the Keres and Jémez. In testimony whereof I signed with my said secretary of government and war. Don Diego de Vargas Zapata Luján Ponce de León. Before me, Alfonso Rael de Aguilar, secretary of government and war.

The governor of Cochití sends his war captains to receive the people I had taken as prisoners in accordance with the request that he had made of me, said governor and captain general, as recorded on the day of the entry there.

On the fourth day of the month of December, the year sixteen hundred ninety-four, the war captains of the pueblo of Cochití, sent by their governor, officials, and the other natives, arrived at this Villa of Santa Fe to request that I order the return to them of the people held as prisoners who were in this said villa, those I had captured in April on their said mesa by fire and sword, conquered and defeated. And since they were subdued and living in their said pueblo, having complied with their promise, by my order I granted freedom to their said people held as prisoners, issuing the order that it be fulfilled to the letter. In testimony of carrying out this measure I signed with my said secretary of government and war. Don Diego de Vargas Zapata Luján Ponce de León. Before me, Alfonso Rael de Aguilar, secretary of government and war.

Proclamation:

General Don Diego de Vargas Zapata Luján Ponce de León, governor and captain general of this kingdom and provinces of New Mexico, its new restorer, conqueror, and reconqueror and castellan of its armed forces and presidio in the name of His Majesty. Having fought the natives of the Keres nation by fire and sword, and having forced them to abandon their mesa, where they had settled, and having reduced them to their pueblo of Cochití as a result of the said triumph, I took a group of their women and children to join the population of this villa, where I had distributed them among the soldiers and some of the residents who participated in the said battle without any time limit but rather with the warning that it was my desire only to keep them as hostages and that for that reason they were given to their masters in trust until the said natives had been reduced to royal vassalage and to their said pueblo. And since this has been accomplished and they are living with and in the Catholic religion, which I saw when I visited them, and royal possession is again reclaimed for His Majesty and also for their minister catechist, they asked me to return and restore to them the said prisoners, which I had promised to do. Therefore, I decree through this proclamation and for this reason that the said people be returned to the said plaza for the purpose of turning them over to the war captains who came in the name of their governor to receive and take the said people to their said pueblo. And in order that this be duly carried out, my secretary of government and war shall obtain from the reverend father guardian of this said villa the list of parishioners who are natives so that the reverend father may identify the ones who should not be returned, separating those who belong under his charge. And this having been done, I order that this decree be proclaimed with his assistance and that of the military leaders and officers, accompanied by the sounding of military instruments. And in testimony of this said order I signed it in this Villa of Santa Fe on December 4, sixteen hundred ninety-four, along with my said secretary of government and war. Don Diego de Vargas Zapata Luján Ponce de León. By order of his lordship, Alfonso Rael de Aguilar, secretary of government and war.

The said governor and captain general goes down to the plaza of this said stronghold to turn over the said prisoners.

And immediately after the said proclamation was publicly issued, I, said governor and captain general, went down to the plaza of this stronghold to effectively assure the release of the said prisoners there and to prevent any of the residents of this villa from stealing a single person and to make clear to the said war captains that I was returning the people punctually in full compliance with my word. And thus, with none of the unaccounted for, and having spoken with them and embraced them, I took leave of them, assuring all of the said people that I would help them. And they left joyfully with their said captains, grateful for the favor I had extended to them by the said return of their people to freedom. In testimony of this action I signed with my said secretary of government and war. Don Diego de Vargas Zapata Luján Ponce de León. Before me, Alfonso Rael de Aguilar, secretary of government and war.

Representatives of the cabildo appear before me in the name of the residents, since on the occasion of the visits of Tewa and Tano natives, the captive people of the said nations residing in this villa are escaping, to the detriment of their owners.

On the sixth day of the present month of December of this year, the illustrious cabildo of the kingdom came to see me, the said governor and captain general, stating that by virtue of the general peace with the Tewa and Tano nations of this kingdom, on the occasion of their daily visits and contact with the Indian women of the said nations who remain captives in this villa since the uprising and our happy victory, some of the captives were escaping with them. And as a result of this representation, in the interest of the said residents and owners of the fugitives I ordered Captain Antonio Jorge and Sergeant Juan Ruiz to go to the pueblos of the said nations to order that their governors and captains appear before me in this villa within three days, telling them that I needed to see them. In testimony whereof I made it of record and signed with my said secretary of government and war. Don Diego de Vargas Zapata Luján Ponce de León. Before me, Alfonso Rael de Aguilar, secretary of government and war.

The said governors come down to this Villa of Santa Fe, and the said governor and captain general gives them the following orders.

On the tenth of the present month of December of this year, the governors and war captains of the pueblos of the Tewas and Tanos arrived at the Villa of Santa Fe, and before me, said governor and captain general, and in the presence of the military leaders and some of the members of the said illustrious cabildo and with the assistance of my secretary of government and war, interpreted by the said Sergeant Juan Ruiz, I told them that which was referred to and requested concerning the flight and carrying off of their said people to their said pueblos in the course of their coming and going to and from this villa. I told them that these people held captive were not and had not ever been hostages taken from their said pueblo, for if they were they would have been returned, as I had done in the case of the Jémez and Keres of Cochití, and that they were legitimately slaves and belonged to this villa, living in this fortress and walled town, having been defeated and captured at the time of their uprising as a result of their rebelliousness and apostasy. And they left to carry out said order, satisfied that what I ordered of them was just and that they should obey submissively. In witness whereof I signed with my said secretary of government and war. Don Diego de Vargas Zapata Luján Ponce de León. Before me, Alfonso Rael de Aguilar, secretary of government and war.

The said governors arrive bringing forty-five prisoners who were the fugitives, and said governor and captain general descends to the plaza and returns them, freeing them in reward for their obedience.

On the twenty-first day of the month of December of this year, the said governors and captains of the said Tewa and Tano pueblos, as well as those of Picurís, arrived at this Villa of Santa Fe in fulfilment of the above order and command made by me, said governor and captain general, bringing the forty-five captives who had fled. And having received them in a most friendly manner, I told them that I wanted them to understand well the kindness of my heart, for through my generosity I was freeing and returning the said people, and that I wanted them to know that I kept my word and that in the planting season I would settle them in the abandoned pueblo of La Cieneguilla, a distance of five leagues from this villa. And I descended to the said plaza, where, through the interpreter, after parleying with them I told them how pleased I was with them and how well I looked upon them as submissive vassals of His Majesty. And showing their pleasure, they thanked me. And embracing all of them and shaking hands with them, I opened to them the said door of freedom so that they could return to their friends and relatives. The said captains left very grateful and happy as a result of my said action. The said governors tarried in festive spirit, and I regaled them and ordered that cloth capes be made for them, and I gave them hats and other gifts. And in witness of the above I signed with my said secretary of government and war. Don Diego de Vargas Zapata Luján Ponce de León. Before me, Alfonso Rael de Aguilar, secretary of government and war.

12. *CARTA PATENTE* OF FRAY FRANCISCO DE VARGAS TO EACH OF THE MISSIONARIES, SANTA FE, DECEMBER 20, 1694[1]

✠

Jesus, Mary, and Joseph

I advise Your Reverence that I have a mandate from our reverend superior prelates in which they order me to inform them of the state in which this holy custody finds itself, and to carry this out I am obliged to turn to Your Reverence, to whom I request that you reply to the following points, answering each one clearly and separately.

1. First, that Your Reverence state what motivated you to go to your mission, and if any prelate forced you to do so.

2. Item, that Your Reverence describe the present conduct of the Indians that you administer, if they attend the instruction in Christian doctrine and follow the other requirements for leading a virtuous life, both in the case of children and adults, and if they assist you with punctuality and obedience at all times.

3. Item, that Your Reverence indicate the success that you have had in winning souls, in having baptized any children, and of these, that you indicate

1. BNM, leg. 3, doc. 6.

how many have died, and also the adults who have received the holy sacraments and have died, and if they seek their minister to administer the holy sacraments when they are seriously ill.

4. Item, if the Indians have built a decent church for the celebration of mass and cells for the residence of the religious.

5. Item, that you indicate whether the said Indians, from the food that they have, in their own way and from their limited amount give help to the minister to help provide his sustenance.

6. Item, that you indicate whether the said Indians, of their own free will, have come to their minister to request the holy sacrament of matrimony, leaving the women with whom they had illicit relations in their apostasy, and those who later wished to place themselves in a state of grace by receiving the holy sacrament of matrimony with only slight suggestion from their minister.

7. Item, that you state whether you expect to have success in the future in winning the souls of the parishioners that you have under your care, administering to them the holy sacraments.

8. Item, that you indicate the bad qualities that you have found in the said Indians, and if you have found them practicing idolatry, and after correcting them lovingly, they remain obstinate.

9. Item, that you state and set forth the dangers that may be found in the future and the hardships and rigors of winter and the other inconveniences you expect to undergo.

10. Item, list all the persons you have as parishioners, both adults and children, so that the number may be known.

All of what is contained in these points I order Your Reverence to respond to, under obedience and in virtue of the Holy Spirit, under oath as a priest and minister of God and without communicating or discussing the said points with any other person but only with your own conscience, signing in your own name and sending me the said statement with a trusted person so that I may be assured in my conscience that the reply is from Your Reverence's conscience, and as a prelate (although unworthy) I may be able to determine what is most fitting in the service of God our Lord. May His Divine Majesty watch over Your Reverence in His holy grace. Villa of Santa Fe, December 20, 1694. I remain, reverend father, your brother who esteems and loves you in the Lord and kisses Your Reverence's hand.

Fray Francisco de Vargas
Custodian

13. LETTER OF FRAY JOSÉ DIEZ, TESUQUE, DECEMBER 22, 1694[1]

OUR reverend father custodian Fray Francisco de Vargas:

In obedience to the just order of our reverend father with regard to my stating the conditions at this mission of San Diego de Tesuque, where I now find myself, I state:

On the first point as to why I asked Your Paternal Reverence to allow me to come to administer this pueblo, it was because I was disconsolate in the villa, both because of habitual attacks of illness, which increased as a result of the humidity of the said villa, and because I was living withdrawn from outside activities, whereas I was more adapted to my institute. For these reasons I earnestly appealed to Your Paternal Reverence, calling attention only to my illnesses, and you granted my request, consoling me with great feeling of concern, as I recognized, and you told me that you had not intended to send me, for which I was grateful and continue to be grateful.

On the second point I state that the Indians attend the instruction in Christian doctrine, and particularly the masses, even though I say them almost every day, for I do not excuse them from attending during this Christmas season, and it is very gratifying to see them coming in the morning through the snow, almost naked. Not all of them always attend, for they say that they are going to the villa to look for food, others to the mountains for wood and to hunt, because of the extreme hunger and poverty that they suffer. They obey me submissively.

On the third point I state that I have baptized twenty-eight small boys and girls, of which two have died, and one girl seven years of age, for whom they called me because she was sick, perhaps unnecessarily, as they considered that she was very young. I have been called to confess several sick persons, which has been very consoling to me. In the villa I saved the souls of seven small children, whom I believe were the ones I buried near the grave of my father companion who served the Tanos. The adults of said villa that I assisted with the sacraments were many, as the records will show. I state this because I have been in this pueblo only a little over one month.

On the fourth point I state that since the Indians made peace in the month of September, and since the winter here has been so severe, it is not possible to work in the fields or build houses at this time. They arranged several separate dwellings for a chapel, tearing down the walls to form the chapel and sacristy, and they plan to build a church in the spring. For the rectory they arranged another capacious house next to that of the governor, with two floors, near which I blessed a cemetery, where the church and rectory are to be built.

1. BNM, leg. 3, doc. 6.

On the fifth point I state that since this pueblo had been the closest to the villa, it was the one most heavily under attack during the war, and the Indians remained without food, and for their survival it was necessary for them to support themselves with wild seeds from the countryside and by making earthenware bowls and pots to sell in the villa in exchange for a little corn and meat; therefore, they cannot support me for the present, although I know that they would like to do so, for when they go to the mountains to hunt they bring me what they can. And one Indian who had gone to Cochití to trade for corn for himself, returning on foot through the snow, gave me some in a gourd [*jicara*] from the little that he brought back on his beast of burden, which I thanked him for, admiring his show of affection. Besides, I am thankful indeed to God, for with the little I obtained in the villa, including vegetables, I am able to manage. Though I am told that some have sheep, probably very few in number, in the *visita*, if I should ask them for any I do not doubt that they would be forthcoming. Also, the governor usually brings me some of the chili that he buys, and I am grateful to him.

On the sixth point I state that the Indian who is said to be the governor of all the Tewas and Tanos, when I used to come here from the villa to say mass, asked me, of his own free will, to perform his marriage, which I did, and I am urging others to do so and will perform some marriages on Christmas day. It is true that I have advised them to do so, saying that if they did not I would separate them.

On the seventh point I state that with God's help I hope that they will be good in the future. I can judge them only from what I see, which appears good. Although the youth who assists me said that the said governor had told him that the Indians of Acoma, Zuñi, and Moqui were crazy, saying that they wanted to fight the Spaniards, but that his people did not want to be crazy, he then asked the boy whether we had a large quantity of powder, balls, and harquebuses. I doubt that he had any designs.

On the eighth point I state that I have not observed bad qualities in them, nor have I caught them practicing idolatry; rather, it is a pleasure to hear the children singing *alabados* throughout the pueblo, and the governor instructs his children in Christian doctrine in the evenings, for I have heard him do so from my house. It is true that in Cuyamungué they had a circle of stones which I judge to be idolatry on their part. I advised them to remove them, explaining the mysteries of our holy faith and that there was only one divine God. And on going to visit them one day, I found that the said stones were there as before. I reprehended them in the church and told them that some backs would burn from lashes if they did not remove them. I now have been told by the fiscal that they removed them, and I will go to see after the heavy snows subside. I also found in the district of this pueblo of Tesuque, near a cross, other stones and what I perceived to be ground corn scattered among them. I threw them away without leaving a single one, which they do not appear to have noticed. It may be that [the stones] were there from the earlier period.

On the ninth point I state that in the future they can be feared if they are oppressed and if there are bad Christians who induce them to rise in rebellion. I say this because I am told that a Spaniard has told them that they will be free for ten years and then they will be killed and their children will be taken away. I state this to fulfill my obligation to obedience. In addition, I refer to my reply on point seven. The sufferings of winter are severe because of the extreme cold, but there is plenty of wood to withstand it, and the Indians bring it to me in abundance, thanks to the Divine Lord.

On the tenth point I state that in this pueblo of both adults and small children there are one hundred eighty-three, with eight who I am told are sick in San Cristóbal and who will return when they recover. I have not counted those in the *visita* because the fiscal has told me that there are only eight Indians there and that the others are in different pueblos and that having written to the *alcalde mayor* of the jurisdiction to bring them, he replied that they were suspicious and that he did not dare to do so; from others I have learned that they do not wish to come, saying that they have no place there to plant; and although I would like to enumerate them, I am unable to do so unless they are at home. However, some of them come to mass despite the winter snow, and the father minister of San Ildefonso has told me that others attend mass there.

All of the above I state to be the truth, and I swear to it *in verbo sacerdotis*. In this pueblo of San Diego de Tesuque on the twenty-second of December, the year sixteen hundred ninety-four.

Fray José Diez

14. LETTER OF FRAY ANTONIO CARBONEL, COCHITÍ, DECEMBER 26, 1694[1]

OUR reverend father Fray Francisco de Vargas, former custodian and present custodian of the Holy Custody of Saint Paul of New Mexico and ecclesiastical judge. In obedience to the mandates of Your Paternal Reverence, I state:

1. On the first point, that the motive for going to the mission was to see if I could achieve the goal for which I came, and I was not forced to do so by any prelate.

1. BNM, leg. 3, doc. 6.

2. On the second point I state that some of them attend the instructions in Christian doctrine and some are obedient at this time and give some assistance to the minister.

3. On the third point I state that I have baptized only two small children and have confessed one sick person, for which purpose I was called.

4. On the fourth point I state that there is a decent chapel, under the circumstances, to celebrate the holy sacrifice of the mass, and a house, with a kitchen and office, for the residence of the religious.

5. On the fifth point I state that the Indians help the religious to a moderate degree with what they have, as the weather permits, for his sustenance.

6. On the sixth point I state that in the one month that I have been in the said *doctrina,* I have not performed any marriages, because no one has requested the said holy sacrament of matrimony.

7. On the seventh point I state that some success in the winning of souls may be expected among the said Indians if they do not again rise in rebellion.

8. On the eighth point I state that I have observed neither good nor bad qualities in the said Indians because I am not sufficiently familiar with them.

9. On the ninth point I state that the winter is extremely severe, and I cannot measure the danger that can be feared.

10. On the tenth point I state that the persons that I have as parishioners total, more or less, five hundred.

In witness of the above, I swear, *in verbo sacerdotis,* that this and this alone is what I perceive to be the truth. Signed by me in this *doctrina* of San Buenaventura de Cochití on the twenty-sixth of December of 1694. Our father custodian, I am the humble servant of Your Reverence.

Fray Antonio Carbonel

15. LETTER OF FRAY GERÓNIMO PRIETO, SAN JUAN, DECEMBER 26, 1694 [1]

☩

STATEMENT of what has been accomplished in this pueblo of San Juan, as Your Paternal Reverence orders me to state individually and candidly.

1. On the first point I state and declare that my coming to the mission of the aforesaid pueblo of San Juan was free and spontaneous, without the intervention or urging or orders of the prelate; rather, I offered to come, without heed to risks nor any other things that might present themselves. The cause has been the desire for the betterment of so many souls and to remove them from the influences of the devil to see if (although facing such a despicable

1. BNM, leg. 3, doc. 6.

instrument) His Supreme Majesty will give them the light that they lacked. This, and my having waited so long, has been the motivation that I had.

2. On the second point I state and declare that not all attend the instructions in Christian doctrine punctually, because there are many (the interpreter tells me) who have not yet entered the church, especially among the old men and women. The others attend, although not regularly, as some do.

3. On the third point I state and declare that by administering the holy sacraments the winning of some souls can be expected, for there are some who appear to be good, and as for the others, since the word of God is so powerful, we cannot exclude them, for we have many examples which encourage us in our effort, although at present they do not appear to be as favorably disposed as we would desire.

4. On the fourth point I state and declare that in the future another uprising by them can and should be feared, as there is reason to believe so. That it has not taken place voluntarily and generally is because many were lost in the war, and they did not act since they did not have the means to fight, as they were suffering from hunger. And whereas they themselves as well as the Tewas accepted peace, shortly thereafter there was a meeting in Picurís with many dances, whether as a prelude to war or not, no one knows. In the opinion of the Spaniards raised in this land, they believe that the latter was not for a good purpose.

The severity of the winter may be readily observed, since we experienced snowfall back in May of the year 'ninety-four, as I well remember.

5. On the fifth point I state and declare that some six children have been baptized, of which one small girl died. Of the adults, one has died, and they called me to confess him, although he was already in his final moments of life; others, although sick, have not called for me, although it is true that they were not suffering from serious illnesses.

6. On the sixth point I state that to the extent they have been able to do so, in view of the weather, they have built a chapel and house, and the chapel is as decent as possible under the circumstances.

7. On the seventh point I state and declare that with regard to provisions they have assisted me to the best of their ability, which has consisted of some five tortillas each day, and others have given me about two dozen, and nothing else, although they could have given me fish which they had to sell. As for corn, they have sufficient, but it is evident that they do not wish to give me any, for when I had meat they wanted to buy some from me in exchange for it, and although I gave them the meat I could spare, I told them that I would not buy anything, that I gave it to them for the love of God, and that they knew very well that it was their obligation to help me with what they had, since I was serving them by administering the holy sacraments. But neither for this

nor for any other reason have they been willing to provide some food, saying that they do not have it to give.

8. On the eighth point I state and declare that during the time that I have served as minister to the said natives, I have seen nothing (that may relate to idolatry) other than some stones of many colors that they pile together, with a large one in the middle, where they place offerings for what they wish to request, either ground corn or *almagre* or feathers or green grass. And when I knocked them down, the interpreter came to tell me that the people said that I should not have done so, that it was their custom, which they had always observed, and that the kingdom had revolted because this had been taken away from them, and that if it were to be taken away from them they would again rise in rebellion. To this I exhorted them that it was a deception of the devil, that the stones could give them nothing, that only God was the all powerful to whom they should appeal for help, and other things which I told them they should believe. He [the interpreter] answered me, do not tire in your work, father, for they should live thusly, for as you instruct them in Christian doctrine, the fathers will eventually teach them this. The following day the people gathered for instruction in Christian doctrine, and I repeated what I had said, condemning them for the evil practice with both kindness and threats, [but] to this day I have not been able to get them to remove them [the stones]. I have torn them down various times, but each time they have again set them up. I have heard of many other errors that persist among them [the people], but I have not seen them firsthand, and for that reason I make no mention of them here, but although I do not know about them, they can be presumed from such barbarous people.

9. Item, I state and declare that of the said natives, up to this day only one, who came to me today, has come to request the holy sacrament of matrimony, after I exhorted them daily that they should marry and that those who were married should leave the women with whom they were living and should join those with whom they had properly lived before (because there was a proclamation when they rose in rebellion that they leave the women with whom they were married and take others), but until this day it has not been possible to remedy this situation.

10. On the tenth point I state that the population of this pueblo, including women, men, young persons, and children, totals one hundred seventy-two. They cannot be listed by name because they are not together at any one time, as they are coming and going each day, and also because most of them are people who were baptized in the year '92, and most of them do not know the names given them and have not been annointed with the holy oil, since they are already adults and do not yet understand the Christian doctrine.

All of that which is contained in this letter, as it has been written, I state and declare to be the truth as to what I have seen, what I know, and what I have heard. And as proof of the truth of all that I have stated, I swear to it *in verbo sacerdotis* (although I am most unworthy), and as minister of this pueblo of San Juan, in which capacity I now serve. I sign this with my signature, on December 26, this present year of 'ninety-four.

> Fray Gerónimo Prieto,
> Minister

16. LETTER OF FRAY FRANCISCO CORBERA, SAN ILDEFONSO, DECEMBER 27, 1694[1]

☩

J. M. J.

Our very reverend father custodian:

I am in receipt of Your Paternity's message in which you order me to reply to various points in holy obedience and in virtue of the Holy Spirit, and, obeying gladly, I answer below, point by point, that which Your Paternity orders of me.

First, Your Paternity orders me to declare what prompted me to go to the mission of San Ildefonso and if I was forced by my prelate to go there. I reply, our father, that having come to this holy custody in the year '91, sent in holy obedience to convert the souls of these barbarians to the True Knowledge, and since there was no opportunity to enter this kingdom immediately, Your Reverence, being the custodian at that time, directed me to seek out the barbarous Indians of the Apache nation, who live a wandering existence, denied the knowledge of our holy law, and I freely and spontaneously offered to accompany Your Paternity, begging that you take me with you to be successful in my vocation, as may be found over my signature at the end of the patent which, for this purpose, Your Paternity issued at El Paso del Río del Norte, inviting the religious to participate in such a holy work, Your Paternity offering to be the first to go so that by your example we would all be inspired. When we were about to leave on this most holy journey, the governor and captain general, who holds that position at present, asked Your Paternity in the name of His Majesty, may God protect him, to delay the journey, believing that very serious dangers might result from it, and so you postponed it.

The following year, the father procurator Fray Joaquín de Hinojosa being president *in capite,* the governor and captain general embarked upon the conquest of this kingdom, and since three religious were to accompany him as chaplains of the army, I asked the prelate that for the love of God I be one of

1. BNM, leg. 3, doc. 6.

those assigned so that I might achieve in a small way the purpose of my vocation. I was given this consolation, being named as president of the religious who came at that time, and I traveled to all parts of this kingdom, including the provinces of Zuñi and Moqui, and baptized very many children and explained the mysteries of our holy faith in various sermons which I gave everywhere and made this journey through uninhabited regions without sleeping under a roof for seven months, with the hardships that can be considered, in the severe cold of winter and over difficult roads. All of this I considered as well employed, having reaped the fruit of having administered these baptisms, for of those baptized most of them died the following year, which was that of '93.

We entered this kingdom a second time, accompanying the reverend father Fray Salvador de San Antonio, and since the Indians rebelled, having been given false information, or for other reasons which only God knows and are not of concern here, I remained at the Villa of Santa Fe for almost a full year, undergoing very great hardships, which of course we all undergo as religious. And all of this I considered as well spent just to reap the fruit of seeing them subdued, as they were, all of these nations having made peace, so it was thought, my desire always having been so great to win these barbarians to true understanding and in seeing them now in their pueblos, peaceful and quiet, and I was assigned to this mission of San Ildefonso. The prelate did not compel me to come here; rather, all of the religious of this custody freely and spontaneously decided to draw up a petition signed by all requesting the father procurator Fray Juan Muñoz de Castro, commissary of the holy office, our father *in capite* at that time, to permit us to go to the missions. And to accomplish our wishes, having gathered us together he told us to present the difficulties that could result, and unanimously and in agreement we all said that there were none and that when they might occur we would willingly expose ourselves to them, even to the point of losing our lives if it were necessary, which we would thereby offer to reap the desired fruit. And we asked and begged the said father president, for greater merit, that he order us in holy obedience, which he did, leaving us all very consoled in the Lord. So that in answering briefly this first point, I state that I was prompted to come to this mission so that the souls of these poor people could not be lost, and that I was not forced by the prelate.

Item, Your Paternity orders me to inform you on the state in which the Indians that I administer find themselves, and if they attend the instruction in Christian doctrine and other spiritual activities, both children and adults, and if they attend punctually and obediently with regard to prayer and instruction. I reply, our father, that all the Indians, both adults and children, in this pueblo of San Ildefonso, know the Hail Mary, the Our Father, the Creed, the Salve, the commandments of God's law and those of the church, the sacraments, confession, and the act of faith. This is what I have been able to teach them in the three months that I have been here, and for proof of this Your Paternity may send here whomever you wish to examine them, and if three of them are found who do not know what I have said they know, I will state that that which is reported is false. They attend the catechism class with such punctuality that they are not content in coming only in the morning, but also come in the evening, with the result that there are catechism classes twice a day, and this is done with so much earnestness that when I told them that Your Paternity ordered (as you ordered in your patent) that they need not attend catechism classes on days of heavy snow and cold, because of their nakedness and poverty, no matter how the weather may be they are not absent, with the result that up to now they have not missed a day of catechism class. And the children attend the morning prayer services, and at twelve noon they recite the Hail Mary, and they sing the *alabado* at the door of the church, as Your Paternity saw the day you came to visit this pueblo. I have two fiscals, who are very solicitous in this particular, as is also the governor of the pueblo, who also helps them, so much so that in ordering the children to attend prayer services he told them that if they failed to do so he would drive them to mass with sticks. None are absent, and there I explain to them, through an interpreter, the mysteries of our holy faith and the prayers in accordance with the orders of the Holy Councils, which they understand very well, as they appear to indicate by the questions they ask me.

Item, Your Paternity orders that I indicate the success that I have had in winning souls, in having baptized some children, and that I report how many of them have died; and also how many adults have received the holy sacraments and then have died; and if when they are suffering from sickness they send for me to administer the holy sacraments. I reply that the success which I have had in the divine service has been much. In this pueblo of San Ildefonso I have baptized eight children, and I am catechizing two adults for baptism. In the pueblo of Jacona I have baptized two children. Three children have died after receiving the water of holy baptism. Two adults have died after receiving the holy sacraments of penance and extreme unction. Although it is true that in this pueblo many have fallen ill with great pains in the side, and all the victims call me immediately when they fall ill, showing signs and demonstrations of contrition, it has been deigned by God our Lord that with some household medicines which with charity I have been able to apply to them, since they had no other remedy, many have recovered, thanks be to God's will. Of those baptized and those who have died I give as good witness the record books of the mission; of those who have made [deathbed] confessions, for the entire pueblo they exceed thirty.

Item, Your Paternity requests me to state whether the Indians of this pueblo have built a decent chapel for the celebration of the holy sacrifice of the mass and if they have built me a cell to live in so that I can live decently, and if they have provided the other needs for the mission. In all of this Your Paternity is a very good witness. What I can say is that a month after winter had set in in all its severity, they finished building the present church, which is quite spacious, large enough to accommodate three hundred persons, with an altar decently decorated, as Your Paternity saw it, with pictures in their glass enclosures, and very beautiful paintings, which I have dedicated to my patroness Our Lady of Guadalupe, whose image is on the altar. And the reason why I do not have a larger church and house are not the fault of the Indians but mine, for considering the rigorous weather I accepted what I considered adequate in the service of the church. I have four sacristans, one of whom already has learned to serve mass, and the other two are learning. I have six singers who perform very well at mass. On the feast day for the dead they sang mass and made the responses very well, and on this day they gave me as an offering some twelve large sacks [*costales*] of corn, and four others of piñon nuts, fish, and vegetables, which lasted me all through Advent. They also sang at the Christmas masses and the matins on Christmas eve very well, celebrating Christmas with dances, and on the vigil of Christmas many assisted me.

Item, Your Paternity requests me to state if the Indians, with the little food that they have, help me by providing assistance for my sustenance. I reply that as Your Paternity knows, with the war they were unable to plant, and the little they planted they lost, and besides that their pueblo was sacked, so they remained without a grain of corn, and notwithstanding this they have supported me more than I deserve. At noon and in the evening they bring me tortillas, for which I am indebted to them, and they go out to hunt just to bring quail and rabbits for me to eat, and they bring me buffalo meat, and up to now I have not asked them for a single grain of corn. When one of them goes to another pueblo to seek food, he brings me either chili or vegetables or whatever he can. It is true that they are also motivated by my customary friendly treatment, through which I try to please them, for as Your Paternity knows, as a very experienced missionary, which you have been for so many years with the Mansos, such a barbarous people (whom you have known how to convert to organized society and fixed settlement), they are very much influenced by the friendly treatment and love which they see in their ministers, and more so in his personal abnegation.

Item, Your Paternity requests that I state whether of their own volition the Indians have come to ask me for the holy sacrament of matrimony, leaving the women with whom they had been living illicitly during their apostasy, and whether others later have sought to place themselves in the state of grace by receiving the holy sacrament of matrimony with slight urging from me. I reply that after I entered this pueblo two Indians came to me, the governor and the interpreter, to ask that they be joined with their own wives, stating that they were living with women out of wedlock. I acted immediately to carry this out, and it is to be noted that if they had not stated their situation of their own volition it would not have been possible, morally speaking, for me to know. Until the present time I have only performed one marriage. I have some to perform shortly, which have been asked of me.

Item, Your Paternity requests that I state if in the future success is expected in the winning of souls among the parishioners that I have under my charge, to whom I am administering the holy sacraments. I reply that the success that I expect, with Divine Grace, is much. And if it would be no greater than that already attained, I would continue for a thousand years, if I lived to attain that age, administering to these poor souls. Apart from that, from what I see I know that success in the future will be great. And I believe this from seeing them receptive to the things pertaining to God, fond of prayer, and listening attentively to the Divine Word. And if their intention should be deceitful, *de ocultis indicate ecletia,* and everything goes wrong, it will only be a benefit to us, as they would take our lives, which I consider difficult from what I see, and what greater gain could we achieve than to lose our lives for the salvation of souls?

Item, Your Paternity requests that I indicate the bad qualities I have found in the said Indians, and if in dissuading them in a loving manner from their idolatry, yet they have stubbornly continued to worship their false gods. I answer, our father, that after fifteen years of apostasy from the faith, naturally they must have their false rites deeply rooted in their hearts, and to remove these I have proceeded with great caution, as Your Paternity has ordered in your patent, and in this manner I have attained the goal that I desired. As Your Paternity knows, in all the plazas of the pueblos there are stones where they offer ground corn and feathers, mixing this with many superstitions to request water and other things. One day after mass I condemned them severely for their idolatry and superstitions, and among other things I told them (adapting my words to their crudely developed minds) that if the water they asked for was in the clouds and the stones were in the ground, how could the stones, from below, send forth water which came from above—reasoning which they so fully agreed with that they immediately went to the pile of rocks and in its place they set up a Holy Cross. As Your Paternity already knows, this pueblo was famous as a center of witchcraft, but today they have mended their ways so much that an old man who lived here was thrown out of the pueblo because they said he was a witch [*hechizero*], and he now lives in that villa.

Item, Your Paternity requests that I state and set forth the dangers that may be feared in the future and the hardships and rigors of winter that we are experiencing and other inconveniences presented by the land. The dangers that can be feared, looking at it plainly, are many, because it can be feared that since they have revolted twice, they might revolt a third time, killing the religious and profaning the divine religion, with all that has been accomplished being lost. But if we look only at these problems, nothing will be accomplished. Your Paternity knows well that the celestial shepherd, Christ, notwithstanding that His sheep Adam wished to lose his soul through his sin, left in the desert of heaven ninety-nine choirs of angels to look for it, although he knew that ungrateful mankind would take his life. And going down the scale, Your Reverence knows of the numerous glorious martyrs of our sacred religion in Morocco from the time of our glorious father Saint Francis, and nevertheless our religious continued to go there. And even without such a supreme goal, when a merchant embarks on an enterprise with his riches he must consider the dangers of the changeable elements and cannot achieve his goal of gaining profit without facing them. And thus, as I have verified, the reason why they rose in rebellion this second time was because they were told that we would kill all of them, and as they saw the stoning of all those in the villa, among some Indians, theirs and mine, it is no wonder that they should be afraid. And it appears that they have quieted down and have overcome this fear, with the friendly treatment by the governor and captain general, and since in this second uprising they achieved nothing, for without a loss on our part many of theirs have died and many horses have been taken from them, along with all of their food supplies, as a result they are paying for their sins with the hunger that they are suffering this year, as they themselves admit. Aside from this, if they rise in rebellion where will they go? Not to join the Utes or the Apaches, nations that surround them, for they are their enemies, and eight who joined them for protection were killed by them, and the Apaches, as Your Paternity knows, have not accepted those seeking refuge among them for some time, for they lack food to eat and they sustain themselves by hunting, while these Indians are accustomed to wearing clothing and spending the winter beside the warmth of their ovens, which they could not have living among the Apaches; nor by going to the mesas, because they cannot survive there since they cannot plant crops, and if they did climb to the mesas, it would be with the hope that the Spaniards would leave, and then they would descend, but now they have lost this hope, as they have experienced that the Spaniards defeat and kill them on the mesas. Thus, what basis can there be for presuming that they may again rise in rebellion?

The rigors of winter Your Paternity sees before you, and I doubt that in the lands of Flanders it is as bad, to the point that all of the religious are without clothing whatever, first, because of the lateness of the arrival of the wagons, and, second, because the shipments are so small that they do not meet the needs for a year and they are expected to last for three. None have chocolate to drink, and we have not eaten bread since we left El Paso. And if Your Paternity, with your great charity in providing our needs, had not brought us a small parcel of biscuits and some sheep from El Paso, which enabled each of us to have eight sheep and two goats, we would have perished. Therefore, if His Excellency does not send us help, giving us livestock to enable us to sustain ourselves, we ministers will perish. And if the families are aided with food supplies, clothing, cattle, and all the rest, there should be ample reason for the ministers to express our needs to whomsoever can come to their assistance, for it is in full accord with our holy rule, and we have no other recourse for our survival. Nor is it amiss to say that when we are sent supplies, this is for wax, wine, and oil to say mass, a habit every three years, and a small amount of chocolate, none of which we can eat to sustain ourselves with. And since it is my understanding that all of this has been presented by the governor and captain general of this kingdom to the Royal Junta, there should be reason for presenting this also on our part.

The persons that I have registered in this pueblo of San Ildefonso are:
Men, forty-five
Women, forty-nine
Boys, forty-seven
Girls, forty-seven
In all, one hundred and eighty-eight persons. In my *visita* of Jacona I have:
Men, twelve
Women, thirteen
Boys, eight
Girls, seven
In all, forty persons.

Thus I have obeyed Your Paternity. But I wish to make clear that all that which I have stated refers only to this pueblo, as the situation in the others may not be the same, for I know from some of the others quite the contrary, and I, too, am experiencing this, for what I have stated is what is occurring in this pueblo. And in my *visita* Jacona the situation is the contrary, for there I have not yet been able, with the efforts that I have made, to see them all together at mass; at most only four attend. When I wished to go to their pueblo to teach them to pray, they said that they had no food to give me; when I said that I would take my own, they said that they did not have a place for me to stay; when I said that I would remain in the fields, they said that the people did not stay in the pueblo because they had no food to eat and went to other pueblos to look for it. But despite all of this, I hope in God our Lord, and in His blessed mother Our Lady, the Virgin Mary, that in time they will be reduced. This is what I feel concerning the points that Your Paternity has requested me to reply to, and for greater force I swear *in verbo sacerdotis* that all that which I have

stated is the exact truth. And in testimony whereof, I signed with my hand on
the twenty-seventh of December, the year sixteen hundred ninety-four.

Fray Francisco Corbera

17. LETTER OF FRAY MIGUEL DE TRIZIO, SANTO DOMINGO, DECEMBER 27, 1694[1]

✝

OUR very reverend father custodian:

With regard to that which Your Reverence orders me in your letter, that I
state certain points for the information of our reverend father superior prelate,
and obeying as is due such a superior mandate:

I state on the first point (our father) that the purpose and motive I had to
come to this holy Custody of New Mexico was to better serve God our Lord,
dedicating myself to teaching the Christian doctrine to the Indians of this land
to see if I could reduce some unbelievers, or apostates of our law, to the body of
our holy mother church. And I had this same end and motive to come to this
pueblo of Santo Domingo without being forced to do so in any way by any
superior prelate. On the contrary, I was disposed and ready to go obediently to
whichever pueblo I would be sent.

On the second point I state that up until now I have always experienced
prompt obedience by these Indians in whatever I have ordered them to do,
especially in coming to church, to catechism, and to mass, only those who are
actually busy at work failing to do so.

On the third point I state that since the day I entered this pueblo, twenty
persons have been baptized, all small children, none of whom have died. Of
the adults I have no case to report, since there has been no sick person to attend, although there was a Tiwa Indian who lived with those of this pueblo
who got sick, and they asked me to see him, and since he was not able to confess, he did not do so, but the next day they notified me that he was dying and
[asked] that I give him extreme unction, which I did. I have nothing more to
say on this point.

On the fourth point I reply that the natives of this pueblo have built a
chapel, although not very large, and accommodated so that mass may be said
under decent conditions; the same may be said of their minister's cell. However, all are ready to build a suitable and appropriate church when the weather
improves.

1. BNM, leg. 3, doc. 6.

With regard to the fifth point, I state that up until now they have come to my aid with sufficient corn for my sustenance.

On the sixth point I state that neither voluntarily nor after my having spoken to them many times in the church have any of them come to me to request the holy sacrament of matrimony and thereby leave their evil condition.

On the seventh point I state that as I proceed, and as I observe them, many souls will be won, both adults and small children.

On the eighth point I reply that until now I have not observed any bad traits in any of these Indians, nor have I seen nor heard said that any of them have bad habits, especially with respect to idolatry.

On the ninth point I state that as for future dangers I cannot recognize any, and since they are now peaceful, I judge that they will always remain so. Of the sufferings and rigors of winter I have nothing to say, because they do not exist.

On the last point I state that the persons who live in this pueblo usually number at some times twenty, at other times more, at other times less, because all of the others live on the mesa of San Juan; and the day when most of them were gathered here, they numbered eighty-six. Therefore, the number of persons who are inhabitants of this pueblo cannot be estimated with certainty until they come down from the mesa.

This, our father, is what I perceive in good faith concerning the points that Your Paternal Reverence orders me to report on, and thus I swear to it under oath, *in verbo sacerdotis,* as a priest and minister of God, so that Your Paternal Reverence may be assured in conscience of the truth. May God protect Your Paternal Reverence felicitous years. From this your pueblo of Santo Domingo, December 27, 1694.

Your most humble son, who kisses the hand of Your Paternal Reverence.

Fray Miguel de Trizio

18. LETTER OF FRAY JUAN ALPUENTE, ZIA AND SANTA ANA, DECEMBER 28, 1694[1]

VERY reverend father custodian and ecclesiastical judge, Fray Francisco de Vargas:

With regard to the order from Your Very Reverence contained in your letter in which you request me to reply to, and certify as my conscience dictates, the following points, I state, reverend father, without departing (to my knowledge) one iota from the truth, as follows:

1. BNM, leg. 3, doc. 6.

1. What were my motives for coming to the pueblos of Zia and Santa Ana, and if a prelate forced me to come.

I, Fray Juan Alpuente, declare and certify that my only motive was to see if by being present here I might have good fortune and success by baptizing the small children and through the mercy of God our Lord lead some adult to confess his sins, at least when such a person is approaching the moment of death; also because I had learned about the Villa of Santa Fe, and since I am by nature irascible, I know in my conscience that I only live when I live alone. Since I had no other motives, it is clear that I came freely and without being forced to do so by any prelate.

2. That I describe the present status of the Indians, if both children and adults attend the instructions in Christian doctrine, and if they obey me.

I state and certify on this point that at present, and from my observation, the said Indians are well behaved, and both children and adults attend the catechism classes except that in the case of the adults it is sometimes necessary to scold them for their tardiness. With regard to their due obedience, I state that to get them to obey as they should it is sometimes necessary to show anger, but in a manner that attracts them, not by yelling, which causes them to withdraw.

3. That I state the success that I have had in baptizing some children and adults and that I indicate those who have died; and if, when they are sick, they immediately seek the minister to administer the blessed sacraments to them.

I state and certify that in the two pueblos of Zia and Santa Ana I have baptized 32 infants, all less than a year old, and of these five have died. As for adults, I have not baptized any, and none have died. As regards their seeking assistance when they are sick, I state that it is necessary for the minister to send the fiscal daily to find out if anyone is sick, for they are by nature negligent. They are that way even when they are about to die, and there seems to be no way to get them to prepare for death.

4. That I state whether the said Indians have built a decent chapel for the celebration of the divine services, and if they have built cells for the minister so that he can live decently as a religious.

I state and certify that in the pueblo of Zia the Indians have build a decent chapel for the present, and also habitation for the minister. In Santa Ana the chapel is not satisfactory, although the residence for the minister is adequate. It should be pointed out, however, that the poor people have worked hard to construct the church, with very little help from the weather, which has limited what they have been able to do.

5. That if the Indians, with the little food that they have, assist me so that I can sustain myself.

I state and verify that the poor people assist me with the food that they have, which is at least something, since they have very little, and this suits me very well. I know that if they had more they would give it to me, for up to now the poor people have not denied me what they have.

6. That if the Indians, of their own free will, have asked to leave and abandon their sinful marital status, and with only slight urging from the minister.

I state and certify that about nine have married after I only told them that they should see that they now had a priest to marry them and thereby place them in the joyous state of grace, that they either marry or remain apostates. Others have left those illicit relationships and are living with their own wives; and there are others who neither leave their present condition nor marry, no matter how much the father tells them to do so, and that is the largest portion of them.

7. That I state whether I expect to have some success in the future in winning the souls of those who are under my charge in the pueblos of Zia and Santa Ana.

I state and certify that I hope and trust in God our Lord, with His help, to have much success in winning said souls, because I see many good signs after the ugly blotting out for such a long time.

8. That I indicate the qualities of the said Indians, and if I have seen or found any idolatry, and if after admonishing them they have stubbornly persevered.

I state and certify that the said Indians, excepting that by nature they are negligent and lax and have other defects as stated above, otherwise have very good qualities. As for the point regarding idolatry, until now I have not found any Indian, nor anyone else, engaged in this kind of evil practice.

9. That you state the dangers that can be expected in the future and the severity of the winter.

I state and certify that during this present winter more hardships than relief are expected. On the other point, I do not know, and I say the same with regard to the fear that they may have.

10. That I list all the persons who are my parishioners.

I state and certify that in Zia I have 279 and in Santa Ana 168.

Since all of that which I have stated above is true, and according to my conscience, and does not depart (to my knowledge) one iota from the truth, I swear to it *in verbo sacerdotis* and sign on December 28, 1694.

Fray Juan Alpuente

19. LETTER OF FRAY DIEGO ZEINOS, PECOS, DECEMBER 28, 1694[1]

✝

OUR very reverend father custodian, Fray Francisco de Vargas. My dear father,

I received the letter from Your Paternal Reverence, and with the esteem that is due to your paternal love I respond in filial obedience to the ten points that Your Reverence orders me to resolve. I reply subjecting myself not only to my will but to my limited intelligence in the following manner.

On the first point I state that the motivating, and even final, cause for my having come to this pueblo of the Pecos was that which brought me to this holy and venerable custody, which was the goal to convert the souls redeemed by the precious blood of our Redeemer. And my coming to the said pueblo was not the result of force by any prelate; rather, all the missionaries, awaiting the slightest suggestion, went willingly to their designated districts.

On the second point I state that the condition of the Indians at this time is good, that they attend the instruction in Christian doctrine whenever they can, adults as well as little children, although in regard to prayer I found them so ignorant that most of them did not know how to make the sign of the cross, and it is necessary to teach them very slowly for them to learn its meaning.

On the third point, which has four parts, I state that thanks to God our Lord I have succeeded in baptizing seven infants, besides two hundred thirty whom I have annointed with the holy oils who were baptized by the reverend father Fray Francisco Corbera in the year '92. And of the infants who were baptized, nine have died and were buried in this pueblo. Of the adults, three have died, having received the holy sacraments before their deaths. In regard to the fourth part of this third point, that if when they are seriously ill they call for their minister, it is true that one woman, an adult, died without receiving confession (which saddened my soul), because when they called me she was already dead, and when I scolded the women of the house, they said that it was not their fault, saying that there was nothing more that they could do, since the attack was sudden.

On the fourth point, in the order of the questions, I state that the Indians of this pueblo have built a chapel which is not large, but decent and well proportioned, to celebrate the holy sacrifice of the mass, and also they have made cells for the unworthy religious who administers to them.

On the fifth point I state that these natives do for me what they can to help me and provide me with food.

On the sixth point, I reply that none of these natives has come to me to ask me to marry them in accordance with our holy mother church. Because it is my

1. BNM, leg. 3, doc. 6.

desire, as it is my obligation, to place them in grace, with little effort I have succeeded, for I have married thirteen young men with those with whom they were living illicitly, and I hope with God's help that soon many others will marry.

On the seventh point I hope, not by me, but by the all powerful One, to reap much fruit in the future and that these natives on their part will not disappoint me.

On the eighth point I state that I have not seen at the present time serious practice of idolatry among these natives, although I have indications that it takes place, and I ask the Father of all mankind to give me the light to recognize it and remedy it.

On the ninth point I reply that we should always fear the dangers of the future because of the great fickleness and inconstancy which we experience in the Indians, but this fear has not been sufficient for us to waver from our main purpose, for we are ready to die, if it should be necessary, for our Lord, who, without sin, gave His life for ours. And with regard to the remaining part of this ninth point I state that the winter is very severe and the poverty of the land is great, but there is no human recourse until new provisions are sent, but (with honor and glory to God our Lord) none of this deters us from following the road that has been opened to us.

On the tenth point I state that the number of parishioners under my charge totals seven hundred thirty-six persons: one hundred eighty-six men, two hundred thirty adult women, and three hundred and twenty small children from their earliest years to twelve or thirteen years of age.

And I, Fray Diego Zeinos, president of this pueblo of Pecos, state that all of what I have stated above is what I feel in God and in my conscience, and I swear, *in verbo sacerdotis*, that all of what I have stated is the truth, as far as I am able to perceive it. In witness whereof I signed in said pueblo on the twenty-eighth day of December, the year sixteen hundred ninety-four.

Fray Diego Zeinos

20. LETTER OF FRAY JUAN ANTONIO DEL CORRAL, SAN FELIPE, DECEMBER 30, 1694 [1]

✠

VERY reverend father and superior:

Fray Francisco de Vargas, my father and superior:

I received a message from Your Very Reverence, issued in the Villa of Santa Fe on the twentieth of December of the year sixteen hundred ninety-four, in

---

1. BNM, leg. 3, doc. 6.

which Your Paternity orders me, in holy obedience and in virtue of the Holy Spirit and as a minister of God, to reply, under oath, to the points that are asked of me.

And carrying out the order of Your Paternity, I turn to the first point. I reply that it was in holy obedience that I came to this pueblo of San Felipe, without being forced to do so by the prelate.

On the second point I state that as to the status of the Indians to whom I administer, they attend the instruction in doctrine and mass and the other religious exercises, but since they have lost fourteen years of instruction, they are ignorant; but with time and prudence they will begin to understand what they are taught. The assistance received by the ministers is very good, and they bring wood and water and assist all day in the minister's cell.

On the third point I reply that I have not baptized anyone, because my predecessor baptized seventy-six, and of those two have died. With regard to the winning of souls, there has been one sick person for whom I was called to administer the holy sacrament of penance.

On the fourth point I reply that the chapel is not one of the most decent ones, but it is adequate, since there is nothing else available in the place where it is located. They are already carrying timber and stone to improve it, but the winter impedes them in their work. The minister's dwelling is sufficient for now; it is decent and has three rooms.

On the fifth point I reply that in food supplies they have an abundance of corn, beans, and squash, but when they can they bring me four tortillas in the morning, four at midday, and four in the evening, and nothing else.

On the sixth point I reply that in seeing the obstacle of so much sin, in knowing that they are living with the women they had taken in their apostasy, I ordered the fiscals to make publicly known that they should return to the state of grace, explaining to them the sacrament of matrimony, and after the second suggestion seven came forth whom I married after I had carried out the decrees as ordered by the Holy Council.

On the seventh point I reply that it may be that God will enlighten their understanding so that they may know His divine precepts and that there may be hope in the future to save their souls.

On the eighth point I reply that as to the qualities of these Indians, with their dances and songs in their *estufas,* I have not seen any idolatry among them, although I have asked them about it. Besides this I have seen nothing more than the dances and singing, which is their custom, and I have no knowledge that they do so with malicious intent.

On the ninth point I reply that I cannot speak with assurance, for after all, after a hundred years converting them they rose in rebellion. The sufferings of winter are many, for they are exceedingly severe, and the land is very sterile.

On the tenth point I reply that of adults and others, old and young, I have two hundred forty persons.

All of the above, in God's name, is the truth, and I swear under oath, *in verbo sacerdotis,* that there is nothing of malice in my statement. And I ask that God protect and keep Your Paternity so that your efforts may be amplified in so holy a mandate. From this your pueblo of San Felipe, December 30 of the year 1694. Your most devoted servant, who kisses your hand.

Fray Juan Antonio del Corral

21. LETTER OF FRAY JOSÉ GARCÍA MARÍN, SANTA CLARA, DECEMBER 31, 1694[1]

✠

HAVING received an order from Your Very Reverend Paternity on December 24, 1694, in which you order me to state and verify the following points, specifying each one separately, in their own individuality and distinction, I obey gladly as a true son and subject of Your Very Reverend Paternity, and I will make my statement and certification as I have known and experienced it, as our Lord God and my own conscience dictate.

FIRST POINT

First, that Your Reverence state what directed you to go to the mission of the pueblo of Santa Clara, and if any prelate forced you to do so.

To answer and make my statement on this point, I believe that while I was a preacher, although unworthy, in the holy province of Burgos in the year 1692, a patent arrived in said province from our most reverend father provincial commissary Fray Julián Chumilla in which the religious were notified that in New Spain the kingdom of the Texas had been discovered, where there was an infinity of souls desiring to receive holy baptism, to live and die in our holy law. Moved by the zeal inspired by God that so many souls should not be lost for lack of priests but be redeemed by the precious blood of our Lord Jesus Christ, I decided to leave my holy province, country, parents, brothers, relatives, and friends to sail the expansive and dangerous seas that lie between Spain and New Spain only to achieve the goal that said souls not be lost. I came, then, with the zeal inspired by God for this purpose, and having been frustrated by events which I am ignorant of, I stopped over at the College of the Holy Cross of Apostolic Preachers until a patent arrived from our most reverend father com-

1. BNM, leg. 3, doc. 6.

missary general in which he lovingly encouraged the religious to go as volunteers to the missions of the holy custody of New Mexico. Having listened to the reading of said patent, I begged His Most Reverence to do me the favor and charity of granting me his blessing and permission to come and accomplish the most holy goal for which I had left my holy province, country, etc. The very reverend father granted me his permission, and with it I came gladly to this holy custody.

And after I arrived at said holy custody, the reverend father Fray Juan Alonso, who at that time was vice-custodian, assigned me to reside at the convent of our father San Antonio at the pueblo of Senecú, where the said reverend father vice-custodian was serving as guardian and minister. He helped me and assisted me with great love and affection, providing me with the abundance of needs that I have always been assisted with since I left the holy college and until the time I arrived at this convent; and all the other reverend fathers who were in the convent of El Paso assisted me in the same manner, for I received the greatest assistance from all of them, and they helped me in every way possible, as true and genuine brothers.

I served in this said holy custody, awaiting momentarily for good and certain news of the pacification and submission of those unfortunate souls, apostates of our holy Catholic faith, and it was the wish of His Holy Majesty that all this should come about, as we all saw. And so, with this good news, I went to the convent where Your Most Reverend Paternity resided to ask you if the news that had arrived was true, and if so, as a favor and charity, to send me, with your blessing, on the mission I hoped for. The other fathers and brothers at the convents in El Paso did the same. And Your Very Reverend Paternity, granting our just request, was the first to decide to come with the said fathers, and Your Very Reverend Paternity left with them on the seventh of October of the year 1694, and we arrived at the Villa of Santa Fe on November 1.

What Your Very Reverend Paternity did for us in the course of the journey only God knows, and it is well known to all those of this kingdom, and therefore I cannot fail to mention how ungrateful it would be not to refer to the favors received. And, therefore, I say that Your Very Reverend Paternity continued to assist us on the journey with all of our needs, at your own expense, for which purpose it is of record that you sent to Parral for chocolate and sugar and other necessary provisions for the trip.

Having arrived at the Villa of Santa Fe, then, and having seen that the news that was received in El Paso was true, and seeing also that all the other fathers and brothers were already in their pueblos administering to the Indians and that other pueblos were without ministers and were asking for them, we made the same request that we made in El Paso, that Your Very Reverend Paternity do us the favor and charity of giving us your holy blessing and permission to put into execution the most holy goal which we desired, and agreeing with our request, Your Very Reverend Paternity was the first to go out with His Lordship, the governor and captain general, to place each religious in the pueblo to which he had been assigned.

I reply that my reason for coming to this mission was the zeal inspired by God, and the supreme desire that I had to achieve such a greatly desired goal. And my coming to this place rather than another was that with regard to the missions that were without ministers, some fathers were attracted to some, and others to others, and Your Very Reverend Paternity, as always, wished to give this comfort to the religious. From all of which it is clear that no prelate forced me to come to the said mission.

SECOND POINT

Item, that I indicate to Your Reverence the extent to which at the present time the Indians, both children and adults, attend instruction in Christian doctrine and other religious exercises and if they render due obedience to their minister.

To answer this point, first I believe that I came to this pueblo of Santa Clara on November 26 of the said year referred to. Second, I believe that said pueblo was always a *visita* administered from the pueblo of San Juan, and it is not now the same as a pueblo that is a *visita,* as it has its own direct administration, this being my understanding.

I respond that the present state of the Indians, as regards their inner thoughts, only God can know. But in my opinion I see affection in many of them in their demeanor and outward appearance, and in others such as the young boys, who have never seen or known the priests or Spaniards; I also see in some apparent affection, and in others I note that they are somewhat confused in seeing what they had never seen before. In response to the second part, if they attend, etc., I reply that on some occasions I have had the singular pleasure of seeing them recite the catechism, while I assist them by listening to them as they recite; and although they recite in unison, not all of them know the Christian doctrine, which is not easy for them in the short time (as I have noted) that they have been under my administration. Nevertheless, some of them do know it, and those who do not are being instructed by me. I also state that every day (except those on which I excuse them because of the severity of the cold and snow) nearly all of them attend, with one or another in the habit of being absent, and their absence seems to be because they are temporarily away from the pueblo. In response to the third part, if they are, etc., I state that until now I have not found anyone who has resisted my order or request.

THIRD POINT

Item, that Your Reverence state the success obtained in the winning of souls by baptizing some children, and of these, indicating those that have died; and also those adults who have received the holy sacraments and have subsequently died; and if, when they are seriously ill, they immediately seek their minister to administer the holy sacraments to them.

I reply to the first part, that up until the present day I have baptized eighteen boys and girls, none of whom have died. And I have not baptized any adults, because I have not been sufficiently satisfied that they know the catechism and other mysteries of the faith necessary for them to receive holy baptism. And if, finding themselves, etc., I say that two, *ex propio motu,* called me to confess them, which I did; and I have no knowledge of any others in serious illness besides these two, neither of whom died.

FOURTH POINT

Item, if said Indians have built a decent church for the celebration of the holy sacrifice of the mass, and if they have built cells for the residence of the religious.

In reply, I refer to that which has been stated under the second point that I believe that I entered this pueblo on November 26; and also, as to the extremely cold climate of the region, I will refer to this below. This being understood, I state that without any scruples I say mass in the chapel which the said Indians have built amidst cold weather and in such a short time. With regard to the cells, they are adequate for the present. I hope with God's help that in the spring a very decent chapel and cells for the religious will be built.

FIFTH POINT

Item, that I state whether the Indians, in their own way, with the little food that they have, contribute to the minister for his sustenance.

In reply, I understand that the said Indians are those who withdrew from the *mesilla* [small mesa] of San Ildefonso, which is about a half a league from said pueblo, and on this said *mesilla* they were rebellious and obstinate, fighting against the Spaniards until the day of the Nativity of Our Lady the Blessed Virgin. I also understand that with the continuous wars that the Spaniards carried out against them, they were unable to plant very much, and of the little that they planted, the Spaniards who came to fight against them seized their ears of corn, from which it is clear to me that they cannot have much food supplies. Nevertheless they have provided me with twelve *guaiavas* each day for my sustenance and a boy to assist me as an altar boy for mass, and since the fifth of December, when I received a small amount of corn from Your Very Reverend Paternity, since that said fifth day I have not asked the said Indians for any more food. But I have advised them that when the said corn is exhausted, and if no more aid is forthcoming (which I expect, as I always look to Your Very Reverend Paternity for assistance), it will be necessary for them to help me to the extent that they can. They say that they, also, are destitute, but that they will do what they can. I cannot be assured that they will, but I hope, with the help of our Lord Jesus Christ, that in response to the friendly treatment that I am extending to them, with some talks that I had with them, they will help their minister to the extent that they can with their limited means.

SIXTH POINT

Item, that I state whether of their own volition the Indians have requested the holy sacrament of matrimony, leaving the women with whom, in their apostasy, they lived in illicit cohabitation, and indicate those who have sought to place themselves in a state of grace by receiving the holy sacrament of matrimony with only slight urging from their minister.

I reply that of the five that I have married during this short time, three asked me to marry them *ex propio modo* and the other two came to me after I had admonished them and urged them to marry so that they would not offend our Lord Christ, our King and Lord. On the second part, and those that follow, etc., I state that none of the said Indians has asked to receive the holy sacrament of penance, whereby they could be in the state of grace, although many times I have exhorted them to do so as best they could. But I must point out that neither do I know their language nor is there an adequate and competent interpreter in the pueblo, for the available one lacks full knowledge of the language of the said Indians and is also limited in the Spanish language.

SEVENTH POINT

Item, that I state if in the future I expect to have success in winning the souls of the parishioners under my charge, in administering the holy sacraments.

I reply that with God's grace I hope to save the souls of all the children who die, that is, if they die convinced and baptized. With regard to the adults, only God knows, but under the assumption that the said Indians will not rebel, I hope in the Lord that by instructing them, little by little, in the sovereign mysteries of the holy Catholic faith, and on my part with all my love and affection, seeing that they obey the laws of our holy Catholic faith and those of our mother church, that I will win the souls of a large number of the said Indians.

EIGHTH POINT

Item, that I state the bad qualities that I have found in said Indians, and if I have caught them in idol worship, and after correcting them in a loving manner, they stubbornly persist.

I reply that up to now, through the mercy of God our Lord, I have not seen bad qualities in them, nor have I caught them in idol worship. Although it is true that said Indians, as in the other said pueblos, as I have learned from many persons, had some evil practices with regard to stones gathered in the center of the plaza of the pueblo, the first time that I admonished them to remove them, they did so very obediently.

NINTH POINT

Item, that I indicate the dangers that may be expected in the future, and the sufferings, rigors of winter, and other inconveniences that I may be experiencing.

In reply I wish to point out that on the first item, said pueblo of Santa Clara is contiguous to and on the edge of the Río Grande, isolated on its west bank a distance of six leagues from the sierra of the Navajo Apaches, enemies of both the Spaniards and the Indians of other nations, and the other nations which are closest to the said pueblo of Santa Clara are those of the pueblos of the Tewas, on the east bank. I wish to point out, with regard to the second item, that the rigors of winter are very great, for although in Spain, in the lands of Burgos, Segovia, and Avila and in the Pyrenees Mountains that separate our Spain from France, just as much, if not more, snow falls as in this country; despite the cold and ice of those places they cannot compare with those of this country. Not even the coldest weather of Flanders can be compared with the severity of the cold in this country, for in no part of Spain nor in Flanders does it reach the point where any river carrying a great volume of water reaches the stage of being blocked by ice, as does this Río del Norte, which is covered from bank to bank to such a degree that it can only be crossed by passing over the ice, and this I state as an eyewitness.

With regard to the third item, I am aware that the said holy custody, from what I have observed and experienced, is exceedingly poor, for in early March the convents that are located in El Paso, which seemed to be the ones where the religious could live with a degree of decency, were without food supplies, and it was necessary to obtain them from Casas Grandes, as Your Very Reverend Paternity did when you were guardian of the convent in El Paso. And the other father guardians of the said pueblos of El Paso did the same in order to support the religious with decency, and this was by ordering corn in place of other principal items for shipment, such as chocolate and sugar, Your Very Reverend Paternity and the other fathers depriving yourselves from drinking chocolate only for the sake of having a small amount of corn. And I also saw and experienced that in all of the other needs for the necessary support of the religious, such as a few sheep and some cows, the said convents are indeed quite impoverished.

I reply that as for the dangers that can be feared in the future with respect to the Indians of the said pueblo of Santa Clara, only God can know, for only His Divine Majesty can know their intentions. But if they do not rebel and persevere in our holy law, I do not fear any danger from the said Indians. With respect to the Navajo Apache Indians, I can fear some harm, for the Indians of this pueblo fear them continuously, especially when the river is flowing, at which time the Apaches make raids on this pueblo, but usually its warriors are readied for their defense at that time. And as to the hardships and rigors, etc., I say that the hardships and rigors of winter suffered here can be inferred from what is already stated above. I have served five years in the region of Burgos, and I have never experienced half the cold as in this region, and it should be noted that Burgos, in the general opinion of the Spaniards, is the coldest land in Spain. As to the inconveniences that, etc., I say that only for the love of our God and Lord and the great desire that I have to assure that these miserable souls are not lost can one suffer that which is suffered here. I have been asked to refer to what I am actually experiencing, and since it is an order, I have answered the said points specifically and separately as requested. From the day that I entered this pueblo until the present day I have resided here only with a ten-year-old boy in my humble cell, and if we need something to eat, the boy and I prepare it, and we give many thanks to our Lord for whatever we may have to prepare. Also, I thank Your Very Reverend Paternity for your great charity in assisting me as much as you can within the limits of your resources.

POINT 10

Item, that I list all of the persons I have in my parish, both adults and children, so that the number may be known.

I reply that the families of said pueblo of Santa Clara total 32 and the number of persons totals 249, as follows: 49 young men, 79 young women, and 121 small boys and girls, totaling 249 in all.

All of what I have answered and declared on said points I confess and certify, *in verbo sacerdotis,* to be the truth with respect to what I have experienced and seen. Therefore, I swear to it *in verbo sacerdotis.*

In this pueblo of Santa Clara, December 31 of the year 1694.

Fray José García Marín
Apostolic preacher, guardian and
minister of the said pueblo.

22. LETTER OF FRAY JUAN MUÑOZ DE CASTRO, SANTA FE, JANUARY 4, 1695 [1]

JESUS, MARY, AND JOSEPH

Our reverend father custodian, my father and lord, I have seen the order and call for obedience from Your Paternal Reverence, to which I reply promptly in obeisance.

Question one. First, state what motivated you to accompany the governor of this kingdom, taking with him the religious subjects, and why you decided to leave them in their ministries without taking precautions against the dangers that might beset the said ministers by his not having left a guard of soldiers for their protection?

On the first point I state that what motivated me to leave with the lord governor and captain general of this kingdom, bringing with me the religious ministers, my subjects and companions, to place them in the ministries without taking precautions against the dangers which the said ministers might face without military protection, was to respond immediately to my obligation in conscience, seeing that the kingdom was already at peace and without any evidence of danger at this time; and also, seeing that the said father ministers were so desirous and ready to carry out their holy and apostolic vocation, as is evident in the paper signed by all of them which I presented to Your Paternal Reverence, in which, without considering dangers, calamities, and hardships, they clamored for the good of souls, imitating, like good ministers, the Good Shepherd who for the love of His sheep gave His life. In addition to the above reason, I acquiesced in the name of our seraphic religion, carrying out the summons to me by the governor and captain general in the name of the king, our lord, that we provide him with ministers as royal chaplains to administer the holy sacraments, to teach the Christian doctrine, to provide spiritual nourishment of the souls there, and to bring peace, with God's mercy, to their pueblos. And seeing, in the spirit of said Indians, security and humble submission, it did not appear necessary to be guarded by soldiers for safety, and we did not want them to suspect mistrust or fear of them on our part and be saddened by the sound of arms and soldiers in the pueblos when they had submitted peacefully to our holy and evangelical faith. For we saw them so prompt in rendering royal obedience that before the time limit which they were given to settle and join together, they were already together in their

---

1. BNM, leg. 3, doc. 6. Father Muñoz de Castro was vice-custodian and commissary of the Holy Office following the departure of Father Salvador de San Antonio, and he was succeeded by Father Vargas. At the time of this inquiry he was the pastor at Santa Fe. Thus, his reply to Father Vargas was more general than those of the friars stationed at their missions.

pueblos, rebuilding them, and with friendly communication and trade among all of us.

Question two. Item, state the degree of respect and affection with which the Indians of said pueblos received you and the reverend ministers who accompanied you.

On the second point I state and declare that in receiving us in their pueblos they were extremely courteous in their behavior, with great demonstrations of pleasure, having arranged arches overhead, shading the roads and over the plazas and at the entrances and doorways of their houses, and extending to us all kinds of attentions and courtesies, and the ministers assigned to each pueblo were received with great demonstrations of affection and joy.

Question three. Item, that if any of the religious were forced to remain alone in their administration.

On this third point I state that I did not force any minister to remain alone in his ministry, and in the manner in which the reverend father general Salvador de San Antonio assigned them, I placed them in accordance with their wishes, conferring the designation of the fathers for the pueblo to which each one of them had been assigned previously because of the fondness that they had acquired for the said assignments to the pueblos.

Question four. Item, if you have information directly from the ministers that they have had any success in winning souls for God, our Lord.

On this fourth point I state that I have received very certain reports that during the time since the said pueblos have been administered, the father ministers have been successful with both small children and adults, some of those baptized having died, others having been administered the holy sacraments. And in addition there are many who have married, leaving the women with whom they lived illicitly during their apostasy; and there are others entreating with those who were their legitimate wives before their apostasy in order to live with them; and also there are others receiving voluntarily those with whom they were living in an illicit state and marrying them; this is information obtained from some of the said father ministers.

Question five. Item, if you know directly from the ministers that their parishioners attend instruction in Christian doctrine and follow the other practices of a virtuous life.

On this fifth point I state that I know from the father ministers that said Indians attend their instructions in Christian doctrine and obligatory masses with punctuality, and they have told me that in the pueblos of San Ildefonso, San Lázaro, and Santa Clara they know how to say their prayers on their own. Their attendance at their instructions in Christian doctrine varies according to the information that I have: that of the small children in the pueblos all attend, but not all of the adults, nor do they attend as frequently, many of those of the Tewa and Tanos pueblos failing to do so because they are traveling about soliciting food, since they are suffering seriously from hunger, for during the course of the war they had no harvests whatever.

Question six. Item, if you know whether they have decent churches in which to celebrate the holy sacrifice of the mass, and if they have built cells for their ministers in which they can live.

I state on this sixth point that all of the said father ministers have in their pueblos decent churches or chapels where they can say mass, which are adequate temporarily, small and large in construction, and also they have ample and clean cells and living quarters, which were immediately prepared for them, which I saw when I went there with the father ministers, and I was very impressed with the brevity and love with which they proceeded to do this.

Question seven. Item, that in view of the scarcity of food in which the Indians find themselves, if you know whether they assist their ministers with what little they have for their sustenance.

On this seventh point I state that I have been told by said fathers that with the great scarcity of food in which the Tewa, Tanos, and Jémez Indians find themselves, they do not fail to assist their minister with the help of a few tortillas, and those who are better supplied, such as the Pecos and Keres nations, assist the said fathers in greater abundance, but this is entirely limited to corn and tortillas and nothing else. And without the plan and foresight of Your Paternal Reverence, we would not have been provided with the livestock and biscuit which you brought from El Paso and would have endured without that help and sustenance. But it is understood that for those who are engaged in such an elevated and sacred calling, seeking above all the kingdom of God, an activity so pleasing to God, nothing can be lacking for sustenance, for our Lord Himself promises it to us in His Gospel: *querite primum regnum Dei.*

Question eight. Item, state if you have learned that the said Indians have been admonished for the sin of idolatry, and if after being admonished they persist in worshiping their false gods.

On this eighth point I state that the father ministers have done so, with apostolic zeal and discretion, preaching to and exhorting the Indians, their parishioners, the detestation of the sin of idolatry, abuses, auguries, and banal observations and their deception and blindness. And I have learned that in only one pueblo, San Juan de los Caballeros of the Tewa nation, they have persisted with some rebelliousness in keeping, in parts of said pueblo, some piles of stones where they offer ground corn, feathers, and other articles by means of which the common enemy corrupts their minds, and I know that their minister has admonished them with holy and discreet zeal and has prudently managed to rout out the diabolic and corrupting vice. I know of no other pueblo where such a thing is to be found.

Question nine. Item, if you know whether the said Indians are obedient and respectful to their ministers.

On this point I know that all of the reverend ministers are obeyed, respected, and loved by all of their Indian parishioners.

Question ten. Item, that you set forth the dangers that may be feared in the future and also the hardships of this kingdom resulting from the severe weather, and if, under these hardships, any of these ministers, although in good health, leaving aside their holy vow of obedience, would leave of their own free will because of the above mentioned circumstances, although it is known that souls can be saved.

On this tenth point, to which I am ordered to reply, I state that the dangers that may be feared in the future are (not because I affirm that they may occur) that because of the fickleness of these miserable Indians and their natural rebelliousness, having lived for fifteen years in liberty, feeling the suppression and reduction which they must have in submitting to Christian and politic ways of life, the enemy might perturb their spirits, resulting in some tumult among them. And if there is indiscretion at some time by oppressing them in their work, damaging their property and sown fields and insulting them with oprobriums as apostates, rebels, and witches, much can be feared of them that the goal that we have worked so hard to achieve might end in failure.

The extreme hardships that characterize this kingdom, on which you also request a reply under this point, manifest themselves very clearly and are well known by virtue of the severe extremes of its unsteady weather, in cold spells, snows, and barrenness, and the recourse for help so difficult that it appears to me almost impossible, because of the great remoteness of the location of this kingdom, for the closest place to it to which to appeal for anything (as Your Reverence knows) is more than two hundred seventy leagues away over rough roads full of danger from enemies. During the greater part of the year, extreme hardships are suffered from the cold and snow, and my only source of help and consolation is the winning of souls for God, which is the only goal to which we aspire as ministers of the gospel, sons of our seraphic father Saint Francis, without aspiring to greater worldly goods or conveniences and offering gladly to lose our very lives to achieve this goal.

Speaking for myself, I state (because it is asked of me) that with the help and grace of our Lord amidst these inconveniences, hardships, and needs, and finding myself in good health to serve His Divine Majesty, who rules in heaven (as to leaving aside the holy obedience, to which I am an unworthy son, I am ready to do whatever is wished of me), I, of my own free will, would not leave this calling and ministry, recognizing the harvest of souls awaiting us and which will be awaiting us in the future. And even under much greater hardships and dangers to my life that might confront me, I would not abandon the cultivation of God's vineyard, with its abundance of fruit.

Fulfilling humbly the obedience to your order, I swear and declare, *in verbo sacerdotis,* that all of this is true, as I feel in my conscience. And as an unworthy minister of the Lord, I pray and ask that He watch over Your Paternal Reverence for many most happy years, for the spiritual and temporal wellbeing of your humble sons. Villa of Santa Fe, January four, the year 'ninety-five.

Your humble son and subject, who loves you in Christ our Lord, kisses the hand of Your Paternal Reverence.

Fray Juan Muñoz de Castro

23. GOVERNOR VARGAS TO THE VICEROY, LETTER OF TRANSMISSION, SANTA FE, JANUARY 10, 1695 [1]

IN the Villa of Santa Fe, capital of the kingdom of New Mexico, on the tenth day of the month of January, sixteen hundred ninety-five, I, Don Diego de Vargas Zapata Luján Ponce de León, governor and captain general of this kingdom and castellan of its armed forces and presidios for His Majesty. Having seen these *autos,* one may see that many visits were made to the vanquished Keres nations of Cochití and San Juan, who had been gathered on the mesas and who have now returned to settle in their pueblos of San Juan and Santo Domingo, and those of the *ciénaga* of Cochití to theirs on the bank of the Río del Norte three short leagues from Santo Domingo. And that in each I left and granted possession to their minister catechists in the name of His Majesty, as designated by their present vice-custodian and custodian, Fray Francisco de Vargas. In like manner I left the two missions of Tesuque and Santa Clara resettled. On said visit I also left the Tewa and Tanos pueblos persevering in their submission and vassalage, with their chapels and residences for their ministers. And also, by virtue of their punctual obedience, I returned, for reasons which I considered to be in the interest of good government, the fugitive Tanos Indian women who were slaves of the residents of this said villa. To strengthen the obligation of the said natives and nations, I returned them openly, granting to them their freedom on condition that they recognize the absolute authority of His Majesty and as his vassals that they recognize that his

1. AGI, *Guadalajara,* leg. 140, doc. 5. This report of Governor Vargas to the viceroy contains the earliest known documented reference to the Third Order of Saint Francis in New Mexico (1694). See also fn. 2, document 87, below.

strong arm and sovereign power reaches all parts. And I apprise His Excellency the Count de Galve, viceroy, governor, and captain general of the entire kingdom of New Spain, of the addition of the said four missions, the newly achieved subjugation of the said two pueblos, and that a total of twelve have been resettled to date. And with the lack of sufficient ministers, it is hoped that additional ones will be sent from El Paso so that those of the remaining nations may be resettled, such as those of Picurís and Taos, whose natives are also ready to resettle their pueblos and receive them. I have sent the said *autos* to Your Excellency with this *auto* of transmission, which I ordered my secretary of government and war to copy to the letter, in testimony thereof, and concordant with them, in the proper form to accompany the said letter of transmission, with the various matters contained therein for His Excellency the viceroy. And that it be of record, I signed in this Villa of Santa Fe on the said day, month, and year with said secretary of government and war. Don Diego de Vargas Zapata Luján Ponce de León. Before me, Alfonso Rael de Aguilar, secretary of government and war.

Excellent sir, I have sent to Your Excellency the testimony of the *autos* I have prepared, in which you will observe the felicitous success with which, wind right aft, this kingdom sails forward, with an increase in the number of missions and in divine worship. The newly elected vice-custodian and present custodian, Fray Francisco de Vargas, arrived on November 1, past, bringing with him four religious. He set out on a visit, accompanied by me, to establish the settlement and possession of the four missions and *doctrinas,* two of them pueblos that had been abandoned and whose natives I subdued by force of arms on their mesas, where they had gone to live, and the other two missions in the two pueblos of Tewas, so that there are now twelve. And the said father custodian has designated for himself that of Santa Ana. At the same time, four other missions are ready for four religious who will come from El Paso with the wagons that bring the supply of corn. Thus there will be seventeen here, and only three missions will remain to be settled.

Thus, I give Your Excellency this report in accordance with your order directing me to indicate the number of pueblos that have been subjugated, which include all of those in this kingdom. They are as follows: This Villa of Santa Fe is at this time occupied by the complete garrison [presidio] of soldiers, the previous inhabitants of the kingdom, whom I moved from El Paso, and those I brought from other localities, along with the military forces, and also the sixty families which, at Your Excellency's expense, entered this villa on the wagons of the father procurator Fray Francisco Farfán. And although some of the said residents have inspected their ranch sites in order to occupy them this summer, I have not moved them, nor are they able to move, because of the

severity of the present winter weather, and also, because of the sparse food supply it is necessary that all eat at one table. Thus, I will wait until next summer,
with the arrival also of the new people who are being solicited by order of Your
Excellency through the chief commissary, named by me, at which time the
division and settlement will be made in accordance with the plans I have made
to assure that the strength of our forces will be able to resist any unforeseen or
unexpected invasion by the surrounding enemy nations, which is why I have
not moved them, although these nations have not been engaged in hostile activities on these frontiers. Thus I have responded to Your Excellency on the
said point.

Also, this villa has its guardian and father minister catechist and his companion, who is also the minister for the brothers of the Third Order. For the
pueblo of the Pecos nation I have appointed as *alcalde mayor* and military captain one who also speaks the native language and is an old resident of the kingdom, and he has his minister catechist, and when more religious arrive he will
need a companion, since it has a large population. The Tewa nation is composed of the following pueblos: Tesuque, which has its minister catechist;
Cuyamungué, without a minister; Pojoaque, without a minister; San Ildefonso, which has its minister, with the pueblo of Jacona as a *visita;* Santa Clara,
which has its minister; and San Juan de los Caballeros, which has its minister,
and for it and the said pueblos noted above I have placed as *alcalde mayor* and
military captain an old soldier and old resident of the kingdom who knows the
Tewa language of the said nation. Of the Tano nation the pueblo of San Cristóbal is without a minister; the pueblo of San Lázaro has its minister, and here I
have placed an *alcalde mayor* and military captain to assist the two, and he
knows the said language and for this reason is of great help, like those mentioned above, in assisting the said ministers, which is the reason why I selected
him. The pueblo of the Picurís nation is without a minister; the pueblo of the
Taos nation is without a minister; the pueblo of Santo Domingo, of the Keres
nation, has its minister; the pueblo of Cochití has its minister; the pueblo of
San Felipe has its minister; the pueblo of Santa Ana has its minister, and I have
appointed an *alcalde mayor* for the said pueblos and the silver mining area [*real
de minas*] six leagues from this villa, to be settled where the ore has been found,
ore having been assayed and found to contain fine silver, with the advantage of
alloy, so that it can supply other mines that may be found, and may it serve
God our Lord that it provide what is needed with regard to the said alloys. At
this time the very rigorous snow and ice have not made possible its inspection,
which I will make in person at the opportune time this summer, encouraging
the enterprise as much as possible, as I have done with respect to the said discovery and the three assays that have been made, in all of which I have observed
that the quality of the metal is very tractable, of much richness in alloys, and

the silver appears to be very solid, showing in one of the said three assays four ounces per quintal, even though with the bad weather the said ore flowed over the vessel. Thus, I give Your Excellency this brief report because it may be that in the course of time something may come of it, and I plan to name the mine after you, in Your Excellency's memory, as a reminder that in your time not only was this kingdom restored to the royal crown, but also the mines for its aid. The pueblo of Zia, of the said Keres nation, has its minister; half of the said Keres nation of the pueblo of Santo Domingo remains on the mesa of San Juan, the other half residing there being of the Jémez nation, which has its pueblo on the mesa of San Diego, with its minister, whose parishioners are composed of four hundred five persons, and I have named an *alcalde mayor* and military captain and also one for the said nation of the pueblo of Taos.

I wish to advise Your Excellency, for Your Excellency's consideration, that through the letter I received from the chief commissary, whom I sent to the outlying areas to enlist families in accordance with Your Excellency's order, he advises me that the effort will be greatly delayed because the royal treasury of Zacatecas appears to have been shorter in funds than we had been given to believe by its royal official judges, and this will be of the gravest damage if the families arrive after the time when they can plant their crops. Therefore, in that Royal Junta let them not present obstacles to the cost of their support, and thus Your Excellency could enliven the said royal official judges in that business, who in their capacity can obtain sufficient means so that those in Sombrerete may provide the said assistance and payment to the families who might volunteer in the said mining town, for since it is populated by persons with no fixed abode it should be possible to enlist them there. And thus I also advise the said chief commissary on this said point, ordering him to assure their entry into this kingdom in mid-April so that they will arrive in time to plant the crops for their support in the ensuing year.

Your Excellency also states in your said order that the said residents of this villa can plant many crops with the farm implements that they have, to which I respond that in the consultative letter I indicated what they needed, as well as other points, which I proposed therein to Your Excellency, sent on January twenty-one of the past year with the testimony of the campaign *autos* concerning the victory at this villa which was seen by the junta of the royal treasury and war that Your Excellency convened on the twenty-third of March of said past year, in which Your Excellency determined and ordered with respect to one of those points that through your agent I be sent the iron goods that I requested and set forth in said letter, including hoes, spades, axes, plowshares, and padlocks, to be distributed among the said residents for the cultivation of their fields. With the most essential need, the oxen still lacking, for they were not granted, and not even the said iron goods having arrived, unless we are advised that they have been sent by the said agent of the royal officials, they will hardly be able to till the soil, or they will have to sow by hand, requiring much unnecessary work, for only these barbarous Indians are accustomed to raising their crops in this way. Thus I hope that Your Excellency has sent said letter to His Majesty and his supreme council, for I have no doubt that he will order that all be fully carried out and that Your Excellency will order that the goods be provided. I am inspired by my desire for the wellbeing of these residents and that they be sent the needed relief so that they may establish themselves on a firm basis in their accustomed way of life, for without this material I do not see how this can properly come about. And thus it is necessary that I make this reference to my said letter, especially since I am motivated by reason of the aforesaid point of the said order and resolution of the juntas, stating that farm implements would be made available but not having granted them, and deciding upon and designating what would be sent but not following up on the action. Thus I trust that Your Excellency will give most serious attention to this reply of mine, made with due respect and just obeisance to your greatness and to those honorable ministers of that royal junta. May they take proper note, humbly thanking Your Excellency for the aid given of the three thousand *fanegas* of corn to help feed this population, ordering that the payment of its value and the cost of its transportation be made without cost to the royal treasury of that court.

Would that my fortune and luck, Your Excellency, were such, through the discovery of fine ore in this kingdom, that it could serve to recompense the disbursement made from royal funds. What I promised was to risk my life and offer my life as necessary in the restoration of this kingdom. I never proposed that which might be impossible to accomplish without cost. In the case of my first entry and conquest, in the course of which I entered the remote provinces of Zuñi and Moqui and sent you samples of red earth or vermilion and ascended the rock of Acoma, I presented that universal conquest to Your Excellency in the service of His Majesty at my own expense and reported clearly that which was needed. And thus I recall to Your Excellency's memory, as set forth in said report, the great amount that it would be necessary for His Majesty the king, our lord, may God preserve him, to provide in order to solidify this kingdom on a firm basis, restoring it to his royal crown, and above all for the establishment of our holy faith. And thus it will never be possible for me to facilitate, without cost, the task of again acquiring and conserving it.

Thus I have responded to the points included in said order. And with respect to my solicitude for the wellbeing of this kingdom and the fostering of its development, you may be certain that I will give it my attention and esteem as a cause close to my heart, my only resource for its betterment being my imperfect judgment and mind, and I shall endeavor, on my part, to present to Your

Excellency all the suggestions and requests which I feel necessary for its conservation. May God preserve Your Excellency many happy years, which I wish for you. In this Villa of Santa Fe, the tenth of January of the year sixteen hundred ninety-five.

This testimony is in accord with the military campaign journals [*autos de guerra*] to which I refer, which remain in the archive of this government office, which I, Captain Alfonso Rael de Aguilar, copied to the letter by order and command of General Don Diego de Vargas Zapata Luján Ponce de León, distinguished and meritorious governor and captain general of this kingdom of New Mexico, its new restorer and conqueror at his own expense, reconqueror, and castellan of its armed forces and presidios for His Majesty. It is sent certified and true and corresponds with the said original, and present to see, correct, and finalize it were Juan de Ulibarri and Domingo de la Barreda. It goes forward on twenty-five pages written on ordinary white paper, as that with seal is not available in these parts. Completed in this Villa of Santa Fe on January the eleventh of the year sixteen hundred ninety-five.

In testimony of the veracity of the above, I hereby place my accustomed signature and rubric.

Alfonso Rael de Aguilar [rubric],
Secretary of government and war

PART FOUR

Warnings by the Franciscan Missionaries to Governor Vargas of Secret Plans by Pueblo Indian Leaders for a General Revolt, December 13–20, 1695

24. OPINION OF THE *DEFINITORIO* [DEFINITORY, GOVERNING COUNCIL] OF THE FRANCISCAN COMMUNITY, SANTA FE, DECEMBER 13, 1695 [1]

IN this Villa of Santa Fe, the thirteenth day of December of this year 'ninety-five, our very reverend father Fray Francisco de Vargas, former and present custodian of this Holy Custody of the Conversion of Saint Paul, His Paternal Reverence having received reports through letters both from some of the religious, missionaries of the said custody, as well as from civilian settlers of this kingdom, in which they have stated that they had reports of an impending general uprising and of meetings in the pueblos of the Indians of this kingdom with other nations, who had gathered together to incite the natives for this purpose; and although these reports have been at variance with a variety of opinions which the military leaders have brought to this Villa of Santa Fe, nevertheless, for the greater protection of the lives of the religious missionaries, the very reverend father had appealed to the lord governor and captain general of this kingdom, showing to His Lordship the letters that he has received from the religious in which they report on the said uprising. And apart from this action, the very reverend father has, on many and repeated occasions, called upon the said lord governor to safeguard the lives of the religious, who are alone at their missions, requesting that His Lordship provide the protection necessary to forestall the very grave dangers that can result from the said uprising, since these rumors are so widespread. And it would not be the first time that the Indians of this kingdom would have carried out the killing of the religious of this holy custody. For these reasons the most reverend father requested of His Lordship that mobile squads, with arms and horses, be sent to rapidly reconnoiter and inspect the said pueblos.

And since the very reverend father saw that his request was not being carried out and was looked upon as mere expression of opinion, His Reverence decided under the circumstances not to take action on his own but to do so jointly with the venerable *definitorio* of this holy custody, and the most reverend father, on the day indicated above, ordered it to assemble in this convent of the Villa of Santa Fe. And before the assembly gathered together, the most reverend father asked, in view of the widely known current rumors of a revolt by the Indians, whether or not it would be desirable to withdraw the religious who are alone at their missions and join them together in one place. He also raised the question that if they should gather together in this Villa of Santa Fe, or at some other convent, the fathers would be without food to sustain themselves as

1. BNM, leg. 4, docs. 15, 24.

well as lacking in adequate living quarters. And apart from these inconveniences it would follow that the religious might well be calumnied for abandoning their missions, because the variety of rumors and opinions may be either true or false. And if they are false and the religious leave, it would discredit our holy religion.

All of the above having been discussed with the venerable *definitorio* in order to reach a decision on the matter, it was decided that the religious should not leave their administrations, for the above reasons, and that the reverend father custodian should go to the palace of the lord governor and captain general of this kingdom and, in the name of the venerable *definitorio,* again protest, as the father had done before, requesting that His Lordship take action in sending mobile squads with military equipment to inspect and reconnoiter the pueblos and missions of this custody. And after the very reverend father was prepared to carry out the above decision of the venerable *definitorio,* to protest to the lord governor all of the dangers that could arise if there were any delay in the departure of said squads, which His Lordship had promised would immediately go forth as the venerable *definitorio* requested and the reverend father custodian hoped would be acted upon. But since these measures so essential for the safety of the lives of the religious were not carried out, it was decided to pursue another more expedient course, namely, to juridically make our statement in writing to the lord governor, which was not done before, in recognition of the attention, civility, and respect due to the word of His Lordship, in which we judge that he will not fail, may it be God's will. Thus the venerable *definitorio* decided and ordered, jointly with the reverend father custodian. Signed by him and by his very reverend fathers on said day, month, and year. Fray Francisco de Vargas, custodian. Fray Antonio de Azevedo, *definidor* [member of the *definitorio*]. Fray Juan Daza, *definidor;* Fray Juan Alpuente, *definidor.* By order of the *definitorio,* Fray Antonio Carbonel, *definidor,* and secretary of the *definitorio.*

25. *CARTA PATENTE* OF FRAY FRANCISCO DE VARGAS,
SANTA FE, DECEMBER 18, 1695 [1]

REVEREND fathers and ministers of this holy custody, my fathers and brothers. Jesus, Mary, and Joseph.

Inasmuch as there has been clamor that the Christian Indians of this kingdom and other pagan nations have the intention of calling a general gathering for the purpose of planning to kill the Spanish people of this kingdom and the

1. BNM, leg. 4, doc. 24.

missionary ministers of the gospel who reside in this holy custody and to desolate the land, and although these are rumors, they have been reported from a variety of sources, some being uncertain and others affirming that the said uprising is true, it is my duty to be concerned for the lives of the religious. I have determined that since it is widely reported that it is said to be the intention of the Indians to carry out this evil act on the evening of the birth of our Lord, on that night we will seek to protect ourselves to the extent possible, and this will be done by the gathering together of all the religious who are administering the Indians of the Keres nation and those of the Jémez nation at our mission of the Immaculate Conception at the pueblo of Zia, for the protection of which I have called upon the lord governor and captain general of this kingdom, requesting him to assure me of the safety of the religious. Wherewith, His Lordship, in my presence, commanded that an order be sent to Captain Juan Olguín to set out with fifteen men armed with military equipment and that it be on guard at the said pueblo of Zia on Christmas eve and through Christmas, and that the Spanish people at the place [*paraje*] of Bernalillo should also gather at the said pueblo. With this decision I have decided that each father minister go to the said pueblo of Zia and as brothers spend Christmas eve there, each one taking with him from his mission that which is necessary for his sustenance so as not to burden the father minister of that mission. And in the morning, God our Lord willing, each father minister shall request the said military leader Juan Olguín to provide the men that he needs for his protection, and each one of Your Reverences shall go with them to say mass for your parishioners. And if after arriving in your mission you should observe evil activities among your Indians, you should return to the said mission of Zia and report to me what each of you may have experienced so that the most appropriate action may be determined. And this *carta patente* shall be sent with a reliable person, without entrusting it to any Indian, and shall be passed along as directed, with each religious signing at the foot of the letter so that we will know that this notice has come to the attention of all.

And those father ministers who might find some inconvenience or harm that might result from their withdrawal and of their own will and good spirit might wish to remain in their mission, considering that which has been decided and referred to, let him so state in his own writing, signing with his own name, placing the statement along with the others at the foot of this our *carta patente* so that it will return to our attention and we will be consoled in knowing that Your Reverences are in some degree of safety, for whom I wish a very happy Christmas honoring our Lord and Redeemer Jesus Christ, with much success in winning souls and spiritual benefits, praying that the Divine Majesty our Lord grants it and protects Your Reverences in His holy grace.

Villa of Santa Fe, December 18, the year 1695.

To Your Reverences, fathers and brothers, from one who loves you in the Lord and kisses your hands.

Fray Francisco de Vargas, custodian

26. REPLIES OF THE MISSIONARIES TO THE *CARTA PATENTE* OF FRAY FRANCISCO DE VARGAS, DECEMBER 20, 1695[1]

SANTO Domingo, seen and obeyed; Cochití, seen and obeyed; San Felipe, seen and obeyed; Zia, seen and obeyed; San Diego de Jémez, seen and obeyed; San José de Jémez, seen and obeyed.[2]

I, fray Juan Daza, preacher and member of the *definitorio* of this custody, minister and president of the mission of our father Santo Domingo, state that in obedience to the *carta patente* I will withdraw from the mission to the place that may be most fit for me (by the special order that I have to do so from our very reverend father custodian), and I am preparing to leave in compliance with the permission given to me by my superior prelate, and it will not be easy for me to support myself at the mission of Zia. And attesting that this is the truth, I signed on December 20, the year '95. Fray Juan Daza.[3]

27. LETTER OF FRAY FRANCISCO CORBERA, SAN ILDEFONSO, DECEMBER 20, 1695[1]

OUR very reverend father custodian. My father:

It will please my soul to know that Your Paternal Reverence may be in very good health. Mine, I offer at the feet of Your Reverence with the fervor of your humble son. Our father, I have not failed to keep Your Paternal Reverence informed of what is occurring with regard to the Indians; Your Paternal Reverence is well aware of the reports that are current. I am fearful of what may happen. I have gone every night, wrapped in a buffalo pelt, to the door of the *estufa* to see what the elders are discussing, and I have not been able to discover anything of importance except that last night I heard some words that are very suspicious: that if they leave they will not go to the mesa, but rather to the mesas of the Navajos. That is what they themselves say, although in their actions I have not seen any movement. But since they are so cautious, we cannot

1. BNM, leg. 4, doc. 24.
2. These acknowledgments are written in the margin of the first page of Father Vargas's letter as it was returned to him.
3. This fuller acknowledgment is on a separate sheet of paper attached to the letter.
1. BNM, leg. 4, doc. 10.

rely so much on their actions as on their intentions. I will find out exactly what they have in mind, with the utmost caution, and will inform Your Paternal Reverence of everything that I find out, for it is much easier for me than for others, for I know their language. And therefore, as long as I do not advise Your Paternal Reverence of a certainty, do not be disturbed. I give you this report only so that you will be on your guard. In any case, I will let you know if the Moquis have come, for they are awaiting help, from where I do not know, and finally, I cannot write all that I know until I have more definite information from what I hear. What I do know is that the Spaniards will not find out, much as they try.

Even if I learn for certain of the uprising, I will write to Your Paternal Reverence but not to the lord governor, so that the leaders will not be punished, for although I know who they are (and they are those least suspected), it does not become me, as a priest, to expose them. The uprising will take place sooner or later, and although I know the day for which it has been set, I will not leave my mission if I am not ordered to do so in holy obedience. What I do know is that they will kill me or they will take me with them, as they have promised me; in either case there can be no doubt. What I risk is my life. What can be achieved in their reduction? If they leave, they will be afraid to return in submission, and by my remaining with them I may be able to remove their fear and I would at least have doubts about whether they will take me with them. Because it appears from the signs that I see that not only the Indians of my pueblo but also those of other pueblos seem to love me, by the indications that I observe, for I am indebted to them for some kindnesses, *nies obice,* and although there were such great and virtuous ministers in the year '80 of their revolt, they took none of them with them. For God is powerful, making from stones the sons of Abraham, and the power of God will shine more brilliantly if I am seized as an instrument, rather than seizing a saint, for the power of the agent shines that much brighter when the instrument through which it works is more inadequate and useless.

Thus, Your Paternal Reverence will act in all things as you deem most appropriate, as I know from your experience and wisdom. May God preserve Your Paternal Reverence many years for the consolation of your subjects.

San Ildefonso, December 20, the year '95.

Your humble son and most devoted subject kisses your hand.

Fray Francisco Corbera

PART FIVE

Repeated Warnings and Pleas to Governor Vargas for Military
Protection of the Missions, March 7–April 21, 1696

28. PETITION OF FRAY FRANCISCO DE VARGAS AND THE *DEFINITORIO* TO GOVERNOR VARGAS, SANTA FE, MARCH 7, 1696[1]

PETITION. Lord governor and captain general. Fray Francisco de Vargas, apostolic preacher among the barbarous nations of these kingdoms of New Mexico, former custodian and present custodian of this Holy Custody of the Conversion of Saint Paul of these kingdoms of New Mexico.

The venerable *definitorio* of this holy custody has examined closely the claims, information, and fears which have been expressed in letters and through other means by all the religious missionaries in these missions, indicating the certainty of a general uprising and revolt by the Indians of this kingdom, attested to by many evil demonstrations which give cause to suspect that they might treacherously kill the ministers of the gospel, that they have had this intention deeply in mind since the beginning of the month of December of the past year, and that now they find themselves with more certainty of success, and it also has been apprised of the statements which many Indian men and women have made to their ministers, moved by compassion to notify them of the betrayal planned at this moon to treacherously take the lives both of the religious and of the Spaniards of this kingdom, seeing them short of food supplies and of sufficient arms and military equipment. Also, it has been learned that the apostolic preacher and father Fray Blas Navarro, missionary minister of the pueblo of Picurís, who understands the language of the said Picurís Indians, overheard the Indians, who entered the kitchen of the convent, speaking to a boy of their nation, to whom they gave a chamois skin, asking him if the said father was sleeping, and the said boy answered that he was not and asked why they asked him, and they said to him, because they had come to kill him, and that he notify them when he was asleep. And the evidence seems to be the same in the case of a statement made by the governor of the pueblo of Tesuque, Domingo the Tewa, who, accompanied by the father preacher Fray José Diez, minister of the said pueblo, came and stated before Your Excellency on the twenty-sixth of February of this year that all of the nations were planning to rise in rebellion (and this cannot be denied).

And recognizing that the said religious are alone in their missions, undaunted, without any means or manner to safeguard their lives, and also seeing and recognizing that the Indians have a considerable amount of Spanish arms which should not be in their possession, and with the repetition of such bad reports, they [the religious] are fearful, for each one of them is dealing with so many Indians, and hearing reports of an uprising, we should not reject all of

1. BNM, leg. 4, docs. 15, 24.

these portents. For we saw by experience what happened in the year 'eighty, when the treason was discovered and the information was given to the governor and captain general of this kingdom many days earlier, even by the Indians themselves, and by many of the religious, their ministers, and since full credence was not given the desolation and destruction of this kingdom took place.

And fearful of these reports and experiences, some of the religious have come together in this villa to ask for help in this difficulty, and if they had not been cognizant of the obvious risk in which they find themselves at this time, they would not have withdrawn.

As Your Excellency and all of this kingdom know, the said religious have been administering in their missions without any protection for a year and six months. And although they could have been fearful when they first arrived at their missions, despite the risk of losing their lives they decided to go to said missions because they saw the overpowering strength of Spanish arms, whereby the said Indians were routed, dispersed, and forced to abandon their pueblos and without food were fought vigorously by the Spaniards. But now the situation is quite the opposite, for the Spaniards find themselves lacking in food supplies and arms, and also some of the soldiers with whom the Indians had tested their strength in battle have died in the epidemic of the past year. And the said Indians now have the necessary food supplies, for which reason it can be seen that they have the capability to rise in rebellion and become apostates of our holy faith, and the beginning of the said uprising will without doubt be to take the lives of the priests, their ministers, who are alone in their pueblos without the protection of the Spaniards. For although Your Excellency may reconnoiter with soldiers throughout a large area, in which there is a great distance from the first to the last missions, when Your Excellency wishes to remedy the damage at one extremity you cannot do so at another. And also we have the experience of the short period in which they carried out their treachery in the year 'eighty.

Besides this, these miserable Indians must find themselves in contempt of and unwilling to again accept our holy faith and law, in view of their rebelliousness and the repeated deaths they have committed. For they have already profaned the temples which were built at the request of the reverend father missionaries a year and a half ago, as well as the sacred vessels and the articles of divine worship. And also they have seized the cattle and sheep, which, at my request and that of this holy custody, have been placed at these missions: over sixteen hundred head of cattle and sheep and one hundred fifty mares, and all of this is in their possession. This can only give them greater strength and leave them better prepared to attack the Spaniards with greater force in the uprising which is expected with full certainty.

For all of these reasons I request and the venerable *definitorio* of this holy custody requests of Your Excellency that without delay, as the situation requires it, you provide each mission with the military escort necessary for the safety of the lives of the religious and the conservation of the holy temples and articles related to the divine worship. And if Your Excellency provides this military escort, the religious will not abandon their missions and will be able to pursue the spiritual nourishment of souls. We ask Your Excellency to send us an authorized statement in writing in reply to our petition. And so that this my petition will be of permanent record, I signed, along with the reverend and venerable *definitorio* of this Villa of Santa Fe, on the seventh day of March of the year sixteen hundred ninety-six.

Fray Francisco de Vargas, custodian. Fray Antonio de Azevedo, *definidor*. Fray Juan de Alpuente, *definidor*. Fray Juan de Zavaleta, *definidor*. Fray Antonio Carbonel, *definidor* and secretary of the *definitorio*.

29. *AUTO* OF GOVERNOR VARGAS, SANTA FE, MARCH 8, 1696 [1]

AUTO. In this Villa of Santa Fe, on the eighth day of the month of March, the year sixteen hundred ninety-six. Before me, Don Diego de Vargas Zapata Luján Ponce de León, governor and captain general of this kingdom and provinces of New Mexico, its new restorer and governor, at his own cost, reconqueror and settler of the region and castellan of its forces and presidio for His Most Excellent Majesty, [the petition] was presented by the reverend father *definidor* Fray Antonio Carbonel, minister missionary and guardian of the pueblo of Nambé. And as it was seen by me, said governor and captain general, I state that in the said month of December, having recovered from the serious illness from which I was suffering, I was given the said news of the reports that were widespread about the said uprising, which compelled me to get up from my bed, as I was recovering from the fever, and I ordered the governors and war captains of all of the pueblos, whom I had summoned, to appear before me to tell them that I now had regained my strength sufficiently to go and visit them at their pueblos and that I had news about the Indian *tlatoleros* [spokesmen, carriers of news] who were going about agitating the people and that they should tell them that they are my children and that they should remember the war that they had suffered so that they should be at peace. I told them that they had undergone good and bad times and had benefited during the period of my presence, both from the said war by which they had provoked me and the peace that they have enjoyed, and that now they were enjoying living in their

1. BNM, leg. 4, docs. 15, 24.

pueblos without danger whatsoever from either me or the Spaniards and that they should apprehend any Indian *tlatolero* who might go to disquiet them. And they left happily, for in taking this action I urged them to cast aside their treacherous intentions, if indeed they had any.

And on the aforementioned twenty-sixth of February I had news through a letter written by the reverend father Fray José Diez, missionary minister and guardian of the pueblo of Tesuque, which I received at midnight of said day, Sunday, brought to me by hand by the lieutenant governor and captain general, the *maese de campo* Luis Granillo, that the Pecos wished to rise in rebellion. And also, on the following day, Monday, the twenty-seventh, the governor of the pueblo of Tesuque came to bring me the news that a Tewa Indian of the pueblo of Nambé had come from the said pueblo of Pecos, saying that the said Indians of Pecos wished to rise in rebellion, saying that they had said this to him and that the said Tewas also should do so, and that in fear, because he was alone, and so that they would not kill him, he had said yes. And he said that the captain of the said Pecos and the leader of the said tumult was Don Lorenzo, the son of de Ye, and that it was his [Don Lorenzo's] intention to kill the father first and then come to do the same to the Spaniards and that they would go to Piedra Blanca, where they have an old pueblo, and that the said Indian left to spread the same information among the rest of the pueblos of the Tewa nation.

And this news and declaration is of record in the campaign *autos* as well as the record of my having left this villa on the twenty-eighth of February to visit and express my good will to the natives, using this said pretext with the said Governor Domingo to assure the said natives in their said pueblos, not revealing that the reason was because of the said news and statement given by the aforementioned Indian of Nambé, so that they would not become restless. And on the said visit, as I observed in their outward demeanor, the natives received me with the humble compliance of vassals of His Majesty, and also I saw that the chapels and churches of said pueblos were in good condition and that they were responding to the services of their ministers and reverend fathers. And in San Cristóbal, of the Tanos nation, I ordered them to move to Galisteo, which was their ancient pueblo, and they replied that they would obey, although I had previously granted them, by request from their reverend father minister and their *alcalde mayor,* the gift of the place and location of Chimayó, which in the past year of 'ninety-five had been designated for them, by virtue of my order, by my said lieutenant. And with regard to the said pueblo of Picurís, the reverend father, its minister, will recognize, and must have recognized, the intention of the said Indians. All I know is that in September past, of 'ninety-five, they were pleased with the said father.

And with regard to those of the pueblo of Taos, which is on the frontier, as is that of Picurís, I know that the said nations were prompt in attending the divine services and instruction in Christian doctrine, and they have with them their *alcalde mayor,* placed there over a month ago, and thirty soldiers for fear that the Utes might make an attack there. And the said *alcalde mayor,* accompanied by the said soldiers, went fourteen leagues distance into the interior and found only three foot tracks of the said Utes, which were the ones discovered in the pueblo of Taos, which was the reason why I, said governor and captain general, sent the said troops and why the said lieutenant of the cavalry, Roque Madrid, was sent to reconnoiter in San Juan, since thirteen horses had been stolen from there by the said Ute Indians, four from the reverend father minister and nine from the said Indians. And having gone out and ridden inland as far as the San Antonio River in the land of the said Ute Indians, accompanied by the soldiers I had sent him, he only found and saw nine foot tracks of the said Utes, which were those of the ones who had stolen the said thirteen horses. And with regard to the reverend father missionaries who are at the missions of the Keres and Jémez nations, with the fear resulting from the news given by the chief war captain and governor of the pueblo of Santa Ana of the Keres nation, Bartolomé de Ojeda, and given by the Jémez Indian Cristóbal to the *alcalde mayor* and captain Juan de Olguín, that a *junta* [meeting] was being held at the rock of Acoma composed of the Apaches, Chilmos and Faraones, Janos, and Mansos, who were awaiting the arrival of the Zuñis and Moquis, to come to destroy this kingdom, and that by a knotted cord they indicated the next full moon as the said time and date designated to initiate the war, I am prepared to set out tomorrow to reconnoiter the said pueblos, as well as that of Zia, where, following what Bartolomé de Ojeda says in his letter, the *alcalde mayor* was going down to investigate.

And thus, on my part may be seen the punctual vigilance which I will observe in the visit to and reconnoitering of the said pueblos, although I lack, with my limited forces, the men necessary for this task, as one part is being employed to guard the horses and cattle and another part in the convoy to escort the beasts of burden that convey the food supplies and other needs for this settlement, these two parts being taken from the total of one hundred soldiers that compose this presidio. You can see how short-handed it will be for me to go about to the places where help might be needed. Nevertheless, recognizing that the said reverend father missionaries are asking for the assignment of soldiers for their protection, I will do so, although I realize the inconveniences and difficulties in dividing the said military force in order to assist with it at any place where necessary to assure that the administration of the holy sacraments and the teaching of Christian doctrine will not cease. And if the said Indians are absent from their missions, they can have no confidence in me and in the said Spaniards, and our presumption that they have planned to revolt will have been confirmed. And so I repeat, on my part, that to provide assistance I will enter and reconnoiter the said pueblos and will provide the said military escorts, distributed within the capabilities of the small number of said soldiers, and you, very reverend father, shall apprise me of the very reverend fathers of the missions who request them so that in consideration of this, and of the number requested, I may provide and send what help is most appropriate in the service of both Majesties.

That this said reply to the said petition may be of record, my secretary of government and war will present to the said reverend father minister custodian the testimony that he requests, copied to the letter along with his said petition. And I signed, with the said. Done *ut supra*.

Don Diego de Vargas Zapata Luján Ponce de León. Before me, Domingo de la Barreda, secretary of government and war. It is in accord with the original, which I, Domingo de la Barreda, secretary of government and war, by order of the lord governor and captain general, Don Diego de Vargas Zapata Luján Ponce de León, of this kingdom and the provinces of New Mexico, its new restorer and conqueror at his own cost, reconqueror and settler, and castellan of its armed forces and presidio for His Majesty, took and copied to the letter. It is true and exact, and present to see it corrected and compared were the captain of the presidio, Don Antonio de Valverde, and the *alférez* Don Martín de Urioste. It is on six pages on ordinary white paper because there is no paper with seal in these parts. And that it be of record, I signed in the said Villa of Santa Fe on the said eighth day of March, the year sixteen hundred ninety-six. In testimony of the truth, I place my signature and my rubric.

Domingo de la Barreda,
secretary of government and war

30. *CARTA PATENTE* OF FRAY FRANCISCO DE VARGAS, SANTA FE, MARCH 9, 1696[1]

REVEREND fathers and ministers of this holy custody. My fathers and brothers:

Since very intense clamor has been widespread, proclaiming and declaring a general state of rebellion among the Christian Indians of this kingdom and among the other surrounding pagan nations, it is feared, and can be feared, that as in the year '80, the religious missionaries of this holy custody might be killed, for, as we saw, the said Indians began by treacherously killing their ministers. And today, as already indicated, and from the declarations which some of the father ministers of this custody have made to me in person and to

1. BNM, leg. 4, docs. 15, 24.

the venerable *definitorio,* stating that they were withdrawing to this Villa of Santa Fe to give me the news and expressing their fear of the evil actions they have seen among their parishioners, for which reasons, and on the basis of letters and other documents that are in my possession which in substance contain that which the reverend fathers declare, and so that I may not be accused of neglect or omission in seeking the protection and safety of the lives of the religious, I determined that on the seventh day of·this month the venerable *definitorio* should gather together and meet to decide and determine what is most appropriate for the credit of our holy religion and the safety and the lives of the religious. And having come to a decision on the matter, it was decided that the lord governor and captain general be requested, by legal petition, to provide soldiers as guards for the safety of the ministers, of the articles of divine worship, and of related activities necessary for the missions, to which the governor replied in the following words:

" . . . Nevertheless, recognizing that the said reverend father missionaries are asking for the assignment of soldiers for their protection, I will do so, although I realize the inconveniences and difficulties in dividing the said militery force in order to assist with it at any place where necessary, to assure that the administration of the holy sacraments and the teaching of Christian doctrine will not cease. And if the said Indians are absent from their missions, they can have no confidence in me and in the said Spaniards, and our presumption that they have planned to revolt will have been confirmed. And so I repeat, on my part, that to provide assistance I will enter and reconnoiter the said pueblos and will provide the said military escorts, distributed within the capabilities of the small number of said soldiers, and you, very reverend father, shall apprise me of the very reverend fathers of the missions who request them, so that in consideration of this, [and of the number requested,] I may provide and send what help is most appropriate in the service of both Majesties."

Thus, after you have read this, with the attention and care which is required for our credit and for the service of God our Lord, I suggest to you, reverend fathers, each one individually, that you measure and weigh the matter which we now have in hand, without abandoning the missions or stopping from administering the holy sacraments, especially with the promise that the lord governor and captain general makes to provide the necessary guard of armed soldiers for each mission where it may be required.

Therefore, each of you, reverend fathers, should ask for the soldiers which you believe to be necessary at each mission for its protection, and you shall place at the foot of this, our *carta patente,* in writing, and signed with your name, the number of soldiers that are necessary at each mission. And if any of you, reverend fathers, should conclude that you do not need a military guard, indicate it in the same manner. As I have stated above, in doing this I request and beg, with complete love and humility, that none of you, reverend fathers, fail to write at the foot of this, our *patente,* that which has been mentioned above, because if there is any negligence or omission in this matter, I will be responsible for it and will present my failures in responsibility to our reverend fathers who are our superior prelates. And since the seriousness of the situation requires preciseness on our going to the lord governor to request the soldiers asked for by each of you, I entrust to each of you, reverend fathers, that when this our *patente* arrives at the mission it be read and answered without delay and passed on to the next mission, as directed by you, finding a trustworthy person for its transmission; and from the last mission it will be sent to us so that we will be certain that it has been obeyed and of what each one of you reverend fathers requests, and thereby may ask the lord governor to provide the help which he has promised.

May the majesty of God our Lord preserve the lives of Your Paternal Reverences in His holy grace and give you the spirit and tolerance so that you may be able to toil in the vineyard of the Lord. Villa of Santa Fe, March the ninth, the year sixteen hundred ninety-six.

I address you, reverend fathers and brothers, as one who loves you in the Lord, and I kiss your hands.

Fray Francisco de Vargas, custodian

[Marginal notation:] Seen and read: Cochití, San Felipe, Zia, San Juan de los Jémez, San Diego de los Jémez, Pecos. Seen in person.[2]

31. LETTER OF FRAY JOSÉ ARBIZU, SAN CRISTÓBAL, MARCH 9, 1696[1]

OUR very reverend father custodian, Fray Francisco de Vargas, my lord and father:

It will be most pleasing to me if you, very reverend father, are in good health and have had more rest. I humbly offer that which I am enjoying in the service of Your Very Reverend Paternity, our father custodian. Yesterday I wrote to that villa to Fray José, unaware that our very reverend father was there, which is the reason why I did not carry out my obligation, which I do now, notifying you, most reverend father, of the situation in this my mission of San Cristóbal.

2. A copy of the same *carta patente* of Fray Francisco de Vargas, of the same date, was sent to the other eight missions and returned to him with the marginal notation: "Tesuque, seen; Nambé, seen; San Cristóbal, seen; Picurís, seen; Taos, seen; Santa Clara, seen. Seen in person." Although not listed in this notation, the replies to the *carta patente* include letters from Father Corbera of San Ildefonso, Father Prieto of San Juan, and Father Zavaleta at Santa Fe.

1. BNM, leg. 4, doc. 12.

The situation is that the natives of the said pueblo, with Chimayó as their destination, are leaving me, and in the sierra they have placed their corn supplies and clothing, because *el Cacacha,* or Pinjui, has made them do so, as well as three or four others who are his followers, who are openly in rebellion, and what is worse, all of the young men of said pueblo support them. The sierra, I know, has an abundance of water, for the said river which joins that of the Chimayó flows down from it. Many traps have been set, with stockades; this I have learned from Don Cristóbal Yope Tete, who says that the said natives are hostile to him because he did not wish to help them on the past Christmas eve, which I believe from things that I have seen. He has promised to protect me with all his pueblo of San Lázaro. And what I know is that only those of San Lázaro have done what little is being done with regard to Chimayó and that they will go out with the Spaniards with all of their households because they fear that they also will be killed, because on the mesa, four times they were about to take his life, and from what is now to be seen, they can well do so, for they have not had any dealings with him concerning the treachery which he informs me of, or with the *alcalde mayor* so that he could warn His Lordship to enable him to know the truth and punish the evil ones.

I have believed him because I have seen that they guard against him and that they have quarreled with him, telling him that what is known [about this plan] is from his mouth, and that although he is their enemy, it is well to listen to him, but that when he speaks in our favor, it is not well to do so. I have spent a most terrifying night, at times awaiting death, although they did not wish to perpetrate it. Since His Lordship was here I have not had the least moment of pleasure or rest, for last Thursday all of the people left me for the sierra, with the feigned threat of Galisteo. And the Pecos, brought by His Lordship, told them that they came to kill all of them. Consider, most reverend father, what would be necessary to return them to the pueblo? What extreme risks would I not take to get them to understand that we wished them no harm? Especially when I know, from the mouth of His Lordship, that it did not even pass through his mind to have them go to Galisteo, when he urged me to write to him requesting that they remain in Chimayó, and with many other imprudent actions (which I may call them) I again embraced them and placed my life in great jeopardy, all so that today no one would have fear. Does Your Very Reverend Paternity not see what a situation I am in? By what I have said and in what I have said? What I do state is that if this departure of those of San Cristóbal is not corrected, I see no end to the treachery, especially when it is known that they are instigating the others. What can we expect to come of all of this? For if it had been God's will that the two pueblos be dispersed, there would no longer be any memories of me or of the pueblo of San Cristóbal. And what most afflicts me and preys on my limited intellect is to consider that if I am killed, would it be true martyrdom or not? For should it come to pass that I might be able to flee, if I do so would it be cause for them to become more obdurate? On the other hand, in seeing that Don Cristóbal Yope Tete and Pecuchillo, without being asked, warn me about the said people and beg of me for the love of God, can I leave them alone and forsake them? What can I do in this situation? Very reverend father, as prelate, and assisted by the Holy Spirit, I beg of you to order me what I should do and as your most humble servant I will obey you. And may God watch over you for many years, for my protection and consolation, with my best wishes.

San Cristóbal, March 9, of the year 1696. Our very reverend father, your most humble subject kisses Your Reverence's hand.

Fray José Arbizu

32. LETTER OF FRAY JUAN DE ZAVALETA, SANTA FE, MARCH 9, 1696[1]

IN fulfilment of that which has been ordered and commanded by Your Reverence in this *patent,* ordering that the ministers specify the protection needed for the divine religion and for their persons, through the petition that was presented to the lord governor in which he was requested to provide soldiers for their protection and his reply that he would do so to the extent possible, in order not to commit an error in my judgment, I state that I leave it to the decision of the captain who the said lord governor may have on the said frontier of the pueblo so that the one who sees the situation at first hand may judge accordingly and may decide to ask for the soldiers he considers necessary. After this has been carried out and I have improved in health, I will go to said pueblo with the blessing of my prelate. And since this is the truth, I signed in this Villa of Santa Fe on the ninth of March of this year sixteen hundred ninety-six.

Fray Juan de Zavaleta

33. LETTER OF FRAY JUAN ALPUENTE, PECOS, MARCH 9, 1696[1]

OUR very reverend father custodian. Assuming that the reports of the uprising are correct, as I suspect, and having seen and read carefully the *carta patente,* which with care and solicitude Your Very Paternal Reverence sends throughout this holy custody, I reply and in conscience request, for the protec-

---

1. BNM, leg. 4, docs. 15, 24. Father Zavaleta had withdrawn to Santa Fe from his mission at Taos.
1. BNM, leg. 4, docs. 15, 24.

tion of the holy vessels and of my person, six soldiers, under the following conditions: First, that they be equipped with arms, powder, and bullets; second, that they be God-fearing, so that they will not bring unrest and scandal to the pueblo, for I tell and preach to the Indians that they should leave the women with whom they are living in sin and live according to God's commands; let them not be seen by the Indians talking with the Indian women, only to have them tell me in my face, "So why are you scolding us, Father, for aren't the Spaniards doing the same thing?"; and third, that the support for the said six soldiers be from their salary, because the convent cannot support them. This is what I request, as others will be requesting, with regard to what I need. Signed by me on March 9, 1696.

Fray Juan Alpuente

34. LETTER OF FRAY ALFONSO JIMÉNEZ DE CISNEROS, COCHITÍ, MARCH 9, 1696[1]

OUR father and very reverend custodian. I have seen and read carefully all the sentences in this *carta patente,* and I state that at present I do not need any military protection for the safety of my person or for anything else, and this is my reply. On the ninth day of March, the year sixteen hundred ninety-six.

Fray Alfonso Jiménez de Cisneros

35. LETTER OF FRAY BLAS NAVARRO, PICURÍS, MARCH 9, 1696[1]

HAVING read the *carta patente* of our very reverend father custodian, in which the ministers of this holy custody are requested to ask for the military guard necessary to assure the divine worship and the protection of their persons, I reply:

That with regard to the pueblo of Picurís, I have seen true acts of rebellion, and since I have heard them, in their language, threaten to take my life, and also have seen them continue to profane the sacred vessels, I request and beg of His Lordship that he grant me twelve soldiers in full readiness and expert in soldiery, and under these conditions I will go to the said mission with God's blessing and that of my prelate. And confirming that this is the truth, I signed in this Villa of Santa Fe on March 9 of the year '96.

Fray Blas Navarro

1. BNM, leg.4, docs. 15, 24.
1. BNM, leg. 4, docs. 15, 24.

36. LETTER OF FRAY JOSÉ GARCÍA MARÍN, SANTA CLARA, MARCH 9, 1696[1]

IN fulfilment of the *carta patente* of Your Very Paternal Reverence, I reply that with certainty and with evidence I can report that the uprising is planned for this present moon, in view of the public reprimand made by Domingo, the captain general of the Tewas, in the pueblos of his jurisdiction, naming by their names the instigators of the revolt, who fled to the hills of San Ildefonso. And the pueblo of Santa Clara is on the frontier of the enemy Apachs and Utes, and it is probable that the Indians of the provinces of Zuñi and Moqui are coming by way of the said pueblo of Santa Clara. And since in earlier days, without a presidio, there were six residents stationed as guards at said pueblo, I request that I be provided with ten well-armed soldiers. And I urge that their leader be the *ayudante* Juan Ruiz, because he knows the language of the said Tewas, by means of which he will be able to investigate day and night if we are in danger, to protect the sacred objects and, after that, our persons. With this detachment of soldiers I will go with God's blessing and that of my prelate. This is how I see it. And I signed in this Villa of Santa Fe on March 9 the year '96.

Fray José García Marín

37. LETTER OF FRAY JOSÉ DIEZ, TESUQUE, MARCH 9, 1696[1]

IN fulfillment of this *carta patente* from Your Most Paternal Reverence I reply that I have notified His Lordship of the report from Domingo Thuogue, governor general of the Tewas and Tanos, in which he states that the Pecos are in rebellion, and that it is to protect themselves from a feared invasion of the pueblo by the Spaniards, as it was the closest, and that I have learned that a Tano Indian of the pueblo of San Lázaro stated in the presence of Captain Roque Madrid that the revolt was certain, and that they were awaiting the full moon to carry it out, which will be about eight days from now. And it is so certain that the said Indian states that they have removed their food supplies and clothing to the mountains. And the said captain has seen with his own eyes that only a small amount of food supplies is to be found in the houses. And the said Indian states that those of the said pueblo of San Cristóbal have prepared covered pits and traps at the ascents to said mountains so that the horses of the

1. BNM, leg. 4, docs. 15, 24.
1. BNM, leg. 4, docs. 15, 24.

Spaniards will fall into them. And they are awaiting the full moon to carry out their evil intent. And although I know that the father minister of said pueblo is not unaware of this, nevertheless, with so much risk to his life, he continues in its administration. And the father minister of Pecos, knowing that the Indians of his said pueblo are carrying their food supplies to the Peña Blanca, persists in ministering to them. It is not temerity to say that the revolt is a certainty even if the ministers were to leave them, for although we know this and much more, we continue to remain, and it is a certainty to take place before we leave. Later, then, the revolt cannot be attributed to us, when, with danger to our lives, we are among our enemies, for they are already in revolt.

Moreover, I do not know how, in conscience, I can say mass to apostates, which I know they already are in their knowledge of the uprising, nor can I communicate with them, as I know that they are (I have so stated). By word of the *alcalde mayor* Francisco de Anaya, in the presence of the lord governor and four priests, I know that two Indians of my mission are telling the Pecos: "There is only a short time remaining, only you are lacking, the Spaniards are dropping with hunger, there are only twenty brave ones." For this reason, the said *alcalde mayor* whipped, or ordered to be whipped, those referred to, this I know. And I know who the two are, and I consider that they alone are the evil ones. If they are excommunicated and cast out of the church, they will say that it is because of the imprudence of the minister that they are in rebellion; if not, I cannot celebrate mass before them.

Thus, I state that my help can come only from God, for, with respect to the above, I find myself with great doubts, and I find that only by withdrawing to the Villa of Santa Cruz can I live consoled until the kingdom is restored and they are absolved, if I am still alive, for there is so little time remaining for its preservation. And since the lord governor is with the Keres with almost all of the soldiers, the military guard will arrive when there is nothing for them to guard, for many days have passed since I requested it and it has not been given to me. I state, moreover, that it cannot be said that if the religious abandon their missions the revolt will take place, for in addition to what is stated above, since the month of August I have known that at my mission some Indians have gathered in the house of a witch doctor [*hechizero*] and, singing war songs, they were saying: "Death to the Spaniards, what good are the Spaniards? We were better off before." And this witch doctor is the adviser to the previously mentioned governor, Domingo Thuogue.

And finally, if you, most reverend father, notwithstanding what I have related here, order me to serve at my mission, I request (with a clear conscience), for the safety of our divine religion and of my life, twelve well-armed soldiers and that they provide their own sustenance from their salaries, for I have no corn. This is my opinion. And that it be of record, I signed this at this mission of San Diego de Tesuque on the ninth day of the month of March, the year sixteen hundred ninety-six.

Fray José Diez

38. NOTE OF FRAY DIEGO DE RAMÍREZ, BERNALILLO
[CA. MARCH 9, 1696][1]

BECAUSE of the extremely bad health in which I find myself, it was read to me, in Bernalillo.

Fray Diego de Ramírez

39. LETTER OF FRAY DIEGO DE CHAVARRÍA, TAOS,
MARCH 9, 1696[1]

IN fulfilment of that which has been ordered and commanded by Your Very Paternal Reverence in this *carta patente,* to the effect that the father ministers request protection for the divine worship, for our persons, and for the other things relating to the safeguarding of the missions, in accordance with the petition that was presented to the lord governor and captain general, and His Lordship having decided that he would place the guards necessary for protection, with regard to all of that which is referred to above, I state:

That in the pueblo and mission of the Taos, where I reside, a very considerable detachment is necessary because of the great distance from this villa to the said pueblo and because it is a very dangerous frontier, in view of the hostility that the residents of the said pueblo have experienced from the Indian nation of the Utes, who have committed hostilities against them on many occasions, from what the said residents have told me, and that they have killed many residents in their cornfields [*milpas*].

This is what I feel. And that it be of record I signed this in this Villa of Santa Fe on March 9 of the year '96.

Fray Diego de Chavarría

1. BNM, leg. 4, docs. 15, 24.
1. BNM, leg. 4, docs. 15, 24.

40. LETTER OF FRAY JOSÉ ARBIZU, SAN CRISTÓBAL, MARCH 10, 1696[1]

IN compliance with the order from you, very reverend father, in your written *carta patente,* I state that although His Lordship refers to the general revolt of all of the bad Christian Indians of this kingdom as merely presumption on our part, and that we should not fail to administer the holy sacraments to our parishioners, it is not presumption or fear on the part of the ministers. What I do state is that the Indians of this place of San Cristóbal, whom His Lordship ordered to go to the sierra of Chimayó, where there is no place to live, but only open land, have made many complaints, and the said Indians presume that His Lordship wishes to take their lives, as the Indians themselves have told me in person, saying that a year ago their pueblo was taken from them for the Spaniards. And now he is sending them to open land? What can they presume other than that their lives are at stake? Besides, when on his visit His Lordship ordered them to go to Galisteo, having promised them earlier the said lands of Chimayó, they believed that this was the greatest evidence that His Lordship planned to kill them, which is the reason why they left when His Lordship departed from here to go to Santa Clara, leaving me alone, and ascended the sierra of Chimayó, where they had, and still have, all of their food supplies and weapons of war and have set up stockades to make themselves invincible. This I know from some Indians, even though they are enemies, from which I infer, as a legitimate conclusion, that their uprising is a certainty, not presumption, since I know about it directly from them and from their own mouths and not be presumption, since they themselves say so not only with words but with works, for I know and His Lordship knows about El Pinjui, who is a declared rebel, with four others, for he is one of those of the *junta,* and His Lordship is aware of it, and not by presumption. For it is written in a letter to the *alcalde mayor* Roque Madrid that he should capture him, and that if he is unable to, to shoot him. Is this presumption or not? If it is, why does His Lordship order that he be killed? If it is not, let him alone until the presumption is verified. Thus, it is clear that what the father ministers have written and said is true.

Moreover, when the said *alcalde mayor* of the said Indians went to trade for corn, which His Lordship was requesting of them, to feed the Spaniards of the Villa of Santa Cruz, the said Indians, with a letter from me, went to ask him not to move them to Galisteo (a petition that I would not have made if His Lordship himself had not asked me to do so, since I know that in this kingdom they rebel for the slightest reason and say that the Indians rebel because of the

1. BNM, leg. 4, docs. 15, 24.

ministers). And when His Lordship asked the said Indians to provide two hundred sacks [*costales*] of corn and that he would pay them for it, as in fact he did pay them with hoes, bridles, and spurs for the little that they collected, and when the said *alcalde mayor* saw the small amount of corn that they were giving, as they had promised, he decided, at the request of the Indians, to inspect their houses, and he found in them (there being five hundred persons who inhabit this pueblo, of San Cristóbal, San Lázaro, Tewas, and Piros) only thirteen sacks of corn, which, for the support of so many people, do not total two *fanegas,* for which it was presumed that they were acting in bad faith. And having investigated, it was found that the presumption was true and that their uprising was a reality and that since Christmas they had it [their corn] stored in the said sierra of Chimayó for their planned revolt. All of this was verified by their *alcalde mayor,* and he notified His Lordship of the person from whom he had learned this. Therefore this is not presumption, it is evidence, and if it is not, I ask, what is presumption? It is for one to think evil of one's neighbor when he is innocent or when the truth is concealed, but this is not concealed, hence it is not presumption, but rather, the revolt is real and true.

With regard to what His Lordship tells us, that we should administer the holy sacraments to our parishioners, I state that I will give my soul for any of them, but if the Indians take advantage of our ministering to them as a pretext to take our lives and, after the minister is dead, to profane the temples and sacred vessels, what will His Lordship do? By not believing what he has been told on different occasions by you, most reverend father, and by all of the father ministers, who are the ones who suffer and who suffered in the year 'eighty from the same incredulity by shedding their blood? If His Lordship wishes to remain well guarded and protected with his troops while the ministers are spilling their blood helplessly, without any benefit, of what use will it be for us to be among them, making them all more obstinate, administering the holy sacraments to those who are unworthy and who do not believe in God's law? For I know that when they attend mass, when I raise the holy body of Jesus Christ they despise it and say that they do not believe it. What benefit do we gain from this, other than irritation and obstinacy? This is what we are accomplishing today by our administration.

As for the armed guard which His Lordship promises for each mission, both for the protection of the sacred vessels and our lives, I state that to make possible the administering of the holy sacraments (although to unworthy ones, as stated) if His Lordship finds it possible to do so, he assign to my mission Lieutenant General Luis Granillo with all the men that His Lordship might deem appropriate. And if the rebels do not carry out their intentions at this time, which is presumed, only because they already have been discovered, let His

Lordship not argue about their being sent, because it [the impending revolt] is certain. And when the guard comes, they should know that they will eat at their own expense, not at the expense of the convents, for these are in great need, and we do not need to have them take from us the little that, at great expense and through hard work, you, most reverend father, have given to us and that we have saved.

This is my opinion. Done at this devastated mission of San Cristóbal, the tenth of March of the year sixteen hundred ninety-six, and signed by me.

Fray José Arbizu

41. LETTER OF FRAY GERÓNIMO PRIETO, SAN JUAN, MARCH 10, 1696 [1]

TO obey the order from you, most reverend father, it is necessary for me to begin back in the year sixteen hundred ninety-five in the month of August, and although there is a popular proverb that says, "water that has passed does not make the mill grind," [2] I state that it appears to me to be necessary to proceed logically with the report which I attempt to make, which is as follows, and which will be brief, for the truth does not require much proof.

Your Reverence had been informed by Reverend Father Fray Juan Daza, who (since Your Reverence was absent) was vice-custodian of this custody, that in said month and year I discovered a planned uprising of all the Christian pueblos, and although at that time I was not certain about one pueblo, which was that of the Indians of Pecos, later, in the course of discussing the matter, I came to know that half of that pueblo was in support of this terrible wickedness, and I notified the lord governor and captain general Don Diego de Vargas of the said uprising, and it was all clear to him, just as I had referred it to the said lord governor, for he sent, or there came, the military officers Captain Antonio Valverde and Sergeant Juan Ruiz with others, and they found out what I had said from the same person who had given the information to me. And we now know what has been remedied, because nothing was done. This is what happened in regard to this uprising.

As for the planned uprising at Christmastime, I could say much, but since I did not know about it with the certainty that is required to give a true report, I say no more.

With regard to what we now see concerning the present uprising, which

1. BNM, leg. 4, docs, 15, 24.
2. Agua pasada no muele el molino.

they tell us is fear on the part of the ministers, I would like for those who attribute it to fear to tell me that if it is fear, is it unfounded? For what we know is that the Indians of Tesuque went to the pueblo of the Pecos with the *tlatole* and that the said Pecos, having reported it to the *alcalde mayor* of said pueblo, were badly whipped, and they [the Indians of Tesuque] angrily attributed to the Pecos that they wished to rise in rebellion, as it is known that the governor, Domingo, went to tell this to the father president of the mission of San Diego de Tesuque that it was the Pecos who were the ones who wanted to rise in rebellion. And if this is not sufficient to presume, without presumption I add what was said by the Indian Domingo, governor of the pueblos of the Tewas and Tanos, on Tuesday before Ash Wednesday in the church of this pueblo of San Juan of the Tewas, which was as follows: The said governor said to the Indians, without fearing me, and I left immediately so that he could express himself freely, that three Indians of the pueblos of San Cristóbal and San Lázaro, two from the pueblo of Santa Clara, two from Nambé, two from Jacona, two from Cuyamungué, and two others from Tesuque had gathered in some hills next to the mesa that lies midway between the pueblo of San Ildefonso and that of Santa Clara to make final plans for the revolt. I now ask, Is this presumption? When an Indian says this publicly, is it presumption when he designates the time that has been fixed, affirming that it is set for this next full moon; is this presumption? When the said Indian feared that it might be reported to other Indians who were absent and that they might notify the Spaniards? Is all of this mere presumption? What are we waiting for? For it to happen? May God not permit it. Moreover, is it presumption, which it cannot be, nor is it ill-founded fear, when some crafty Indians who give the appearance of wishing to live as Christians report to me that the Moquis, the Zuñis, and the Acomas are coming and that they have spread the news that they are coming to the pueblo of Santa Clara to trade and they bring this information to my attention—why don't they go to see the governor of the villa? For so many people to come to this pueblo to trade is not good. We are very fearful, and if we could, we would go to the villa to join the Spaniards there.

I do not wish to waste more paper, for with this, I believe, all that we ministers can say has been said. As for the guard, I state, since I am on a frontier, and with aid more difficult than is presumed, that I leave it to the zeal that I can devote from one who in such spirit is devoted to the propagation of the faith. This is what I believe and request. Done at this mission of San Juan of the Tewas, March the tenth, the year sixteen hundred ninety-six.

Fray Gerónimo Prieto

42. LETTER OF FRAY FRANCISCO CORBERA, SAN ILDEFONSO, MARCH 10, 1696[1]

OUR father, in compliance with the order from Your Paternity, the revolt is certain and firm, there is no doubt of it, nor is it only a presumption as the lord governor states. I have evidence and proof to provide, with only two reasons, although I could affirm almost an infinite number of them which prove this. The first is that every night I go to the *estufa* of the Indians of my pueblo, which is the place where they discuss their affairs, as Your Reverence knows in your place of residence, and I have heard them discussing the revolt while I was hidden so that they could neither see nor recognize me. Alone among themselves they would not be lying, and, moreover, an interpreter could not deceive me, because I have no need for one, as I understand the language of the Indians. I also know that they went to the meeting [*junta*] that was held opposite Santa Clara, and they asked my permission, saying that they were going hunting, which was false, as I found out. This reason alone appears to be sufficient, but I now present the second: it is known that there are no pueblos in which some Indians have not at least notified the minister; these Indians are of their own people and would have more love for their companions of their own nation than for the Spaniards; therefore, this evidence of the revolt is not presumption. And if no one dares to tell His Lordship, it is for two reasons: first, because the one who tells him loses standing with His Lordship and is considered an enemy, and in addition, it is said that there is nothing to gain by it; this is a reason that I have heard many give in saying to His Lordship that the Indians will not rise in rebellion although they know otherwise. The second reason is that on the occasions when His Lordship has been notified, he has called in Indians and has asked them, and they say that they are not rising in rebellion, and His Lordship regales them, so what else are the Indians to say, as they also know that His Lordship might have them shot?

Already His Lordship has been notified many times by those who speak in plain language and truthfully. The same thing happened in the year '80, when there were fewer warnings, and since they were ignored, all the religious died, the holy faith was profaned, His Majesty lost this kingdom, and the souls of the Indians perished. If it is finally to be believed when it is unavoidable, as in the year '80, when there was less advance notice, there is better reason to believe it now, when there is still some hope for avoiding it. And if *oculus tuus scandilizatte absinde es et projiceabste,*[2] scripture gives this counsel, I do not say so.

---

1. BNM, leg. 4, docs. 15, 24.
2. "If your eye is an occasion of scandal pluck it out and cast it away." Paraphrase from Matt. 18:9 and Mark 9:46.

What I know is that if there is cancer in one arm, it is cut off so that the rest of the body may be cured. God inspires whoever can provide a suitable remedy.

What I know, our father, is that even if the ministers should leave their missions, this will not be the reason for the Indians to rise in rebellion, as His Lordship insinuates, for two reasons. One is that in the year 'ninety-three, when we entered, the Indians rose in rebellion, and there were no ministers at the missions, although they wished to go; therefore, neither the ministers' leaving nor their not leaving is a reason for the Indians to rebel, for in the year 'eighty the ministers did not leave the missions and the Indians rose in rebellion. The other is that, as Your Reverence knows, the uprising has been verified three times already, and the ministers have not left their missions, and, nevertheless, they persist in rebelling, therefore it is not because of the departure of the missionaries.

What I believe, our father, is that the Tanos are already in the mountains and that the uprising is set for this full moon, and if it is not prevented soon, there will be no way to avoid it. First of all, each pueblo will go its own way, and to conquer them later, should this be accomplished, at least two years will be required. During this time what will the Spaniards eat? They do not have a single grain of corn, and they rely on the Indians to provide it for them, nor will they find it in the pueblos, as was the case the last time, for the Indians have already made known that they do not have any, and it is clear to me that they have gathered it together and carried it off.

I do not know what we are waiting for. After we are dead we will come to believe it in eternity. It is not for the above that I shun dying at my mission, if my death assures the saving of some of my parishioners, but rather, I know that they will be more obstinate after my death. Nor would this be a rigorous martyrdom, for two reasons: martyrdom is a crowning glory, and I do not deserve it; the other reason is that it would be rigorously an act of hatred of the faith. Therefore, it would be rashness not to preserve my life while able to do so, assuming all of this.

I state that the military guard that I need is this: that His Lordship see and come to a mission with as many people as he considers necessary for the safety of his person, and in the quietest mission let him venture to stay eight days. I would be satisfied with that kind of protection. And I refer only to what His Lordship would need only to protect his person, while I protect the holy faith, which is the most important thing in the world, and my person secondarily. My life is cheap; let His Lordship protect the holy faith, which is the intention of His Catholic Majesty and for which he spends his royal resources so generously.

This is my judgment, and I request that the decision be made as soon as possible. And that it be of record, I signed this in this mission of San Ildefonso on the tenth of March, the year 'ninety-six.

Fray Francisco Corbera

43. LETTER OF FRAY ANTONIO CARBONEL, NAMBÉ, MARCH 10, 1696[1]

OUR very reverend father custodian. I have read with due reverence and attention the *carta patente* of Your Reverence, and in obedience I state that the only military guard I need (assuming the uprising) is that which may be assigned to the other missions neighboring this one, for if they are safe, this one will be safe. Moreover, I am not disposed to abandon the mission, as I would rather die as a Catholic and religious friar. This is my opinion. And I signed this on the tenth day of March, sixteen hundred ninety-six.

Fray Antonio Carbonel

44. LETTER OF FRAY PEDRO DE MATHA, ZIA, MARCH 10, 1696[1]

HAVING seen this from Your Very Paternal Reverence, I state that in this pueblo and mission of Zia a guard of six or eight well-armed soldiers is needed for safety against the awaited enemy. And I signed this on the tenth of March, the year sixteen hundred ninety-six.

Fray Pedro de Matha

45. LETTER OF FRAY FRANCISCO DE JESÚS MARÍA CASAÑAS, SAN DIEGO DEL MONTE DE JÉMEZ [CA. MARCH 10, 1696][1]

OUR reverend father custodian. I have seen the letter of Your Paternal Reverence, and I obey your orders. And from what is said, I do not doubt that it is true, in view of the intentions that are seen throughout the entire kingdom, with the news that is rampant, including these parts, and sufficient to believe their treacherous and evil intent. And in view of this I have made known to His

1. BNM, leg. 4, docs. 15, 24.
1. BNM, leg. 4, docs. 15, 24.
1. BNM, leg. 4, docs. 15, 24.

Lordship the dangers that can result from the declarations that have been made by some of the Indians of these pueblos. And since it has been recognized by His Lordship that it is suitable, he leaves four soldiers as guard at the pueblo of San Diego. And in testimony of the truth, I sign in person.

Fray Francisco de Jesús

46. LETTER OF FRAY MIGUEL TRIZIO, SAN JUAN DE LOS JÉMEZ, MARCH 11, 1696[1]

OUR very reverend father custodian. In obedience to what Your Paternal Reverence orders, I reply that according to what is taking place in these parts and what is being said and what I am experiencing in this pueblo, eight or ten well-armed soldiers are needed as guard, no less. This I believe in conscience and to be the truth. I signed this on March eleven, 1696.

Fray Miguel Trizio

After I had signed this, His Lordship told me that he was leaving four soldiers at this pueblo of San Juan, and I will remain with them until we see what happens.

47. PETITION OF FRAY FRANCISCO DE VARGAS TO GOVERNOR VARGAS, SANTA FE, MARCH 13, 1696[1]

PETITION. Lord governor and captain general:

On the seventh day of this month of March a petition was presented to Your Lordship by me and by the reverend *definitorio* of this holy custody in which Your Lordship was apprised of the manifest dangers in which the religious missionaries of this holy custody have found and still find themselves in administering the holy sacraments to the natives, of whom it is feared, and has been feared, that they will succeed in treacherously taking the lives of the said father ministers. For this reason Your Lordship agreed in substance that to prevent the termination of the administration of the holy sacraments to the said natives you would provide military guards necessary for the safety of the lives of the said religious, and Your Lordship requested that I ask each religious individually to indicate the guard needed in his mission for the preservation of their lives and of the sacred vessels and other articles pertaining to the divine reli-

1. BNM, leg. 4, docs. 15, 24.
1. BNM, leg. 4, docs. 15, 24.

gion. And having carried this out with *cartas patentes* which I sent to each of the religious, asking them to request the guard necessary and specifically stating that those who considered that they had no need for it should so state in writing, each of them signed his reply with his signature at the foot of the *cartas patentes,* and the said religious, in obedience to what is stated above, requested the guard that they need, taking into consideration the frontier character of their locations and the distances from recourse to Spanish residents, as follows:

The reverend father preacher and *definidor* and minister president of the mission of Taos states that he will be pleased with whatever guard the *alcalde mayor* of the said pueblo requests of His Lordship without determining the exact number it might be; Father Fray Diego de Chavarría, his companion, requests a much larger guard, for the reason that it is on the frontier of the enemy Utes, for fear of the two nations which they assist in said pueblo and because the source of help to them is very distant. The father preacher Fray Blas Navarro, minister of the pueblo of Picurís, requests ten well-armed soldiers, and for this request he gives very good reasons. The father preacher Fray José García requests ten well-armed soldiers and asks that Your Lordship provide *ayudante* Juan Ruiz as their leader, because he knows the language of the Tewas, which is that of his mission of Santa Clara. The father preacher Fray José Diez requests twelve well-armed soldiers for the protection of his person in his mission of Tesuque. The father preacher Fray Francisco de Corbera, minister of the pueblo of San Ildefonso, states that he will be pleased wth the guard that Your Lordship would need to be able to reside in the most quiet and peaceful pueblo of this kingdom. The father preacher Fray Gerónimo Prieto, minister of the pueblo of San Juan of the Tewas, states that he leaves it to the Catholic zeal of the one who has such a great desire for the propagation of our holy faith, believing that he will provide the needs, especially knowing that the said pueblo is on the frontier. The father preacher Fray José Arbizu, minister of the pueblo of San Cristóbal, requests as leader the lieutenant general of this kingdom Luis Granillo with all the soldiers that Your Lordship may consider necessary. The reverend father preacher and *definidor* Fray Antonio Carbonel, minister of Nambé, states that he does not need a guard if all the other missions have what is necessary. The reverend father preacher and *definidor* Fray Juan Alpuente, minister of the pueblo of Pecos, requests six well-armed soldiers. The father preacher Fray Alfonso Jiménez de Cisneros, minister of the pueblo of Cochití, states that he does not need any guards. Father Fray José Ramirez, assistant at the mission of San Felipe, who is ill at this time, does not request military guard since he is living with the Spaniards at Bernalillo. The father preacher Fray Pedro Matha, minister of the mission of Zia, requests six to eight well-armed soldiers. The father preacher Fray Miguel Trizio, minister of the mission of San Juan de Jémez, requests eighteen well-armed soldiers, since he is on a frontier. The father preacher Fray Francisco de Jesús, minister of the pueblo of San Diego de Jémez, indicates that he is satisfied with the four soldiers he says Your Lordship left with him.

And finally, most of these father ministers who request military guards state that they do not have food in their missions to be able to feed the said soldiers who are stationed there as guards, indicating that they only have what is essential for their own support, for if the meat that Your Lordship provides for the said father ministers were not available, they would be in very bad straits, for with it, although it does not last for the period for which it is provided, they supplement their needs for a few days and provide for the sick Indians and other very needy ones who come to their kitchens. And if this is not sufficient to support them, in the long run how can the missions be expected to support the said soldiers stationed as guards? Your Lordship will surely provide what you consider appropriate to meet this requirement. Also, it behooves me to state to Your Lordship what all of the religious request in their letters, that the said soldiers and their leaders not act in such a way in the pueblos that they will exasperate the ministers. And under all of these circumstances referred to, said father ministers are resigned, with the spirit and fervor that becomes them as ministers of the gospel, to provide the spiritual needs for the souls of their parishioners without failing to carry out any of their work.

Lord governor and captain general, may Your Lordship provide what is most appropriate, examining closely what has been requested and presented in the sentences written above. And in order that this petition may be of permanent record, I signed it in the name of all of the religious of this holy custody in the Villa of Santa Fe on the thirteenth day of the month of March, this year sixteen hundred ninety-six.

Fray Francisco de Vargas, custodian

48. *AUTO* OF GOVERNOR VARGAS, SANTA FE, MARCH 15, 1696[1]

THE request for military guards made by the reverend father missionaries, referred to therein, having been seen by me, said governor and captain general, and recognizing the impossibility of being able to comply with the number of soldiers which each of them requests and proposes, I refer to what is of record in my reply to the said request of the seventh of March of this present year which deals with the petition of the aforesaid very reverend father custodian referred to therein, to which Your Very Reverence was given my testimony and I, said governor and captain general, repeat that I have at my disposal one

---

1. BNM, leg. 4, docs. 15, 24.

hundred soldiers, which is the complement of this presidio, and of these the body of two squads of thirty men each, who comprise sixty, is needed to guard the horses, which are in danger and in no way secure, and of the remaining forty, ten of them are employed in guarding the gate to this villa, and of the remaining thirty, those who are being sent with the beasts of burden to El Paso to bring the aid in food supplies and livestock comprise two squads of twelve men each, with their leaders, which total twenty-six, with four remaining, who are the only ones at the top level, my lieutenant general, the captain of the presidio, the *alférez,* and the *ayudante,* and this without the position of sergeant. So there is nothing more that I can say in reply with regard to the guard that is requested by the said reverend father ministers in their said petition other than that, on my part, I will provide the following, although it will be at my own cost and credit.

For the following fathers: For Reverend Father Fray Gerónimo Prieto, who is on the frontier as missionary minister at the pueblo of San Juan de los Caballeros, four armed men; and as for the reverend father Fray José García, who is at the pueblo of Santa Clara, which was its *visita,* for which reason the said minister was placed there as well as for the reason that its people are even greater in number than those of the said pueblo of San Juan, he may leave there and join him because of the high running river, which lasts two months, and being there with the said minister Fray Gerónimo Prieto, he can go out with the said guard to administer the holy sacraments and to say mass to them on feast days and return with it, since he is so close to the said pueblo.

And for the pueblo of San Ildefonso, which is approximately two and a half leagues from the Villa Nueva de Españoles of Santa Cruz,[2] I will provide four men so that, along with the pueblo of Nambé two leagues from San Ildefonso, and four from this said Villa of Santa Fe, with the continuous communication with those who come and go from one villa to the other and the visits which their residents make to the said pueblos, they will be safe because of the close proximity to the Spaniards of the said Villa Nueva, and this same advantage is enjoyed and can be enjoyed by the pueblo of San Cristóbal, since it is so close by. Thus I have stated for these missions in this manner, and if it is the desire of the reverend father ministers, they can continue in their said duties.

And with regard to the pueblo of Tesuque, its minister may withdraw to this villa, serving it as a *visita,* which it was as you, reverend father, determined at the end of last year, since you realized that the reverend father guardian and minister could not go there from this villa without the service of the

---

2. The town of Santa Cruz was formally founded on April 22, 1695, with the title Villa Nueva de Santa Cruz de los Españoles Mexicanos del Rey Nuestro Señor Carlos Segundo. It is referred to in the documents in several shorter forms, as noted previously. It is most frequently referred to in the documents as the Villa of Santa Cruz and the Villa Nueva. See also fn. 2, document 1, above.

said Indians, and they, on their own, asked their said minister, the reverend father preacher Fray José Diez, if that was the reason for leaving them, and if so they would assist in providing the said service, as was customary, and by virtue of this they designated the pueblo of Cuyamungué so that they might assist the said reverend father guardian of this villa, and thus, withdrawing to it, the said minister and reverend father preacher can from there administer to them the holy sacraments and say mass on feast days, for which I will provide the necessary military escort.

And with regard to the pueblo of Pecos, it is my experience that the said Indians are very loyal, for it is of record and is commonly and widely known throughout all of this kingdom that they have assisted in notifying us of the insurrections of the said natives, and I consider it to be undesirable, apart from not having the soldiers, to provide the said guard of six men requested by the reverend father Fray Juan de Alpuente. To send the said guard would lead the said Indians to believe that we do not place trust in their proven loyalty, and as for my part, I believe that it is better that they not have a minister if the said reverend father *definidor* does not wish to go there to administer to them than that the bad consequences follow from their presuming that we do not have the said confidence in them. For this reason I reply that I be supported in my view that it should be considered, and so on my part I urge the said reverend father *definidor* Fray Juan de Alpuente that His Reverence acknowledge the kindness with which they treated his predecessor, the father secretary and *definidor* Fray Diego Zeinos, who, while examining a harquebus, which he was sure he had not loaded but was loaded by another's hand, had the misfortune of discharging it and inadvertently killing an Indian. And when the said religious withdrew to this villa to report the incident to his prelate, all of the pueblo sought his return with expressions of tenderness and with such determination that three months after the said misfortune (although in suspense) they welcomed and assisted him as their minister, and when they learned that he had been ordered to return to Mexico, they asked me, said governor and captain general, to request his very reverend father custodian to return him to them, as I did, going in person with the said Indians, from which the extent of their loyalty can be deduced and seen, for the fact of the said death could have led them, as barbarous people, to carry out some disrespectful act against the said reverend father, and not only did they not do so, but they grieved over the death for the sorrow it caused to the said religious. And thus can be seen, for the said reasons and experience, how we can live and have lived with them. The need for protection can only be justified by the said reverend father because of the frontier location, but not because of the said Indians.

And passing on to the distant Picurís and Taos nations, as their reverend father ministers indicate, since they are on the frontier of the Utes and Apaches, and although they recognize that they must be suspicious of and can have little confidence in the said natives there, I do not have the forces to provide all that they ask for. But I will designate four men for each of them so that the said Indians may not distrust me and the Spaniards; although they may not be sufficient, if on my part I promise to provide them, and if the said reverend fathers are prepared to return there at the time when they are requested, I will provide them.

And passing on to the nation of Jémez, in the same manner I will provide four men, both for the reverend father Fray Francisco de Jesús and for the reverend father Miguel Trizio. And because the Keres are friends, and since they fought on our side in the war of the conquest of this kingdom, there is no reason, because of our experiences with them, to provide said guard, apart from the fact that I do not have it to provide. As for the reverend father Fray Pedro Matha, minister of the pueblo of Zia, he can avail himself of the guard of the said eight men and the *alcalde mayor* of Jémez, since the first pueblo of San Juan is a distance of two leagues from there and that of San Diego del Monte a distance of four, and also his mission is protected by the Keres Indians, who are among the most highly esteemed in this kingdom in valor, skill, arms, and horsemanship.

Thus, in the interim, until a decision is made by His Most Excellent Lordship the viceroy of the entire kingdom of New Spain after he has seen the testimony of the two petitions, including the one cited in the one of the seventh of March of this year, sixteen hundred ninety-six, I will assist and maintain, with arms and horses, at my expense, the said twenty-four men so that the said reverend father missionaries may continue in the said missions in the manner as indicated above and on the presumption that on my part I will be vigilant and will reconnoiter and scout the area, either in person, if our Lord gives me the health and strength to do so, or by a person selected by me to go in my place. In this way the said Indians will be moved to realize that there is apprehension and distrust of them on my part when the said reverend father missionaries are provided with guards, if they are willing to accept them and receive them in the said manner. And I will expect that Your Very Reverence will cooperate with me in every way, encouraging the said missionary ministers of said pueblos, as chaplains of His Majesty the king, our lord, may God keep him, who will consider himself well served by their assistance and the assistance they have had from the said Indians, who have built their churches, chapels, and convents and have cultivated their cornfields and provided other services even without armed guards for a year and six months of possession. It would appear that with the said guard they can be even safer, and they can

confide in my word that I will assist them by the said reconnoitering and visits
to their pueblos in the interim until, as I repeat, the most excellent lord viceroy of all the kingdom of New Spain shall determine and provide the help of
the people, to the number of five hundred families, which I have requested of
him and which has not yet been agreed upon, along with the representation
that I will make to his greatness with regard to the soldiers who died in the
epidemic of the past year as well as those who died in the reconquest.

And that this said reply be of record both for the said most excellent lord
viceroy and for the aforsaid very reverend father preacher Fray Francisco de
Vargas, custodian and ecclesiastical judge, *in capite,* of this holy custody, I
signed this in this said Villa of Santa Fe along with my secretary of government
and war, whom I ordered to provide the testimony, in accord with both the
said petition and my reply, copied to the letter, made by me, said governor and
captain general. Done on said day, *ut supra.*

Don Diego de Vargas Zapata Luján Ponce de León. Before me, Domingo de
la Barreda, secretary of government and war.

This copy is in accord with the original, from which I, Domingo de la
Barreda, secretary of government and war, by order of the lord governor and
captain general Don Diego de Vargas Zapata Luján Ponce de León, the new
restorer, conqueror at his own expense, reconqueror, and settler of this kingdom of New Mexico and castellan of its frontiers, forces, and presidios for His
Majesty, drew the information and copied it to the letter. And it goes forth
certain and true on seven pages of ordinary white paper, because sealed sheets
are not available in these parts, and those present to see it corrected and agreed
upon were Captain Don Antonio Valverde and the *alférez* Martín de Urioste on
March fifteen of the year sixteen hundred ninety-six. In testimony of the truth,
I sign with my customary rubric.

> Domingo de la Barreda, secretary of
> government and war.

49. *CARTA PATENTE* OF FRAY FRANCISCO DE VARGAS TO ALL THE MISSIONARIES, SANTA FE, MARCH 16, 1696[1]

REVEREND fathers and ministers of this our holy custody. This is to inform
you, reverend fathers, that on the thirteenth day of the present month I presented to the said governor and captain general of this kingdom the petition of
all of you reverend fathers with regard to the soldiers that each of Your Rever-

1. BNM, leg. 4, docs. 15, 24.

ences needed for your protection, in accordance with the letters from each of you. And although the reply from the said lord governor in his letter is very diffuse, in substance that which His Lordship replies, and indicates that he will provide, is to say:

That of the one hundred soldiers that he has in this presidio, they are distributed in squads to guard the horse herds, the transportation of the food supplies and cattle from the pueblo of El Paso, and those who are posted as guards, and broken down numerically, he has only four positions left, and these are for the officers of the presidio, including his lieutenant general. But His Lordship promises in his letter to provide (although at his own expense) the assignment of soldiers to guard the missions so that the father ministers may be able to continue to administer the holy sacraments, and his promise is as follows: [Here follows a copy in quotes of relevant portions of the *auto* of Governor Vargas of March 15, 1696, doc. 48 above.]

And from all that which is referred to by His Lordship, each of you, reverend fathers, will examine closely what can be done, but I do warn you (may you fathers and religious pardon the expression) that you have asked for the number of soldiers that each of you needed for your protection in the missions, and that if the second petition is not as urgent and immediate as was requested at the beginning, and if some of Your Reverences decide to return alone to your missions or with less than the number of soldiers previously requested, we will be placed in the position that it could be presumed of the father ministers of this holy custody that their representations and the fears that they had of the Indians were unfounded and were only unnecessary cause for the agitation of the residents of this kingdom. And therefore, my fathers and brothers, Your Reverences should premeditate this point and recognize wisely that in the present case it is my obligation (unworthy as I am as the prelate of this holy custody) not to force any of Your Reverences to go to your missions without the safety of your lives or to prevent any one of you who has the ardor to go alone to do so. For I judge as very holy the zeal of each of you fathers and religious. Therefore, anyone who does not go will not be deemed cowardly, especially since it is realized what little fruit can be obtained from the souls of these apostates of our holy religion; and if a minister should offer his life of his own accord, they will gloat over his sacerdotal blood, and it would be another of the many sins and sacrileges which they have committed and will prepare them for the next occasion for them to relapse into vice, causing them to fall into greater sins, for which the greatest punishment of condemnation will be brought upon them. This, reverend fathers, you know better than I, as well as that if one or some of you reverend fathers, with divine inspiration, should be embued with the spirit and fervor to be willing to accept death for preaching the gospel of our holy religion, offering for God our Lord to suffer and sacrifice your lives, in doing so you will be assured the everlasting good fortune and crown of our holy religion. And I call to your attention, reverend fathers, that His Lordship also promised to make visits to inspect conditions in the pueblos, in person or by a person of his choosing. Thus, my reverend fathers and brothers, may you, reverend fathers, with the most judicious resolution, zeal, and spirit, do what God our Lord inspires in you.

I request of you, reverend fathers, that each of you place at the foot of this our *carta patente* your final resolve, signing it with your name as was done with regard to the preceding one, so that with said decisions I may again appeal to the lord governor and may thereby present our final decision. And so that this our *carta patente* may come to the attention of all, all of the religious of the Jémez and Keres will gather in the town of Bernalillo, where it will be read to them so that each one may place, by his own hand, the opinion that he considers to be advisable. The same will be done with those who this day are in this Villa of Santa Fe, to which they have withdrawn. And finally, our *carta patente* will be sent to the Villa Nueva of Santa Cruz, and all of the religious gathered there in the same manner will give their opinions. And when all have placed their opinions at the foot of the letter, they will be transmitted to me by a trustworthy person so that we may examine closely the statements of each of the father ministers and their obedience.

May the divine majesty of God our Lord keep you, reverend fathers, many years, and may His Divine Majesty grant you patience and tolerance so that you may be able to cultivate the vineyard of the Lord.

From this Villa of Santa Fe, March 16, the year 1696, I remain, reverend fathers, your brother and servant, who loves you in the Lord and kisses Your Reverences' hands.

Fray Francisco de Vargas, custodian

50. *CARTA PATENTE* OF FRAY FRANCISCO DE VARGAS TO THE MISSIONARIES OF THE JÉMEZ AND KERES PUEBLOS, SANTA FE, MARCH 16, 1696[1]

REVEREND fathers and ministers of this holy custody.

My reverend fathers and brothers:
I inform you, reverend fathers, that on the thirteenth of the present month

1. BNM, leg. 4, docs. 15, 24.

and year I presented to the lord governor and captain general of this kingdom the request from all of you reverend fathers regarding your needs as set forth in each of your letters. And although the reply from the lord governor in his letter is very diffuse, in substance what His Lordship indicates that he can provide is to say that of the one hundred soldiers that he has in this presidio, they are distributed in squads for the protection of the horse herds, the conveyance of food supplies and livestock from the pueblo of El Paso, and those who constitute his personal guard, and that breaking down the entire number, only four positions remain, and these are those of the officers of the presidio, which include his lieutenant general. But His Lordship promises in his letter to provide (although at his own personal cost) the support of soldiers to protect the missions so that they will not be without missionary fathers for the administration of the holy sacraments, and the promise is as follows:

"And passing on to the missions of Jémez, in the same manner I will provide four men, both for the reverend father Fray Francisco de Jesús and for the reverend father Fray Miguel Trizio. And because the Keres are friends, and since they fought on our side in the war of the conquest of this kingdom, there is no reason, because of our experiences with them, to provide the said guard, apart from the fact that I do not have it to provide. As for the reverend father Fray Pedro Matha, minister of the pueblo of Zia, he can avail himself of the said eight men and the *alcalde mayor* of Jémez, since the pueblo of San Juan is a distance of two leagues from there and that of San Diego del Monte a distance of four; and also his mission is protected by the Keres Indians, who are among the most highly esteemed in this kingdom in valor, skill, arms, and horsemanship, and thus in the interim. . . ."

All of the above refers to the missions of the Keres and Jémez, excepting the Tewas, Tanos, Picurís, and Taos, which, so as not to delay matters, I will not discuss here. And of all that which is referred to by His Lordship, each one of you reverend fathers will recognize what could be done, but I only wish to warn you (with your pardon, reverend fathers) that each of you has requested the soldiers that you needed for your protection in your missions, and if the second request is not of the urgency and immediacy indicated at the beginning, and if some of Your Reverences should decide to go to your missions alone or without the number of soldiers requested earlier, we will be placed in the position that it can be presumed of the father ministers of this holy custody that their representations, and the fears that they had of the Indians, were not true and were only unnecessary cause for restiveness and worry on the part of the residents of this kingdom.

And so, my fathers and brothers, Your Reverences should meditate carefully on this point, recognizing the wisdom that is required in this case, for I (unworthy prelate of this holy custody as I am), cannot force any of you, reverend fathers, to go to your missions without protection for your lives, nor can I prevent any one of you who has the spirit to go alone from doing so, for I judge the zeal of each one of Your Reverences as very holy; nor will it be considered cowardly if anyone does not wish to go, especially since it is realized, as regards these apostates of our holy faith, that little fruit can be obtained from their souls by a minister offering up his life; rather, they would gloat over his sacerdotal blood, and it would be another of the many sins and sacrileges that they have committed, and it would prepare them for the next occasion to do the same again, causing them to commit greater sins, for which they will condemn themselves to the greatest punishment. This, reverend fathers, you know better than I, as well as that if one or some of you reverend fathers should be divinely inspired with the spirit and fervor to accept death in preaching the gospel of our holy faith and law, offering for God our Lord to suffer and sacrifice your lives, in doing so you will be assured the eternal good fortune and crown of our holy religion. And, therefore, my reverend fathers and brothers, may Your Reverences, calling upon your best judgment, do as God may inspire you to do.

And I request of Your Reverences that each of you place at the foot of this our *carta patente* your final resolution, signing with your name as was done with regard to the previous one so that with these said opinions I may again return to the lord governor with our final decision. And so that our *carta patente* may come to the attention of all of you, all of the religious among the Jémez and Keres will gather in the settlement of Bernalillo, where it will be read so that each one may write, by his own hand, the opinion that he deems appropriate. And when all of this is done, this, our *carta patente,* will be returned to this Villa of Santa Fe by a reliable person and presented to me in person so that we may examine the reports of each of the father ministers and their obedience.

May the Divine Majesty of God our Lord watch over you, reverend fathers, many years, and may His Divine Majesty bestow patience and tolerance so that you may be able to cultivate the vineyard of the Lord.

From this Villa of Santa Fe, March 16, the year 1696. And I advise Your Reverences that, likewise, His Lordship promises to make inspection visits on horseback throughout the pueblos, either in person or by persons selected by him.

From your servant, very reverend fathers and brothers, who loves you in the Lord and kisses the hands of Your Reverences.

Fray Francisco de Vargas, custodian

51. LETTER OF FRAY JUAN DE ZAVALETA, SANTA FE, MARCH 16, 1696[1]

OUR very reverend father custodian. In obedience to what Your Very Reverence has ordered, I reply and state that since I am not in good health, which is needed in such a cold place as is the region of the Taos, and also since His Lordship is unable to provide the guard that is needed on such a frontier, for His Lordship promises only four soldiers, I state that I am not disposed to go to serve there. And that it be of record, I signed in this Villa of Santa Fe on the sixteenth of March, the year 1696.

Fray Juan de Zavaleta

52. LETTER OF FRAY DIEGO DE CHAVARRÍA, SANTA FE, MARCH 16, 1696[1]

IN compliance with that which has been stated and proposed by Your Most Reverend Paternity in this your just *patente,* I reply and state (because my conscience dictates) that if I were to return to the mission of Taos, where Your Most Reverend Paternity has assigned me to reside, and should the said Indians carry out what it is presumed that they intend to do, with the advance warnings that are so evident since they are brought to our attention daily, concerning the general revolt of all of the natives of this kingdom and the treacherous plan to kill me, and recalling the treacherous manner in which in the year 'eighty they killed the religious who ministered in this holy custody for the welfare of souls, I believe that they will only be made more obdurate (if they carry it out), and I believe that no fruit whatsoever will be gained from the sacrilege that they can commit. And I, in my opinion, am obligated to prevent them from such a sacrilege, and of two dangers I know that I must choose the least, knowing that they will kill me, *mere in odiu fidei,* and with the grace of our Lord I would be prepared to return to the said pueblo. This is the way I see all of this, since the lord governor does not wish to grant or provide the guard which has appeared to me to be necessary for the protection of all that which I have mentioned. This is my reply, and I signed in this convent of Santa Fe on the sixteenth of March, the year 'ninety-six.

Fray Diego de Chavarría

1. BNM, leg. 4, docs. 15, 24.
1. BNM, leg. 4, docs. 15, 24.

53. LETTER OF FRAY BLAS NAVARRO, SANTA FE,
MARCH 16, 1696[1]

IN order not to fail in my obedience to our very reverend father custodian, in whose [*carta patente*] we are informed that it is not possible to obtain the guard which we requested of the lord governor for the protection of the holy religion and of our lives, I reply that in conscience I cannot go, for besides what I answered previously, I have seen that they are enemies of our holy religion, for one day they stoned the saint whose image is on the altar, as all can see, because they broke one side of it. And if they do this to the saints, they will be more likely to do it to me. And in testimony of the truth, I signed in this Villa of Santa Fe on March sixteenth, the year 'ninety-six.

Fray Blas Navarro

54. LETTER OF FRAY JOSÉ DIEZ, SANTA FE, March 16, 1696[1]

IN obedience to Your Very Reverend Paternity, I state that as for my withdrawing to the Villa of Santa Fe I have already done so because the sending of the guard was being delayed and the voices of rebellion are growing louder, and today is the day of the full moon, when they say that they will carry out the revolt (but there is no definite moon for them, because they have intended to do so three times, from last August to now). To administer the pueblos of Tesuque and Cuyamungué from this said villa with the escort that His Lordship promises, as though it were a *visita*, I cannot decide on my own, for I am sworn to obedience and will do only as Your Very Reverend Paternity so orders of me, and you have placed me as minister president of Tesuque and its *visita*. I cannot go to administer to them and say mass for them with the escort because all of the road for three leagues is through forests and canyons, where many [Spaniards] were killed by Apaches at Alto de Cuma before the revolt of the year 'eighty, and today they will be more ready to do the same, with the revolt that is certain, as many Indians have stated. Besides, those who cooperate [at these pueblos] are excommunicated and I cannot celebrate mass before any of them because I do not know which ones are in this state, nor can I communicate with them because I know that some of them are impenitent, and if they go on this way I cannot absolve them.

And with regard to His Lordship's position that he does not have sufficient people to provide the guard of twelve men that I request, and having heard

1. BNM, leg. 4, docs. 15, 24.
1. BNM, leg. 4, docs. 15, 24.

that the governor of my mission is on the side of the Spaniards, and despite the fact that I have heard the Tanos of San Cristóbal threaten to kill him because he does not support their evil intentions, and I being in the said pueblo defenseless, and there being many there who are on the side of the said Tanos, I request one-half of the ten guards that I requested in reply to the *carta patente,* with which I will be satisfied for the protection of the divine worship and of my person. This on the supposition that those of my pueblo who have publicly proclaimed their intention of participating in the revolt repent and ask for absolution, and after this has been given to them, I will minister to them, and likewise on the supposition that I am assured of the permanence of Christianity in this kingdom, both on the part of the Spaniards, who are without food, as well as on the part of the Indians. If this is not to be the case, the children cannot be baptized, for it is less undesirable that they remain pagans rather than apostates of our holy religion. In conscience, I can do no less than this.

This is my reply in this Villa of Santa Fe on the sixteenth day of March, the year sixteen hundred ninety-six.

Fray José Diez

55. LETTER OF FRAY JUAN ALPUENTE, SANTA FE, MARCH 16, 1696[1]

OUR very reverend father custodian. Since I have requested of the lord governor six gentlemen soldiers for the protection of the sacred vessels and of my person for the mission and the administration of the pueblo of Pecos, and since His Lordship has replied that he cannot provide me with the said guard, I state and reply, on the basis of many reasons that I have, that in conscience I cannot serve there without the said guard. And that it be of record, I signed in this Villa of Santa Fe, March sixteenth, the year sixteen hundred ninety-six.

Fray Juan Alpuente

56. LETTER OF FRAY ANTONIO CARBONEL [SANTA CRUZ], MARCH 21, 1696[1]

OUR very reverend father custodian. In obedience to the orders of Your Very Reverend Paternity, I state the same as what was contained in the previous petition presented to the lord governor, that, assuming the general revolt, the

1. BNM, leg. 4, docs. 15, 24.
1. BNM, leg. 4, docs. 15, 24.

guard that I need at this mission of Nambé for the protection of my person, the ornaments, and the sacred vessels is the same as that which would be needed in the other neighboring missions so that they might be given succor. And if the said missions are left without guards, and assuming that the revolt will take place, I state that the ministers should withdraw to a place where they will not perish, more from hunger and need than from the Indians. This is my opinion. And also, I would not be prepared to feed the soldiers who would come to inspect, because on my part I do not have it to provide even for myself. And in testimony of the truth I signed this on the twenty-first day of the month of March, the year sixteen hundred ninety-six.

Fray Antonio Carbonel

57. LETTER OF FRAY MIGUEL TRIZIO, BERNALILLO, MARCH 18, 1696[1]

REVEREND father custodian. In obedience to the order of Your Reverence I state that the order of the lord governor giving us four soldiers is good to escort a minister from one pueblo to another on a particular day, but for safety against an uprising as is feared, not even twelve or fourteen are sufficient. If the lord governor places fifty soldiers for the protection of the three father ministers of Zia and Jémez, we will be very pleased to serve there. Otherwise we would be courting danger or death without hope of winning souls and with much damage to our bodies. This is my opinion, all depending on what Your Reverence should order us to do. Bernalillo, the eighteenth of March of the year sixteen hundred ninety-six.

Fray Miguel de Trizio

58. LETTER OF FRAY ALFONSO JIMÉNEZ DE CISNEROS, BERNALILLO, MARCH 18, 1696[1]

OUR very reverend father custodian. I have seen and read this *carta patente,* with all of its points and particulars, and I reply that in the state of affairs in which things are found at this time, a large armed guard is necessary for the protection of the holy vessels and the other articles pertaining to the divine worship, and therefore if His Lordship is to provide protection for what is re-

1. BNM, leg. 4, docs. 15, 24.
1. BNM, leg. 4, docs. 15, 24.

ferred to above, I state that twenty or twenty-four are necessary, and I still am dubious, because the treachery of these pagans can be such that even with the said, nothing can be remedied, and we will see the sacred vessels profaned by such rabble because their traitorous acts are such that nothing else can be expected of them, for of those who carried out the last revolt which took place no other outcome can be expected. Therefore, if His Lordship is to station the necessary guard as I have indicated, the twenty-four soldiers, it is not because I am afraid, for I am awaiting death at all times and wish only to die as a Catholic and for the religion of our Lord Jesus Christ as an old Castilian.

This is my opinion, but above all I will act only as you wish, although I have had reports from trustworthy witnesses that an Indian of this my mission plans to drink from the holy chalice. Having heard this from Spaniards who stated that an Indian of this pueblo of Cochití has said this, I do not know what we are waiting for. Finally, if I, who am his minister, should die only to permit this dog to commit this perfidy, I state that it is for this reason that I request the soldiers referred to. This is what I state at this time. May our Lord keep Your Very Reverence the many years that my affection wishes for you. Bernalillo, March eighteen of the year 'ninety-six. Your humble servant who kisses Your Most Reverend Paternity's hand.

Fray Alfonso Jiménez de Cisneros

59. LETTER OF FRAY PEDRO DE MATHA, BERNALILLO, MARCH 19, 1696[1]

I reply, most reverend father, as I replied to your last *patente,* that for the protection of the holy vessels and of my life, six or eight [soldiers] paid by His Majesty are not sufficient, and that I have reasons for fearing my parishioners, for even if I should see them put to death their children and brothers in defense of the Christian religion, I would say that it was to palliate themselves for their determined treachery against the Christian religion. Your Reverence will do what is proper, and may the heavens watch over you many years. Bernalillo, March 19, the year 1696.

Your Very Reverend Paternity's humble servant, who kisses your hand.

Fray Pedro de Matha

1. BNM, leg. 4, docs. 15, 24.

60. LETTER OF FRAY FRANCISCO DE JESÚS MARÍA CASAÑAS [BERNALILLO, CA. MARCH 19, 1696][1]

OUR father custodian, I have seen and obey the *patente* of Your Most Reverend Paternity, and I respond to the aforementioned points that with regard to the recent occurrences relating to the statements that I have heard from some of the Indians, I stated my opinion clearly to His Lordship at San Juan de los Jémez, namely, that for my complete safety the entire presidio would be required. To this His Lordship responded by declaring and making clear to me that "he did not have that much bread for that big a wedding,"[2] and he designated four gentlemen soldiers, for "he who does not have bread should be satisfied with tortillas."[3] This is of the past; at present His Lordship has given other orders to the said soldiers for certain reasons resulting from the state of insurrection in the kingdom, and it is still a burning issue, and from what the wind brings it appears to be burning even hotter. And so for the safety of my person I have no need for a guard, for if what is feared occurs, much strength is needed, and not having it, I will endeavor to seek safety. To place myself at the mouth of the wolf, so that he may swallow me and drink my blood, my mother did not bear me to be another minister (although unworthy) for that purpose. For I did not come to seek death but rather the lives of these miserable ones. And if His Divine Majesty wishes to grant me the prize, he will do so even if it is in the public square of Mexico. Therefore, if His Lordship wishes to provide for my protection so that I may administer the holy sacraments to them, His Lordship will do so as he sees fit, and when he finds a way and manner for it, I will go. As I have indicated, if I am called to administer the holy sacraments, I will go, recognizing that morally I am able to go and that their snares are easy to comprehend. This is my opinion, and as a chaplain of His Majesty I respond to what His Lordship, as governor and captain general, desires.

Fray Francisco de Jesús

61. LETTER OF FRAY JOSÉ ARBIZU, SANTA CRUZ, MARCH 17, 1696[1]

VERY reverend father custodian. I obey, answering what Your Very Reverend Paternity orders of me, and state that His Lordship the lord governor and captain general of this kingdom was notified on the tenth of March of this year of

1. BNM, leg. 4, docs. 15, 24.
2. No tenía tanta pan por tanta boda.
3. Quien no tiene pan se contenta con tortillas.
1. BNM, leg. 4, docs. 15, 24.

the state of affairs in the mission of the pueblo of San Cristóbal (as stated by me in my reply to the *carta patente* of Your Most Reverend Paternity), that the Indians of the said pueblo and mission of San Cristóbal have already openly indicated their intentions and in effect would have killed me and profaned the holy vessels had not an Indian interpreter advised me to leave, which I did at nine o'clock Sunday night, on foot, with the church ornaments and the sacred vessels that I was able to take with me and nothing else. Otherwise, today I would be giving my account to His Divine Majesty.

The revolt of the said Indians is real and true, as His Lordship and all the kingdom are aware (although little so, it would appear), having seen, with their own eyes, said pueblo desolated, with said Indians in the mountains, summoned to come down not one or three times but many times, and at this moment they are very rebellious. I state that since His Lordship has not promised, as he does not do so now, any guard for the said pueblo of San Cristóbal, with so much evidence under no circumstances can I return to the said pueblo, even though some of the Indians should descend from the mountains, because without the said guard that I requested (although I did not designate a specific number) I believe that since I have removed the sacred vessels (as stated), they would return to profane those that remain there and would spill my innocent blood without my attaining any benefit whatever.

And so I repeat that the Villa of Santa Cruz lies one league from the said pueblo of San Cristóbal and that its residents, like me, are without arms and virtually naked, and in no way can they protect me or themselves, so the promise of His Lordship is of no use to me, which leads me to say and to repeat that in conscience I cannot return to administer the holy sacraments to openly declared apostates without the guard that is needed for a pueblo of five hundred persons. This is my opinion; so be it. Done in this Villa of Santa Cruz on March 17, the year 1696.

Fray José Arbizu

62. LETTER OF FRAY JOSÉ GARCÍA MARÍN, SANTA CRUZ, MARCH 18, 1696[1]

OUR very reverend father custodian. I reply, obeying the order of Your Very Reverend Paternity, and state that at present I find myself in such poor health that I am unable to administer, even should I be provided the guard that I have requested. But if our Lord grants me sufficient health to administer, I state that if I should recognize that this kingdom is finally quiet and peaceful, I will

---

1. BNM, leg. 4, docs. 15, 24.

go to administer without any guard whatsoever, as I have done until I observed the restlessness and evil intentions of the Indians. But in the absence of such peace and quiet I state that under no circumstances will I go, and there are very many reasons why it is not possible licitly for me to administer to apostates openly declared against our holy religion. This is my opinion. In this Villa of Santa Cruz, the eighteenth of March of the year 'ninety-six.

Fray José García

63. LETTER OF FRAY FRANCISCO CORBERA, SANTA CRUZ, MARCH 18, 1696[1]

OUR very reverend father custodian. In obedience to what you have ordered, reverend father, I state that, as in my previously stated opinion, I do not ask for a specified number of armed guards. Now I am more specific, and I say that the four men that His Lordship promises me are too many and too few. Too many because if this kingdom were at peace, they would be too many; too few because this not being the case, they do not provide sufficient armed protection. And the reason is clear because in the year 'eighty there were more than four armed guards in some of the pueblos, and both the guards and the minister perished. Hence, with the land not at peace (as it is not), four men are not sufficient guard, and therefore the guard that I requested then, and which I again request now, is that I be assured that the Indians are at peace and that this peace be proclaimed by common voice and not by an individual only, and then I will go to the mission which holy obligation has assigned to me without any guard. Without said security I will not go unless Your Reverence orders me to do so, in which case I will obey. This is my opinion, and that it be of record I signed on March eighteen of the year 'ninety-six.

Fray Francisco Corbera

64. LETTER OF FRAY GERÓNIMO PRIETO [SANTA CRUZ, CA. MARCH 18, 1696][1]

OUR reverend father custodian. As sworn to obedience, I reply and state that I will go to the mission of San Juan of the Tewas, where I am assigned as minister, when the kingdom is at peace, for otherwise I feel an internal repugnance that I cannot easily overcome, and it is based on the fact that this kingdom is

---

1. BNM, leg. 4, docs. 15, 24.
1. BNM, leg. 4, docs. 15, 24.

rent by many disturbances by many evil persons who go about agitating, and it has been my opinion that this is very clear. And under these circumstances the lord governor assigns to me a guard of four men, and these to escort me to and from the pueblo of Santa Clara, from which I infer that it is not really a guard of four, but rather none at all, seriously considered, because I would remain alone in the pueblo. But leaving this aside, I only state that if the enemies whom we fear so justifiably were strangers, and not local residents, there might be some consolation, even though it might be instantaneous, but being as they are from these parts or local residents, all is lost. Therefore, I have come to the conclusion, without failing to do what I can, that I cannot go to assist in serving at the said mission even with the four men. This is my opinion and what I say. So be it.

Fray Gerónimo Prieto

65. DECISION OF THE *DEFINITORIO,* SANTA FE, MARCH 22, 1696[1]

IN the Villa of Santa Fe, in the convent and cell of the reverend father guardian, the reverend father Fray Francisco de Vargas, custodian of this holy custody, along with the venerable and reverend *definitorio,* on the twenty-second of March of the year 'ninety-six, the most reverend father presented the said statements and letters sent by each of the religious missionaries in reply to the last *carta patente,* in which the said father missionaries were notified of the guards that the lord governor and captain general of this kingdom promised and which were so limited, since it was recognized that the entire kingdom was in rebellion, for its natives carry out and have carried out with treacherous cunning many acts which, thanks to God in the highest, have been uncovered by those of their own nation and many manevolent deeds that the ministers have experienced through incidents that can not and should not be concealed. They have scoffed at and scorned the divine gospel of our true God and the images of the saints. And realizing this obstinacy, the said father ministers have withdrawn to the Spanish settlements of this kingdom for the safety of their lives.

And the situation having been presented to the reverend *definitorio* to determine what should be done with the said father missionaries who have withdrawn to the Spanish settlements until it is seen, if it is God's will, that the fire which the common enemy has placed in the hearts of the apostates of our holy faith is quenched so that they will not take possession of the sacred vessels, articles of divine worship, cattle, records of the religious, and other things

1. BNM, leg. 4, docs. 15, 24.

connected with the missions, it was decided to make a petition to the lord
governor requesting him to provide the necessary armed guards that His Lordship would recognize as sufficient so that each minister might remove from his
mission what is referred to above and that all of the contents might be placed in
the Villa of Santa Cruz, in this one of Santa Fe, and in the settlement of Bernalillo in accordance with the proximity of said missions. Also, it was determined that the religious gathered in the said places should not live in the private houses of the residents nor eat outside of their community in said places
and should observe, follow, and fulfill the precept of their divine office by gathering in the churches or chapels of said localities at the hours determined and
designated by the reverend father guardian, helping in the confessions and in
the administration of the holy sacraments, each religious on his own initiative,
and the only ones who will be exempted from all of these duties will be the
religious or those religious who are seriously ill, and these sick ones will be
permitted to eat at the house of the lord governor or be lodged in homes where
they can live comfortably and conveniently during their recovery. All of which
was determined by the reverend and venerable *definitorio,* who signed this and
signed jointly with their most reverend father, said day, month, and year. *Ut
supra.*

Fray Francisco de Vargas, custodian. Fray Juan de Zavaleta, *definidor.* Fray
Antonio de Azevedo, *definidor.* Fray Juan Alpuente, *definidor.* Fray Antonio de
Carbonel, *definidor* and secretary of the *definitorio.*

66. PETITION OF FRAY FRANCISCO DE VARGAS AND THE *DEFINITORIO* TO GOVERNOR VARGAS, SANTA FE, MARCH 22, 1696[1]

LORD governor and captain general. Fray Francisco de Vargas, preacher,
custodian, and ecclesiastical judge of this kingdom and province of New Mexico, by apostolic authority. A joint meeting was held with the reverend and
venerable *definitorio* to examine closely the letters of all of the reverend father
minister missionaries of this holy custody with their replies as to the number of
guards that Your Lordship promised as the result of the petition that was presented to Your Lordship on the thirteenth of the present month, after which
Your Lordship decided that you would provide the guard that was requested,
adjusting the assignment of the soldiers in the manner in which they are now
organized, to which the father preacher minister missionaries, separately and
in person, reply in substance in the following statements:

1. BNM, leg. 4, docs. 15, 24.

The reverend father *definidor* Fray Juan de Zavaleta, minister of the pueblo of Taos, states that both because he is in ill health and because the four soldiers that Your Lordship promises are insufficient, he is unable to go there to administer. The father preacher Fray Diego de Chavarría, resident of said pueblo of Taos, states that he finds that they are more obstinate, and since the guard is not sufficient, he is not disposed to go there. The father preacher Fray Blas Navarro, minister president of the pueblo of Picurís, states that he is not disposed to go to the said mission, as he has seen the titular saint stoned, and the guard of four soldiers is too little. The father preacher Fray José Diez, minister president of the pueblo of Tesuque, states that it is difficult to go to administer there because it can be reached only through mountain forests and canyons, and some of them are declared apostates; he requests the five soldiers, provided that they [the natives] are absolved and it is assured that they can be baptized without danger of subversion. The reverend father *definidor* Fray Juan de Alpuente, minister president of the pueblo of Pecos, states that he cannot go there without the six guards that he requested.

The father preacher Fray Francisco Corbera, minister president of the pueblo of San Ildefonso, states that the guard he needs is that the guard should be the Indians themselves, safe and at peace by common agreement among them and not based on individual opinion, and that under these conditions he would go to his mission without any armed guard. The reverend father preacher Fray José García, minister and president of the pueblo of Santa Clara, states that if he knew that the kingdom was at peace, he would go to administer without any guard, as up to now, but that not seeing said peace and quiet in no way can he go to administer, for serious reasons that he has for not being able to minister licitly to openly declared apostates of our holy religion. The father preacher Fray José Arbizu, minister of the pueblo of San Cristóbal, states that since Your Lordship does not promise him any guard other than the traffic of the Mexicans with the said pueblo, who find themselves as destitute as His Reverence, he can not under any circumstances go to administer without the guard which he requested, especially since they are declared apostates and since most of them have gone up into the mountains and, having been summoned with the offer of peace, have not wished to come down.

The father preacher Fray Gerónimo Prieto, minister missionary of the pueblo of San Juan, states that he will go to his mission only when the kingdom is at peace and that the four soldiers that Your Lordship designates for him are of no use because he would remain alone when the father of Santa Clara goes to say mass. The reverend father *definidor* Fray Antonio de Carbonel, minister president of the pueblo of Nambé, states that when the other missions are safe, his will also be safe, and that if guards are not provided for the other missions the ministers should go where they will not perish from hunger.

The father preacher Fray Francisco Jesús, minister president of the pueblo of San Diego de los Jémez, states that he told Your Lordship that he would need the entire presidio for his protection and that since Your Lordship replied that this was not possible, he states that he did not come to seek death but rather the spiritual life of these poor souls, and that therefore he will not go, and that in case he should be called to administer, he will go, knowing morally that he can go, and that without guard he will endeavor to protect himself. The father preacher Fray Miguel Trizio, minister president of the pueblo of San Juan de los Jémez, states that neither twelve nor fourteen men are sufficient and that if Your Lordship provides fifty men for Jémez and Zia, he will be pleased to serve there, but that otherwise he would be going at the danger of his life without hope of winning souls. The father preacher Fray Pedro Matha, minister president of the pueblo of Zia, states that for the protection of the holy vessels and of his life not even eight soldiers are enough. The father preacher Fray Alfonso Jiménez de Cisneros, minister president of the pueblo of Cochití, states that for himself he requests nothing but that he knows from trustworthy persons that an Indian of his pueblo states that he will drink from the chalice, and thus, for the protection of the sacred vessels and the divine religion, he requests twenty-four soldiers. The father Fray Domingo de Jesús, resident of the pueblo of Pecos, states that they made fun of him while he was preaching with a holy crucifix in his hands, and that though he placed the vessels in his cell for safekeeping last night, the twenty-first of March, at midnight, the Indians went to his cell and carried them away, along with the keys to the entire convent and church, and that two Indians urged him to flee from the pueblo, begging him not to reveal who they were. And he also states that there is a camp of Faraones in the pueblo and another at the river of the said pueblo of Pecos, which is very near to it, and that a heathen Indian [*infiel*], crying, told him in signs that they wished to behead him.

After all of the above had been examined, registered, and read with the attention required in the present situation, in order to decide on the inconvenient circumstances facing our service to our Lord God, it was decided to represent to Your Lordship, in the name of this holy custody, the damage that is taking place in leaving in the possession of apostates of our holy religion the sacred vessels and images of saints and other articles of divine worship, which we know for certain, from reports, will be profaned and abused by them, this without a doubt. The lives of the ministers have been spared from the hands of the apostates of our holy religion and are safe in part but not entirely so, since most of them are now in Spanish settlements; we say that they are not entirely safe because the Spaniards in the Villa Nueva of Santa Cruz are without necessary arms and horses, for there are very few available, and the forces of the enemies of this kingdom are well equipped, since they have all that is necessary, and besides, the Spaniards are lacking in food supplies.

And so that they [the enemy] may not be given more strength and power, we request that Your Lordship order the necessary guards to be sent with the means to remove from the missions everything pertaining to divine worship, and the cattle and sheep that at the cost of this holy custody were placed in the missions for their improvement, under the supposition that the Indians of this kingdom would be at peace. But at present it is obvious that they are in rebellion, for those of the Tanos nation are in the mountains and more intent to make war than peace, and so there is no reason to believe that they would not dare to rebel without the help of other nations. Therefore, we again request Your Lordship to order the removal of the belongings that the religious have at the said missions, the little food that has remained in their possession, and the sheep, so that they may provide them with sustenance, and we beseech Your Lordship, as our brother syndic, to place these in safety where Your Lordship has yours.

This is what relates to the father preachers and ministers, who have withdrawn to this Villa of Santa Fe for the contact that they have there to enable them to be helped. If it is God our Lord's will, the said father preachers will be prompt in continuing the said administration of their pueblos when the Indian parishioners who inhabit them are quieted down and they are given the guards they have requested. For as loyal vassals of His Majesty, the said father preacher ministers will not forsake this kingdom, nor will they leave their missions. But at present this is not possible for the reasons that each one of the said father preachers have given for not being among the said Indians, as can be seen by their statements referred to. And I, unworthy prelate of this holy custody, can not force them nor order them to return alone to administer their missions, nor can I impede from going at the manifest risk of their lives those who are disposed and have reason not to leave their parishioners, for some are more feared than others. What I clearly recognize is that if these said religious are alone, in some pueblos the Indians will have no other object than to make a thousand false calumnies against their ministers, for these parishioners only wish to have and enjoy the liberty that they had for the previous fourteen years, and they do not wish to acquiesce in the efforts of the missionaries to correct their excesses of idolatry and many other evils. Nor do they recognize that the exhortations are for their spiritual good. And since they were reduced by force of arms and not by the word of the gospel, which has not been wanting, and respond more to sternness than to the love of their ministers of the gospel, the ministers do not dare to punish them for evil acts, because they are alone. For they fear only the force and rigor of Spanish arms and their *alcaldes mayores*. But if the said *alcaldes mayores* are not continually assisting in the missions, how can the ministers have recourse? Or the Indians have fear? For many of them live as though they were not Christians and always with hatred toward the father preacher ministers who preach the gospel.

Lord governor and captain general, we request of Your Lordship and beg of you that you see fit to provide what we have requested in our above-mentioned petition, as stated above, and that you also send us a copy of all that which is authorized so that it may be of permanent record. And so I sign, and the reverend father preacher *definidores* of this holy custody also sign, on the twenty-second of March of the year sixteen hundred ninety-six.

Fray Francisco de Vargas, custodian. Fray Antonio de Azevedo, *definidor*. Fray Juan de Alpuente, *definidor*. Fray Juan de Zavaleta, *definidor*. Fray Antonio Carbonel, *definidor* and secretary of the *definitorio*.

Presentation of the petition, Santa Fe, March 22, 1696.

In this Villa of Santa Fe on the twenty-second day of the month of March of sixteen hundred ninety-six, before me, Don Diego de Vargas Zapata Luján Ponce de León, governor and captain general of this said kingdom, the reverend father *definidor* Fray Antonio Carbonel, minister president of the pueblo of Nambé, presented to me the petition in the name of the very reverend father Fray Francisco de Vargas, custodian of this holy custody and ecclesiastical judge *in capite* of this said kingdom, signed today, said day and date, by the very reverend father and the reverend father *definidores* Fray Antonio de Azevedo, Fray Juan de Alpuente, Fray Juan de Zavaleta, and the aforesaid father Fray Antonio Carbonel, *definidor* and secretary of the *definitorio*.

67. *AUTO* OF GOVERNOR VARGAS, SANTA FE, MARCH 22, 1696[1]

AND seen by me, said governor and captain general, it having been presented to me, I reply to the points and statements concerning the guards that are being requested by the reverend father missionaries along with the said reverend *definidores,* each of whom, with respect to the guards I promised, presents his views in his reply. And I, said governor and captain general, recognizing with due attention the gravity of the said petition, can only say that I do not have the means to provide the said soldiers and to again take them with me to each of the missions of the said reverend father *definidores* and minister presidents of the said pueblos referred to in the said petition as I did in most cases at the end of September and in October and November of the year sixteen hun-

1. BNM, leg. 4, docs. 15, 24.

dred ninety-four, which, as will be noted, I left without guards, as they were not requested of me, and they have remained in the said missions; and if now they are fearful because of rumors, reports, and presumptions, it is not possible for me to provide, all at once, assistance that will assure their protection. I can only provide, on my part, that which I can designate to the extent that it can contribute in part to said assistance, which I have reasoned in the following manner:

For the reverend father *definidor* Fray Juan Alpuente, minister president of the pueblo of Pecos, I will provide the said six men for up to three weeks, during which he can be thus protected from the said Indians for the reasons set forth by the religious who is his companion, Father Fray Domingo de Jesús, as well as because of the presence of the camp of pagan Apaches which was found in the immediate neighborhood of said pueblo, and of others in the pueblo, and after the said period of the said three weeks I will withdraw four of the said six men, and the two remaining ones I will leave to guard his person and to accompany him at night when he might be called to administer the holy sacraments.

For the reverend father minister presidents of the pueblos of Santa Clara, San Juan de los Caballeros, and San Cristóbal I do not have guards to give them in accordance with their reply, and I can only conclude that they should withdraw (as they have done), along with the reverend father minister president of San Ildefonso, to the Villa Nueva de Santa Cruz de Españoles Mexicanos, and from there, if they see fit, they can administer the holy sacraments with the eight soldiers which I left allotted under the command of the *alcalde mayor* of the said Villa Nueva, who also serves in that capacity for the said nations of the Tewas and Tanos. And since the said pueblos are in such close proximity, they can bring their food supplies for their sustenance, along with the sheep which they might have, the sacred vessels, religious ornaments, clothing, and their other belongings, to the said Villa Nueva, and the same may be done in the case of Santa Clara, since the river is running high, with the danger of being invaded by the Utes, their enemies. In view of this I notified the Indian leaders [*principales*] who came to see me at the time that I made this decision so that they would not be alarmed if their said reverend father José García Marín should ask them for the said livestock and ask them to help him take away his belongings. And he should tell the said Indians that the reason was because of the said Utes, their enemies, fearing that they might be able to make an invasion, since the river is running high, which is expected to take place at the next full moon.

And the same reason can also be given to assist Father Fray Gerónimo Prieto, minister of the pueblo of San Juan, so that he may tell the said Indians discreetly that on two successive full moons they [the Utes] have carried off horses, that on the first occasion they carried off four horses belonging to the said reverend father, and that with the said experience he does not wish to risk losing his cattle and his other belongings and wishes to remove them to the said Villa Nueva, giving said reasons and others in his discretion to satisfy the spirit of the said Indians so that they may not be suspicious and see evil intent, for their reasoning, although it is that of barbarians, is very subtle, which confuses me, because I do not want them to conclude that I, said governor and captain general, and the Spaniards are acting with evil intent and that they continue to stir up rebellion as a result of this.

And the said minister president reverend father Fray José Arbizu, of the pueblo of San Cristóbal of the Tanos, which includes the people of San Lázaro, can, being in the said Villa Nueva, which is so close to the said pueblo, support himself with his supply of provisions. And I feel that he can not remove his livestock from there, nor anything else, since the said people of San Lázaro have been reduced to the said pueblo with those gathered there with a few others, and this can not be done simply because some of the people that belong to the said San Cristóbal are absent from there—they have been informed that the aforesaid who remained are pardoned, and since they have their planting already at hand, this should move them to return to their said pueblo to adopt a moderate way of living rather than that in rebellion they be led to seek liberty by choosing to live with the Apaches and their Navajo friends; and since the land there is impoverished and without water, they should find it more in their interest to decide to again return submissively to their said pueblo. The resolution of the problem will be left entirely to be determined by the said reverend father Fray José Arbizu.

And with regard to the minister president and reverend father of Picurís, Fray Blas Navarro, I do not have the guards that he proposes. Not because of the reasons which he attests regarding his said Indians, but since it is a frontier of the Apaches and Utes, I will call in the governor and the other Indian leaders of the said pueblo of Picurís to tell them that it is because of the said Utes that the said reverend father does not wish to return, and that is what should be told to the said people of the pueblo, and that his said belongings and what sheep he has should be transferred, for which I will provide the said escort.

Also, with regard to the pueblo of Taos, for the reverend minister Your Very Reverence may select I will provide the *alcalde mayor* with five soldiers to guard the said pueblo, and if he should consider this to be sufficient for the protection of his person, whoever is selected may go, and should so request of the said very reverend father custodian. Otherwise it will be necessary to rely on the governor and other Indian leaders, making use of the said explanation referred to in regard to Picurís, that of the said Utes. In this way the said reverend fathers will be able to remove their livestock and what other possessions they have, which leaves me with considerable qualms about the bad consequences which might follow amid such preventive arrangements and satisfaction of wishes because of the shrewdness and malice of the said Indians, and even though this kingdom finds itself alone, there should not be so much fear of a few people who are glib speakers and who from a single statement may pretend that it is made for reasons other than those intended by us. And so I will provide the pack mules and personnel for the said escort and transportation of the said belongings on the arrival of the mule trains from El Paso del Norte that have been sent to transport the aid in food that can be carried for part of the residents of this said kingdom.

And the said father of San Ildefonso, Fray Francisco Corbera, may, from the said Villa Nueva, if he so wishes, assist his said Indians and enjoy the presence of the soldiers who are stationed at the said Villa Nueva. And the one at Nambé, the said reverend father *definidor* Fray Antonio Carbonel, since his mission is located between the two villas, with the continuous entry and departure of the respective residents in their communication with each other, as has been seen and recognized with regard to their said Indians, can be safe and can remain at his said mission, if he so wishes, recognizing this reason, for otherwise it would only arouse suspicion on all sides.

And likewise, the reverend father preacher Fray José Diez, of the pueblo of Tesuque, if he so wishes, and with even more justifiable reason, finding himself at a distance of three short leagues from this Villa of Santa Fe and on the route to the said pueblos, can do without the said guard that he requests and which would not be denied to him if I had it. And so, acknowledging this reason given, he should consider himself safe, because he will be protected by my said measures from the suspicion of the said Indians and their desire to rise in rebellion. On my part I am not telling the very reverend father to remain at his said mission but that I leave it to the fervor of his zeal to serve there.

And passing on to the minister president of the pueblo of the Keres of Cochití, Fray Alfonso Jiménez de Cisneros, who asks for twenty-four men, I state, of course, that I do not have them to provide, and therefore it would be impossible to protect his livestock and belongings. The only thing that can be done is to pretend that he is withdrawing with his possessions because of orders from you, the very reverend prelate and friar custodian, and for him to go to the mission of the pueblo of Santo Domingo, which he is assisting, since it does not have a minister. And thus, since I only have the means to remove the said cattle and belongings, at the same time the said reverend father will not undergo the risk that he attests of the intention which he has been told, that they will drink from the chalice and that the said Indians as well as many of their people are so bellicose, since they were conquered by fire and blood. Since they are now quiet, moving the said cattle and belongings without the said reason, which is so honest, would only stir them up. Thus, when the said minister president goes down to the said pueblo of Santo Domingo to administer to its natives, he can go from the said pueblo of Santo Domingo to that of Cochití, where he now is assigned. In this manner the said reason for this move will pass unnoticed by the said Indians until the aforesaid father can live in safety with the said Indians, which I have seen can be expected of them, as it would appear from their outward actions.

And as for the reverend fathers of the pueblos of San Juan of the Jémez, Fray Miguel Trizio, and San Diego of the Mesa del Monte, Fray Francisco de Jesús, with the four men that I have offered to provide to each of them, they can be assured of their protection by having the said father [Fray Francisco de Jesús] move to the pueblo of San Juan, and with the said people united there, in the company of the *alcalde mayor* he can go from the said pueblo to administer the holy sacraments, as it is one long league away, and said father Fray Miguel Trizio of the said pueblo of San Juan can in this manner also be protected by the said guards, united in the said pueblo of San Juan, the aforesaid father Fray Francisco de Jesús being there. And in this manner the livestock that they may have can be honestly moved there, and they can avail themselves of this source of food for their sustenance.

The reverend father Fray Pedro Matha, of the pueblo of Zia, being so close to the said pueblo of San Juan, with its said guard of soldiers with their *alcalde mayor,* can live very safely with the Keres natives, for they are our friends, as are those of Santa Ana, and in this manner the said section will find itself protected by the said guards so that its said ministers and reverend father missionaries may be able to serve in their said missions without causing the said Indians to be disturbed by their absence and the moving of their said livestock as well as their belongings by reason of their leaving or to infer that our peace is perfidious and feigned, causing the chiefs who are guilty of past crimes, as well as those others who are suspected at the present time, to become agitated through fear and stir up the said people, since their leaders find it so easy and certain to bend them to their will.

And with regard to all of the help of the said families that are needed, up to the number of five hundred that the most excellent lord viceroy Conde de Galve had been requested to provide, in my repeated reports, which are on record in the Office of Government and War in the secretariat of the court and city of Mexico, I again repeat to His Excellency, the most excellent lord viceroy of all the kingdom of New Spain, that, after seeing the testimony of the three petitions of the very reverend father presented in his name and the replies, he provide and order that this help be sent, for it is his obligation to preserve not only this said kingdom but also its Christianity, for our lord the king (may

God keep him) through his royal *cédulas* so strongly repeats, requests, orders, and decrees its said restoration, as it is his royal pleasure and desire.

Therefore, we cannot expect that such a royal master and lord will fail, or can fail, to provide the means. On my part, it is my obligation only to notify and send the said testimony to the said most excellent lord viceroy, whomsoever he may be, and that it also be provided to the said most reverend father custodian as he and the reverend *definitorio* of this holy custody have requested.

With regard to their said petition and that which I provide, resolve, and determine, I, said governor and captain general, order that it be given to my secretary of government and war and that it be copied in accord with the original, as has been determined. Done and signed by me, that it be of record, with my said secretary of government and war in this Villa of Santa Fe on said day, month, and year, *ut supra.*

Don Diego de Vargas Zapata Luján Ponce de León. Before me, Domingo de la Barreda, secretary of government and war.

It is in accord with the original, from which I, Domingo de la Barreda, secretary of government and war, by order of the lord governor and captain general Don Diego de Vargas Zapata Luján Ponce de León, who at present holds that office in this kingdom and provinces of New Mexico, its new restorer, conqueror at his own expense, reconqueror and settler there, and castellan of its forces and presidio for His Majesty, copied it to the letter, and it is a certain and true copy of the original. It is on thirteen pages of ordinary white paper, because sealed paper is not available in these parts.

And that it be of record I signed on the said twenty-second of March of the year sixteen hundred ninety-six. In testimony of the truth I place my signature and customary rubic.

Domingo de la Barreda,
secretary of government and war

68. *CARTA PATENTE* OF FRAY FRANCISCO DE VARGAS, SANTA FE, MARCH 26, 1696[1]

REVEREND fathers and minister presidents of the Tewas and Tanos. I inform you, reverend fathers, that having reported to the lord governor and captain general of this kingdom what is contained in your letters, giving him the reasons why each of you reverend fathers has left your mission, and also requesting that His Lordship provide the guards that each of you reverend fathers has re-

---

1. BNM, leg. 4, docs. 15, 24.

quested, and if he cannot provide them (as in effect His Lordship cannot provide them, nor does he promise to do so) that he make them available to remove the sacred vessels and other articles of divine worship as well as the sheep and all of the other things relating to the said missions, His Lordship replies as follows:

"I can only say that I do not have the means to provide the said soldiers and to again take them with me to each of the missions of the said reverend father *definidores* and minister presidents of the said pueblos referred to in the said petition as I did in most cases at the end of September and in October and November of the years 'ninety-four, which, as will be noted, I left without guards, as they were not requested of me, and they have remained in the said missions; and if now they are fearful because of rumors, reports, and presumptions, it is not possible for me to provide, all at once, assistance that will assure their protection. I can only provide, on my part, that which I can designate to the extent that it can contribute in part to said assistance, which I have reasoned in the following manner. . . ."

And he continues: "For the reverend father missionaries, presidents of the pueblos of Santa Clara, San Juan de los Caballeros, and San Cristóbal, I do not have the guards to give them in accordance with their reply, and I can only conclude that they can withdraw as they have done, along with the reverend father minister of San Ildefonso, to the Villa Nueva de Santa Cruz de Españoles Mexicanos, and from there, (if they see fit), they can administer the holy sacraments with the eight soldiers that I left allotted under the command of the *alcalde mayor* of the said villa."

Item, he continues that said fathers of Santa Clara and San Juan should undertake the task of removing their cattle, and belongings, explaining to the Indians that it is being done because of the incursions that have been made by the Utes. This is in substance what he has said. He continues: "This will satisfy the spirit of the said Indians so that they may not be suspicious and see evil intent. For their reasoning, although it is that of barbarians, is very subtle, which confuses me, because I do not want them to conclude that I, said governor and captain general, and the Spaniards are acting with evil intent and that they continue to stir up rebellion as a result of this.

"And the said minister president reverend father Fray José Arbizu, of the pueblo of San Cristóbal of the Tanos, which includes the people of San Lázaro, can, being in the said Villa Nueva, which is so close to the said pueblo, support himself with his supply of provisions. And I feel that he can not remove his livestock from there, nor anything else, since the said people of San Lázaro have been reduced to the said pueblo with those gathered there with a few others, and this can not be done simply because some of the people that belong to the said San Cristóbal are absent from there—they have been informed that the aforesaid who have remained are pardoned, and since they have their planting already at hand, this should move them to return to their said pueblo . . . rather than that in rebellion they be led to seek liberty by choosing to live with the Apaches and their Navajo friends; and since the land there is impoverished and without water, they should find it more in their interest to decide to again return submissively to their said pueblo. The resolution of the problem will be left entirely to be determined by the said reverend father Fray José Arbizu."

And farther on: "And the said father of San Ildefonso, Fray Francisco Corbera, may, from the said Villa Nueva, if he so wishes, assist his said Indians and enjoy the presence of the soldiers who are stationed at the said Villa Nueva. And the one at Nambé, the reverend father *definidor* Fray Antonio Carbonel, since this mission is located between the two villas, with the continuous entry and departure of the respective residents in their communication with each other, which has been seen and accepted with regard to their said Indians, can be safe and can remain in his said mission, if he so wishes, recognizing this reason, for otherwise it would only arouse suspicion on all sides.

"And likewise, the reverend father Fray José Diez, of the pueblo of Tesuque, if he so wishes, and with even more justifiable reason, finding himself at a distance of three short leagues from this Villa of Santa Fe and on the route to the said pueblos, can do without the said guard that he requests and which would not be denied to him if I had it. And so, acknowledging this reason given, he should consider himself safe, because he will be protected by my said measures from the suspicion of the said Indians and their desire to rise in rebellion. On my part I am not telling the very reverend father to remain at his said mission but that I leave it to the fervor of his zeal to serve there."

In addition, when I presented an earlier petition to His Lordship urging him to provide the guards that you, reverend fathers, requested, he indicated that he has the soldiers distributed in the following manner, saying: "I have at my disposal one hundred soldiers, which is the complement of this presidio; and of these, the body of two squads of thirty men each, who comprise sixty, is required to guard the horses, which are in danger and in no way secure, and of the remaining forty, ten of them are employed in guarding the gate to this villa; and of the remaining thirty, those who are being sent with the beasts of burden to El Paso to bring the aid in food supplies and livestock comprise two squads of twelve men each, with their leaders, which total twenty-six, with four remaining who are the only ones assigned at the top level." Thus far, the statement of the said lord governor.

I ask you, reverend fathers, to examine, consider, check closely, and weigh this matter of such great importance, keeping in mind the name of our holy religion. And at the foot of this letter you are requested to reply with your opinion, signing your name so that we may have it of record and may make the appropriate representations to His Lordship. May God watch over your lives, reverend fathers, with happiness and consolation and all good wishes.

Villa of Santa Fe, March 26, 1696. Your brother and servant, reverend fathers, who loves you in the Lord and kisses your hands.

Fray Francisco de Vargas, custodian

69. LETTER OF FRAY JOSÉ DIEZ, SAN DIEGO DE TESUQUE, MARCH 29, 1696[1]

OUR very reverend father custodian and ecclesiastical judge. Although in the affliction and sorrow in which we find ourselves, and have found ourselves, for fear not so much of the lives of your sons as the profaning of that which is sacred, for the defense of which the giving up of one's life is a small matter, it is seen that there is no human aid forthcoming, for the lord governor neither provides me with guards nor gathers up the sacred vessels. Ignoring others, His Lordship states that it is presumption to believe that the uprising will take place when His Lordship himself went on various occasions to beg the rebellious Tanos to come down, and finally departed leaving most of them in their insolence; and when His Lordship obtained a statement from the governor of my pueblo in which, before the lieutenant general Luis Granillo and the *maestre de campo* Lorenzo Madrid, he stated, in my presence, that the Pecos were rising in rebellion and other things, and that they could not be acting alone without a confederation of all the nations; and when a Tano Indian told me, in front of Captain Roque Madrid, that at the next full moon they planned to kill the Spaniards; and when the Indians who are the movers of the betrayal are fugitives; and His Lordship acknowledges that thirty soldiers are necessary to guard the horses, and this because they are in danger and not safe, from which it follows that the uprising is certain, since previously fifteen soldiers sufficed, and now the horses are in danger with thirty (how can it be that the poor minister is not in danger without a single soldier?). Therefore, the uprising is presumptuous on the part of the ministers and not on the part of the precautions to protect the horses!

So, I state, our very reverend father, that without this supposition I find help only from heaven and that writing only serves to tire us in vain, because His Lordship does not reply to the points made in our letters. So that this may be of permanent record four our very reverend prelates and for the entire world, that in defense of our holy law and of the sacred vessels and for the glory of our holy religion I am prepared to die (if the revolt should take place), I state the

1. BNM, leg. 4, docs. 15, 24.

reasons and motives which have led me to return to my mission, as Your Very Reverend Paternity will see from this letter, which I had already written yesterday and had not sent to you because I was awaiting a trustworthy messenger.

I only say, with regard to His Lordship's answers in the part referring to this mission, that "since it is on the road used by the pueblos, and is a distance of two short leagues from the villa, it can, if it is his desire, remain without the said guard," that it is three leagues from the villa, and that it is near a [well-traveled] thoroughfare is of no help to me, because at times when we hear rumors of an uprising, as I have seen on two occasions, and also when the Indians can kill me during the night at will, as we have the example of Father Pío [in 1680], who on coming as their minister to say mass to them (even with military guard) was killed by them in this pueblo, therefore, neither the nearness nor that it is near the thoroughfare are of any help to me.

With regard to His Lordship's statement that it is suspicion of said Indians and of their desire for rebellion, as if the suspicion and desire are mine, I do not believe that he could presume that in his Catholic heart. I only desire the salvation of all, and I risk my life for it. If it is suspicion on my part and desire on the part of the Indians, I have already proved that it is not only suspicion, but that there is evidence (for if they do not carry it out at present it is because their plans have been uncovered) that the Indians desire it. I already have stated this in the letter, to which I add that since the time for planting is approaching, this is another reason why I am obliged to come to my mission, because of need, since I will have nothing to eat (if I live) if I do not till the soil, as His Lordship will not be able to provide it for me, as he does for the settlers, nor will I be able to carry out the parturition of the livestock to aid me in my needs. And therefore, for this reason and the others that I state here I will return to my mission. This is my letter:

My very reverend father custodian and ecclesiastical judge. Recognizing the paternal love with which you look upon the welfare of your sons, the ministers of this holy custody, at this time when the rumors of a general uprising have increased day by day, and with the rumors accompanied by growing evidence, consider the following: The Tanos of the pueblo of San Cristóbal have withdrawn to a mountain, where, lying in ambush and entrenched, they have declared war, as is known, because they said that they wanted to fight; and on the occasion when I sent to Your Very Reverend Paternity the statement of Domingo Tuhogue, the governor of my pueblo, which was made in the presence of two Spanish witnesses and signed by them, in which he said that the Indians of Pecos were rising in rebellion, and with this warning Your Very Reverend Paternity immediately sought protection for your sons as well as for the sacred vessels, requesting, jointly with the reverend *definitorio,* that the lord governor provide help in the face of the great dangers that were expected from so much hostility on the part of the Indians—as occurred (what sorrow!) in the year 'eighty—His Lordship replied that he would provide guards to the extent possible within the limits of his forces; and when I requested six soldiers for this mission, His Lordship replied that he could not provide them for me or remove the sacred vessels or the livestock, which, with great pains and solicitude, Your Very Reverend Paternity placed at the missions, or the supplies that our lord the king (may God protect him) bestowed to us for the celebration of the holy sacrifice of the mass and to alleviate our needs.

I state that I have decided to return for now to my mission (notwithstanding that the revolt is feared momentarily, and that since the month of August, last, they have made the attempt three times) for the following reasons:

First, because although I know that two Indians from my pueblo went to incite the Pecos to rise in rebellion, I also know that the said governor of my pueblo is on the side of the Spaniards to the extent that the declared enemy Indians attempted to kill him because he made peace with the lord governor, both at the time when he made his first expedition into this kingdom and when they came down from the mesa of San Ildefonso, which I myself saw near the said mesa. For this reason I cannot in conscience leave the said Indian without mass and without the administration of the holy sacraments or do so with regard to the other Indians who to my knowledge may not have concurred in the said revolt, for there is no reason for the just to pay for sinners, and especially when they wish to go to confession to fulfill their religious obligations.

The second reason is that although the lord governor does not provide me with the guard that I requested, he told me verbally that he was placing the horse herd near this mission, and since thirty soldiers are guarding them (as His Lordship affirms in his letter), the public worship in the church and my person will be protected better than by six soldiers. I warn, however, that if the horses are not placed there, as he has promised, I will gather the sacred vessels and withdraw to the Villa of Santa Fe, from which I will administer this mission with the armed guard that His Lordship promises to me, and if this should not be sufficient, *nullo modo,* they might commit some iniquitous act while I am saying mass.

The third reason is that if I do not remove the sacred vessels from the mission while I would be in the villa they would be in danger of being profaned without my being able to remedy such an act, for His Lordship states that he does not wish to have them removed so as not to stir up the Indians or destroy their confidence in His Lordship—as though they were not already stirred up before we ministers departed from the missions, for I say that they already were, and in my mission the governor of this pueblo made the statement that I have indicated. So I have the choice of being able to return, or to hide the sacred vessels if I again withdraw, or to die as a Catholic Christian in their defense in the event that I am unable to flee; not that I consider flight as cowardice, since it would be rashness (for that is what I feel) to offer oneself to be killed only for the sake of their desire to kill without reaping any fruit for God if they only remain more obstinate.

Nor can my return accomplish much with regard to what I stated in my reply to this second *carta patente:* that since there are some in my mission who are perverse, I could not celebrate mass before them unless they should repent and ask for absolution, nor could I administer baptism until I could be assured of the permanence of Christianity in this kingdom. The first is no hindrance, for since I know those who are, I called them before saying mass, and exhorting them, I indicated that at their request I would absolve them. The second does not hinder me, for I will not baptize without said assurances except in the case of extreme need to prevent the danger of apostasy.

These are, our very reverend paternity, the reasons that have motivated me to return to this mission, where I will await a few days to see if the horses are placed nearby (as was promised to me), and if they are not, I will again withdraw to the villa. For although the full moon has passed, when it was feared that the Indians would carry out their treacherous betrayal, the mad ones [*locos*] become infuriated with each full moon, especially these evil Indians, who are tolerated, for if "the mad man becomes sane when he is punished,"[2] that will never be, for they lack any punishment, while we ministers have an excess of sorrow in seeing that they leave whenever they wish, and we cannot get them to fulfill the obligation to assist their ministers, for their negligence is continual, and it appears that this is done on purpose to annoy us. I only grieve that so little fruit is being gathered for God from our tireless efforts. May His Divine Majesty remedy it, and may He guard over Your Very Reverend Father Paternity many years. From this mission of San Diego de Tesuque, March 29, the year 1696. Your humble son and subject who loves you and kisses the feet of Your Very Reverend Paternity.

Fray José Diez

70. LETTER OF FRAY ANTONIO CARBONEL, NAMBÉ, MARCH 31, 1696[1]

OUR very reverend father custodian and ecclesiastical judge. I am grateful for the paternal love and watchfulness with which Your Paternal Reverence seeks

2. El loco por la pena es cuerdo.
1. BNM, leg. 4, docs. 15, 24.

the good of your sheep, as the vigilant shepherd over the small flock which our holy mother church has entrusted to Your Paternal Reverence. I state below what motivated me to return to the mission of Our Father San Francisco of Nambé even without the guard that was requested of the lord governor and captain general of this kingdom, who did not grant it because he indicates that he does not have sufficient soldiers for his own protection and that of the horses, despite the fact that His Majesty (may God protect him) spends from the royal treasury for soldiers to protect the ministers of the gospel when wars are taking place, as they are taking place in this kingdom. As His Lordship knows and has witnessed, for three days he was summoning [*requiriendo*] the Tanos Indians of the pueblo of San Cristóbal, who were in the mountains in rebellion, and they said that they wanted only to fight, and most of them are still joined with the bandits, who have no intention of coming down. This I know, for I saw it with my own eyes, having gone to said pueblo in the company of Reverend Father Fray José Arbizu and the lord captain Roque Madrid, and of the over six hundred Indians of that pueblo there were only ten or twelve who, because of fear, did not go, because they were certain that they would be killed for having given advance notice to the Spaniards; therefore, this is evidence of revolt and not presumption or rumors. I also know for certain that an Indian *tlatolero* of this pueblo went with them to the mountains with ten or twelve Indian men and women who do not appear to be from this pueblo, and on various occasions they have come to stir up the Indians of this pueblo to revolt, and although they say that they have not admitted the said *tlatoles,* "if the jug goes too many times to the fountain, it finally is broken."[2] And when all of these people act like bandits, I do not know what protection there is for a poor religious alone at his mission, for even if the Indians of this pueblo might wish to defend me, assuming that they are good, "What can an ant do against a thousand bloodthirsty wolves?"[3]

Notwithstanding all of what has been referred to above, I returned to my mission so that they would not profane the sacred vessels and vestments and the other articles pertaining to the divine religion and in case a child might be born in danger of not being baptized, so that he might be saved, but without applying the holy oils, because being close to apostates I do not know whether I may administer any other holy sacrament, because in administering it we should follow the surest course, following the published apostolic decrees.

I recognize manifest danger for the ministers, because punishment is lacking for those who so much deserve it. Some eight months ago, while I was engaged in my holy duties in the mission of Cochití, an Indian slapped me in

2. Mas tantas veces va el cántaro a la fuente que por último se quiebra.
3. ¿Que hará una hormiga respecto de mil lobos carniceros?

the face, and it was the same day that the lord governor paid a visit to the said pueblo, and having notified him of the said boldness and impudence on the part of the said Indian, the lord governor gave it the same notice as one would give to a corpse. When this is overlooked and His Lordship lets apostate rebels go without punishment, what can the poor ministers do, seeing their sacerdotal dignity thus outraged? What can be presumed other than that the vile acts and wickedness of the said Indians are swept aside and they are left to commit other greater shameful acts, for which the ministers are continuously struggling with the Indians, as they know and experience their dissoluteness and wickedness? What the lord governor experiences on a one-hour visit, accompanied by one hundred armed men and only passing through, is not the same as being there over a period of time, alone, contending with the Indians. On a passing visit they act like gentle sheep, and over a longer period they are wild bears. Idolatry is continued, they continue their depraved concubinage, and the time has come to remedy all of this, for we have been among them now for three years, and every day they are worse, because the Indians know who should punish them and who is observing and suffering their wicked acts. And so it is my view that what is taking place is going more against the crown of our royal monarch than in his favor.

I say, as for me, that when they took me from my mother the Province of Santo Evangelio, it was to go to a conquered and pacified land, which it is not nor has it been nor will it be until it may serve God our Lord to free it from danger. And if they had told me then that I was coming to die among infidels, I would have premeditated the undertaking and would have followed the dictates of the Lord. I now confess that I was deceived, because if the goal that our Catholic monarch (may God keep him) hopes for is not attained, how can we justly receive the very considerable alms which he spends from his royal treasury, with so much generosity, on the ministers of the gospel only for the purpose of teaching these Indians the catechism and instructing them under the impression that much fruit is being harvested, whereas there is none because of the very many thorns and brambles? These can not be pulled out, because the strength to do so is lacking. I also state that since I am a poor friar minor without a house or home or anything else from which I can pay back to my king what he is spending on me from the treasury, in the belief that I am gathering some fruit, and I know that I have accomplished nothing, these are points that weigh very heavily and are a burden on my conscience. I unburden it in this letter for the rigorous tribunal, our father. I speak with all of this clearness so that at no time may it be said that our sacred religion has deceived its king, to whom we should look with piety, for he looks upon us with compassion.

I recognize that the said Indians do not seek peace but rather to perturb the peace, for every day the ministers are on the verge of being lost. The same day that the lord governor and captain general made a visit to this pueblo, the Indians killed the best cow of three that Your Paternal Reverence charitably gave me for this mission, and during the period of three months they have stolen twenty-seven head of sheep, not small ones but large ones and the best ones, and I fear that they may consume all of them, for they go unpunished. This was the payment I received from them for having them place their trust in the lord governor. Also, twice they have broken into the convent and have stolen from me a quantity of food, chocolate, and sugar. Does this show that the Indians are good? When they look for incidents to confound the minister so that they may say that it is because of the minister that they are in rebellion? It appears to me that all of their ill will is toward the ministers, because they are the ones who seek to lead them to live as Christians. Their idolatries continue, and it is very difficult to root them out. They do not like Christians nor those who subject them to the law of God; rather, they wish to flee to freedom. This should not be permitted, because of what I have said, that the reason that His Majesty (may God keep him) is spending from the royal treasury is in conformity with the successful winning of souls. To deal and bargain with the Indians is not the same as to teach them the law of God, for the heretics deal and bargain with Christians, but in dealing with the matter of whether they wish to be Catholics, most of them refuse. I speak from experience.

They mock the ministers and even Christ transubstantiated in the host. If this is tolerated among Catholics, ponder on it as a point to be given thought. Although they have not yet revolted, because their plan has been foreseen, sooner or later they will carry it out, and they will begin with the ministers, who are alone at their missions. And so, if it is going astray to change one's opinion, I change mine, and I state that it is now of concern to change such opinion, because if these few Indians of this pueblo are communicating with the many perverse and evil ones for fear of these others, they will kill millions of priests, who cost dearly and are not found easily, whereas soldiers are found abundantly. Your Reverence may be sure that your ministers have their reputation guaranteed by my mother religion and not by the boldness of the lord governor, who in wishing to pursue difficult undertakings must support them with the spilling of the blood of ministers of the gospel, who could in another land profit in the winning of souls. It is not my word but that of the gospel, when Christ ordered us, in our lives as ministers of the gospel, that if we should find ourselves in a city where the people refused to accept the divine law, we should flee to another where we would be received and welcomed, and since these people do not wish to accept it, let us go to another place where they accept it. And our father Saint Francis orders us likewise: Ubi no fuerint accepti fugiam in alia terra cum benedictione Dei.[4] We read the same in the writings of many other saints, and therefore we are not the ones who flee when we are thus ordered, when finding no success for conversion to our holy gospel among these natives.

I cannot speak more clearly, because I am not able to do so with my limited ability. Your Very Reverend Paternity knows very well what should be done; I only say that we are spending our time writing letters, nothing is being carried out, help is very distant, the travails and needs are very great, and death is very close at hand; all rests on entrapping time, and it will entrap us in our tombs. For already two of the religious have died within a short time, and perhaps one has died more from grief and the other from being bewitched than from anything else, as is presumed. And there are others who walk about with the same ailment, and if here they kill us and bewitch us to flee from being among these people, before they destroy us and make us unfit for service, let the will of God be done, from whom I request the good direction and wisdom of Your Reverend Paternity.

At this mission of our father San Francisco of Nambé, March thirty-one, the year sixteen hundred ninety-six. Our very reverend father custodian, your most humble and lowly son and subject kisses your feet.

Fray Antonio Carbonel

71. LETTER OF FRAY JOSÉ ARBIZU, SANTA FE, APRIL 2, 1696[1]

I have now stated to you, very reverend father, three times, including this time, concerning my departure from the mission, and I state, unburdening my conscience, that I can not go to the mission of San Cristóbal of the Tanos for the reasons that I have already given as well as because His Lordship will not provide me with any guard, and with five men (which are not eight) for five missions, which are those of San Juan, Santa Clara, San Ildefonso, San Cristóbal, and the *visita* of Pojoaque, it will not be possible to administer. And when he provides it, I will go to administer the holy sacrament of baptism for some child when I see and know morally that he will die, because for the present there is danger of subversion among the others, and when the danger ceases— that is, if they are at peace and not in the mountains provoking war—I will go. But if they continue as they still are, I state that it is not possible for me to do so, because by my death no benefit is gained at all.

---

4. "Where you have not been accepted flee into another land with the blessing of God." Paraphrase from Matt. 10:14, Mark 6:11, and Luke 9:53. Paraphrased in Spanish by Fray Francisco de Jesus in document 76, below.

1. BNM, leg. 4, docs. 15, 24.

And I also state that if the sacred vessels should be profaned because His Lordship does not wish to provide the said escort to remove them, I salve my conscience, as I do with regard to what I have received from His Majesty, if he should use some means for my support, for no guard is provided nor is any help being given in any way, and if I should return to the said mission alone, it will be to protect the sacred vessels, and the only protection I will have will be to die with them, and this will be no protection whatever. What I am saying is that the return to my said mission will be when they are not at war, as they are. May God grant us peace, and may God keep you, very reverend father, many years with all good fortune.

From this Villa of Santa Fe, April 2, the year 1696. Your humble son and devoted subject, who kisses the hand of Your Very Reverend Paternity.

Fray José Arbizu

72. LETTER OF FRAY GERÓNIMO PRIETO, SANTA CRUZ, APRIL 2, 1696[1]

OUR very reverend father custodian. What I reply in this letter is what I have stated in two others, stated and replied to, and I have nothing more to say. I only affirm that I will not return to the mission to live there without a large armed guard, for two reasons: one is because of the Utes, and the other because of those of the pueblo. This is what I feel, as I unburden my conscience. Salve.

In this Villa of Santa Cruz, the second of April, the year sixteen hundred ninety-six.

Fray Gerónimo Prieto

73. LETTER OF FRAY JOSÉ GARCÍA MARÍN, SANTA CRUZ, APRIL 2, 1696[1]

OUR very reverend father custodian. I have already replied with what I have recognized in accordance with my conscience. I have seen that nothing has been remedied, and so I state now that I can not go to administer, first, because I find myself in bad health, and second, because it is not licit for me to baptize except in extreme need, and to do this I need protection for my life, and if such protection is not provided, it is not licit for me either, and since it is not licit, I

1. BNM, leg. 4, docs. 15, 24.
1. BNM, leg. 4, docs. 15, 24.

can not carry out such work or administer even if all the religious should lose their reputation. For God does not order that for the credit of anyone I should commit a mortal sin. Besides, in this matter there cannot be any loss of credit, but rather much credit for our Christian order, or any other particular one, not to baptize when it is not licit. I state this founded on the very firm principles of the very learned Villalobos,[2] and since it is not licit for me, I unburden my conscience on that of Your Very Reverend Father Paternity, informing you that all of the sacred objects are at the mission of Santa Clara and, therefore, Your Very Reverend Paternity may resolve what should be done in these matters. And if on any occasion I should go to the said mission, it will be to see if by chance they have done, or are doing, some outrage to the things pertaining to God. And if I should remain there one or several days, it will be because in the interim that I am alive I could not permit that the sacred objects be profaned. This is what I feel at this time and will feel in the future if the situation is not remedied.

Villa of Santa Cruz, April 2, of '96.

Fray José García Marín

74. LETTER OF FRAY MIGUEL TRIZIO, BERNALILLO, APRIL 17, 1696[1]

OUR reverend father custodian. After having read with attention each clause in the letter from Your Paternal Reverence, and especially the explanations and replies of the lord governor in answer to the petition which Your Paternal Reverence has made to him as prelate of this holy custody in the name of its religious, I find that His Lordship makes no mention of those of us who live in these parts on this bank of the river, such as the Jémez and Keres, for His Lordship speaks only about the fathers who assist among the Tewas and Tanos, and His Lordship could have included the risks and dangers which can come about among us and which are feared daily. For on the one hand we have the obstacle of the river, and in the season when the level of the water is at its peak we find ourselves isolated, without any recourse or help other than that of God, and on the other hand we are near so many enemy nations, such as those of

---

2. It would appear that this reference is to Fray Enrique de Villalobos's *Summa de teología moral y canónica,* Lisbon, 1623, and later editions, in two-volume folio, listed in the inventory of books left by Diego de Peñalosa, governor of New Mexico, 1661–64. When the books were auctioned in 1669, Fray Francisco de Ayeta, who was later a custodian of the New Mexico missions, bought forty-three of the books for 46 pesos. Eleanor B. Adams and France V. Scholes, "Books in New Mexico, 1598–1680," *New Mexico Historical Review* 19 (1944): 40–41.

1. BNM, leg. 4, docs. 15, 24.

Acoma, Zuñi, Moqui, and the many other nations of the Apaches, and although some of them at the moment appear to be at peace and act as friends, at the slightest movement that may be made by the natives concerning their uprising, they will all unite with them, because after all they are changeable Indians and enemies of the Spaniards. And although we are subject to so many risks, and besides, with the many things that I am experiencing and undergoing in this pueblo of San Juan de los Jémez, of which the lord governor already has been informed, His Lordship provides no help whatever; rather, he pays no attention to any of it. For when all of the inconveniences we are experiencing, and the very great risk that we are threatened with, were addressed to him, he left four soldiers to protect the sacred objects and the precious articles of divine worship, but they were so poorly equipped with arms, horses, and clothing that they not only did not instill any fear in the Indians, but rather gave them strength and spirit to carry out their evil deeds. For in recognizing the little defense that [the soldiers] offered, [the Indians] must have judged (as they might well have) that all of the soldiers and Spaniards were like them [the four] and that they could safely carry out what they had planned.

Therefore, our father, I state that if His Lordship wishes that this place be lost and that the father ministers perish, I do not have that valor and spirit, for although shedding one's blood in defense of the holy gospel and in the name of Jesus Christ is very pleasing to His Divine Majesty, and martyrdom is pleasing to our souls, it is understandable when some gain is expected, but here the gain is expected only in increasing their sins and in suffering more hell, for their only purpose is to kill the fathers, for it appears to them that with this they are free and that the Spaniards will leave them. And although His Lordship has said that the full moon has passed and that the gathering at Acoma has been broken up, there will be another and another and many more full moons, and we do not know which one will become the waning for us and the crescent for them.

And so, considering all of this, and having requested twice that His Lordship provide the necessary guard and it has not been provided, nor has he even shown the disposition to do so, it is my view that it is wiser to leave the pueblos before [the Indians] leave them. For to administer the holy sacraments, according to the most reliable opinion when there is danger of apostates, as at present, it is understood that this can not be done with regard to the sacrament of baptism, and in speaking of penance, experience shows that one in a hundred go to confession, and they do not make a good confession or even a suitable one, for if they do so it is not to free themselves of their sins but because they feel forced to do so, fearful of the punishment which they are afraid they might undergo when they confess their sins.

But so that it never can be said that the fathers are the cause for the disturbances and that they instill valor in the Indians, and since it is planting time, I will assist at the mission on the days that I can, and especially on Sundays, to say mass, and then return to Bernalillo unless Your Reverence should decide on some other course. May God protect you as He can and as I desire.

From this town of Bernalillo, April 17, 1696. Your most humble son, who loves you in the Lord and kisses the feet of Your Very Reverend Paternity.

Fray Miguel Trizio

75. LETTER OF FRAY PEDRO DE MATHA, ZIA, APRIL 17, 1696[1]

OUR very reverend father custodian and ecclesiastical judge. Although the lord governor makes no mention (in statements which Your Very Reverend Paternity shares with me) of the mission of Zía, I have seen that he wrote to its *alcalde mayor* in which he states that the said mission appears not to be in danger and that with the soldiers who are stationed in the Jémez pueblos I am protected. To this I state that little can I be helped (may God not will that it be needed) by armed men who are dying of hunger, and they will first help the fathers of the missions where they are located before they help me.

I also state that the pueblo of Zia has needed and now needs guards, because His Lordship does not know with certainty if the Acomas and Zuñis are at peace, for the Acomas said that an Indian he sent has died (to which I state that this is possible, because it is natural to die), but it is also possible that they killed him, and there is not much doubt of this, since they kill the religious with witchcraft or poison. For if justice had been carried out (and they would fear it), an inquiry would have been made into the cause of the death of the father preacher Fray José Ramírez, and it would have been verified, because it is an obligation perhaps that we all should see how these rebels kill the ministers of the gospel. More so when His Majesty, may God guard him, in his royal *cédulas* entrusts his judges to take care of his ministers of the gospel.

The very illustrious Doctor Montenegro states in his *Itinerario,* book 1, treatise 5, section 5, to prelates and superiors, that it is clear that the superior who does not forestall the danger of corporal death to a subject on the occasions when he can and should do so is held culpable for it and therefore deserves the name of homicide and should be punished as such, because it would be voluntary homicide *in causa* for not having prevented it when he should have done so in his official capacity, as is commonly stated by the doctors of the church and

1. BNM, leg. 4, docs. 15, 24.

by many saints. This is one of the passages of the said author. And so, our father, Your Paternal Reverence, discharge your duty by reporting the manifest risks in this kingdom, and may God guard your life many years.

Zia, April 17, the year '96. Your subject, who holds you in esteem and kisses your hand.

Fray Pedro de Matha

76. LETTER OF FRAY FRANCISCO DE JESÚS MARÍA CASAÑAS, BERNALILLO, APRIL 18, 1696[1]

OUR father custodian. I have examined the aforesaid clauses and points, and from what I see in them I recognize from all of them that nothing is being remedied, only that time is being lost in responding, for nothing is being remedied. I am now tired of requesting and notifying His Lordship in writing and by word of mouth, and I see no reason to tire myself more even if the mountains should open, because it is my experience that in his replies His Lordship does not answer the points that I have written to him. I have had twelve years of experience with Indians in America, with infidels as well as Christians and apostates who are enemies of the evangelical law, as are these in New Mexico, and others that I have seen with different nations mixed among infidels who are baptized Christians, and these find themselves better off with their liberty rather than under the yoke of the evangelical and Catholic law. And with regard to these of New Mexico, one can only believe that they still are drawn more by their idolatry and infidelity than by the Christian doctrine, for we see in them that with their little loyalty, at every full moon they rise in rebellion, foaming at the mouth. From that it is inferred that what they learn in one week, on Saturday, when they go to the river to bathe, they wash away the good that they have gathered from the teaching of the ministers through their daily instructions. This is not without foundation, for I have sufficient experience, from what I have seen and observed among different nations, to know that in matters of idolatry and superstition they are all alike, as in the other aspects of their nature. On this matter I have made a report to the Audiencia, and it was sent to Spain by order of His Most Excellent Lord and my superior prelates, who ordered me to present in detail an account of all that which I had experienced in two years which I spent traveling only on foot among different nations and provinces of the Texas and the empire of the Canse. And for my sins I have fallen among apostates in New Mexico who if they do not revolt, it

---

1. BNM, leg. 4, docs. 15, 24.

is not because they do not wish to, as they only await to do so at the safest opportunity. That the Christian law will stop them, it is clear that it will not. Ergo, if they do not revolt today, they will tomorrow. This is what can be feared from the stirring which is seen among them every day.

To await more signs will be to ask unnecessarily for miracles, for God has given us the gift of reason, and he has given us enough warnings directly from them for us to be watchful and fearful of the danger to our lives and of the outraging of our churches and sacred vessels. And thus, in this situation may His Lordship provide the help that he deems appropriate. The guard of four soldiers, unarmed, that he has placed at my mission is not a guard or protection whatever; rather, it is a burden on the Indians, protecting them and eating the little that they have, as they themselves say. If only it would be requested that one of them see what he could find that is bad here and report on it, because if they themselves [the Indians] should go to report, His Lordship would think that they were *tlatoleros* and liars. But they themselves have requested this, not I, and so that the situation might be better reported, on their own they asked Ventura de Apodaca, for the other three [soldiers] were never able to reach this pueblo, as they went astray. And one time when I went to say mass, they were away, and only one attended with the *alcalde mayor;* if this is the soldiering that the kingdom has to preserve the peace, I have no doubt that it will soon be in ruins.

We know that the reconquest of the kingdom was a great miracle. Its preservation is in our hands, with the grace of God, if we await another miracle. I do not know if this will come to pass, in seeing the little benefit gained in this evil land of apostates against the word of God and that of our Catholic king, for they are very remote from the power and lordship of His Majesty. For even the oldest residents ask about the king from Parral, Puebla, Mexico City, and other towns of New Spain. If they say that not all of the pueblos are bad, that some are peaceful, like the one that I administer, I say that when the occasion arrives, all will be coming with the *tlatole,* as when they crucified Jesus Christ, and if anything is expected of them, it will be manifest deceit.

If His Majesty should see this kingdom at present, I have no doubt that he would order the ministers of the gospel to withdraw, or that they should go where benefit would follow and the Holy Gospel would be accepted. Our Lord advised this when He sent out the apostles to preach the Holy Gospel, and we know that in some places it was accepted and they were welcomed and in other places this was not the case, and from these they fled, shaking the dust from their sandals, leaving and abhoring that land. And we have the same advice from our father Saint Francis. But so also may Your Very Reverend Paternity, as father and successor of our father Saint Francis, consider, through your paternal direction, that which is most appropriate, for I am very ready to obey and to give up my life if necessary for the salvation of souls and to carry out my holy obligation.

This is my feeling, and may God, through His most holy Passion, remedy the situation for the good of these souls, if it is His wish, and if it is not, let Him place us where profit may be gained, which His Majesty our Catholic king seeks, and where the expense which he has invested in his payments and in his ministers of the gospel may be rewarded. For it is clear that in this kingdom this needs to be made up for and questioned, in view of the many hardships which all of the kingdom suffers from lack of food without any recourse from the pueblos, for His Lordship knows in person that the Indians are eating and the Spaniards are fasting at such great expense.

Done at this villa of Our Father San Francisco of Bernalillo,[2] today, April 18, 1696.

Fray Francisco de Jesús María

77. LETTER OF FRAY JOSÉ ARBIZU, SANTA CRUZ, APRIL 18, 1696[1]

AVE MARÍA

I trust that thanks to God our Lord you have had a good Holy Week, and I wish you a most happy Easter, with spiritual exaltation that I, the most worthless son of Your Very Reverend Paternity, wish for you. Our father, in reply to the three *cartas patentes* of Your Very Reverend Paternity I have stated the reason for my leaving the mission of San Cristóbal of the Tanos, which Your Very Reverend Paternity has presented to the lord governor. And His Lordship saw with his own eyes that the pueblo is desolated, in rebellion, and summoned by the said Tanos Indians to fight. The general uprising is not feigned on our part; it is verified and confirmed by His Lordship; yet he has not only paid no attention, as he has not provided the guard which I requested for the said rebellious and incited pueblo, but has also answered only with words, which His Lordship has chosen to use in generalities. And the reply that His Lordship gives to the fathers of San Ildefonso and to those of the Tewas he also gives to me, as though my petition were the same as those of the said fathers, and although the said fathers seek the same purpose as I do, the *tlatoleros* and principal movers for the general revolt are in their pueblos, they are not in the mountains, as the Tanos were and now are, and most of them scattered, not among the Apaches, as it is said, but in the pueblos of Taos, Picurís, and the Tewas, hidden, await-

---

2. Bernalillo is erroneously or inadvertently referred to as a villa. It is referred to in all other instances as a *paraje, puesto,* or *población.*

1. BNM, leg. 4, docs. 15, 17, 24.

ing, and like bandits inciting the others to flee and to rise in rebellion, which has been attempted not one time but four times, and which they would have carried out many days ago if they had not been found out.

And with all of this I have caught the Indian who was going to the provinces of Moqui, and I saw a Tiwa in my mission hidden in some houses, making a count of the people of the pueblo and feigning that he was a Moqui, and when he told them to talk to him, they said that they did not know his language, and they told me that he had been for a month in my said mission of San Cristóbal, which has been the source of all this evil. I see, our father, that not only will no attention be given, but this His Lordship replies that I should not remove the holy vessels and the other subjects of divine worship and the livestock that Your Very Reverend Paternity personally has solicited and provided for our sustenance, as well as that which His Majesty (may God protect him) gave us, because it would anger the Indians; as though the Indians were not already stirred up and as though His Lordship had not seen the pueblo on the feast day of Saint Joseph devastated, the people having fled to the mountains, and with messages from the Indians to His Lordship that they wanted to fight—Can they be more stirred up, can there be greater unrest? This is not feigned on my part, for all of the soldiers heard the message from the said Indians to His Lordship.

And finally, what is happening and has been happening is that not only their corn supplies, but also that which I have for my sustenance they have carried off, as well as the chocolate which I had, and they have left me with nothing to eat and without any hope of obtaining it. Your Very Reverend Paternity knows that we are all aware of the hunger that we are suffering, not only the religious but also all of the kingdom, for there is not a grain of corn, and the only ones who have it are the Indians. All of this has occurred because His Lordship has not wished to provide the escort to remove the most holy vessels and the provisions. As a result, these living temples of God are undergoing the most calamitous times that have been seen. For the church finds itself persecuted by these apostates of our holy faith and with its ministers as fugitives, without any place where they can stay, along with the general famine which all of us Spaniards are suffering, with the little food that we had acquired being carried away by the senseless ones who are tolerated, although their purposes are known with their wicked and depraved customs, rooted in fifteen years of apostasy, and now more apostates than then. Yes, the priests perished by their sacrilegious hands, and now, not only is that their intention, but also that our death be by a prolonged knife in our side, and they, because of our fear, performing iniquities.

For all of which, as I see it, I appeal to Your Most Reverend Paternity, for I know of no other help than that of God, who is the One we await, and none other, which is why I intend to have this letter of mine kept in the archive of this holy custody so that it may serve, although written by a simple person like me, in the future defense of our sacred religion. And I state, our very reverend father paternity, that because of the sacred vessels and other articles of divine worship and because there is no guard or improvement or wherewithal to improve my situation, because I am already perishing from hunger, that I am going to the mission of San Cristóbal not to administer, because today there is no purpose in administering, with respect to what I have said, and with the danger stated, not doubtful or presumed but verified. And so I state that should I die, it will be in defense of that which is sacred because I am not provided with guards for its defense or to remove it. This is my intent. Your Very Reverend Paternity should advise me if it is to be carried out. And if the danger is so evident in this pueblo of San Cristóbal that I should perish and the sacred vessels should be profaned, it will not be the fault of the order but that of His Lordship, to whom I make and have made known these considerations in my replies. May God console us, and may He grant Your Very Reverend paternity the health and patience to suffer so many tasks, and may God protect you many years with much happiness.

Villa of Santa Cruz, April 18, the year 1696. Our very reverend father. Your most humble subject kisses the hand of Your Reverence.

Fray José Arbizu

Our very reverend father custodian, Fray Francisco de Vargas, my father and lord.

78. LETTER OF FRAY ALFONSO JIMÉNEZ DE CISNEROS, COCHITÍ, APRIL 21, 1696[1]

OUR very reverend father custodian and ordinary ecclesiastical judge. With regard to the *carta patente* which preceded this one, I requested and all of the fathers requested guards, and they were provided to some and not to others, for which there was no reason. Nor will they be provided now, although they are requested, because previously there were more soldiers than there are now, for those who went to El Paso to conduct the food supplies are now absent.

And so I reply that I have read carefully all of the points and passages in your letter, and if the lord governor and captain general is of the opinion that all is very quiet, he deceives himself. For the statement that was made by the Indian who went to Acoma, Zuñi, and Moqui to report on the revolt is true, because

1. BNM, leg. 4, docs, 15, 24.

his statement is not wanting. And if the lord governor should say that he confessed because of the torture they indicated, and that which he confessed was a
lie, he is deceived. I ask: Why did the Indian woman confess the same thing
without the threat of torture, and if they did not agree in the said torture it
would be true, that the revolt was not true? But since they agreed, there is no
doubt whatever that the revolt was a certainty. And to better confirm the
above, consider what that Indian woman said, or says, which is thus: "Take
notice, Spaniards, the Indian has not said once that there will be a revolt and
that they plan to kill all of the Spaniards. Do not tire, because what the Indian
says once, he always carries out, so do not trust them; when the least you expect
it they will strike you over the head." These are the exact words said by the
Indian woman, and if the opportunity presents itself, I can provide enough and
sufficient witnesses. And when she was asked why she was leaving, she replied
that since she was tired of going from mountain to mountain, dying of hunger,
she was going to Moqui, since she had relatives there. But none of this is of
any weight for the lord governor, because His Lordship keeps himself well
guarded, but not the ministers, because they are left to the inclemency of the
heavens.

I ask, if all of these premises to which I have referred and those to which I
will refer below are true, that in Picurís the Indians wanted to kill, as *de facto*
they themselves confess; that in Pecos the father was removed to safety by a few
of the good ones that were there because this is what the world is made of; and
that in San Juan de los Jémez the same occurred, for their own guilt accused
them, and many of them abandoned the pueblo because they were so malev-
olent. And after all of this, the lord governor says that they are good and that
they are his sons, and he remains very content with this.

I ask a second time, Why did the said governor and captain general bring
legal charges against the Spaniards who fled from this kingdom? So that those
who remained here would bear in mind an abhorrent act, to prevent its re-
occurrence, or because it was possible to do so, and now, with regard to those
who left San Cristóbal and those who left San Juan, all of whom are fomenting
sedition and creating disturbances in the kingdom, why have they not been
brought to justice? It must be for the lack of something, because the crimes of
these Indians are much greater than those committed by the Spaniards who
fled. I do not say that they should be killed, for there are other punishments
without killing, but to do absolutely nothing to them is an abundance of kindness and the placing of much confidence in them. But I am weary of hearing it
stated, time and again, that it is for lack of people that he does not do anything
about it. Why should I tire myself in asking, as I asked the time before, when
the lord governor paid no attention?

And therefore I stated that I make no request, for obedience placed me in this mission of San Buenaventura of Cochití, and I will remain here until Your Most Reverend Paternity may order something else, and if it is necessary for me to die, I will die, and that now and always I offer myself to remain in the said pueblo as I have remained amidst so many disturbances and insurrections that have occurred. For to this moment they have not missed a mass or a feast day, and they will not in the future, if God gives me the health and strength to be able to tolerate the atrocities of these pagans and rebels against the faith of Jesus Christ our Redeemer. But if my inconstant frailty with regard to what is stated above leads me to believe that the peril is too great, and if I am unable to endure this rabble, I will withdraw to the safest place to protect myself, which might be my salvation, sparing me from death at the hands of these traitors.

This is what I have to say. May God free us from them and enlighten our understanding so that we may be freed from their treachery. And may our Lord watch over you, very reverend father, for the many years that my love wishes for you.

Done at this mission of San Buenaventura of Cochití on the twenty-first of April, the year sixteen hundred ninety-six. Your subject, who esteems and loves you, kisses the hands of Your Very Reverend Paternity.

                                                    Fray Alfonso Jiménez de Cisneros

79. LETTER OF FRAY FRANCISCO DE VARGAS TO THE FATHER COMMISSARY GENERAL, SANTA ANA, MAY 17, 1696[1]

OUR most reverend father commissary general, my father and lord.

On this occasion it is necessary for me to inform you, most reverend father, of the departure of the apostolic fathers Fray José Diez, Fray Gerónimo Prieto, and Fray Domingo de Jesús, missionaries who have belonged to this holy custody of Your Most Reverend Paternity, who leave with licenses sent by the reverend father minister provincial of the province of Michoacán, and from the tenor of these licenses, in which you state, most reverend father, that it is a

---

1. BNM, leg. 4, docs. 13, 23. The orders of Commissary General Fray Manuel de Monzabál to Fray Francisco de Vargas for the return to the College of Santa Cruz de Querétaro by the three friars mentioned in this letter were dated January 17, 1696. Fray Francisco de Vargas's letters of compliance were dated May 15 and May 16. The three friars arrived at Querétaro on August 19 and 21 (*ibid.*, leg. 4, docs. 19, 22).

The orders were received at a moment when the Franciscan missions in New Mexico could ill afford the departure of three of their missionaries, but Father Vargas reluctantly complied with them. Soon after the three missionaries arrived at Querétaro, they learned of the reason for their withdrawal from New Mexico. It appears that some of the Majorcan friars of the college at Querétaro had left the community, thus depleting its ranks, as a result of an administrative dispute between Spanish and Majorcan friars of the college concerning the holding of office in the community (Michael B. McCloskey, *The Formative Years of the Missionary College of Santa Cruz de Querétaro, 1683–1733*, 74).

special order from you, most reverend father, that these fathers leave this custody, attending to it with due orders of Your Most Reverend Paternity, as your humble and devoted subject, I permit their departure, although I find myself with a lack of ministers in this custody.

But I have the hope and promise that our father provincial of the [Province of] Santo Evangelio, Fray Clemente de Ledesma, plans to send from the holy province the religious necessary for the administration of the holy sacraments in the missions where ministers are lacking. But for those that are now currently served, although with the great task at hand, they are provided for with those missionaries who are in this custody. For although there are other missions that are without ministers, these are very distant from recourse to the Spaniards, and I do not dare, nor have I dared, to provide them with a minister because of the fickleness of the Indians, from whom we have had the problem of their relapsing into apostasy because this kingdom finds itself with very little strength of Spanish arms and with the very serious need for food, while the Indians are supplied with arms, horses, and food, and the latter is obtained from them with difficulty, even when purchased from them. For this reason we have not been spared of many rebellious and evil rumors that they wish to revolt, and with these reports I have gathered together the religious whom I have recognized to be in the greatest danger of losing their lives at the hands of the Indians. And after these evil reports of an uprising were calmed and extinguished, the religious who from their spontaneous desires have wished to return to their missions have been permitted to do so, recognizing their zeal and good spirits, to insure that the administration of the holy sacraments not be wanting, for the honor of our sacred religion and service to God our Lord, for only through His holy love can one undergo such dangers and risks, of which Your Most Reverend Paternity is well aware.

The missions where the father missionaries are stationed are in operation, thanks be to God, and with the hopes that some food can be gathered from what they have planted there. Each mission has a beginning in sheep, which at my request I have placed there, so that from their nourishment the fathers of the custody may have some relief, as they have had. And so, in this regard, and with this assistance, religion will not falter in preventing the abandonment of the kingdom and the loss of the many souls that are there. I give this brief account to Your Most Reverend Paternity so that you may be informed of the present situation in this miserable kingdom.

The apostolic father Fray José Diez is one of the religious included in the license, and he will inform Your Most Reverend Paternity in greater detail on many points that I do not mention so as not to bother you with diffusive writing. The said father, in what he has been called upon to do in holy obedience in this holy custody, has performed his duties with the most careful attention, and although his conduct does not require my certification, I would not obey my conscience if I did not state to you, most reverend paternity, how well the said father has carried out his duties and the difficulties he has faced during the time that he has been in this holy custody.

May our Lord keep Your Most Reverend Paternity many happy years, for the consolation of your sons and subjects, and especially for mine, and for the protection of this holy custody.

Mission of Our Lady, Santa Ana. May 17, the year 1696. Your Most Reverend Paternity's humble son and devoted subject, who kisses the feet of Your Most Reverend Paternity.

Fray Francisco de Vargas

PART SIX

The Pueblo Indian Revolt of 1696

80. LETTER OF FRAY ALFONSO JIMÉNEZ DE CISNEROS TO GOVERNOR VARGAS, SAN FELIPE, JUNE 4, 1696[1]

LORD Governor and Captain General Don Diego de Vargas Zapata Luján Ponce de León. My dear lord:

What I wish to report to Your Lordship in this letter is to tell you that the entire pueblo of Cochití has gone up to the mesa, and with this circumstance they took with them all of the sheep and the other livestock as well, and all of the horses, so that on foot, at four o'clock in the morning, I left for this pueblo of San Felipe, where I found Señor Don Fernando, its *alcalde mayor,* with other neighbors, where I joined them.

I state, Your Lordship, that we have reached Flanders, and there is no more Flanders than what has happened. For it has been by the grace of God that I was able to escape alive from among so many hungry hounds and hypocrites. There is nothing more that I can say, so "keep your saddle in close view and your hat on your head,"[2] for they have become this bold. On another occasion I will speak at greater length.

May God protect Your Lordship many years. San Felipe, June the fourth of the year 'ninety-six.

Fray Alfonso Jiménez de Cisneros

81. LETTER OF GOVERNOR VARGAS TO FRAY FRANCISCO DE VARGAS, SANTA FE, JUNE 9, 1696[1]

MY very reverend father and dear lordship. I have just received a letter from the principal captain [*capitan mayor*] of the Keres, the governor of the pueblo of Santa Ana, Bartolomé de Ojeda, in which he informs me of the meeting [*junta*] which was being held by the Acomas, and that they were awaiting the Moquis, Zuñis, and Utes, and therefore, for said reason, he does not wish to

1. AGI, *Guadalajara,* leg. 141, doc. 19; SANM, Governor Vargas's journal.

2. Pues la silla delante de los ojos y el sombrero de la cabeza.

EDITOR'S NOTE: A detailed account of the prompt and effective actions taken by Governor Vargas imme-diately upon receipt of news of the outbreak of the revolt on June 4, 1696, is included in document 88, below. This document is the long letter of transmission from Vargas to the viceroy, July 31, 1696, which was accompanied by the transmission of a copy of his day-to-day campaign journal and other related papers. The letter of transmission summarizes the contents of his day-to-day journal from June 4 to July 31, 1696. It describes every important event during that period and refers to each specific document included in the day-to-day journal, relating the events in perspective as reported to him or as he witnessed them.

A translation of Vargas's day-to-day journal for the period June 4 through June 17 was made by Ralph E. Twitchell based on the damaged copy available in the Spanish Archives of New Mexico, Santa Fe, published under the title "The Pueblo Revolt of 1696," *Old Santa Fe,* III (1916), 341–72.

1. AGI, *Guadalajara,* leg. 141, doc. 19; SANM.

take any chances, since I am unable to provide the guard necessary for the safety of the families of Bernalillo. I am giving a hasty order, to be executed immediately, in His Majesty's name, to Captain Don Fernando de Chávez, *alcalde mayor* of Bernalillo, to send its inhabitants to the pueblo on the mesa of San Ildefonso and to have the rafts prepared for their crossing, advising me when they are on the said mesa and the rafts are ready in order that I may send an escort so that they may withdraw to this Villa of Santa Fe. And when they are there, from the tower [*torreón*] they can build their corrals for the livestock. And I, to this end, will have a squad on patrol, and in this way the enemy will not succeed in getting in without being observed and the safety of its defense will be insured. And therefore, in view of the said danger, you, most reverend father, and the other fathers can withdraw and find safety in this said villa, because war having broken out, I do not have a large enough army to separate even a small part of it and remain completely undefended. May God protect you, my most reverend father, for the happy years I wish for you.

Done at this Villa of Santa Fe, the ninth of June, the year sixteen hundred ninety-six. Your most unfailing servant kisses Your Very Reverend Paternity's hand. Don Diego de Vargas Zapata Luján Ponce de León. Very Reverend Father Custodian Fray Francisco de Vargas, my most esteemed lord. And that it be of record that this letter is faithfully copied, I certified it and signed it with my secretary of government and war.

Don Diego de Vargas Zapata Luján Ponce de León. Before me, Domingo de la Barreda, secretary of government and war.

82. LETTER OF BARTOLOMÉ DE OJEDA, INDIAN GOVERNOR OF THE PUEBLO OF SANTA ANA, TO FRAY FRANCISCO DE VARGAS, SANTA ANA [JUNE 10, 1696][1]

TO the very reverend father custodian Fray Francisco de Vargas. I inform Your Paternity that it now appears that the ambuscade has been broken up, not be-

1. AGI, *Guadalajara*, leg. 141, doc. 19; SANM. Ojeda was one of Governor Vargas's most loyal Indian allies, one of the unsung heroes of the Spanish reconquest of New Mexico. He had fought with great valor against the Spaniards at the time of Governor Cruzate's foray from El Paso and attack on Zia in 1689. Fearing death from wounds, he gave himself up to the Spaniards, from whom he sought a Franciscan friar to hear his confession. He was taken to El Paso for questioning and remained there for a time. Following the recapture of Santa Fe and the year of bitter warfare that followed, bringing a period of tenuous but eventual peace, Ojeda, in the fall of 1694, became governor of Santa Ana pueblo with Governor Vargas's special blessing (see document 11, above). Santa Ana became a model Christian pueblo, and Ojeda constantly kept Governor Vargas apprised of rebel Indian activities. Ojeda had Spanish blood. He wrote, spoke, and read Spanish quite well and was described as being very intelligent. Several of his letters to Spanish authorities, written in Spanish, are included or cited in the documents translated above. For additional data on Ojeda see J. Manuel Espinosa, *Crusaders of the Rio Grande*, 20, 134, 163–64, 179, 185, 199, 248, 249, 261, 276.

cause we know for certain, but because I sent scouts to reconnoiter the ground, and some tracks were seen going toward Acoma. But I inform you of it so that you may take care, since there is much in this to reflect upon, because in the direction of the Río Puerco some smoke has been rising, and it is thought that they have not yet gone, and we do not yet know whether they will strike here or there. And this morning we received news of those tracks, and the night before there were two horsemen riding about who perhaps were spies, who are spying on us, and yesterday two were riding about. And if anything happens to us here, which God our Lord forbid, it will not be for lack of care but because the hour has come that God our Lord has willed. I also inform our father guardian that we have moved what you had in the convent, because the devil does not sleep. As Your Paternity well knows, the pueblo is large and the people few, and we think that they may come and set fire to it, and no one but Jesus Christ could save it. And if Your Paternity should say that there was no one to warn you, you may advise them that everything [that was in the convent] is now in safety, at least in the best way possible, in a house covered over with mud, by obstructing the door and all other means to remove it. I have nothing else to inform you except that all the people are good, and much to be praised. I remain in poor health, and I believe that I have been caught with the fever [*tabardillo*]. And nothing more, except that may God our Lord guard you the many years I wish for you. Your Paternity's servant and godchild.

Bartolomé de Ojeda

83. VICEREGAL ORDER TO FRAY FRANCISCO DE VARGAS, MEXICO CITY, JULY 4, 1696[1]

TO the reverend father Francisco de Vargas, custodian, and the other religious of that our custody of New Mexico, health and peace in our Lord Jesus Christ. Since we have received some letters from religious of that our custody in which it was signified to us that you were in great danger because of the revolt of some Indians, and in fear of most of them, and that the bloody fury of said Indians could be expected to fall upon the lives of the said religious, for which reasons we were requested permission and our blessing to leave the said custody, on all of which we notified His Most Excellent Lord Bishop, viceroy of this New Spain, as is our obligation, and with this notice His Excellency has seen fit to dispatch to us the following request and charge:

Don Juan de Ortega y Montañés, bishop of the holy church of Valladolid, of His Majesty's council, the viceroy and lieutenant governor and captain general

---

1. AGI, *Guadalajara*, leg. 141, doc. 19; SANM.

of this New Spain, president of its royal *audiencia*. For the present, in conformity with the resolution in *junta general,* which I held today, on this date I had
before me a request and charge to the reverend father commissary general of
the Order of Saint Francis, Fray Manuel de Monzabál, that he encourage the
religious to assist in the provinces of New Mexico in obligation to such a holy
institute as is the conversion of so many souls that it is hoped will be reduced
and the preservation of those reduced, inspiring them to persevere and to continue in such a laudable task, consecrating to God and His Majesty the risk of
the dangers that they insinuate, for the merit that they achieve is so great in
the existence and continuation of their apostolic ministry.

Mexico, July four, sixteen hundred ninety-six.

Juan, bishop of Valladolid. By order of His Excellency, Don Francisco de
Morales.

84. *CARTA PATENTE* OF THE COMMISSARY GENERAL TO THE MISSIONARIES IN NEW MEXICO, QUERÉTARO, JULY 19, 1696[1]

BY copy of these presents, written in my hand, sealed with the great seal of our
office, and countersigned by our secretary, we request and beg and charge Your
Reverences that you be encouraged in the Lord to continue the work that you
have begun, considering the good zeal and ardent desire that accompanied you
when you went there, and that the crown is not won unless it is fought for to
the finish, nor is it achieved if having placed the hand to the plow, it is turned
back. My beloved sons, the occupation in which you find yourselves is no less
than the goal of the blood of our Redeemer Jesus Christ to win souls for heaven,
and for greater solace you should scorn your corporal lives. With this seraphic
desire our seraphic father Saint Francis founded his religious order and saw in
his lifetime the achievement of his ardent desires. With the blood of your five
religious, with the shedding of this blood in the continuation of martyrs, the
religion will be multiplied and extended throughout the entire world. And in
that New Mexico, although the blood that was shed with constancy and valor
by twenty-one of our brothers is not yet dry, it has been a seed that has borne
fruit in the garden of God. Fortitude is necessary while the battle lasts. Put
aside, my sons, the fear of those who can only kill the body. Perfect charity
casts out all fear, and there can be no greater charity than to risk one's corporal
life to convert an idolater and to maintain in the faith those who are already
converted, nor greater reward for Your Reverences. For if it should happen that
in your work you should lose your corporal life, you would be assuring the

1. AGI, *Guadalajara,* leg. 141, doc. 19; SANM.

eternal life of your soul. May the blessing of God and our father Saint Francis, and mine, be bestowed upon you, my constant and persevering sons. I beg of you to commend me to God, for I am making special prayers to His Majesty so that He may give you courage, valor, and fortitude and assist you with His Divine Grace.

Given at this our convent of Santiago de Querétaro on the nineteenth day of July, the year sixteen hundred ninety-six. With this our *patente* all of the religious of the missions of New Mexico will be notified, and necessary copies of it will be made. And in testimony of its receipt and notification, the original will be returned to us, at the first opportunity, to the City of Mexico so that we will have record of its having been carried out.

Fray Manuel de Monzabál. By order of His Very Reverend Paternity. Fray Miguel Gonzales, secretary general.

85. LETTER OF FRAY FRANCISCO DE VARGAS TO THE COMMISSARY GENERAL, SANTA FE, JULY 21, 1696[1]

OUR most reverend father commissary general, Fray Manuel de Monzabál, my father and lord.

Our most reverend father commissary general. I have written to Your Most Reverend Paternity on May 17 of this year, in which I reported to Your Most Reverend Paternity the state in which this holy custody found itself, and now, on July 21 of this present year, I write to report to you, with sorrow in my heart, the sad and unfortunate death of five religious of this holy custody who passed away at the hands of the apostate Indians of our faith. The deceased are: father preacher Fray José Arbizu, secretary general of this custody and minister president of the pueblo of San Cristóbal, and in his company they killed the father preacher and *definidor* of this custody Fray Antonio Carbonel, of the province of Valencia, and in the pueblo of San Ildefonso the father preacher Fray Francisco Corbera, minister president of the said pueblo, died along with some Spanish men, women, and children who took refuge in the convent, which was surrounded by the Indians and set afire on all sides, and not being able to escape, they huddled in a small cell, but it was to no avail because of the fierce flames, and they were suffocated by the smoke and all of them died. In their company was the father preacher Fray Antonio Moreno, who that day had gone to the convent for spiritual consolation. The said father was the minister president of the pueblo of Nambé, in which pueblo the Indians killed some other Spaniards and one woman. In the pueblo of San Diego de Jémez they

1. BNM, leg. 4, docs. 13, 15, 20.

killed the apostolic father preacher Fray Francisco de Jesús, son of the holy province of Catalonia, and in the said pueblo they killed a soldier who had the rank of captain, three Spaniards, and three children. And in the pueblo of San Juan de los Jémez, they killed the *alcalde mayor* and two of his servants. So that of all of the Spaniards who died in different places there were about thirty persons.

The other religious who were at their missions miraculously escaped with their lives. There are no words to magnify the outrages they committed with regard to the objects of divine worship, profaning the sacred vessels; inspired by the devil, they pulled off even the crosses and rosaries that they had hanging from their necks and threw them to the ground. With such diabolical actions we cannot have much hope that there will be any emendation of these missions, for they have relapsed so many times in their apostasy, and it is known that they acted in *odiu fide* in carrying out the above outrage, and the said Indians prefer to die in rebellion and apostasy rather than to yield or subject themselves to the yoke of the church.

Furthermore, so that it may not be said that the religious are the first to abandon this kingdom, I have them gathered safely where the Indians can not kill them until Your Most Reverend Paternity comes to a decision on what I should do after Your Most Reverend Paternity has seen and recorded the dispatches that I send with the father preacher Fray Juan de Alpuente. In them Your Most Reverend Paternity will see what I have done, and the implications of the governor of this kingdom in his replies, not providing and not having provided any help whatever on his part, for although I warned him in ample time to remove the sacred vessels from the missions, as well as the food, livestock, and the records and equipment of the religious, he promised to do so but never carried it out in order not to intimate to the Indians that they were believed to be confederated for the purpose of rising in rebellion, and he would only presume that the religious were the restive ones. Yet the said governor had no lack of reports and evidences, even from the Indians, but he gave this little regard until the event occurred.

And if the religious returned to their missions after I had gathered them together, it was to look after the objects of divine worship. And because in the Spanish settlements where they were staying they were undergoing many hardships, as I had no food to give them, and that which was available was in the missions and the governor did not wish to remove it, in spite of this I, on my part, made every possible effort to sustain them by stretching what little I had. And finally, if the religious returned to their missions it was because of their spontaneous desire, for never did I force them and order them to go; rather, I left it to what God our Lord would inspire them to do.

And it should be noted that the last *carta patente* that was circulated was on the 16th of March, and the replies were in my hands on April 21 of this year, as Your Most Reverend Paternity will recognize, and before I responded to their said letters for a final decision, they were already in their missions, so I did not have the opportunity to take any steps other than those that had been taken previously.

Of the deceased religious, two, Father Arbizu and Father Carbonel, were buried in the church at San Cristóbal. For days these two lay thrown on the ground, placed in the form of a cross, face up. When they went to bury them, they were found only in their underclothing, and the body of Father Arbizu was very easy to handle, soft, and not heavy, but rather very light, an occurrence which was noted by many soldiers who saw him, and Father Fray Blas Navarro and Father Fray Juan de Alpuente both are in complete accord. And also an Indian woman who was in the said pueblo of San Cristóbal at the time when they killed the two said fathers states that it took place at sundown. And she states that after the bodies were thrown on the ground, the old Indian women and other women put their arms around them and wept over them tenderly, sorrowful over the death of the said two religious and lamenting the hardships which they expected to undergo in the mountains with their children. And some of the Indian men were of this same sentiment. But the leaders of this treachery silenced them and chided them. The two fathers who died in San Ildefonso were not buried because their bodies were very fetid and rotted, so some walls were placed over them to hide them from the Indians, designating the location so that at an appropriate time the bones will be taken out and buried. When the soldiers went to the pueblo of father Fray Francisco de Jesús, they found that his body had been consumed by animals, but they gathered some of the bones, which they carried away and buried in the church at Zia.

And with regard to the preservation of this kingdom, I find, from what knowledge I have, that it is impossible to preserve, with the Spanish people who are now there perishing from hunger, the rebellious Indians in the mountains, all of the cultivated fields lost, the rigorous winter close at hand, recourse for help very distant, and the roads infested and harassed by the enemy, so that on every side there are difficulties.

And if I had not brought in the sheep to this custody as I did, the religious would have perished, because we have supported ourselves with those that remain. And of all that was stolen by the rebellious Indians, the governor was able to recover only eighty head of livestock. The losses that have been suffered by this holy custody in this uprising are very considerable, and this at the cost of what the holy custody had, including the part that was obtained through my request, endeavoring not to increase the expenses of our lord the king (may

God keep him), for His Majesty has given us the alms of the religious articles only every three years, and this has been since the foundation of the said custody. And up to the present time we only receive from His Majesty ten sacred vestments, with all of the effects to say mass, ten bells, ten iron moulds for hosts, and nothing else. And since there are twenty-seven missions, including those of El Paso, one may readily see the loss that the custody has suffered and the setback to its development at the cost and solicitude of the missionaries.

On all of these matters I have sent to His Excellency the lord viceroy, Count de Galve, a testimony and certification of the governor of this kingdom and other instruments which give honor and credit to our sacred religion, all of which passed through the hands of the most reverend father provincial, Fray Clemente de Ledesma, so that he might examine them closely and place them in the hands of His Excellency, and I have a reply from Your Very Reverend Paternity of having received them.

I send all these reports to Your Most Reverend Paternity in case some of the points might be necessary for the most excellent lord viceroy. And so as not to bother nor tire Your Most Reverend Paternity, I implore and request that you read the letter I am sending to our most reverend father minister provincial, to whom I report other points that are not contained in this one.

May God our Lord keep Your Most Reverend Paternity many happy years for my protection and that of this holy custody.

The convent of our father Saint Francis, Villa of Santa Fe, July 21, the year 1696. Your Most Reverend Paternity's son and humble servant, who kisses the feet of Your Most Reverend Paternity.

Fray Francisco de Vargas

86. LETTER OF FRAY FRANCISCO DE VARGAS TO THE FATHER GUARDIAN AT EL PASO, SANTA FE, JULY 21, 1696[1]

COPY of the letter written by the father preacher Fray Francisco de Vargas, custodian of this holy custody of New Mexico, to the father minister of the mission of the convent of El Paso del Río del Norte.

My father guardian Fray Miguel Aviniz, my friend and dear brother. If I had displeasures with the lord governor, it was in the effort to have him remedy that which no longer can be remedied; therefore, I do not regret my break with His Lordship with the uprising of these obstinate Indians who killed our

1. BNM, leg. 4, docs. 13, 16, 21.

brothers and friends Fray José Arbizu, Fray Antonio Carbonel, Fray Francisco Corbera, Fray Antonio Moreno,[2] and Fray Francisco de Jesús. The other ministers escaped miraculously, not because of the means provided by the lord governor, because he provided none, but because of Divine Providence. I was caught at Santa Ana the fourth day of June, which was the day of their fatal misfortune. And with the river running so high, it was difficult to cross even on a raft, and since I was aware of the malice, I did not give occasion for Bartolico or the others to carry out their purpose, because since they realized that we had foreseen their aim, their intentions, which were general among all those involved in the uprising, were frustrated. I give many thanks to God and to the Mansos, who were distributed in this kingdom among the pueblos and who a few days later, it being God's wish, all gathered in Santa Ana. They totaled eight, with my servant Lorenzo and with Felipe, who are famous in valor, and only with them, without a single Spaniard, I have defended and protected myself in Santa Ana and even done harm to the Jémez enemies, for of them they killed five men and captured eleven persons, five men and the other youths and two women, one of whom was the wife of Diaguillo of Jémez and the other his mother-in-law, who I have in my possession.

I removed from the pueblo of San Juan de Jémez, where I arrived on the fifth of June, at noon with some from Zia and Santa Ana who followed me, many objects of divine worship, and our allies seized horses, clothing, and much corn. At this time we were noticed, and the Jémez came down from their retreat above, with Apaches and Acomas, to attack us inside the said pueblo. And although they were a great multitude, God did not permit them to fall upon us, and this was under the leadership of Diaguillo, who came with the harquebus and leather jacket of Juan de Olguín, whom they had killed the day before in the said pueblo with two of his servants. But the said Indians thought that those who accompanied me were Spaniards, and they fled and were unable to take the captives from us. Felipe was wounded with a dart that struck his eyebrow, but there was no other casualty. My Mansos fought bravely, and the Keres of Zia and Santa Ana and Señor Bartolo all were engaged with the Mansos, and with the five deaths that they wrought on the Jémez, I assured myself which ones were the enemies of others, although at first they were all together. But it can no longer be said that all of them are bad. I risked my life alone without a single Spaniard at my side, but thanks be to God, I came out very well, and my Mansos came out very well dressed and with horses they captured. If the lord governor had endeavored to carry out this type of action with-

2. Fray Antonio Moreno, who died at San Ildefonso, was visiting there from his post as minister guardian of the mission at the pueblo of Nambé (see documents 87 and 88, below).

out giving the Indians time to fortify themselves in the mountains, so much would not have been lost, as has been lost, in the custody because of vain and foolish incredulity.

As for my part and my measures, let not Vargas's words but rather the written records speak for themselves,[3] which I send to our father prelates with a copy of all the petitions which I presented to the lord governor, and these are authorized by his secretary of war. If I had not found myself with so many protective actions and signatures of the religious, I might now be in a position to lose after having escaped from the Indians, but thanks be to God, all proceeds in the proper manner. And if the religious returned to their missions, it was because of their pleasure and not mine, for I always left it to their wishes, and of this I have writings in my possession in addition to the originals which I send. So I do not know in what way they can slander me as being neglectful. And if such should occur, it will be my misfortune, because on my part I have done all in my power to prevent what has resulted in deaths.

I beg of Your Reverence to show this to our Father Alvarez, because I cannot write to His Reverence at length about all of that which has happened. The omissions of the lord governor in reporting on this revolt are many. And although after the event took place, at different times I placed in the current of the river four small wooden boxes with papers reporting to that pueblo of El Paso, I believe that none of them arrived, and I feared that the uprising might have extended to El Paso. And since no mail was being dispatched at the time, I was ready to have two Mansos go to report on the state in which we found ourselves and to find out if things were quiet in El Paso, and if so that Your Reverence send me, if they should acquiesce, the Mansos referred to in the above papers, and with them at Santa Ana, along with those I have, I would have no fear of these treacherous ones.

May God our Lord keep Your Reverence many years. Villa of Santa Fe, July 21, 1696. Your Reverence's brother and friend, who holds you in esteem and kisses your hand.

Fray Francisco de Vargas

---

3. The traditional Spanish saying paraphrased here is "callen barbas y hablen cartas." In his letter Father Vargas writes instead, with sarcasm, "callen barbas o Vargas y hablen cartas," adding the name of Governor Vargas. The words "callen barbas o Vargas," which rhyme in Spanish, present the obvious note of sarcasm in Father Vargas's elaboration of the traditional Spanish saying.

87. LETTER OF FRAY FRANCISCO DE VARGAS TO THE
PROVINCIAL, SANTA FE, JULY 21, 1696[1]

OUR very reverend father minister provincial Clemente de Ledesma, my father and lord.

Our very reverend father minister provincial. The last letter which I sent to Your Very Reverend Paternity was on the eighteenth of the month of May of this present year, carried by the apostolic father preacher Fray José Diez, whom I entrusted to notify you of the state of affairs in this holy custody, for at that time we feared a revolt by the Indians of this kingdom. And in a letter which I dispatched to Your Very Reverend Paternity from El Paso del Río del Norte in the month of September of the past year, 'ninety-five, I wrote to Your Very Reverend Paternity that I feared that there might be many fatalities in this kingdom because of the lack of food supplies available to the Spaniards of this kingdom and the few arms and horses to restrain the enemies, who had taken possession of everything, leaving the Spaniards very destitute and with recourse to remedy the situation very far off, from which I inferred that the Indians might follow with deaths to avenge those that had been incurred on them.

And although they palliated their depraved intentions by assisting their ministers punctually and with other external demonstrations, which in appearance deceived many who were not familiar with their evil nature, they persevered in their continual ceremonies until the time came for them to carry out their treachery, which, fired by the devil to the perdition of their souls, they carried out on the fourth day of June, taking the lives of the father preacher, secretary of this custody, and minister president of the pueblo of San Cristóbal Fray José Arbizu, and in his company they killed the father preacher, *definidor* of this custody and minister president of the pueblo of Taos Fray Antonio Carbonel, who had come to the said pueblo of San Cristóbal for some of his belongings; and in the pueblo of San Ildefonso at about eight in the evening the Indians of the said pueblo, united with those of the Apache nation, surrounded the pueblo, and, fearing the few Spaniards who were there, set fire to the entire place, and since neither the father preacher and minister of said pueblo, Fray Francisco Corbera, nor the father preacher Fray Antonio Moreno, minister president of the pueblo of Nambé, who had gone there for spiritual consolation, could escape, they both died from the fire and fierce flames, suffocating from the smoke in a small room that they had entered to protect themselves, and with them a few lay persons; and in the pueblo of San Diego de los Jémez

1. BNM, leg. 4, doc. 18.

on that day at about eleven in the morning they took the life of the apostolic father preacher Fray Francisco de Jesús, whom they called, deceitfully, to go out to confess a sick person, and the Indians, waiting in advance at the door of the convent, caught him and killed him next to a cross that the said religious had set up in the cemetery; and on many occasions the said religious was heard to say, and I heard him say, that he had it so that they could crucify him on it, and although these wishes were not attained, he succeeded in expiring at the foot of the cross after he had been wounded many times, as they ended his life.[2] Oh what sorrow! These were the ones who died.

The others in the other missions escaped miraculously, for neither by the force of Spanish arms nor by protection provided by the governor of this king-

2. Since Fray Francisco de Jesús María Casañas was the first martyr from the Missionary College of Santa Cruz de Querétaro, he was the special subject of biographical accounts written by Franciscan historians, some published and others in manuscript, the most important being those of Fray Francisco Hidalgo, ms., 1707, and Fray Isidro Félix de Espinosa, published in Mexico in 1746. These sources, and other bibliographical items in manuscripts, are discussed in the notes for the chapters on Fray Francisco de Jesús María in Lino Gómez Canedo's edition of Espinosa's work entitled *Fray Isidro Félix de Espinosa, O.F.M.: Crónica de los Colegios de Propaganda Fide de la Nueva España* (Washington, D.C.: Academy of American Franciscan History, 1964). The chapters on Fray Francisco de Jesús in Gómez Canedo's edition comprise pages 459–94.

Fray Francisco de Jesús was born in 1656 in Barcelona, Spain, where he became a friar in the Franciscan province of Catalonia. Like most of his Franciscan contemporaries in New Mexico, he was a seasoned missionary in America, with many years of experience among the Indians. Since the early 1680s he had served as a missionary in Vera Cruz, Yucatán, Chiapas, Guatemala, Campeche, Mérida, Querétaro, and Texas. He spent two years in Texas from 1690 to 1692 (see documents 76 and 85, above; Espinosa, *Crónica,* Gómez Canedo edition, 459–66, 469–79; McClosky, *op. cit.,* 56–60, 66–72). He entered New Mexico with the Franciscan missionaries who accompanied Governor Vargas on his colonizing expedition of 1693 (see document 3, above).

Fray Francisco de Jesús was recognized by his fellow religious at the convent in Querétaro as a saintly person. In the privacy of his cell, and before his fellow religious in the convent, he inflicted severe bodily punishment on himself, including flagellation and, during the Lenten season, the carrying of a large heavy cross on his shoulders while wearing a crown of thorns that pierced his temples, emulating the suffering of Christ. It can be assumed that he continued these penitential practices while in New Mexico, since they were a part of his personal religious life. When he left El Paso for New Mexico, it is said that he was in a happy mood and that when he was asked why by a resident of the town, he replied, "Goodbye, brother, don't forget me in your prayers, for I am going to be killed by the Indians." At his mission among the Jémez, near the church cemetery he set up a cross on which he hoped to be crucified should it be his fortune to die at the hands of hostile Indians, and when he was betrayed by them, he managed to get to the foot of that cross, where he was brutally clubbed to death by Indian warriors (see documents 89 and 90, above).

Fray Francisco de Jesús and other Franciscan missionaries in their penitential practices undoubtedly influenced devout New Mexicans of their day, especially those who were members of the lay brotherhood of the Third Order of Saint Francis, the ritual of which centered on the Passion of Christ and which is also referred to in contemporary documents as the Third Order of Penance, "la tercera orden de penitencia." The establishment of the Third Order in 1694 under the direction of a Franciscan chaplain is recorded in document 23, above. It can be assumed that under the Franciscan friars as their mentors, members of the Third Order in seventeenth-century New Mexico in expiation for their sins practiced severe types of penance not unlike those performed by Fray Francisco de Jesús as described by Espinosa in his *Crónica,* Gómez Canedo edition, 481–83. The similarities to these forms of penance found later in New Mexico in the religious practices of the Hermanos de Nuestro Padre Jesús Nazareno, known as the Penitentes, lend support to the view that the Penitentes had their origin in the Third Order of Saint Francis as it evolved in New Mexico.

dom on the occasion were they delivered, but only by Divine Providence, for most of them were alone in their pueblos, unguarded by soldiers which I had petitioned of the lord governor, and all of the religious had made the same petition, which was never answered because of the incredulity of the governor, who never placed any credence in the pleas of the religious and only did so with regard to the feigned outward formalities of the Indians in his presence.

At that time I was at the pueblo and mission of Santa Ana alone, unaccompanied by any Spaniards, and only accompanied by some Indians of the Manso nation, who assisted me in every service that I needed because days before I had recognized that those of the pueblo were very agitated, from which I recognized that much evil was afoot, and I was cautious in dealing with them, living with very much apprehension and having the servants do likewise so that neither they nor I should perish. And in the impossible situation in which we found ourselves on the other side of the Río del Norte, which was flowing very high, so it could only be crossed on a raft, and this with great difficulty and manifest danger, amidst all of these inconveniences I notified the five religious who were on the other side of the river by letters that they should assemble at Bernalillo, where some Spaniards reside. And with the four now together, and certain that the Indians were in the mountains in revolt and that Father Fray Alfonso Jiménez de Cisneros, minister at Cochití, had left on foot accompanied only by a boy, awaiting until the middle of the night to go to the said place of Bernalillo, as he did, escaping miraculously, these religious were now safe.

And seeing that Father Fray Francisco de Jesús was late in replying to the letter I sent him telling him to come to the mission of Santa Ana, I presumed that he was with the *alcalde mayor* of his pueblo and two other Spaniards, locked up in the convent and defending themselves from the multitude of hostile Indians, and I judged that they had not come in answer to my call, even though there still was time, because they had no horses to do so.

Therefore, I decided to go and rescue them, taking with me the servants who accompanied me, who are experienced and brave, and these were joined by some Indians of the pueblo of Santa Ana and others of the pueblo of Zia, and so from all of them I had some consolation in seeing that they offered to accompany me even without my asking them to do so. All together, some forty persons were gathered, and I exhorted them to take heed that they were Christians and that they should realize that they were pursuing the cause of God our Lord, because it was my intention to go and rescue Father Jesús and the Spaniards and the sacred vessels, for I had no other motive. To this they displayed great bravery and said that they would follow me, as they did with their arms and horses. But despite all of these demonstrations I did not fully trust the said Indians, and I ordered the domestic servants who accompanied me personally not to leave me but rather to be always at my side, to be sure that I would not be taken by surprise by some treacherous act.

And having traveled about six leagues, we arrived at the pueblo of San Juan de los Jémez, where the minister was the apostolic father preacher Fray Miguel de Trizio, who a few days earlier I had granted permission to go to the pueblo of Pecos at the request and for the consolation of the father who was stationed there. And on coming in view of the said pueblo of San Juan, the Indians who accompanied me decided, themselves, to lay siege to the pueblo to see if they could capture an Indian from whom they could find out if Father Fray Francisco de Jesús was alive or dead, because the pueblo of San Juan is only one league from that of San Diego, where he resided. And having placed this plan in operation, the advance to the pueblo was made, and eleven persons, children, men, and women, were captured, and these later stated that Father Jesús and the Spaniards had been killed with the help of other nations.

But the said Indians who accompanied me were not satisfied with the eleven persons taken prisoners, and some of them went out to explore the roads, where they found many Indians who were fleeing to the mountains loaded with food supplies and clothing, and when they were seen, they opened battle and killed five of them, and of the Indians who accompanied me, only five were wounded, but not dangerously. And they took from the apostates many horses, clothing, and corn. And during the time that they were engaged in this activity, with the few Indians who remained with me I ventured to the convent to remove what I could of what pertained to our divine religion, and what I found was the images of the saints destroyed and in pieces and the crosses broken. And in the church it was the same, the rosaries thrown on the ground and covered with feathers, ashes, and some rabbit skins, leaving no trace of anything Christian, a mockery which caused very much affliction in my heart and which would cause the same to any Catholic on seeing the little benefit that had been derived from these souls. And passing on to their houses and dwellings, I searched them and removed many articles of divine worship, some of which they had buried and others hidden. And while we were engaged in this activity, we were already noticed by the pueblo above, from which many Indians came on foot and on horseback, some armed with harquebuses and leather jackets, but it was the will of our Lord God that on reaching about four squares from the pueblo, where we were, seeing the large number of their adversaries and judging that all those who were accompanying me were Spaniards, they returned in flight to their pueblos, for which I give many thanks to His Divine Majesty, because the removal of the articles of divine worship, which I have referred to, was accomplished. Women and children were captured besides the men, who were five. Three of the Indians had an untimely end for their little heed, because the governors and captains of the two pueblos of Santa Ana and Zia together decided to send them to the lord governor, and that night one of them escaped from the *estufa* where they had been imprisoned, and in the morning when they were inspected two were found who had hanged themselves by their own hands. They are so obstinate that they prefer to die in despair rather than live under the yoke of our holy religion.

And returning to my distrust of these Indians who accompanied me, as was shown by the action they carried out I was assured that the three pueblos of Zia, Santa Ana, and San Felipe would not rise in rebellion, for these, in all of the battles that have taken place, have helped the Spaniards, as has been the case with the Pecos nation and those of the pueblo of Tesuque, for only these five pueblos have helped and have not rebelled and have fought against the apostates of our holy faith, and they are administered the holy sacraments in the following manner: at the pueblo of Tesuque, which serves as a *visita* of the Villa of Santa Fe, which is three leagues distant, its minister, accompanied by a military escort, goes to say mass; at the pueblo of Pecos, which is four leagues from this villa, it is visited every fifteen days in this same manner; at that of Zia, the minister assists, since he has eight soldiers as guard; at the pueblo of Santa Ana, I assist because of the love they have for me and also because I find the said place good for my health; at San Felipe, Father Fray Alfonso Jiménez assists at the *visita* on Sundays and feast days and then returns to the settlement of Bernalillo, where some Spaniards reside. And it is to be noted that these religious are in these administrations of their own free will without having forced them or ordered them to do so; rather, these reverend fathers offered and requested of me to remain there, because with what occurred, it was my intention that the ministers should remain only in the Spanish settlements and not in Indian settlements.

And in this Villa of Santa Fe at present the following religious are found: as minister guardian, Father Preacher Fray Antonio de Azevedo; Father Preacher Fray Juan de Zavaleta; Father Preacher Fray Diego de Chavarría; Father Preacher Fray Juan Antonio del Corral; Apostolic Father Preacher Fray Miguel de Trizio; Apostolic Father Preacher Fray José García; and Apostolic Father Preacher Fray Blas Navarro; and at the Villa Nueva de Santa Cruz, Father Preacher Fray Antonio de Obregón. These have been withheld until I know Your Very Reverend Paternity's decision and order. In the meantime, "the choir continues," with all the rest, as is in keeping with the monastic life.

The only thing that torments me is the lack of food supplies, for these, at the cost of much work and solicitude on my part, have been brought from the Pecos mission and from no other pueblos, because all that there was at the missions was stolen by the Indians who rebelled, leaving no livestock or other things of use to the religious. And those who escaped with their lives I am now supporting with the little that I can provide for their needs, for they remained completely destitute. And the Indians are interested only in obtaining the equipment of the ministers, the livestock, and everything with regard to the divine religion, all of which they broke to pieces and profaned, and very little of it has appeared in the battles that have been fought up to this time. And of the deceased religious, only a few pieces of religious jewelry of father Fray José Arbizu have been recovered, which were distributed among the religious, and over one hundred masses have been said for him. The livestock lost in this revolt must be about fourteen hundred head of sheep and about one hundred large livestock, including horses, cows, and oxen. Of these, about eighty head of sheep have perished. And the pity is that both the lives of the religious and everything else could have been saved by the lord governor. For with my requests and letters, which I presented to His Lordship since the month of December of the past year, 'ninety-five, he could have corrected the situation in time, as Your Very Reverend Paternity will recognize from the letters that I am sending to our most reverend father commissary general so that the honor of our sacred religion may be guaranteed and so that the excellent lord viceroy and the royal *audiencia* may recognize the charges that have been made against the said governor and that which has been achieved by the ministers of the gospel in this holy custody, which can be no more than to sacrifice their lives and to have placed them in the hands of the sacrilegious apostates of our holy faith only for the purpose of protecting the holy vessels and objects of divine worship, since the lord governor did not wish to remedy the situation in time. And so that Your Very Reverend Paternity may know that the religious were motivated by this zeal, I transmit those three original letters, and in them Your Very Reverend Paternity will recognize the zeal which motivated the said fathers to return to their missions. For I, as I have written to Your Very Reverend Paternity, had them gathered together and protected in the Spanish settlements, although with practically no food, because what there was of it in the missions the governor did not wish to remove. He only wished that by their wits, without any help, they should find some food. And since His Lordship did not venture to do so himself with his soldiers and beasts of burden, fearing the Indians, how could the poor religious not be afraid? And so I have no doubt that it was because of their dire needs in the Spanish settlements and to protect the sacred vessels, as already referred to, that some of them returned to their missions.

I was not able to have the food supplies that I had collected in El Paso brought in wagons or by beasts of burden, not for lack of orders which I sent for that purpose to the father procurator Fray Francisco Farfán, as well as to the brother procurator Fray Buenaventura de Contreras, but because the wagons must have been in such bad condition to wheel that the transportation of the said food supplies was not attempted. And what I foresee in the future is the war that has continued since the revolt up to the present. The horse herds have destroyed the cultivated fields and the wheat that was ripening, and since the needs that the Spanish people are suffering are so great, as are those that we suffer, it is being cut even before it is ripe, and it is becoming impossible to send any to El Paso del Río del Norte or to be stored in this Villa of Santa Fe. It is a pity to see men, women, and children, famished with hunger, eating roasted cow hide, and even this is scarce, and they even kill the dogs to eat them, a situation which has obliged me to have some lambs killed to help these poor people, and with those that remain I am sustaining the religious. And I am reserving, for whatever might happen, at the pueblo of Santa Ana and the place of Bernalillo about two hundred fifty head, and at the pueblo of San Felipe, one hundred, so that if they are needed in one place, by accident of war from the enemy, they will not be lacking in the other, and with them we will be able to support ourselves if we have to leave. If the said livestock had not been brought up from El Paso at the opportune moment, we religious would have perished.

As for any prospect of winning over the rebellious Indians in the mountains, there is no hope that they will submit to our holy faith. And although the governor of this kingdom, in the campaigns he has made with his soldiers and Indian allies, having punished and killed up to eighty Indians, having captured some women and children, and having seized their food, even with all of this it is evident that the enemy is very rebellious and contumacious in their relapse to apostasy. And they are well aware of the little military strength of the Spaniards and that the rigors of winter are near at hand, at which time the Indians can make war against the Spaniards in full safety without any harm being done to them. And what is most regrettable is that the governor, seeing the wickedness that they have carried out up to now, is sending a mission of peace, as he has done with three Indian women of those taken captive, whom he sent to the mountains with some crosses to negotiate peace with them, as though the said apostates, being enemies of our holy faith, would venerate or adore the holy cross, especially when they have just completed the outrage that they committed on the priests. And I recognize that if they should come down peacefully, what minister will want to assist them, when it is seen how little progress is gained in the attempt to win their souls, and what can be expected in living with them in the future? And if the governor aspires to pacify them only by his point of honor and standing, and if this peace is only to be a pretense to cover up their wickedness, as bloodthirsty wolves in sheep's clothing, we ministers of the gospel can not profit from such evilness. And now that God our Lord has been served, with only five religious and approximately thirty Spaniards having perished, with the women captives who have remained with them, we cannot place ourselves under the risk of having all of the priestly ministers perish. For the only ones who can be administered will be those who have been proven to be loyal; these I would not fail to have assisted. And if I have not granted permission to the religious who are now in this Villa of Santa Fe to leave for El Paso del Río del Norte without being assigned to administer, it has been with the consideration that it not be said at any time that the religious are the first who have forsaken the kingdom and that the Spanish people have followed them. In short, if God our Lord gives us life, it will be seen that the Spanish people, even contrary to the dictates of the governor, will leave for El Paso del Río del Norte, for they are ready to go there, and if that should occur, we will continue with our parishioners with the help of God, subject to the orders and mandates of Your Most Reverend Paternity, which I will carry out with prompt obedience.

For the above reasons I have decided to dispatch this packet of papers and reports to you, most reverend father, with Fray Juan de Alpuente of the holy province of barefoot friars of San Diego of Mexico, who had presented a petition to me, which, from the tenor of the license that he carries, Your Very Reverend Paternity will recognize, and I do this on this occasion so as not to entrust a letter of such consequence to a civilian messenger or to permit it to fall into the hands of the governor and endanger the loss of the said dispatches or that they be hidden or that anyone obscure the truth which is so clear and evident, as is the case of the others that I have written to Your Very Reverend Paternity. And if on some occasions I have written of successes in this kingdom, it has been according to the times and in accordance with what appeared to be good signs on the part of the Indians. Therefore, in this respect Your Very Reverend Paternity will examine my letters and those of the religious and will sort out the certain and the doubtful ones and will be prepared for the future on the basis of my experience.

And in order that Your Most Reverend Paternity may be fully informed of what has happened up to the present I am sending the said father Fray Juan de Alpuente, who will report more extensively and as a first-hand witness of all that has occurred. And said father, with your resolution, most reverend father, and that of our most reverend father commissary general, having seen the letters that I send, and it being the wish of Your Most Reverend Paternity that it be appropriate to reply, that it be brought by the said father Fray Juan de Alpuente returning to this holy custody after leaving your most reverend paternity. For this purpose he carries the necessary provisions to go there and return. And if it is possible for him to return as soon as possible, I will be grateful, so that I may carry out, at the proper time, that which you, most reverend father, order me to do. For to make your decision you have at your disposal the writings to Your Most Reverend Paternity. Copies of all of them remain in the archive of this custody, and I send the originals. Since these writings are so diffuse I am not sending an extra copy for you, most reverend father, whom I request that God our Lord may protect many very happy years, for my aid and that of this holy custody.

Convent of Our Father Saint Francis of Your Most Reverent Paternity. Villa of Santa Fe, July 21, the year 1696. Your son and humble servant, who kisses the feet of Your Most Reverend Paternity.

Fray Francisco de Vargas

88. GOVERNOR VARGAS TO THE VICEROY, LETTER OF TRANSMISSION OF *AUTOS* AND REPORTS, JUNE–JULY, SANTA FE, JULY 31, 1696[1]

MOST excellent lord. My lord, on the twenty-eighth of March past, of the present year, I transmitted to Your Excellency the *autos* which, by virtue of the three petitions presented to me on the part of the very reverend father custodian, the *definitorio,* and the reverend father *definidores,* refer to them, and they are recorded therein. They refer to the rumors and opinions that the Indians of the nations of this said kingdom were prepared to revolt. These said rumors and opinions have spread among the citizens of the kingdom and also among the reverend fathers of some of the missions since July of the past year sixteen hundred ninety-five. And through my action and attention I caused the said Indians to desist in their desire and to abandon their plans. In fact, they assured me of this as I observed their activities, for in going to visit the various nations in their pueblos of the Jémez, Pecos, and Keres, and those of the Tiwas on three occasions, I found that they were well along in planting their abundant *milpas,* both with crops and vegetables, and the gardens of the reverend fathers in the said pueblos and missions were also in a prosperous condition. And I left each of them pleased and living free from the said fear, confusion, and opinions resulting from rumors. This was reinforced by my having placed in the Villa Nueva nineteen families in addition to the group of settlers who entered under the leadership of Captain Juan Páez from Zacatecas, which entered this Villa of Santa Fe on May 9 of the past year 'ninety-five. And so in both cases I left them with their lands and corn seeds distributed so that they all could do their planting. And in this Villa of Santa Fe I did the same for the families who had come from outside as well as those of the kingdom who are residing together there. And living with this confidence, they are entering and leaving to and from all the pueblos, even including the most remote and distant ones of the Taos, Picurís, and Jémez. And the captain of this presidio,

1. AGI, *Guadalajara,* leg. 141, doc. 19.

Don Antonio Valverde, went with the *alférez* and other soldiers to the pueblo of Taos, and leaving there very early in the morning on Monday, the fourth of the month of June, he went to the pueblo of San Cristóbal, where he visited the reverend father Fray José Arbizu, minister of the said perverse nation of the Tanos, and in his company as guest was the reverend father Fray Antonio Carbonel, who was on his way to his mission of Taos and whom he [Father Arbizu] had asked to spend the day there. And the said captain and *alférez* were at the said pueblo, and they told me that they had left Taos with its said people in good spirits, and that it was the same at Picurís, through which they passed and where the said Indians were building the house for their reverend father minister. And they were in the said pueblo of San Cristóbal with the aforesaid reverend fathers, with whom they drank chocolate at six in the evening, with their leather jackets and arms removed, which they left with their horses in the plaza in the care of the said Indians, along with their firearms. And they said that they remained there until about six-thirty in the evening, and from there they passed through the said Villa Nueva, and from there they came here, arriving at eleven o'clock that evening, and on the following day they gave me this report.

On said day, Monday, the fourth of the said month of June past, of this present year 'ninety-six, I received, at six in the evening, two letters, which go forward at the beginning of the *autos,* sent with an Indian of the Keres nation of San Felipe, our friends, one from the reverend father Fray Alfonso Jiménez de Cisneros, minister catechist of the pueblo of Cochití, and the other from the *alcalde mayor* Don Fernando de Chávez. The said father stated to me that in the morning of the previous day, after mass, the said Indians had taken his large and small livestock up to the mountains, as well as the horses that he had, leaving him on foot, and that it was only by the grace of God that his life had been spared, and that he left the said pueblo at four o'clock in the morning and arrived before daybreak at the said pueblo of San Felipe, where he came upon the said *alcalde mayor,* who was traveling with some residents of the locality of Bernalillo. The reason why the said *alcalde mayor* was there, on said day Sunday, at mass, as he said in his letter to me, was to carry out the task of sending me four bachelor residents who, without my permission, were discovered to have gone to live at the said pueblo of Cochití. And the reason to seek them out was that during the previous week they had succeeded in stealing some oxen from a resident of this villa in the evening, and when his servant went to gather them to enclose them in the corral, he saw the tracks indicating that they had been taken away by someone on horseback. And with the said news, which he gave to his master, he took his harquebus, and with his said servant he followed the tracks. And by the grace of God our Lord, traveling until the next day until sundown he came upon the said oxen in a hidden meadow near the bed of the river facing the mesa and mountain slopes near the pueblo of Cochití. And he also found the head of a horse that they had killed, reddish in color, and the meat which they had cut into pieces for roasting fresh horse meat, which provided food for him and his servant. And in the said meadow he also found two horses hobbled with ropes of Tehuacán, from which it was recognized that the said theft had not been made by Indians. And he mounted one of them and his servant the other, bareback, and in this way he brought back his oxen, and it was found that one of the horses had been stolen from a soldier and the other from a resident. And for this reason I gave said order to the said *alcalde mayor* Don Fernando de Chávez to send me as prisoners the said four settlers, judging that they were the ones who had stolen the said oxen and horses. And on said day Sunday, the third, after mass, he found three of them in the said pueblo. Being told that they would be brought to me, they were allowed to come to tell me that Antonio de la Torre was in hiding and that he did not live with them in the said pueblo but in the one occupied by the Indians on the said mesa, and that those from Cochití helped them willingly to cross the river on rafts, and that for fear of being drowned they did not cross. And the said Antonio de la Torre had arrived at the said pueblo of San Felipe in the morning of said day, Monday, wounded by lances and arrows, scalped, and left for dead.

And after I received the said letters, which I had placed at the head of the campaign journals [*autos de guerra*], I ordered the military leader Juan de Ulibarri, accompanied by an old soldier named Juan de Perea, to go to the Villa Nueva with the letters, which contained the information for the said *alcalde mayor* and the reverend father guardian so that the reverend fathers of those missions could withdraw to the said villa, since it was so near by, or, if they preferred, to come to this Villa of Santa Fe. I also dispatched ammunition of powder and bullets to the said lieutenant general in charge of the horses. At the same time, I sent an order to the military leader Juan de Archuleta, who was in charge of the horses that were between the said Villa Nueva and the pueblo of the Tewas of San Juan de los Caballeros, to provide the said *alcalde mayor* and lieutenant general in charge of the horses, Roque Madrid, with two of my saddle horses, which I designated, and eight of the soldiers so that he would be reinforced with the said soldiers, and I ordered that he be on guard for the defense of the said villa. And I also gave orders to the said military leader Archuleta to withdraw with the horses to this Villa of Santa Fe. I also sent the said information and order to the *alcalde mayor* and military captain of the pueblo of Pecos, Sergeant Francisco de Anaya, so that he could notify the two father missionaries who were in said pueblo, and under the pretense that the reverend father Fray José García Marín was ill, that he be brought up here with his companion and that he should tell the governor, Don Felipe, that I awaited him here to come on Wednesday with one hundred Indian warriors and that they be here by noon and that they should come well armed with their weapons and with their horses and food supplies. I gave him the same instruction regarding the bringing of the said fathers for the reason that on the one hand it was not good to give the Indians to understand that we did not confide in them, and on the other hand to confide in them that their warriors were being brought to fight against the said enemy, and I ordered that he come very cautiously.

All of this I included in my reply to the said two letters, which I sent with an Indian of San Felipe, indicating that there were no new developments in these pueblos and that it appeared that only that of Cochití was guilty of the aforesaid theft of the oxen and horses and that on Thursday afternoon I would be at the edge of the ford of the river in front of the pueblo of Santo Domingo with the said Indian warriors I had summoned and with the soldiers. And I also ordered that the residents of the said place and *alcaldía mayor* of Bernalillo be asked to provide six milk cows that they now have for food for the said soldiers, and that I would pay for them. And thus I sent the said Indian courier, rewarding him and paying him for his work. And also, in this villa I examined the arms and opened two boxes that I had in reserve, which were among those not currently for use, as well as the ammunition of powder and bullets, which were for all of the people so that they would be ready in case of a battle, and I had the horses that slept outside of the plaza brought in from the outside so that I would be ready to meet the enemy if he should come. And I also withdrew the people who were scattered in their cornfields within a short league in the surrounding area.

With these arrangements and preparations I retired to my room, exhausted from sleepless nights, where a short while later, at about eleven at night, I received a letter carried by an Indian named El Tempano who lives in the said villa, who is apt as a linguist and who, on the said day, Monday, was at the aforementioned pueblo of San Cristóbal, where the Indians were entertaining him, and he said that after the said captain and *alférez* had left, the people gathered in the said pueblo, and he saw that they were in revolt, and he escaped by telling them that he would help them and that he would return to do so. And by this means of leaving he went immediately to the said Villa Nueva, where he arrived after dark, as the said *alcalde mayor* and lieutenant Roque Madrid reported that he had been notified that the Indians of San Cristóbal had revolted, along with the Keres, Apaches, Moquis, and Pecos. And by virtue of this report he [Roque Madrid] had had the horses of the said residents brought in, and he prepared to go to the said pueblo of San Cristóbal because he was told that the father might already have been killed. At the same time, I received the other letter from the Indian Domingo, who said that he had been notified from Cuyamungué by the singer Francisco that all of the nation was in revolt, including also the Taos, Picurís, Acomas, Zuñis, and Jémez, and that only the people of his pueblo of Tesuque were under control and on our side. And I ordered that the said letters also be placed at the head of the said *autos*.

On Tuesday, the fifth, I sent a military escort to the other ranches of Los Cerrillos, El Alamo, and La Ciénaga and the help of beasts of burden to the *alcalde mayor* of Los Cerrillos so that he could withdraw to this said villa. I also sent the military leader Juan de Archuleta with five soldiers and a letter to the *alcalde mayor* of Bernalillo, telling him to confer with reference to the information contained in the said letters and ascertain whether the revolt of the said Indians of these pueblos was true, and I ordered him to find out if the people were safe and, if not, [tell them] that they should withdraw to this said Villa of Santa Fe, as I had sent them the said military escort for this purpose, as is of record in the letter contained in the said *autos,* a copy of which I sent to the said *alcalde mayor.*

On that day the military leaders Juan de Ulibarri and the one in charge of guarding the horses arrived, bringing me the news that the Tanos Indians of the pueblo of San Cristóbal had killed there the reverend father preacher Fray José Arbizu, their minister catechist and the guardian of said convent, and the reverend father *definidor* Fray Antonio Carbonel, guardian and minister president of the pueblo of Taos, having killed them outside of the said convent, and that they also had killed Simón de Molina and Diego Betanzos, a singer, who had come with the Mexican families and whom the above-mentioned reverend father Fray José Arbizu had in his employ making the doors for the church and repairing the said convent, and also a young Mexican Indian servant, fourteen or fifteen years of age, of the said Father Arbizu, and also another young Indian boy, nine or ten years old, who spoke Spanish, from the town of El Paso del Río del Norte. And that at the pueblo of San Juan de los Caballeros, with the news of all that which is referred to above, Juan de Archuleta, who was in the canyon, immediately had gone to the said pueblo of San Juan de los Caballeros, where the reverend father Fray Blas Navarro, who had locked himself in with a soldier named Matías Lobato, was sleeping in his convent, where they had gathered the sacred vessels and ornaments. And he [Archuleta] said that the people of the pueblo had already left and it was uninhabited. Thus, he left, bringing with him the said father Fray Blas Navarro and the said soldier to the Villa Nueva. The latter had left his horse, saddled, at the door of the said convent, and they stole it, leaving him the saddle. And that having passed on to the pueblo of San Ildefonso, he [Archuleta] found the church and convent burned, and in a room of the said convent and church they had killed, suffocated by the smoke, because they had closed up all of the windows and skylights with straw, the reverend father Fray Francisco Corbera, minister catechist and president of the said convent, and the reverend father Fray Antonio Moreno, missionary minister and guardian of the pueblo of Nambé, who on that day, Monday, had gone to see him and had remained for the night. And in the said pueblo they also found the dead bodies of Doña Juana de Almazán with her son Alonso, seventeen years of age, and her daughter Doña Leonor, who was married to a soldier, with a daughter and a son, and a soldier named Mateo Trujillo. And they passed on to Nambé, where they found that the sacred vessels and ornaments had been carried off, the said convent had been looted, and they [the Indians] had killed Juan Cortés, his daughter, and his son-in-law, named José Sánchez, all of the said having come with the families from Mexico.

On said day at midnight, the *alcalde mayor* of Pecos arrived with the two fathers who were at said pueblo, and he said that the said Indians, with their governor Don Felipe, would be at this said villa on the following day, Wednesday, at noon. On Wednesday, the sixth, at two o'clock in the afternoon, the governor Don Felipe arrived at this villa, bringing with him the said one hundred Indian warriors with their captains. I welcomed them, served them chocolate, and gave them tobacco, and I told them how loyal they were. I then told them to rest until the next day and that the *alcalde mayor* would keep them advised. Thus, they left, very pleased, to set up their camp and a place for their horses beyond the cornfields of this villa. On said day in the afternoon, the *alcalde mayor* and war captain Don Alonso Rael de Aguilar arrived from the mining town of Los Cerrillos and the jurisdiction of El Alamo and La Cieneguilla, its pueblos, and that of Cochití. He informed me that the previous night he had slept with the residents of other localities at the hacienda of El Alamo, and he brought prisoner the Indian governor of said pueblo of Santo Domingo, who was found outside the said hacienda. And on questioning him, after making sure of his own protection, since he was armed and on a swift horse, [the governor] told [Aguilar] that he had first gone to the said place of Los Cerrillos, and not finding it, he had gone to La Ciénaga, and not finding it, he was on his way to the said hacienda of El Alamo. And the said governor was telling the truth, but not about the purpose of his search, for it was probably to find the rebellious Indians of his said pueblo, who were lying in ambush, and finding the people of the said places gathered together in the said hacienda, he did not dare to enter, nor did he have time to look further for the place where the ambush was left, which must have been in a well-hidden place difficult to find, because the location of the said hacienda of El Alamo is on open land and without woods where the enemy could hide.

By the said day, Wednesday, the sixth, the people of said hacienda and ranches had been withdrawn and were safe inside this said fortress and Villa of Santa Fe, where all the windows and open doorways to the outside of the said fortress were covered over and well enclosed with adobe bricks and the entrances to the said houses in the two plazas were closed from the inside. At the same time, I named as military leader the inactive sergeant José de Contreras and gave him from the muster roll twenty-four soldiers, assigning to him the bastion, intrenchments, and fortified tower, where he was to place them as sentinels, all with their arms and ammunition, alternating them at the regular change of guards. And with everything in readiness and prepared, I took muster of the soldiers with the officials, leaders, and my lieutenant, leaving the thin horses that could be an impediment guarded by six soldiers in the villa so that they would be kept away from their cornfields and kept enclosed in the plaza of the villa after sundown. And I ordered the said captain and *ayudante* that the said people should be mounted at daybreak and that he should so advise the *alcalde mayor* of Pecos so that his people likewise would be ready to leave with me at that time.

On Thursday, the seventh of said month, I left with the said people indicated above to reconnoiter the pueblos of the said rebels, both of Nambé and of San Ildefonso, and to bury the dead, which I had already done with regard to those of the pueblo of San Cristóbal and the Villa Nueva, the said *alcalde mayor* and lieutenant general of the cavalry Roque Madrid having taken them, along with some religious articles of the said reverend father Fray José Arbizu and everything concerning the divine religion and the sacred vessels, all of which were received by the reverend father Fray Antonio Obregón, guardian of the said Villa Nueva. And having entered the pueblo of Tesuque, I found its governor Domingo with all of his people, and they received me submissively, indicating their loyalty and assuring me that they were not accomplices or plotters of the said revolt, since the people had left the pueblo of Cuyamungué, where Francisco the singer had come to sing, as has been written in the letter that is of record in the said *autos*. And responding to them, having lined up in the said plaza the twenty men in the squad that accompanied me, I made known to them how important it was for them to be loyal to His Majesty the king, our lord, may God protect him, who had great power, and that I would follow those who fled as far as Gran Quivira.

And I took leave of them and passed on to the pubelo of Nambé, where I saw and recognized the four dead bodies of the persons who assisted the reverend father Fray Antonio Moreno, minister catechist and president of the said convent, and it is of record that they are the ones indicated in the report of the fifth made by the military leader Juan de Ulibarri. I, said governor, ordered that the said bodies be buried in an old fallen-down house next to the cemetery of the said church, since the cemetery had been profaned. The other bodies were so decomposed and rotted that they emitted a sickening stench. And so they were buried, the services being performed by the reverend father lector and *definidor* Fray Juan de Alpuente. I asked him to inspect the said convent and to gather whatever religious articles he might find, and entering with him, I saw some broken boxes and two bottle cases, and I found only the missal and some books and the broken box of the holy oils, the contents of which had been poured out on the ground. And in the church we found, in place on the main altar, Our Lady of the Conception and also the bell, which was hanging undisturbed, and I had it removed and with the said image and the books I took them to the said Villa Nueva, where they were turned over by the said reverend father to its guardian, Fray Antonio Obregón.

At said Villa Nueva I found Don José Manuel de Galdámes, naked, turned into the living image of Lazarus, clubbed and badly wounded, whom the said Indians of Nambé, thinking that he was dead, had thrown into the *estufa* and who, feigning that he was dead, escaped from said pueblo to the said villa in the evening when he heard no signs of life in the said pueblo, and thus he succeeded in escaping, and I sent him as much alms as I could to help him in his dire need.

A short time later, the said *alcalde mayor*, Roque Madrid, arrived from the pueblo of San Ildefonso, which he had gone to inspect with some of the said residents and soldiers, since it was reported that some of the said rebels were about, and in the said pueblo he found a small amount of corn, about fifteen or sixteen *fanegas*, which served them well in their need. And they found there an old woman whom they left hanging in the plaza, and they found the said bodies uncorrupted, and it was observed that they had suffocated from the smoke and heat of the fire in which they had been engulfed.

On Friday, the eighth, I left the said villa with the said squad and soldiers for the pueblo of San Ildefonso, and in the sacristy of the church were found the bodies of the reverend fathers Fray Francisco de Corbera and Fray Antonio Moreno and another body that appeared to be Mateo Trujillo, and that of his son Agustín, recognized as such from his said father, and the aforesaid reverend father Fray Juan de Alpuente ordered Melchor de Herrera, who was with him, to remove from the neck of Fray Francisco de Corbera a very small relic of the *santo lignum crucis,* which the said father had in an octagonal glass locket. And it was seen that the said bodies were badly decomposed, as were the other bodies of the women and the children of Doña Juana de Almazán. As they had been reported on the fifth by the military leader Juan de Ulibarri, they were found in the same form, suffocated in the convent. And since the bodies were so rotted and could not be moved, I ordered the Pecos Indians, with the help of the said soldiers, assisted by the said reverend father, to tear down the walls of the said sacristy and convent so that in this way they would remain buried. And in inspecting the houses of said pueblo, the said soldiers and Indian warriors found a small amount of corn, which was distributed among as many as possible.

I left the said pueblo and proceeded to Jacona, and there we found an Indian, who, being rebellious, was shot with a harquebus after first being absolved by the said father. And returning to this villa, the captain with some of the soldiers traveled around the right bend in the hills and found six Indians, whom he reported had been killed. And in due course I entered the Villa of Santa Fe on said day, the eighth, where I was given the report that the said Mateo Trujillo had arrived naked and had said that he had escaped with his sword in his hand and that it had taken him four days to arrive, as he was barefoot, naked, and faint and had traveled off the course of the road to protect his life, and that at night he slept covered over with many branches. And thus his son Agustín, who had wept over him and threw dirt over him, thinking he was dead, and [the youth's] mother, who thought she was a widow, suddenly found herself with her said husband, who had arrived at this said villa on Thursday, at three in the afternoon on the seventh of the present month. And I also found that I had received a letter that had been written to me by the chief war captain of the Keres nation and governor of the pueblo of Santa Ana, Bartolomé de Ojeda, which is of record in the said *autos,* informing me that they were in very great danger and asking me to send some men to assist them and that their enemies were the Acomas and Jémez, as he was thus informed by a young Indian who had fled from the pueblo of Zia, where the said rebels were gathered awaiting the Moquis, Zuñis, and Utes, and it was presumed that all of the enemy were gathered·at the pueblo of the Jémez.

On Saturday the ninth, by virtue of the said letter, I wrote to the *alcalde mayor* and army captain Don Fernando Chávez at the pueblo of San Felipe as recorded in the said *autos,* ordering him to withdraw with the said residents of the settlement and neighboring ranches of Bernalillo to the pueblo of San Felipe, where they could halt, and go down to cross the river, as they would be safe on the mesa where the said pueblo is located, and that on being informed that they were there I would send them an armed escort to accompany them to this said Villa of Santa Fe, for their children and women and livestock would be safer on the said mesa than on open land. And I asked him to carry out this order without question, as I thus ordered in the name of His Majesty. I also wrote another letter to the reverend father custodian who was at the mission of Santa Ana, close by the said place of Bernalillo and the said friendly Indians, so that His Very Reverend Paternity, with knowledge of the said order to the said *alcalde mayor,* would withdraw to this said Villa of Santa Fe and that he follow the same instructions with regard to the reverend fathers who were at the said place of Bernalillo and the one who was at the above-mentioned pueblo of San

Felipe, since war had broken out and I did not have the forces to distribute the small number available and thereby leave the whole region defenseless, because with the combined enemy forces so far superior, an irreparable calamity could occur. The said letter is of record in the *autos*.

On the said day, Saturday, the ninth, in the morning, the governor of the pueblo of Pecos, the Indian Don Felipe, reported to me, in the presence of the sergeant major and *alcalde mayor* Francisco de Anaya Almazán, after I had closed the door of my room, that a treacherous plan had been prepared for a revolt, along with most of the people of the said pueblo, by the old cacique Don Diego Umbiro and two young warriors with a large following, prominent among whom was the war captain Cachina, who was at the time in Taos, and that for this reason he knew that they were in revolt and gathered with the Jémez, who speak the same language, and most of whom are their friends and relatives, and that if I ordered him to do so, he would hang them, to which I replied that if what he said was true and he had the valor, and had Indians he had confidence in to carry it out, that he do so when the said captain Cachina arrived, to which he answered in the affirmative. And doubting what he said, I replied that it would be well for him to take with him some soldiers that I would provide to carry out the said punishment, to which he replied that with his band of followers he had the means to hang them. And I strongly encouraged him, promising to grant him many favors in the name of His Majesty, and he embraced me and left very pleased. On said day, at about ten o'clock in the night, I received a letter from the lieutenant general of the cavalry and *alcalde mayor* of the Villa Nueva, Roque Madrid, reporting that he had located the said rebellious enemy Tewas and Tanos of the pueblo of San Cristóbal in the vicinity of the said villa in the hills in view of the said pueblo, and that they had raised a large cloud of smoke and that the Tewas of the pueblo of Santa Clara and their allies had raised another one. And he was informing me so that I would sent him more men, four firearms, and ammunition. Therefore, I had the *ayudante* Juan de Cazares arm eight soldiers, and I gave him four firearms in accordance with his wishes and a good supply of ammunition and sent him with a reply to the said *alcalde mayor* in which I told him that with twenty-two soldiers that I had as reinforcements in the said villa, which was protected by embrasures and entrenchments and was well secured, he could defend himself and do great damage to the enemy, who might return here to find resistance and opposing strength. And he was told to have a companion in close communication with those who were guarding the horses so that he could come to notify me if necessary, and if so I would be prepared to give the order to withdraw the horses to the plaza of the said villa to keep them safe there with the soldiers guarding them, who would be ready to mount freshly changed horses to go out and destroy the said enemy. And so I dispatched the said aid, providing a few extra beasts of burden so that it could get there in less than an hour, arriving at said Villa Nueva at daybreak.

On the tenth of said month, Pentecost Sunday, the smoke signals were so widespread that the sky was obscured by thick clouds of smoke on all sides, from which it was deduced that it was the signal that all of the enemy nations from the outer frontiers had been gathered together to make war on us from all sides, or perhaps it was to terrorize us. We were carefully on guard that day and through the night, with vigils and lookout posts, and in this way we spent the day and night, my greatest concern being the said residents of Bernalillo, who, with the order sent and given to the aforesaid *alcalde mayor* on the previous day, the ninth, I judged had been so notified and would obediently seek safety on the said mesa of the pueblo of San Felipe, and I received his reply accordingly. On the eleventh, as is recorded in the said *autos,* he reported to me that despite the inconveniences, he would carry out the order to transfer the said residents of the said locality of Bernalillo to the said pueblo of San Felipe, and the said letter is also thus recorded in said *autos.* And also of record is the letter written by the Indian Bartolomé de Ojeda, who wrote to the very reverend father custodian Fray Francisco de Vargas at the pueblo of Santa Ana, reporting to him that he and his people knew for certain that an ambush and gathering of Apaches and Acomas had been dispersed. And the aforesaid *alcalde mayor* Don Fernando repeated in his said letter that on the following morning my order would be carried out, although with many misgivings on the part of the residents, who had to move with their women and children to the pueblo of San Felipe and all of whom were very sad that they had to withdraw to the Villa of Santa Fe. And it is also stated in the said letter that while it was being written, he received news from the pueblo of Zia, through Bartolito, that the war captains had gone out to reconnoiter the land and had found the tracks of people leading toward Acoma, but that nonetheless he would carry out the said order the following day. And with the aforementioned letters at hand, and since the smoke signals of the rebellious enemy were continuous and repeated, I sent an order to the military leader Miguel de Lara to go with six of the mustered soldiers to the pueblo of Zia, and that having gone to Bernalillo with the military leader Juan de Archuleta, I ordered him [de Lara] and wrote him to turn over the said soldiers he had with him, with the said letter repeating the order to the *alcalde mayor,* the aforesaid Don Fernando de Chávez.

On the twelfth of said month, the reverend father Fray Antonio del Corral, minister of the pueblo of San Felipe, arrived before dawn, not to report that his said Indians were bad, but to say that the Keres of Cochití were their enemies, and he came escorted by Miguel de Lara, who brought me the following letter from the said *alcalde mayor* Fernando de Chávez, which is of record in the said *autos,* in which he [the *alcalde mayor*] informed me of a message sent to him from the Indians of Zia and Santa Ana complaining to him that I had promised to help them and defend them from their enemies in every way possible and that with the abandonment of the aforesaid place of Bernalillo by its said residents, they were being left without the pledge having been carried out, and the said *alcalde mayor* said that he believed that the said pueblos would be abandoned and that since the river was running so high and was flooding the banks, it was not possible for the people or the livestock to be crossed without the risk of many drownings, and that for the third time the said Indians had reported to him that none of them would remain in their pueblos.

On said day, in reply to the said letter of said *alcalde mayor* indicating why he could not cross the said residents on rafts, I told him that it was not desirable to have them endanger the lives of their women and children because of the said livestock, and that I was sending as military leader to the pueblo of Zia, with the title of campaign captain, Miguel de Lara, accompanied by eight armed soldiers from this said presidio, and thus the said Miguel de Lara would have with him more than the eight they had requested, to whom I gave the said title to spur him on in the royal service. And he took with him the said reply to the said letter, in which I repeated to the said Don Fernando that in recognizing the great strength of the enemy, the weather conditions that were in its favor, and what had taken place, I was fearful and suspicious that another great setback might occur: that they [the rebels] might attack the said settlement of Bernalillo and take the horses from the residents, forcing them to defend their women and children from being taken as prisoners, and that [the rebels] would have the advantage, since [the residents] would be left on foot, and thus follow up by succeeding in destroying them, which may God forbid. And therefore I again repeated that the said order be carried out that he bring with him the said residents, the reverend fathers, and our very reverend father custodian, to whom I wrote and supplicated to comply. And I also wrote to the said governors of Zia and Santa Ana that with the protection of the said military escort they would not feel the absence of the said residents and that they were only five leagues from the help that they might request, and I told them that I would pay them two *reales* for the sustenance of the said eight soldiers and their military leader and that they could keep the horses and other beasts that they captured from the enemy as well as the clothing that they should find, which they should gather into one pile and distribute equally with the soldiers. And the said letters are thus recorded in the said *autos*.

On the twelfth of the said month of June, the military leader Juan de Archuleta arrived at about midday and presented himself before me, said governor and captain general, by virtue of my said order that had been shown to him by the aforesaid campaign captain, Miguel de Lara, after which the said enlisted soldiers from the muster list were assigned to him, and in accordance with the said order he went with them to the pueblo of Zia. And at the same time, he handed me the following letters. In one of them it is stated that my order and letter was publicly announced to the said residents of Bernalillo, with the very reverend father custodian and the reverend fathers present, and all of them were in unanimous agreement in their reply that they were not disposed to attempt to take their livestock across the river because of its high level, along with other statements contained in the said letter, which is dated the seventh of the present month. Another letter was from the said Don Fernando, undated, and written and signed by him, in which he states that the reasons why he delayed the departure with his people to San Felipe were the letters that Bartolo is writing daily, stating that if the said place were to be abandoned they would perish, and that they also would abandon the pueblo, as stated in the said letter sent by the said Bartolomé de Ojeda, written and signed by him, which is recorded in the said *autos,* where I ordered that it be placed. The said *alcalde mayor* repeats in his letters, which I had placed in the said *autos* that they be of record, in reply to mine in which I insisted that he carry out the said order to withdraw the said residents with the very reverend custodian, the unanimous agreement in their reply that they were not disposed to attempt to transport their livestock across the river because it was running so high, that they considered that if they left their livestock behind, they would be going to their doom to come to this villa, and that, furthermore, even though the three pueblos of the Keres are in the midst of and border on the said place of Bernalillo, where the said residents have their ranches and settlements, with the convenience of the pastures for their livestock and cornfields, at present they are safe because of the firm peace maintained by the people of the said three pueblos. Another letter states that the cause for detaining the departure and not leaving for San Felipe was because of the letter which he received from Bartolo, which he sent me. It reads as follows:

"Lord Captain Don Fernando de Chávez: We have received the note that you sent us, and it is true that I, and all of us, are very offended by what you have done to us by removing the guard that we had. Either we are friends or we are not; if you know something, or some malice, on our part, why is it not revealed to us? If there is some liar who has gone there with stories, capture him and bring him forward, for we want to know who the liar is, but if you trust in us more than ever, send a military guard, for the good God will protect us, because we are defending the holy law of almighty God. We have followed Him because it seems that we were born without friends, so that other than God we have no one else on our side. For although now everything is safe here, which can be said by those from here, and we know that this must please the lord governor, nevertheless, first for God and then for you we have alienated ourselves from many nations, and now we have no one to defend us, for at any time they put us at a distance and leave us, as we have found out. This will be the first and last letter that I will write to Your Honor, for we have not merited anything from Your Honor, and we see that no matter what we do for you, it seems to appear to you that it is nothing. I ask that you advise me whether or not you will help us, because if you do not, we will order that we leave and go to some other place where there are Christians. I await your reply, and may God protect you at Bernalillo or wherever you may be.

From your honor's servant, Bartolomé de Ojeda."

On the tenth, following my order, the governor of Pecos, Don Felipe, hanged his cacique, Don Diego Umbiro, and Captain Cachina and two others of their Indian followers, since most of the pueblo was ready to go and join the Jémez, who had sent [the rebel] Luis Cuniju [from Jémez] with the reliquary of Father Jesús who had been killed [as a trophy of victory to encourage the rebel partisans there]. And they [Don Felipe and his people] also seized the cacique of the pueblo of Nambé [Diego Xenome], the chief instigator among the said Tewas, whose statements I received in this villa, after which I ordered him to be shot by harquebus. Also, the governor of Santo Domingo was seized by his *alcalde mayor,* Don Alonso de Aguilar, and he ordered him shot by harquebus.

On the seventeenth at twelve o'clock at night I set out to the pueblo of Tesuque at the request of its governor, who was awaiting the people of Santa Clara with their Captain Naranjo, whose purpose was to kill him [the governor] and stir the said people to join him [Naranjo] in the revolt. And therefore I went with thirty-seven soldiers and military leaders to hide in ambush in a ravine, to assure not only that he [Naranjo] would not succeed in his rebellious intention, but also that he would be destroyed. And I remained in the saddle until ten in the morning, and he did not arrive, and after I had decided to withdrawn, the said Governor Domingo insisted that I stay, because he was certain that [Naranjo] would arrive according to the warning his said people had received, and their reply that they would await his arrival, and that he [Governor Domingo] had given orders to his people to climb up to the houses and the he would help them to bring down their clothing, and that in this way he would have time to destroy the said enemy in the plaza of their said pueblo. And making up my mind to await him [Naranjo] I remained in ambush until eleven o'clock that night, when the said Domingo reported that the said enemy was nearby in the hills near the said pueblo, since [Naranjo] had sent a nephew of his, whom [Domingo] held prisoner, to notify the said people to leave, and that they awaited him at said place in fear, being friends of the Spaniards, if they were not there to defend them. And when I went with my said people to take positions at the entrances to the streets, the said Indians of Tesuque made the mistake of tying up the said Indian, who yelled out in his language that he had been captured, and in the silence of the night the said enemy was able to hear him and took flight. And while I was under the impression that he was a native of the said pueblo, the aforesaid Domingo came to me there and gave me the said news, and I was saddened that so much effort had come to naught. And in receiving the statement of the said Indian prisoner in the plaza of the said pueblo, he said that many of the rebels had gone to the pueblo of San Ildefonso to water their cornfields. And although it was five long leagues away, I changed to a fresh horse and went with the said soldiers to attack them at dawn to see if I could succeed in finding the said rebels, but only about eight or nine Indians had remained that night on the other side of the river. A few shots were fired at them, and they took flight. Not being able to follow them because of the swollen river, and returning to inspect the pueblo, I found only a small amount of corn, and it was seen that the cornfields had been irrigated and that the statement of the said prisoner was true; he asked that he be returned to his uncle.

On the twenty-seventh I received the report that many tracks were found leading to Jémez from the direction of Acoma, and I dispatched eight soldiers to Captain Miguel de Lara, who was standing guard with eight others at the pueblo of Zia with the order that with the said people of the three Keres pueblos, our friends, he should go immediately to inspect the said tracks and should follow them and find the enemies. And thus he found the said enemies on a mesa in view of that of the pueblo of San Diego, which they left, and seeing that they were many, with the gathering of Acomas, Zuñis, and Apaches there, they lured them down to advantageous terrain and opened fire on them with many harquebus shots. Our men used the stratagem of fleeing to draw them to more suitable terrain, and [the rebels], thinking that this was done out of fear, followed them to the pueblo of San Juan, where they turned upon them and killed thirty-five Acomas and five Jémez and captured two, who were sent to me at this villa with the news of the said victory. And on arriving at the entrances, one of them escaped, and I ordered my lieutenant to receive a statement from the other one and then to have him shot by harquebus. Much pillage was obtained by our men in the said battle, and our only casualty was the wounding of a soldier on the face.

On the twenty-eighth I set forth to make war against the Tewas and Tanos, and at dawn I reached the mountains six leagues from the Villa Nueva, and since I had not spied on their encampment and was unaware of the place from which the enemy attacked our horses, as the army was moving slowly and was spread out, with the news of their location we attacked them, with the captain and *ayudante* in the lead and the *alférez* and other soldiers following him. Because of the roughness of the terrain of said place and the said time, the crowd of people had time to flee with some of their clothing, although our people took much of what they left behind and was left at their encampment, including over thirty horses used as beasts of burden. And when we were ready to leave the said place and had changed to fresh horses, we were called back to the said place, and the lieutenant general of the cavalry, Roque Madrid, with the *ayudante* and *alférez*, went to inspect the situation, and they found that the alarm resulted only in the discovery of four or six Indians. The said *ayudante* fired a shot at them and knocked down one of them. And when my lieutenant, Luis Granillo, advanced with four soldiers to capture some horses, one of the said rebels came out from among some large rocks and wounded one of them in the shoulder below his leather jacket. This day we took from them a *coscomate* [bin] of corn.

On the following day I returned in search of them in the mountains of Chimayó and in search of their corn supplies, and we found a *coscomate* and in it seven *coas* [tilling sticks] and an *azadón* [hoe]. I returned to the said Villa Nueva as the designated army camp, with the desire to attack the Tewa rebels at the funnel of the river, when the governor of Pecos and his war captains, and those of Tesuque, told me that their horses were exhausted, as well as the said people, who wished to return to their pueblos because of the need to irrigate and weed their cornfields, and since their reasons were very good, and in justice to the said representation, so as not to displease them I granted them permission to return to their said pueblos. And those of Tesuque asked me to leave six soldiers as guard, stating that with them they would be safe not only for the protection of their cornfields but also to enable them to irrigate those that they could that belonged to the said rebels. And thus I left them and returned to this said villa.

Leaving it on the tenth of July to make war against the rebellious Keres of Cochití and to join forces with the friendly people of the three pueblos and the said soldiers at Zia, I traveled under cover of darkness to arrive at dawn in view of the mesa of San Felipe. And I left there on the thirteenth, and on the fourteenth, at dawn, I entered the mountains where the said rebels of Cochití were, passing through a funnel in the mountains and crossing a mountain ridge through rough land, where a large part of the army could have been lost in battle, but by the grace of God our Lord such a misfortune did not take place. And since our army was discovered by the sentinel that the said enemy had posted at the entrance, I attacked at dawn before sunrise, and since their encampment was scattered deep into the canyon, they were able to escape with their said rabble. However, the captain and *ayudante* and my lieutenant, who were in the vanguard, and other soldiers and some of our friendly allies followed them into the said mountains and left six stragglers dead and brought back as prisoners thirty-one women and children of all ages and a large amount of pillage which my people were able to capture because the said encampment had a large number of people from the pueblos of Cochití and Santo Domingo. And also, a large number of sheep, over eighty head, was taken from them, and a cow with its calf which belonged to their reverend father minister. And some of his clothing, and books, and also some precious articles from the church were found. And also some corn was taken from the enemy that they had hidden in the said encampment. And since it was late, I retired to the said old pueblo of Cochití, which I designated to serve as the army camp. And I decided to send an old Indian woman, one of the captives of the said crowd, with a *tlatole* to the said people to request that they come down to their pueblo and that I would pardon them, telling them that they had not committed any crime, since they had not killed the father, and that they could turn over to me the livestock and horses and the jewelry and sacred vessels of the holy church. And thus I sent the said Indian woman, telling her to say to them that if they did not come down I would lay waste to their cornfields and pursue them until they were killed.

On the fourteenth I returned to the said place, going first to climb the mountain to the left of the said canyon, and there we found a *coscomate* of corn, and then we descended a very steep slope, seeking them out, first in the old pueblo on their mesa, and they did not come down either peacefully or to do battle. And that afternoon, in the depth of the said canyon, I took from them the corn that they had moved there that night from the outside and which they had covered with branches, and thus our men obtained some help for their sustenance. And since it was now late, I returned to the said army camp in the old pueblo of Cochití.

On the fifteenth I returned for the third time to look for the said enemy, hoping that they would come down either to make war or peace, and I followed the route along the right side of the mountain. Advancing on, I came upon a steep cliff, which was climbed by most of the soldiers on foot, and I remained on the mesa below with part of the other people. That day brought us repeated good fortune, as we found some *coscomates* of corn, some of which we loaded. It was seen that the enemy was supplying its people from them, although they were at distant places in the gulches and on the ridges of the said mountains, designed to force our men to leave their corn undisturbed, but they did not accomplish their goal, because we loaded all of what we found. And thus at four in the afternoon I ordered that the trumpet be sounded to gather the said army, and together we marched on. And a short while later the said Miguel de Lara noticed that his sword belt was missing, and he returned to the said place, and having dismounted for it, a troop came out, and he fired a bullet at them, and with his harquebus unloaded, one of them pounced on him, and with a blow from his lance [de Lara] left him dead, as he said, which was evident from the fresh blood on its point, and he caught up with me while I had stopped to drink water and gave me this news. Arriving at the said military camp at the said pueblo of Cochití, and measuring the amount of corn obtained during the said three days, it was calculated that the said soldiers and Indian allies had seized over one hundred *fanegas* from the said enemy.

On the sixteenth I entered this villa with the military leaders, leaving the army crossing the Río del Norte and ordering the *ayudante* to spend the night at El Alamo. And at two o'clock that afternoon, shortly after my arrival, I received the report from a Manso Indian, who had been at Taos, that there was a meeting at Taos with representatives of Picurís and the Tewa and Tano nations and that they had set up a forge in the church, which they had converted into a stable for the horses and a corral for the livestock. And therefore, on the seventeenth I ordered that the horses be taken to the said post at El Alamo, where the said army had been sent, and that on the eighteenth they be in this villa. And I again sent the said soldiers to the said pueblo of Tesuque to spend the night there and to be on guard for the spies of the natives, because for the safety of their lives they desired the said war against the said rebels.

On Friday the twentieth, when I was ready to leave early in the morning with the military leaders and officials to join the said army, I was perplexed by a letter I received from the *alcalde mayor* of Pecos, who I had judged, by virtue of my order to him, had gone with eighty Indian warriors to the said pueblo of Tesuque; in the letter he stated that when two young braves went to get their horses to go on the said expedition, they inspected the rough trail they would have to follow and noticed a narrow canyon in which they saw the advancing ambuscade of the said enemies, and for this reason he could not leave or send the said people, who were necessary to remain there to defend their pueblo, and that he was spending the night there to spy on the said enemy. And thus he notified me without asking me for any help other than ammunition. And so it was necessary for me to remain to protect this villa and to send the said report to the *alcalde mayor* of the Villa Nueva of Santa Cruz and an order to the said *ayudante* at the pueblo of Tesuque that he only keep his soldiers mounted to guard the horses, that the others of the army should remain entrenched in the houses of the said pueblo, and that he send the natives who accompanied him to reconnoiter the region through which the said enemy could advance. And since I considered that this villa was their destination, and not the pueblo of Pecos, and that they were advancing under cover of the wooded mountains to ambush us and carry off our livestock, I sent as spies the Manso Indians who were with El Tempano.

And at two o'clock in the afternoon I received a letter from the said *alcalde mayor* of Pecos informing me that he had gone to inspect the area of the said ambush and found that a cross had been left painted by hand on the ground, and tracks returning by way of the trail that leads to Taos, and that he considers that [whoever painted the cross] must have been the cause for the discovery of the said two tracks. And so I arranged for him to come here with the said eighty Indians to spend the night in this villa and [said] that I would be ready to go out with them to pursue the said war. I had more reason to do this after I read a letter that I received that said day from the *alcalde mayor* of the said Villa Nueva in which he notified me that on Wednesday the eighteenth he had seen five objects on the road to San Juan that were moving in the direction of the said *villa,* and that he went out to see what they were, and it was the old Indian who had made the painting, with his wife and two children, who said that since the war captain who was awaiting him had gone to Picurís, he took the opportunity to escape from the said rebel, who had his encampment in the intervening hidden gulch; that only four camps of the said Indians and those of San Juan remained there, since their captain, Juan Griego, had taken most of the people to Taos; that he and his governor had been taken and tied, since they did not wish to participate in the said uprising; that for the same reason they had killed the governor of Santa Clara; and that until nightfall he had remained hidden among some boulders, from where he saw many people descending from the mountains of the Tanos, with their horses loaded with clothing, and crossing the Río del Norte in the vicinity of the pueblo of Santa Clara. And thus I sent this report to the said *ayudante,* ordering that he send out Indian spies from Tesuque to inspect these tracks and find out where they ended.

On the said twentieth day of the month, at five o'clock in the afternoon, the said *alcalde mayor* of Pecos arrived with forty Indians on foot and on horseback, since he was not able to leave the pueblo without necessary defense. And thus I ordered him to tell them to camp near the cornfields, and [I told him] that the next day, the twenty-first, I would order the said forty Indian warriors to go on ahead to the pueblo of Tesuque, where I arrived with the military leaders and officials and some other soldiers to join the said army at eleven o'clock. And at that time two Indians arrived who, by virtue of my said order, the *ayudante* had sent out as spies, reporting that they had discovered the encampment of the enemy, who appeared to them to be Tanos, and that it was in the mountains alongside those near Nambé, and which border on the mountains where on the second day of the present month I attacked the said enemy and did not succeed in killing them for the reason stated previously. And for the present it was resolved, following the opinion given by the said Governor Domingo, that he go out with the said spies and his people, and with twenty soldiers that I provided him as well as the said captain Don Antonio Valverde and the *ayudante* Juan Ruiz. And the *alférez,* Martín de Urioste, asked me to let him go with them, and I complied with his request, adjusting the number to twenty-five. And it was decided that I, said governor and captain general, would go with the rest of the said army to the said Villa Nueva and from there advance at dawn into the said mountains, referred to on the second, to the encampment that had been abandoned by the said enemy. And thus, since the said spies had found that they were in the newly discovered place in the said direction and that the flight must have followed the said ravine, I had decided to take position there and prevent their escape. And after conferring and making plans to open battle at sunrise, the sound of which would surely be heard so that they could attentively await the said enemy, I left at said pueblo of Tesuque the said captain, *alférez,* and *ayudante* so that they could be ready to sally forth at the designated moment as determined. I left and arrived that day at four in the afternoon at the said Villa Nueva.

At dusk, after evening prayers of said day the twenty-first, I set out with the said people of the said part of the army in order to arrive at the said mountain location at dawn, and thus I arrived at daybreak at a deep place which was a part of it, where I remained under cover, so as not to be seen by the enemy, until sunrise, when, it being the designated time as planned, I advanced, climbing the said mountain with the said army and going down to inspect its ravine where the said enemy had its encampment on the second of the present month, and it was found that they had not returned to occupy it. And continuing in search of the tracks, and though I advised the said people to make every effort to see if they could distinguish those of the said captain and *alférez* or if they could hear the sound of the said battle, they found nothing. And with the said people spread out and scattered for an hour, I ordered twelve soldiers, with the lieutenant general of the cavalry, Roque Madrid, to climb the other mountain to see if they could observe at a distance whether the said captain and *alférez* were coming with the said troops under his command. And all they found was a young Indian, about thirty years old, who was with his mother under a tree cooking some purslane with ground corn for lunch. And some of the said swift Pecos Indians who had gone ahead to climb the said mountain killed her, and the said lieutenant captured the said Indian. And discovering that nothing could be seen or heard, they descended to the place where I was, which was in the said ravine, to partake of the water in the small stream. And after receiving a statement from the said Indian, I ordered that he be hanged, and he was left hanging from one of the pine trees. And since it was now approximately midday, I withdrew, considering that the said spies had been deceived regarding the trail that they thought they had found leading from the encampment that they had discovered. And thus I arrived at the said Villa Nueva with the said army at approximately three in the afternoon.

At seven o'clock, the said captain, *alférez,* and *ayudante* and the chaplain of the said army group which I had withdrawn arrived. They said that they had left Tesuque on said day, yesterday, at five o'clock in the afternoon, and that having traveled through the mountain that descends at the other side of the waterfall at the pueblo of Nambé, they were enveloped by the darkness of the night in the depth of a forest, where they were compelled to stop, since the horses could not find their way, and that despite the said circumstances, at daybreak seven horses were missing, and the said captain dispatched two soldiers and four Indians to look for them with orders to proceed with them to the said Villa Nueva. And having gone out at said hour with the said spies, they luckily captured an Indian in a ravine who was carrying some corn from the pueblo of Cuyamungué, and he begged them not to kill him and [said] that he would tell them where the said encampment was located, which the said spies had already located. And thus, in the density and roughness of the said mountains he took them to the said encampment, where the said captain, *alférez,* and *ayudante,* with some others, deployed and killed three boys and a woman and captured eight persons, who totaled nine with a boy they brought alive. And also our people took from the enemy some clothing, two pack horses, a herd of twenty goats, and some lambs and kids, which provided for their lunch. And one of the said women who had been captured said that most of the people of the said encampment had gone out to fight me, as they had discovered the horses of my said army as I ascended the mountain, and that for that reason they had ordered the populace to leave, carrying with them their clothing, which was the reason why they were found, and that the said dead Indians and the others who had fought us were the last of the ones remaining there. And the said captain and *alférez* decided not to pursue them in the said forest, because they left under its cover and also because the horses and the said people were exhausted from traveling since dawn, and it was necessary to rest them until the following day.

On the twenty-third I departed at dusk at the time of evening prayers, with the plan to arrive the next day at dawn with the entire army beside the mountain where the rebel Tewas of Santa Clara and their allies were located. And since I was traveling under cover of darkness, I went toward the pueblo of San Juan, crossing the mountain that descends to the Río del Norte and dropping to the mesa with a very extensive flatland where the said spies from Tesuque led me, and from there they descended into the funnellike canyon [*embudo*] in the said mountain. And it was recognized from the abandoned encampments that the said rebels had first been at that place, and, as we followed their tracks, that they led to the entrance of the funnellike canyon in the said mountains, which was found to be totally closed. A short distance from its entrance, not only from the dense forest, which is heavily wooded, but also from the large trees, the said rebels, aware of the narrowness of the canyon that funnelled through the mountains, cut down many trees to obstruct the passage of our men on horseback and those on foot, requiring them to undergo a great test of valor at the risk of entering the trail at some places under a sort of narrow, covered passageway and at others in the open, and the canyon or ravine that divided the two mountains was the only means of passage to where the rebels were entrenched.

And thus, following the said canyon, the said captain, *alférez,* and *ayudante,* with other soldiers and with Captain Lázaro de Mizquía, agent and council-man of the illustrious cabildo, and other residents in the vanguard, met the said enemy in battle. The latter, with their captain, Naranjo,[2] were waiting in a safe place, entrenched on the cliffs and peaks of the said mountains, ready to fight at the slope of the mountain. Repeated shots were fired at them, and it was our good fortune that the bullet from a shot by one of our men, a resident named Antonio Cisneros, hit [Naranjo] in the Adam's apple and came out the nape of his neck, and when he fell to the ground dead, [Cisneros] decapitated him and carried off his head. I, said governor and captain general, following the trail in the mountain to the right, ascended halfway up with the others, judging that it was the enemy's trail, but when I was told that the tracks were those of friendly Indians, I descended by the same route and entered the said part where the said trees covered the said trail. And as I was leaving, one of the spies of the said enemy began to hurl rocks, and one of them struck one of the Indian allies who was accompanying me on horseback and broke one of his arms. And riding out of the said canyon and funnel, and seeing that the gunfire on the part of our men continued inside the canyon, where the said captain, *alférez,* and *ayudante* were, my lieutenant Luis Granillo came out and told me that I should send him some of the few companions who were with me. And thus my secretary of government and war dismounted, offered to go, and was followed by others, including some Indian allies. And in order to clear out and keep a lookout on the enemy, I had another troop of Indian allies make the ascent with some of our harquebusiers, and I remained guarding the horses that had been dismounted, along with the other members of the army.

And they sent me the head of the said Naranjo, their captain and the leader

2. Governor Vargas's statements in this letter concerning the rebel leader Naranjo, who failed in his attempt to entrap Vargas and some of his best soldiers and annihilate them, paraphrase language used in his campaign journal for July 23, 1696. Naranjo's death at the battle of El Embudo and the defeat of his warriors paved the way for the eventual suppression of the Pueblo Indian revolt of 1696. Other contemporary reports indicate that his first name was Lucas and that he was a mulatto. In the fall of 1694, at the pueblo of Santa Clara, Governor Vargas had confirmed the election "as chief war captain, Lucas Naranjo" (see document 11, above). Villagutierre y Sotomayor, in his unpublished two-volume "Historia de la conquista, pérdida, y restauración de el Reyno de la Nueva México . . . ," ca. 1704, BNS, refers to Lucas Naranjo (Tomo II, libro 10, capítulo 4) as "their captain general the mulatto Lucas Naranjo" (fols. 384–85), "that apostate *lobo* Naranjo urging on his men" (fol. 386; the literal translation of *lobo* is "wolf"; *lobo* is also used as a term to designate a person of mixed Negro-Indian blood), and "their leader [caudillo] Lucas Naranjo" (fol. 386). For the lineage of the Naranjo family in New Mexico, see Fray Angélico Chávez, "Pohe-yemo's Representative and the Pueblo Revolt of 1680," *New Mexico Historical Review* 43 (1967): 85–126.

who had incited them to revolt and who, with four other henchmen of their
said pueblo, had led them to rise in rebellion. And it gave me great pleasure to
see the said rebel apostate dog in that condition. A pistol shot that was fired
into his right temple had blown out his brains leaving the said head hollow.
And the Pecos removed one of his hands to take it to their said pueblo, which
had helped in the said battle. The enemy withdrew, defeated and with many
wounded in addition to those who had been killed. Clothing was taken from
them, and five women and children were captured from them. And then the
said captain, *alférez,* and *ayudante* came out, accompanied by the reverend father *definidor* Fray Juan de Alpuente, chaplain of the said camp, who had entered with the said and remained at their side and was entrenched with his
horse, defended by some of the soldiers so that he would not be killed, because
the said dog Naranjo incited his warriors to aim their shots at the said religious, and his miserable end, I judge, was undoubtedly punishment from
heaven. As a result of this treachery he [Father Alpuente] was struck in the
lower part of the leg by an arrow shot, although the arrow was already spent
and also he was protected by the high leather boots that he was wearing. And
thus they came out with congratulations for the victory. It was estimated that
up to ten had been killed, and from the blood that was dripping from the said
rocks in the ravine it was evident that many others were left mortally wounded.
And when the bugle was sounded to gather our men, it was found that among
those who came out lightly wounded were the sergeant, who received an arrow
shot in the nape of the neck in the flesh under the skin, and the arrow was left
stuck there until it was removed by the lieutenant general of the cavalry, who
fought beside him in the said battle, and also the *alférez,* who was wounded
when he was struck in the face by the branch of a tree, and two other soldiers
lightly wounded. And on leaving the said canyon, on our way to the pueblo of
Santa Clara two others were taken captive, and we arrived at the Villa Nueva at
approximately three o'clock in the afternoon.

On the twenty-fifth, mass was celebrated with the customary military Salve
by the said reverend father chaplain, dedicated by me and the said military
leaders and officials who had taken part in the battle in honor of the lord apostle
Santiago. And leaving mass, the said Indian allies asked my permission to return to their pueblos. I embraced and thanked them profusely, and they left
very pleased with the said victory and the pillage that most of them had acquired. And of the said people taken captive, some of them were requested of
me by the said soldiers, and the others I turned over to the captain and governor of the said pueblo of Tesuque. And I sent one of the old Indian women with
a cross drawn on a piece of paper, as I had done with another of the old women
who had been brought as a prisoner on the twenty-third by the said captain. To
both of them I repeated that they should tell the said people of their said

pueblos that they should come down to them to work in their cornfields and that I would pardon them and defend them against the Indians who had led them to rebel and who had taken them into the mountains, where, if they did not believe me, I would return to kill all of them, and that by the sign of that holy cross the should come down with full assurance that I would pardon them. And so after eating I withdrew to this said villa and left the horses with thirty soldiers at the pueblos of Pojoaque and San Ildefonso, having found nothing else to warrant my concern, other than some tracks.

This is all that has occurred up to the present day, but in all, Your Excellency, with regard to the *cédulas* of His Majesty the king, our lord, which have been repeated concerning the assigned duty to conquer this said kingdom, and having done so to assure its permanence and stability, and the others that may have arrived and may arrive in the dispatch of this mailing period, in reply to the reports and testimony of *autos* sent to the former most excellent lord viceroy, who was the Count de Galve, Your Excellency will determine what you consider most fitting, and I will find that it will always be in the best interest of the said royal service.

May our Lord God protect the most excellent person of Your Excellency in greatness for many happy years. Done at this Villa of Santa Fe on the thirty-first of July of the year sixteen hundred ninety-six.

Most excellent lord, your most unworthy and humble servant, who holds you in the highest esteem and kisses your hands.

Don Diego de Vargas Zapata Luján Ponce de León.

Most excellent lordship and viceroy Don Juan de Ortega Montañés.

PART SEVEN

The Restoration and Expansion of the Franciscan Missions
Following the Suppression of the Pueblo Indian Revolt,
1696–97

89. LETTER OF FRAY FRANCISCO DE VARGAS TO GOVERNOR VARGAS, SANTA FE, NOVEMBER 23, 1696[1]

LORD governor and captain general. Fray Francisco de Vargas, apostolic preacher among the barbarous nations of this kingdom of New Mexico, father of this holy Custody of the Conversion of Saint Paul and its present custodian, and ordinary ecclesiastical judge of said kingdom by apostolic authority.

I have received from my reverend father superior prelates two *patentes*, one in the month of September of the present year and the other on the twenty-second of November of said year, as well as a request and supplication from the most excellent lord viceroy in which he entreats my most reverend father prelate the commissary general to encourage and exhort the missionaries, his subjects, in this holy custody to persevere in the administration of the holy sacraments to the native Indians of this kingdom; and in the second one His Excellency repeats the same entreaty, which was determined in *junta general,* which determined at the same time that twelve religious priests and one lay religious, totalling thirteen, remain to serve in this holy custody and that the other religious should withdraw to the Holy Province, the proposal which Your Lordship made to His Excellency. And so that it be of record regarding the most excellent lord viceroy that the reverend father commissary general duly carried out the full request of His Excellency, I present to Your Lordship their orders and mandates which they presented to me, their servant.

And I, as prelate, although unworthy, of this holy custody, have carried them out, as will be seen in the writings which I present to Your Lordship, requesting and begging of you that you provide me with authorized testimony showing that I have not failed to administer the holy sacraments to the Indians who remained in their pueblos and did not cooperate in the revolt of the apostates of our holy faith, for those who have remained quiet here have had ministers, as do those of the pueblos of Zia, San Felipe, and Santa Ana, where most of the time I have assisted them in the administration of the holy sacraments, providing them with the church and convent, and in the pueblo of Pecos in the same manner, I myself taking on the difficulty and risk of the roads only so that they may not lack spiritual nourishment, and for those in the pueblo of Tesuque, *visita* of this villa, mass has been said to them when there has been the opportunity and manner to be able to do so, as Your Lordship well knows, and that I, on my part, have not omitted any work for the ministry and development of this holy custody and its missions, all of my vigilance and solicitude being the support of the religious of this custody, as is common and public knowledge. Item, how I have assisted the religious who left their missions,

1. AGI, *Guadalajara,* leg. 141, doc. 20.

robbed by the apostate enemy, providing them each month with eight pounds of chocolate, eight of sugar, soap, paper, and the other necessities for their sustenance, as may be seen from their receipts. And also, I request and entreat Your Lordship to order that I be given certification and testimony of the sheep and large livestock to the extent that you can, with those of the missions that were stolen by the apostate Indians, for all of which the king our lord was not called upon to provide any help in their cost, because always my sacred religion has endeavored to spare His Majesty, may God keep him, of greater costs, as the ministers of this holy custody receive only the alms for their religious offices every three years and nothing else, and the meat that Your Lordship has charitably given, when it was available, to the said father ministers of this holy custody.

Lord governor and captain general, for all of this I repeat to Your Lordship that you see fit to provide me with certification in testimony of all of that which has been referred to above, so that it may be of record for the most excellent lord viceroy and my reverend father superior prelates. I await this favor from Your Lordship, which in justice I request so that in the fulfillment of my work this petition will be of permanent record.

I signed this with my signature on the twenty-third day of the month of November, sixteen hundred ninety-six.

Fray Francisco de Vargas, custodian
and ecclesiastical judge

90. *AUTO* OF GOVERNOR VARGAS, SANTA FE, NOVEMBER 23, 1696[1]

PRESENTATION. In this Villa of Santa Fe on the twenty-third day of the month of November, the year sixteen hundred ninety-six. Before me, Don Diego de Vargas Zapata Luján Ponce de León, governor and captain general of this kingdom and provinces of New Mexico, its new restorer, conqueror at his own expense, reconqueror and settler in it, and castellan of its forces and presidio for His Majesty, it was presented to me by the very reverend father custodian Fray Francisco de Vargas, ecclesiastical judge of this holy custody, and I had it in my possession as presented.

Auto. And I, said governor and captain general, certify that the missions of this said kingdom that were without ministers from February of this present year, in March, and including the *entradas* of April, were the following: those of Picurís, Taos, San Juan, San Cristóbal, San Idlefonso, and Tesuque. Also,

1. AGI, *Guadalajara,* leg. 141, doc. 20.

although they had not withdrawn completely, they were in this Villa of Santa Fe most of the time, and likewise, the one at the pueblo of Pecos and those of the two missions of San Diego del Monte and San Juan de Jémez were at the settlement of Bernalillo with the resident settlers, where their ministers are residing. And the said very reverend father custodian, although at that time there were the fears and rumors being spread that the Indians were intending to revolt, did not withdraw to this said villa until the middle of March, returning until Holy Thursday, on which evening he preached the Passion of Christ our Lord, and afterwards he returned to his said mission of Santa Ana, where he remained. And I have knowledge of all of the above because of the forays and visits I was making on horseback, repeatedly, to the said pueblos of this kingdom. And the aforesaid reverend father missionaries, seeing that now, as a result of my action, the said Indians appeared to be safe, and since it was apparent to the very reverend prelate in assisting the said mission, he left to the voluntary decision of the missionaries whether they should return to their missions, which they did, for at that time the said natives also requested their said ministers, treating them with expressions of love, respect, and obedience. For with regard to the two ministers of the said pueblos of Jémez, it is widely known, and is absolutely true, that they [the natives] came down to serve them, bringing them wood to the said settlement of Bernalillo, taking care of their sheep with their shepherds, who alternated each week, and going to ask the missionaries, who were living in the said place of Bernalillo, where they were maintaining themselves with the food that they brought them, to return to their missions. And the same was the case of the said ones of the Tanos of San Cristóbal, San Juan, and Santa Clara, as I know that they maintained themselves in the Villa Nueva de Santa Cruz with their said food supplies. And thus they maintained themselves during that time.

In April, the reverend father Fray Blas Navarro went to the pueblo of San Juan, since Fray Gerónimo Prieto was leaving, as he did with a *patente* from his provincial, to go to the province of Michoacán of New Spain to its college of Santa Cruz de Querétaro. And also the pueblo of Santa Clara was left by its reverend minister, Father Fray José García Marín, and the administration of that pueblo was placed under the reverend father Fray Antonio Obregón, guardian-elect at that time of the said Villa Nueva de Santa Cruz, the said Santa Clara serving as a *visita*. Also at that time the reverend father Fray Domingo de Jesús left for New Spain with a *patente* from his said provincial of Michoacán to the said College of Santa Cruz de Querétaro. And also at that time and in the same manner the reverend father Fray José Diez, who was minister at the pueblo of Tesuque, left, and from then on it remained as a *visita* of the reverend father guardian of this Villa of Santa Fe and under his charge as such, under his administration. And with regard to the said ministers who had withdrawn to the said Villa Nueva de Santa Cruz, I verify, and it is commonly known to its residents and others, that they came and went freely, that the said Indians of said missions brought them firewood, served them in everything their said father ministers and reverend missionaries requested of them, and punctually watched over their convents, livestock, and beasts.

Only in the case of San Ildefonso I cannot certify as to the assistance of food that was provided for its minister, who was the reverend father Fray Francisco Corbera, who is now in the glory of heaven, but from what can be seen of the safekeeping of his said convent, livestock, and beasts, I am aware that they did so. And also the reverend father Fray Antonio Moreno, who is now in the glory of heaven, was elected for Nambé and went to the said mission from the Villa Nueva, where he had been guardian. And the reverend father Fray Antonio Carbonel, who is now in the glory of heaven, went from the mission of the pueblo of Taos to that of Picurís, accompanied by the reverend father Fray Diego de Chavarría. And thus, the said missions were inhabited, as were also those of Cochití, San Felipe, and Pecos, until the revolt of the said Tewa Indians, Picurís, Taos, Tanos, Jémez, and Keres of Cochití and Santo Domingo, after which the only ones that remained inhabited were those of San Felipe, Santa Ana with his very reverend paternity, and Zia, and from Pecos its minister came to this villa because of the danger of the other said Indians who had revolted, who as enemies of the said Pecos might go there to make war on them, as well as for the fear that the said Indians might join the others in the revolt to enjoy the liberty of their idolatry. And it is of record that the reverend father guardian of this villa went down to say mass to them in the month of July and to insure that the food supplies in said mission were brought up, for which His Reverend Paternity requested my aid and the assistance of soldiers as escorts and cargo mules with their muleteers, and along with the said food supplies, to bring up the sacred vessels and other valuable articles of divine worship, and in effect the said reverend father guardian was able to bring them and to transport the said food supplies, for which I provided promptly that which was referred to and requested by His Very Reverend Paternity.

And later, it is of record that in September Your Very Reverend Paternity went down to the pueblo of Pecos when on my return from Taos on my campaign and my journey to the buffalo plains I came out by way of Pecos, and I found there His Very Reverend Paternity, who told me that he had celebrated the Feast of All Saints and of the Dead. And I saw that under his direction and with the plan that he had given to the said Indians and with the assistance that he had from the *alcalde mayor,* he had added to the body of the church, giving it greater height for the skylight, and also had constructed a presbytery with two steps [*gradas*] for the main altar and had the walls for the sacristy and the patio enclosed by a wall with its gate for the entrance to the said convent. And I saw that he had completed the improvements on the one at his mission of Santa Ana, using materials of adobe and wood to build his church, which I saw on my return from the campaign to the rock of Acoma, having brought the carpenters from the said pueblo of Pecos to hasten the work of carving the said wood and also to fit the doors, which the said carpenters measured to do so. And in this manner, those that have been found and are found inhabited are the said one of Pecos, by His Very Reverend Paternity; that of Santa Ana, of which I have known him to be the minister in the period referred to; that of Tesuque, as a *visita* of this villa; that of San Felipe, as a *visita* of Bernalillo; and that of Zía, whose present minister is the reverend father Fray Pedro Matha, who I know assists also at the said Spanish settlement of Bernalillo, to which he goes and comes as many times as he considers necessary for its administration.

And with regard to the sheep, I certify that His Very Reverend Paternity entered in November of the year 'ninety-four, finding at that time all of the said missions already inhabited, except those of Picurís and Taos, which were without ministers until the year 'ninety-five, when in the month of August the reverend father Fray Blas Navarro went to Picurís and in the month of November the reverend father *definidor* Fray Juan de Zavaleta and his companion the reverend father Fray Diego de Chavarría went to Taos. And in the said month of November of 'ninety-four, when His Very Reverend Paternity arrived, I can confirm, since he told me, as was told also by the persons who came on said journey, that five hundred head of sheep and some milk cows and oxen entered and had entered the said mission of Santa Ana. And also, in May of the following year, 'ninety-five, His Very Reverend Paternity left for the town of El Paso, and on his return, early in October of the said year, His Very Reverend Paternity arrived bringing also, as he said, which was very true, one thousand head of sheep, which, as in both cases, he apportioned to all of the said missions. And those that he rescued from the revolt were, I presume, from the missions of Pecos, Tesuque, this villa, San Felipe, Santa Ana, and Zia and also those in the war of Cochití, in which one hundred six head were recovered, and they were handed over to the reverend father Fray Alfonso Jiménez, its minister, who went on said campaign. And thus the very reverend father custodian is the one who can have information on the said livestock, both sheep and large livestock, that he lost in the said missions of the Indians that revolted, of those that there were, because His Very Reverend Paternity had made, and made, an annual visitation. And as for the aid in chocolate, sugar, and the other things with which he has assisted the said reverend father ministers who were robbed, I defer to the receipts which His Reverend Paternity refers to in his said petition or the account he may have made of them.

And as for the assistance for their support, I know that he provided it, the reverend father guardian of this said villa providing their food, and likewise it has been provided at the said mission of Santa Ana, entering and coming to this villa to inspect the said religious and to perform his duties as ecclesiastical judge, undergoing the dangers of the road as he did in going in person to the pueblo of San Juan de los Jémez, going in person with his Indian servants of Zia and Santa Ana to the pueblo of San Juan de los Jémez to remove the sacred vessels and valuable objects from the church and others from the convent, since its minister was at the pueblo of Pecos. And his said Indian servants fought with a troop of those of the said pueblo, some of whom were leaving loaded with their food supplies and others found removing them. And they [the servants] killed and captured on said occasion four of the rebels and one Apache. And on the return they were joined by the *alcalde mayor* of Bernalillo with other residents. And of five Indians [*gandules*] whom they brought back, one hanged himself in the *estufa* that night, one escaped, and the other three were ordered by the *alcalde mayor* to be executed with the garrote because one of them was the one who had killed the *alcalde mayor* and captain Juan Olguín, and the other two for causes of the said revolt. The said very reverend father custodian, on the said occasion, demonstrated great valor, as he always has, with the ardent zeal of his institute in assisting his said mission as well as that of the Pecos at the said times when he has administered them.

For all of which, so that it may be of record to the most reverend father commissary and to the other father superiors, his very reverend prelates, and that he be held in esteem in recognition of his merits, and his having served His Majesty the king, our lord, may God guard him, and his sacred religion, according to his institute, and so that it be of record also to the most excellent lord viceroy of all the kingdom of New Spain, who is His Lordship Don José Sarmiento y Valladares, Count of Montezuma, so that His Excellency may give him due thanks and may esteem his honorable merits and services and may give attention, with the charity and piety of his greatness, to the entreaty which the said very reverend father custodian himself, or through his said superior prelate or very reverend father superiors, may request of Your Greatness. In response to the said entreaty, I will remunerate him in accordance with the said request for the said livestock and sheep as well as the horses. Also, in the aforesaid missions of those who revolted, some lost their lives, the five reverend father missionaries who are now in the glory of heaven, and others escaped, as it was our Lord's will to free them from the said barbarous rebel apostates.

And so that it thus be of record, I certify it in due form, and I signed on said day, month, and year with the assistance of my secretary of government and war, whom I ordered to place the seal of my coat of arms. And it is sent on ordinary white paper because sealed paper is not available in these parts. Done *ut supra*.

Don Diego de Vargas Zapata Luján Ponce de León. Before me, Domingo de la Barreda, secretary of government and war.

91. LETTER OF FRAY FRANCISCO DE VARGAS TO THE VICEROY, SANTA FE, NOVEMBER 28, 1696[1]

MOST excellent lord. May the Divine Majesty of God our Lord be served by Your Excellency's arrival at these kingdoms of New Spain, where, as an humble chaplain of Your Excellency, I wish that you may enjoy happiness and good fortune in your good governance, for I, and the missionary fathers of this custody of New Mexico, as chaplains of Your Excellency, will not fail to request it in the holy sacrifices to Almighty God, for we will be very interested in the good fortunes of Your Excellency, especially in this very remote kingdom of New Mexico, where I, although an unworthy prelate, find myself. And I offer myself with humble compliance to carry out the mandates of Your Excellency, to whom I present a brief account of the state of affairs in this kingdom of New Mexico.

Since the fourth day of June of this present year, more calamities are being experienced than those that were suffered previously, God our Lord placing as the instrument the Indians of this kingdom, who are apostates of our holy religion, at whose hands five of His ministers of the gospel died, their lives taken treacherously and their livestock and sheep stolen, along with the sacred vessels and articles pertaining to the divine worship, for which His Majesty, may God keep him, provided only ten sacred vestments with all of their essentials to say mass, ten bells, and ten molds for hosts, and nothing else. And all of the rest, in the loss referred to, which was considerable, had been obtained through the solicitude of the father ministers without requesting or adding to the expenses of our lord the king, may God guard him. For they have only received the alms of the equipment every three years of wine, wax, and oil and other things required for their needs, which at the present are, and will be, considerable because of what is stated above, with the ministers having no place to resort to to support themselves in any mission, as the Indians who have come down to seek peace have no food. And for this reason they [the Indians] will not attend instructions in Christian doctrine, nor will they be able to support their minister; rather, they will leave him alone in the pueblo, because they will be wandering about in the mountains. Nor will they be able to rebuild the churches that they burned or the dwellings for the religious. And although the said Indians may not take the lives of the fathers, their ministers,

---

1. AGI, *Guadalajara*, leg. 141, doc. 20.

there are other enemy nations who will fight and make war on the pueblos, killing and stealing what they can find.

In these dangers which are so manifest, most excellent lord, the ministers and chaplains of Your Excellency find themselves. But this does not prevent them from taking assiduous measures, to the extent that they can, for the winning of the souls of these rebels of the body of our holy mother church, although with many sufferings and needs, with the thefts made by the Indians, as will be seen by their certification. Therefore, with great humility I request that Your Excellency pass your eyes over it. And the pity is that with all the hardships that have been suffered, these miserable Indians are still very averse to the law of our beloved Christ, for they little accept the Divine Word and Christian doctrine, which, taught by their ministers, only served to instill in them a fatal hatred, cruelly savoring the blood of priests and not responding to love and kindness but only to the rigor and punishment of governors and judges. And so the minister missionaries suffer many insults from the said Indians and spiritual afflictions for the little success in winning souls, for they [the Indians] do not abandon idolatry and bad ways. This, most excellent lord, is what I feel in my conscience from the experience that I have gained from seventeen years that I have served as a missionary in this custody of New Mexico. The said Indians want peace with the Spaniards only for their trade and commerce and not to observe our holy law. For we see by the obvious results the very clear truth.

I have put into effect the order that twelve religious priests and one brother religious should remain in this custody, as the governor of this kingdom requested of the Royal Junta. And after conferring on the matter with the said governor, we find that although at present the twelve religious are sufficient, when the Indians finish coming down to their pueblos they will not be sufficient, and instead, twenty-one will be necessary to be able to administer to them, as will be seen in the separate list that I am sending Your Excellency. And these will have their work doubled, because there are many pueblos, and it is not possible to place a minister in each one of them, because of the inconveniences of the land, dangers, and severe weather. And although previously the said governor requested the twelve religious, it was because of the little hope at that time, but now, since Divine Providence has been served and the said Indians are returning peacefully to their pueblos under the directions of the governor, they can again be rebuilt, with the construction of their churches and dwellings for their father ministers. And at the time when they find themselves with food and the other necessities for their support, which at present they are lacking because of the second war that has been waged against them, the additional religious missionaries should come so that the number of twenty-one priests can be distributed, if it is the wish of Your Excellency, whom I request of our Lord that He protect many happy years.

From this Convent of Our Father Saint Francis, Villa of Santa Fe, the kingdom of New Mexico, November twenty-eight, the year sixteen hundred ninety six. Your Excellency's most humble chaplain, who kisses the feet of Your Excellency.

Fray Francisco de Vargas

92. LIST OF MISSIONARIES NEEDED IN NEW MEXICO, ACCOMPANIMENT TO FRAY FRANCISCO DE VARGAS'S LETTER TO THE VICEROY, SANTA FE, NOVEMBER 28, 1696[1]

List of religious missionaries that are necessary for the administration of the holy sacraments in this kingdom of New Mexico.

The reverent father custodian and ecclesiastical judge.

Villa of Santa Fe, with its two *visitas* of Tesuque and Cuyamungué, which are a little more than three leagues from the Villa—three religious.

Pueblo of Pecos—one religious.

Pueblo of Nambé, with its *visita* of Pojoaque, which is one league from the said pueblo—one.

Pueblo of San Ildefonso, with its *visita* of Jacona, one league away—one.

Pueblo of San Juan de los Caballeros of the Tewas, with the pueblo of Santa Clara, which is two leagues from it—one, with danger of the river when it is frozen and at the time that it is swollen.

Pueblo of Picurís—one.

Pueblo of Taos—two, because of its distance from other settlements.

Villa of Santa Cruz, with its *visita* of the Tanos of San Cristóbal—one.

Cochití, with its *visita* of Santo Domingo, two leagues' distance from it— one, with the inconveniences of the river.

San Felipe, including the administering to Spaniards at Bernalillo, two leagues' distance from it—one.

---

1. AGI, *Guadalajara*, leg. 141, doc. 20.

Pueblo of Zia, with its *visita* Santa Ana, three leagues' distance from it—one, with the inconveniences of the river.

Pueblo of El Paso del Río del Norte, with its *visita* the Real de San Lorenzo, settlement of Spaniards, which is two leagues' distance from it—two religious.

Pueblo of the Piros of Senecú—one.

Pueblo of the Tiwas of La Isleta—one.

Pueblo of the Piros and Sumas of Socorro—one.

The procurator of this custody.

93. LETTER OF GOVERNOR VARGAS TO THE VICEROY, SANTA FE, NOVEMBER 28, 1696[1]

MOST excellent lord. Although it was taken to be impossible to subdue the Indians of the rebellious apostate nations, testimony for which I transmitted in campaign reports [*autos de guerra*] to the most excellent lord bishop viceroy who served in that kingdom, in the prosecution of that war the submission of the eight pueblos has been attained. The situation has changed with this event, and this wild beast has been subdued, for which I am proud, for this was achieved in spite of the contrary opinions of those who saw their [the rebels'] submission as hopeless, stating that they would leave to join the Apache nations. And I saw in the months of June and July that all of my measures to bring them back to their pueblos were thwarted, which was the motive for my consulting, as I did, with the said most excellent lord viceroy to the effect that the number of missionaries to be allotted to the Pueblo of El Paso del Río del Norte should be a total of twelve religious priests, with their very reverend father prelate and custodian and also the father procurator of the said holy custody. And through this consultative letter, which I remitted with said *autos* to the said most excellent bishop viceroy, who was the most excellent lord Don Juan de Ortega y Montañés, His Excellency issued his decree requesting and urging the most reverend father commissary general to leave the aforesaid number of twelve religious missionaries with their very reverend prelate and the father procurator, and that he [the commissary general] order by his *patente* that the said prelate and very reverend father custodian order by his *patente* the withdrawal of the other supernumeraries who were in the province. But since by Divine Grace the eight pueblos have submitted and those of Santa Clara

1. AGI, *Guadalajara*, leg. 141, doc. 20.

also have begun to come down, I am compelled to report to Your Excellency with regard to those religious missionaries who are now required, both those in El Paso as well as those in this villa, in the following manner. . . . [The list that follows here is identical to the one presented by the father custodian of the same date.]

So, according to the number for the said missions and the administering of the holy sacraments to these two villas, they total twenty-one, including the said father procurator. Thus the increase, which will reward His Majesty the king, our lord, may God protect him, over the number of thirteen that was paid for the said allotment for the pueblo of El Paso and those of its district, comes to eight. And Your Excellency, if it is your wish, may request of the said most reverend father commissary general, and in his absence the father provincial of our father Saint Francis of that province of Mexico, whoever he may be, to order that he send here those who are lacking for the complement of the said number, because of those who are leaving for reasons of illness and habitual indisposition. And therefore I propose, most excellent lord, that Your Excellency request the said number.

And the religious who come should come very much of their own free will and aware of the danger to their lives, because I cannot assure them protection from the said recently subdued ones, for amidst rigorous war is born sure peace. For this reason they should not fail to have justifiable fear. Therefore, they should not come with the illusion that guards can be provided to help them to protect their lives, for they should come under the same risk that is also the lot of the fathers of the kingdoms of Vizcaya, Sonora, and Sinaloa, because for me to provide it I would need to have four presidios besides the one at this villa. And therefore, Your Excellency, I wish to note in these proposals, as is my obligation in the royal service and as my experience obliges to me present to Your Greatness, that I do not want them to be making petitions asking for guards for the protection of their lives, either from their very reverend father prelate or in the name of the *definitorio* or from other discreet fathers, saying that if they are not provided they will leave the said missions uninhabited and that if they are unable to assist in administering the holy sacraments and the teaching of Christian doctrine to the said Indians it would be on my account, and as a result the missions would be abandoned. And on my part, what it will be will be to live with the vigilance of repeating my visits to the recently submitted pueblos, sometimes by me and other times by my lieutenant and other military leaders that I will send, as the occasion presents itself, without omitting on my part anything of importance to the royal service.

Your Excellency, in all of these matters, will order what it is your pleasure to determine and resolve. As for me, my only desire is a successful outcome, since Your Excellency has entered your governance with such good fortune, for you are received and welcomed with this new submission of those who in their obstinace were already apostates and who are now returning to the true knowledge under the gentle yoke of our holy faith, a happy prognostication which announces to the greatness of Your Excellency the happy progress under your governance. And may it be accompanied by granting to Your Excellency, our lord, the many years of life that I wish you to enjoy in your superior greatness.

Done at this Villa of Santa Fe on November twenty-eighth, sixteen hundred ninety-six. Most excellent lord, your most humble servant kisses Your Excellency's hand.

Don Diego de Vargas Zapata Luján Ponce de León. Most excellent Lord Viceroy Don José Sarmiento Valladares.

94. ORDER OF THE VICEROY TO THE COMMISSARY GENERAL, TO SEND EIGHT ADDITIONAL MISSIONARIES TO NEW MEXICO, MEXICO CITY, APRIL 3, 1697[1]

DON José Sarmiento y Valladares, knight of the Order of Santiago, Count of Montezuma and of Tula, Lord of Monterrosano de la Pessa, Viscount of Yluacán, of the Council of His Majesty, his viceroy, lieutenant governor, and captain general of this New Spain, and president of its royal Audiencia.

In conformity with that which was resolved in the *junta general* which I held on March 12 of this year, at this time I urge and request the most reverend father commissary general of the Order of Saint Francis, and in his absence the father provincial of this province of Santo Evangelio, that he give appropriate orders that 8 religious priests be sent who are lacking in the complement of 21, which have been stated to me to be necessary by Father Fray Francisco de Vargas, custodian and ecclesiastical judge in the provinces of New Mexico, for the administration of the holy sacraments both in the pueblos that have been restored and the missions of which they are composed as well as for those that are coming down peacefully to their pueblos, as was also endorsed, as referred to, by the governor of said provinces, Don Diego de Vargas. And that the said eight religious who shall go do so much of their own free will, in consideration of their holy and laudable institute, under which they are directed to go to preach the gospel, doctrine, and teaching of our holy Catholic faith to those Indians, with the danger to their lives that they may undergo and suffer with the justifiable fears of the little stability of the said Indians, and with this warning they may go knowing that guards can not be provided to assist them

1. BNM, leg. 4, docs. 13, 26.

in the protection of their lives and missions, in the same manner and form as with the father ministers and missionaries of the kingdoms of New Vizcaya, Sonora, and Sinaloa. For to provide it it would be necessary to have four presidios. So with these means they should not request guards that cannot be provided for them, and they should go with this understanding.

Mexico, April three, the year sixteen hundred ninety-seven.

Don José Sarmiento, By order of His Excellency. Juan de Morales.

BIBLIOGRAPHY

PRINCIPAL ARCHIVES AND MANUSCRIPTS CITED

AASF   Archives of the Archdiocese of Santa Fe, Albuquerque, New Mexico.

AGI   Archivo General de Indias, Seville, Spain.

AGN   Archivo General de la Nación, Mexico City, Mexico (formerly called Archivo General y Público de la Nación).

BC   Bolton Collection, Bancroft Library, University of California, Berkeley, California.

BNM   Biblioteca Nacional de México, Mexico City, Mexico.

BNS   Biblioteca Nacional, Madrid, Spain.

    Juan de Villagutierre y Sotomayor, "Historia de la conquista, pérdida, y restauración de el Reyno y provincias de la Nueva México en la América septentrional," MS. ca. 1703, 2 vols., fols. 1–449, and 1–144. The table of contents of this work is published in P. Otto Maas, *Misiones de Nuevo Mexico* (q.v. below).

CL   Coronado Library, University of New Mexico Library, Albuquerque, New Mexico.

HL–RC   Huntington Library, Ritch Collection, San Marino, California.

LC   Library of Congress, Manuscripts Division, Washington, D.C.

NL–AC   Newberry Library, Edward E. Ayer Collection, Chicago.

    Fray Francisco Antonio de la Rosa Figueroa, "Bezerro general monológico y chronológico de todos los religiosos que de las tres parcialidades, conviene a saber padres de España, hijos de provincia, y criollos ha habido en esta Sta. Pro.a del Sto. Evang.o desde su fundación hasta el pres.te año de 1764, y de todos los prelados, assi nuestros M. Rdos. PP. Comisarios como Rdos. PP. Provinciales que la han gobernado." MS.

SANM   State Records Center and Archives, Santa Fe, New Mexico.

    The principal documents used in these archives are cited in the notes to the translated documents. With reference to the documents in AGN, their location in the archive is indicated on the LC photostats, and the cataloging system is described in Ignacio del Río, *Guide* . . . (q.v. below).

ARCHIVAL GUIDES

Bolton, Herbert Eugene. *Guide to Materials for the History of the United States in the Principal Archives of Mexico.* Washington, D.C.: Carnegie Institution, 1913.

Chávez, Fray Angélico, O.F.M. *Archives of the Archdiocese of Santa Fe, 1678–1900.* Washington, D.C.: Academy of American Franciscan History, 1957.

Díaz, Albert James. *A Guide to the Microfilm Papers Relating to New Mexico.* Albuquerque: University of New Mexico Press, 1960.

Espinosa, J. Manuel. *Crusaders of the Río Grande: The Story of Don Diego de Vargas and the Reconquest and Refounding of New Mexico.* Chicago: Institute of Jesuit History, Loyola

University, 1942. pp. xiii—xx, 374—81. Includes list of headings of the groups of individual documents on New Mexico for the period 1692—1700 used in the present study as they appear at the head of each original grouping in the respective archives.

Jenkins, Myra Ellen, et al. *Calendar of Microfilm Edition of the Spanish Archives of New Mexico, 1621—1821.* Santa Fe: Historical Publications Commission, State of New Mexico Records Center, 1968.

Río, Ignacio del. *Guide to the Archivo Franciscano of the National Library of Mexico.* Mexico, D.F., and Washington, D.C.: Instituto de Investigaciones Bibliográficas, Universidad Nacional Autónoma de Mexico, and Academy of American Franciscan History, 1975.

Twitchell, Ralph Emerson. *The Spanish Archives of New Mexico.* 2 vols. Cedar Rapids, Iowa: Torch Press, 1914.

University of California Library, Berkeley. Card catalog and reference guides to the Bancroft Library.

University of New Mexico Library, Albuquerque. Card catalog of the Coronado Library.

PRINTED MATERIALS

Adams, Eleanor B. *Bishop Tamarón's Visitation of New Mexico, 1760.* Albuquerque: Historical Society of New Mexico, 1954.

———. "Two Colonial New Mexican Libraries, 1704, 1776," *New Mexico Historical Review* 19 (1944): 135—67.

———, and France V. Scholes. "Books in New Mexico, 1598—1680," *New Mexico Historical Review,* 17 (1942): 1—45.

———, and Fray Angélico Chávez. *The Missions of New Mexico, 1776: A Description by Fray Atanasio Domínguez with Other Contemporary Documents.* Albuquerque: University of New Mexico Press, 1956, 1976.

Anderson, H. Allen. "The Encomienda System in New Mexico, 1598—1680," *New Mexico Historical Review* 60 (1985): 353—77.

Arricivita, Juan Domingo. *Crónica seráfica y apostólica del colegio de propaganda fide de la Santa Cruz de Querétaro en la Nueva España.* Mexico City, 1792.

Bailey, Jessie Bromilow. *Diego de Vargas and the Reconquest of New Mexico.* Albuquerque: University of New Mexico Press, 1940.

Bancroft, Hubert Howe. *History of Arizona and New Mexico, 1530—1888.* San Francisco: The History Company, 1889.

———. *History of the North Mexican States and Texas.* 2 vols. San Francisco, 1884—89.

Bandelier, Adolph F. A. *Documentary History of the Rio Grande Pueblos of New Mexico.* Papers of the School of American Archaeology, no. 13. Lancaster, Pa., 1910.

———. *Final Report of Investigations Among the Indians of the Southwestern United States, Carried on Mainly in the Years from 1880 to 1885.* Papers of the Archaeological Institute of America, American Series, vols. 3, 4. Cambridge, Mass., 1890—95.

———, and Edgar Lee Hewett. *Indians of the Rio Grande Valley.* Albuquerque: University of New Mexico Press, 1937.

Bandelier, Fanny R. *The Journey of Alvar Nuñez Cabeza de Vaca and His Companions from Florida to the Pacific, 1528–1536.* New York: A. S. Barnes and Company, 1905.

Bannon, John Francis. *Bolton and the Spanish Borderlands.* Norman: University of Oklahoma Press, 1964, 1968.

————. *The Spanish Borderlands Frontier, 1513–1821.* New York: Holt, Rinehart and Winston, 1970.

[Benavides, Fray Alonso de.] *Benavides' Memorial of 1630.* Ed. and trans. Peter P. Forrestal, C.S.C., and Cyprian J. Lynch, O.F.M. Washington, D.C.: Academy of American Franciscan History, 1954.

————. *Fray Alonso de Benavides' Revised Memorial of 1634.* Ed. and trans. Frederick Webb Hodge, George P. Hammond, and Agapito Rey. Albuquerque: University of New Mexico Press, 1945.

Benedict, Ruth. *Patterns of Culture.* Boston: Houghton Mifflin Co., 1934, 1959.

Bishop, Morris. *The Odyssey of Cabeza de Vaca.* New York: The Century Co., 1933.

Bloom, Lansing B. "The Chihuahua Highway," *New Mexico Historical Review* 12 (1937): 209–16.

————. "Fray Estévan de Perea's *Relación*," *New Mexico Historical Review* 8 (1933): 211–35.

————. "The Governors of New Mexico," *New Mexico Historical Review* 10 (1935): 152–57.

————. "The Royal Order of 1620," *New Mexico Historical Review* 5 (1930): 288–98.

————. "Spain's Investment in New Mexico Under the Hapsburgs," *The Americas* 1 (1944): 3–14.

————. "The Vargas Encomienda," *New Mexico Historical Review* 14 (1939); 360–417.

————. "When Was Santa Fe Founded," *New Mexico Historical Review* 4 (1929); 188–94.

————. "Who Discovered New Mexico?" *New Mexico Historical Review* 15 (1940): 101–32.

————, and Lynn B. Mitchell. "The Chapter Elections in 1672," *New Mexico Historical Review* 13 (1938): 85–119.

Bolton, Herbert E. *Coronado, Knight of Pueblos and Plains.* Albuquerque: University of New Mexico Press, 1949.

————. "The Mission as a Frontier Institution in the Spanish American Colonies," *American Historical Review* 23 (1917): 42–61.

————. *The Spanish Borderlands.* New Haven: Yale University Press, 1921.

————. *Spanish Exploration in the Southwest, 1542–1706.* New York: Charles Scribner's Sons, 1930.

————. *Wider Horizons of American History.* New York: D. Appleton-Century Company, 1939.

————, and Henry Maitland Marshall. *The Colonization of North America, 1492–1783.* New York: Macmillan, 1920.

Bowden, Henry Warner. "Spanish Missions, Cultural Conflict and the Pueblo Revolt of 1680," *Church History* 44 (1975): 217–28.

Boyd, E. *Popular Arts of Spanish New Mexico.* Santa Fe: Museum of New Mexico, 1974.

Chávez, Fray Angélico. *Coronado's Friars*. Washington, D.C.: Academy of American Franciscan History, 1968.

―――. "Pohé-yemo's Representative and the Pueblo Revolt of 1680," *New Mexico Historical Review* 42 (1967): 85–126.

―――. "Santa Fe Church and Convent Sites in the Seventeenth and Eighteenth Centuries," *New Mexico Historical Review* 24 (1949): 85–93.

Documentos para la historia de Méjico. 21 vols. Mexico City: J. R. Navarro, 1853–57. (First Series, III, Mexico City, 1853; Third Series, I, Mexico City, 1856.)

Documentos para servir a la historia del Nuevo México, 1538–1778. Madrid: Ediciones José Porrúa Turanzas, 1962.

Dozier, Edward P. *The Pueblo Indians of North America*. New York: Holt, Rinehart and Winston, 1970.

―――. "Rio Grande Pueblos." In *Perspectives in American Indian Culture Change*, pp. 84–168. Ed. Edward H. Spicer. Chicago: University of Chicago Press, 1961.

―――. "Spanish-Catholic Influences on Rio Grande Pueblo Religion," *American Anthropologist* 60 (1958): 441–48.

Eggan, Fred. *Social Organization of the Western Pueblos*. Chicago: University of Chicago Press, 1950, 1970.

Ellis, Bruce T. "The 'Lost Chapel' of the Third Order of St. Francis, in Santa Fe," *New Mexico Historical Review* 53 (1978): 59–74.

Ellis, Richard N. *New Mexico Past and Present*. Albuquerque: University of New Mexico Press, 1971.

Espinosa, Aurelio M. *The Folklore of Spain in the American Southwest*. Ed. J. Manuel Espinosa. Norman: University of Oklahoma Press, 1985.

Espinosa, Isidro Félix de, O.F.M. *Crónica apostólica y seráfica de todos los Colegios de Propaganda Fide de esta Nueva España de misioneros franciscanos observantes*. Mexico City: 1746.

Espinosa, J. Manuel. *Crusaders of the Río Grande: The Story of Don Diego de Vargas and the Reconquest and Refounding of New Mexico*. Chicago: Institute of Jesuit History, Loyola University, 1942.

―――. "La obra de los misioneros españoles en Nuevo Mexico," *Revista de Geografía Española* (Madrid) 20 (1947): 12 unnumbered pages.

―――. "The Legend of Sierra Azul," *New Mexico Historical Review* 9 (1934): 113–58.

―――. "Our Debt to the Franciscan Missionaries of New Mexico," *The Americas* 1 (1944): 79–87.

―――. "Population of the El Paso District in 1692," *Mid-America* 23 (1941): 61–84.

―――. "The Recapture of Santa Fe, New Mexico, by the Spaniards—December 29–30, 1693," *Hispanic American Historical Review* 19 (1939): 443–63.

―――. "The Virgin of the Reconquest of New Mexico," *Mid-America*, n.s. 7 (1936): 79–87.

―――, ed. and trans. *First Expedition of Vargas into New Mexico, 1692*. Albuquerque: University of New Mexico Press, 1940.

Espinosa, José E. *Saints in the Valleys: Christian Sacred Images in the History, Life, and Folk Art of Spanish New Mexico*. Albuquerque: University of New Mexico Press, 1967.

Fernández Duro, Cesáreo. *Diego de Peñalosa y su descubrimiento del reino de Quivira*. Madrid: 1882.

Forbes, John D. *Apache, Navajo, and Spaniard*. Norman: University of Oklahoma Press, 1960.

Forrest, Earle R. *Missions and Pueblos of the Old Southwest*. 2 vols. Cleveland: Arthur H. Clark Co., 1929.

Goddard, E. P. *Indians of the Southwest*. New York: American Museum of Natural History, 1931.

Gómez Canedo, Lino. *Evangelización y conquista: Experiencia franciscana en Hispanoamerica*. Mexico City: Editorial Porrúa, S.A., 1977.

————, ed. *Fray Isidro Félix de Espinosa, O.F.M., Crónica de los Colegios de Propaganda Fide de la Nueva España*. Washington, D.C.: Academy of American Franciscan History, 1964.

Greenleaf, Richard E. "The Inquisition in Eighteenth Century New Mexico," *New Mexico Historical Review* 60 (1985): 29–60.

————, ed. *The Roman Catholic Church in Colonial Latin America*. New York: Alfred A. Knopf, 1971.

Habig, Marion A., O.F.M., "The Franciscan Provinces of Spanish North America," *The Americas* 1 (1944, 1945): 88–96, 215–30, 330–44.

Hackett, Charles W. "The Causes for the Failure of Otermín's Attempt to Reconquer New Mexico, 1681–1682." In *The Pacific Ocean in History*, pp. 439–51. Ed. H. Morse Stephens and Herbert E. Bolton. New York: The Macmillan Company, 1917.

————. "Otermín's Attempt to Reconquer New Mexico, 1681–1682," *Old Santa Fe* 3 (1916): 44–84, 103–32.

————. "The Revolt of the Pueblo Indians of New Mexico in 1680," *The Quarterly of the Texas State Historical Association* 15 (1911): 93–147.

————, ed. and trans. *Historical Documents Relating to New Mexico, Nueva Vizcaya, and Approaches Thereto, to 1773, Collected by Adolph F. A. Bandelier and Fanny R. Bandelier*. 3 vols. Washington, D.C.: Carnegie Institution, 1923–27.

————, and Charmion Clair Shelby, eds. and trans. *Revolt of the Pueblo Indians of New Mexico, and Otermín's Attempted Reconquest, 1680–1682*. 2 vols. Albuquerque: University of New Mexico Press, 1942.

Hallenbeck, Cleve. *Alvar Núñez Cabeza de Vaca: The Journey and Route of the First European to Cross the Continent of North America, 1534–1536*. Glendale, Calif.: Arthur H. Clark Co., 1940.

————. *The Journey of Fray Marcos de Niza*. Dallas: Southern Methodist University Press, 1949.

————. *Spanish Missions of the Old Southwest*. New York: Garden City Publishing Co., 1926.

Hammond, George P. *Don Juan de Oñate and the Founding of New Mexico*. Santa Fe: Historical Society of New Mexico, 1927.

————. *Expedition into New Mexico Made by Antonio de Espejo, 1582–1583, as Revealed in the Journal of Diego Pérez de Luxán, a Member of the Party*. Los Angeles: The Quivira Society, 1929.

————. *Narratives of the Coronado Expedition, 1540–1542*. Albuquerque: University of New Mexico Press, 1940.

————. *The Rediscovery of New Mexico, 1580–1594*. Albuquerque: University of New Mexico Press, 1966.

————, and Agapito Rey, eds. and trans. *Don Juan de Oñate, Colonizer of New Mexico, 1595–1628*. 2 vols. Albuquerque: University of New Mexico Press, 1940.

Handbook of North American Indians—Southwest. Vol. 9. Ed. Alfonso Ortiz. Washington, D.C.: Smithsonian Institution, 1979.

Hanke, Lewis. "The 'Requerimiento' and Its Interpreters," *Revista de Historia de América* 1 (1938): 1–10.

Hawley, Florence M. "The Role of Pueblo Social Organization in the Dissemination of Catholicism," *American Anthropologist* 48 (1946): 407–15.

Herrera, Alfred Charles. *Transcripción fiel del manuscrito del Libro Segundo de la "Historia de la conquista pérdida y restauración del reino de la Nueva México en la América Septentrional, por Juan de Villagutierre y Sotomayor."* Transcript of fols. 93–181. Madrid: privately printed, 1953.

Hewett, Edgar Lee. *Ancient Life in the American Southwest*. New York: Tudor Publishing Co., 1930.

————, and Reginald G. Fisher. *Mission Monuments of New Mexico*. Albuquerque: University of New Mexico Press, 1943.

Hodge, Frederick Webb. *Handbook of American Indians North of Mexico*. Bureau of American Ethnology Bulletin 30. 2 parts. Washington, D.C.: Government Printing Office, 1907–10.

————. "The Six Cities of Cíbola, 1581–1680," *New Mexico Historical Review* 1 (1926): 478–88.

Hull, Dorothy. "Castaño de Sosa's Expedition to New Mexico in 1590," *Old Santa Fe* 3 (1916): 307–32.

Jones, Oakah L., Jr. *Los Paisanos: Spanish Settlers on the Northern Frontier of New Spain*. Norman: University of Oklahoma Press, 1979.

————. *Pueblo Warriors and Spanish Conquest*. Norman: University of Oklahoma Press, 1966.

Kelly, H. W. "Franciscan Missions of New Mexico, 1740–1760," *New Mexico Historical Review* 15 (1940): 345–68; 16 (1941): 41–69, 148–83.

Kessell, John L. "Diego de Vargas: Another Look," *New Mexico Historical Review* 60 (1985): 8–28.

————. *Kiva, Cross, and Crown: The Pecos Indians and New Mexico, 1540–1840*. Washington, D.C.: National Park Service, 1979.

————. *The Missions of New Mexico Since 1776*. Albuquerque: University of New Mexico Press, 1980.

Kubler, George. *The Religious Architecture of New Mexico in the Colonial Period and Since the American Occupation*. Albuquerque: University of New Mexico Press, 1972.

Leonard, Irving A. *The Mercurio Volante of Don Carlos de Sigüenza y Góngora: An Account of the First Expedition of Don Diego de Vargas into New Mexico in 1692*. Los Angeles: The Quivira Society, 1932.

Lummis, Charles Fletcher. *The Land of Poco Tiempo*. New York: C. Scribner's Sons, 1893.

Maas, P. Otto. "Misiones de Nuevo México," *Archivo Ibero-Americano*, Año IV, nos. 13, 14 (1944): 5–31, 194–237.

———. *Viajes de Misioneros Franciscanos a la conquista de Nuevo México*. Sevilla: 1915.

———, ed. *Misiones de Nuevo Méjico: Documentos del Archivo General de Indias (Sevilla) publicados por primera vez y anotados*. Madrid: Imprenta Hijos de Timinuesa de los Rios, 1929.

McCloskey, Michael B., O.F.M. *The Formative Years of the Missionary College of Santa Cruz de Querétaro, 1683–1733*. Washington, D.C.: Academy of American Franciscan History, 1955.

Moorhead, Max L. *The Presidio, Bastion of the Spanish Borderlands*. Norman: University of Oklahoma Press, 1975.

Ocaranza, Fernando. *Establecimientos franciscanos en el misterioso reino de Nuevo Mexico*. Mexico City: privately printed, 1934.

Ortiz, Alfonso. *The Tewa World: Space, Time, Being, and Becoming in a Pueblo Society*. Chicago: University of Chicago Press, 1969.

Parmentier, Richard J. "The Mythological Triangle: Poseyemu, Montezuma, and Jesus in the Pueblos." In *Handbook of North American Indians—Southwest*, vol. 9, pp. 609–22. Ed. Alfonso Ortiz. Washington, D.C.: Smithsonian Institution, 1979.

Parsons, Elsie Clews. *Pueblo Indian Religion*. 2 vols. Chicago: University of Chicago Press, 1939.

Pérez Balséra, José. *Laudemus viros gloriosos et parentes nostros in generatione sua*. Madrid: privately printed, 1931.

Perrigo, Lynn I. *The American Southwest: Its Peoples and Cultures*. New York; Holt, Rinehart and Winston, 1971.

Porras Muñoz, Guillermo. *Iglesia y Estado en Nueva Vizcaya (1562–1821)*. Pamplona: Universidad de Navarra, 1966.

Prince, L. Bradford. *Spanish Mission Churches of New Mexico*. Cedar Rapids: The Torch Press, 1915.

Rey, Agapito. "Missionary Aspects of the Founding of New Mexico," *New Mexico Historical Review* 23 (1948): 22–31.

Riley, Carroll L. "Early Spanish-Indian Communication in the Greater Southwest," *New Mexico Historical Review* 46 (1971): 285–314.

Sánchez, Jane C. "Spanish-Indian Relations During the Otermín Administration, 1677–1683," *New Mexico Historical Review* 58 (1983): 133–51.

Sando, Joe S. *The Pueblo Indians*. San Francisco: Indian Historian Press, 1976.

———. "The Pueblo Revolt." In *Handbook of North American Indians—Southwest*, vol. 9, pp. 194–97. Ed. Alfonso Ortiz. Washington, D.C.: Smithsonian Institution, 1979.

Saravia, Atanasio G. *Los misioneros muertos en el norte de Nueva España*. Durango, 1920.

Sauer, Carl. *The Road to Cíbola*. Iberoamericana 3. Berkeley: University of California Press, 1932.

Scholes, France V. *Church and State in New Mexico, 1610–1650.* Santa Fe: Historical
    Society of New Mexico, 1937.
————. "Civil Government and Society in New Mexico in the Seventeenth Century,"
    New Mexico Historical Review 10 (1935): 71–111.
————. "Documents for the History of the New Mexican Missions in the Seven-
    teenth Century," *New Mexico Historical Review* 4 (1929): 45–58, 195–201.
————. "The First Decade of the Inquisition in New Mexico," *New Mexico Historical
    Review* 10 (1935): 195–241.
————. "Notes on the Jémez Missions in the Seventeenth Century," *El Palacio* 44
    (1938): 61–71, 93–102.
————. "Problems in the Early Ecclesiastical History of New Mexico," *New Mexico
    Historical Review* 7 (1932): 32–74.
————. "Royal Treasury Records Relating to the Province of New Mexico, 1596–
    1683," *New Mexico Historical Review* 50 (1975): 5–23, 139–64.
————. "The Supply Service of the New Mexican Missions in the Seventeenth Cen-
    tury," *New Mexico Historical Review* 5 (1930): 93–115, 186–210, 386–404.
————. *Troublous Times in New Mexico, 1659–1670.* Albuquerque: Historical Soci-
    ety of New Mexico, 1942.
————, and Eleanor B. Adams. "Inventories of Church Furnishings in Some of the
    New Mexico Missions, 1672." In *Dargan Historical Essays,* University of New Mex-
    ico Publications in History, No. 4, pp. 27–38. Albuquerque: University of New
    Mexico Press, 1952.
————, and Lansing B. Bloom. "Friar Personnel and Mission Chronology, 1598–
    1629," *New Mexico Historical Review* 19 (1944): 319–36; 20 (1945): 58–82.
Schroeder, Albert H. "Shifting for Survival in the Spanish Southwest," *New Mexico
    Historical Review* 43 (1968): 291–310.
————, and Dan S. Madson, eds. *A Colony on the Move: Gaspar Castaño de Sosa's Jour-
    nal, 1590–1591.* Santa Fe: School of American Research, 1965.
Shea, John G. *History of the Catholic Missions Among the Indian Tribes of the United States,
    1529–1854.* New York: E. Dunigan, 1855; P. J. Kennedy, n.d. (ca. 1896).
Simmons, Marc. "History of Pueblo-Spanish Relations to 1821." In *Handbook of North
    American Indians—Southwest,* vol. 9, pp. 178–93. Ed. Alfonso Ortiz. Washing-
    ton, D.C.: Smithsonian Institution, 1979.
————. *Spanish Government in New Mexico.* Albuquerque: University of New Mexico
    Press, 1968.
Smith, Watson. "Seventeenth Century Spanish Missions of the Western Pueblo Area,"
    In *The Smoke Signal,* vol. 21. Tucson: Tucson Corral of the Westerners, 1970.
Spicer, Edward H. *Cycles of Conquest: The Impact of Spain, Mexico, and the United States on
    the Indians of the Southwest, 1533–1960.* Tucson: University of Arizona Press, 1962.
Spiess, Lincoln Bunce. "Church Music in Seventeenth-Century New Mexico," *New
    Mexico Historical Review* 40 (1965): 5–21.
Stoddard, Ellwyn R., Richard L. Nostrand, and Jonathan P. West. *Borderlands Source-
    book: A Guide to the Literature on Northern New Spain and the American Southwest.* Nor-
    man: University of Oklahoma Press, 1983.

Strout, Clevy Lloyd. "The Resettlement of Santa Fe, 1695, the Newly Found Muster Roll," *New Mexico Historical Review* 53 (1978): 261–70.

Thomas, Alfred B. *After Coronado: Spanish Exploration Northeast of New Mexico, 1696–1727.* Norman: University of Oklahoma Press, 1935, 1966.

———. *Alonso de Posada Report, 1686: A Description of the Area of the Present Southern United States in the Seventeenth Century.* Pensacola, Fla.: The Perdido Bay Press, 1982.

———. *Forgotten Frontiers.* Norman: University of Oklahoma Press, 1932.

Tjarks, Alicia. "Demographic, Ethnic and Occupational Structure of New Mexico, 1790," *The Americas* 25 (1978): 45–88.

Twitchell, Ralph Emerson. "The Last Campaign of General de Vargas, 1704," *Old Santa Fe* 2 (1914): 66–72.

———. *The Leading Facts of New Mexican History.* Vols. 1 and 2 of 5. Cedar Rapids: The Torch Press, 1911–17.

———. *Old Santa Fe, the Story of New Mexico's Ancient Capital.* Santa Fe: New Mexico Publishing Company, 1925.

———. "The Pueblo Revolt of 1696: Extracts from the Journal of General Don Diego de Vargas," *Old Santa Fe* 3 (1916): 333–73.

———. "The Reconquest of New Mexico: Extracts from the Journal of General Don Diego de Vargas Zapata Luján Ponce de León," *Old Santa Fe* 1 (1914): 288–307, 420–35.

Vetancurt, Augustín de. *Teatro Mexicano.* 4 vols. Mexico City, 1698.

[Villagrá, Gaspar Pérez de.] *History of New Mexico by Gaspar Pérez de Villagrá, Alcalá, 1610.* Trans. Gilberto Espinosa. Intro. and notes by F. W. Hodge. Los Angeles: The Quivira Society, 1933.

Wagner, Henry R. "Fr. Marcos de Niza," *New Mexico Historical Review* 9 (1934): 184–227.

———. *The Spanish Southwest, 1542–1794: An Annotated Bibliography.* Albuquerque: The Quivira Society, 1937.

Walter, Paul A. F. "Mission Churches in New Mexico," *El Palacio* 5 (1918): 113–23.

Weber, David J. *The Mexican Frontier, 1821–1846.* Albuquerque: University of New Mexico Press, 1982.

———, ed. *New Spain's Far Northern Frontier: Essays on Spain in the American West, 1540–1821.* Albuquerque: University of New Mexico Press, 1979.

Weigle, Marta. *Brothers of Light, Brothers of Blood: The Penitentes of the Southwest.* Albuquerque: University of New Mexico Press, 1976.

———. *A Penitente Bibliography.* Albuquerque: University of New Mexico Press, 1976.

Winship, George Parker, ed. and trans. *The Coronado Expedition, 1540–1542.* U.S. Bureau of American Ethnology 14th Annual Report, Part I. Washington, D.C.; 1896.

Zárate Salmerón, Gerónimo de. "Relaciones de todas las cosas que en el Nuevo México se han visto y sabido, asi por mar como por tierra, desde el año de 1538 hasta el de 1626." In *Documentos para la historia de Mexico*, 3a. ser., vol. 3, pp. 30–38. Mexico City, 1856.

INDEX

Abo Pueblo: 19

Acoma Pueblo: 7–8, 24, 33, 35, 38, 41, 46, 48, 51, 52, 54, 66, 67, 79, 82, 83, 116, 150, 167, 180, 226, 227, 232, 239, 247, 261, 265, 267, 271, 287

Aguatuvi Pueblo: 36, 67

Aguilar, Alonso de: 270

Alameda: 24, 30, 84

Albuquerque: 58

Alcalde: 93–96, 98, 99, 101, 103, 105

Alcalde mayor: 10, 28, 34, 51, 92–94, 148, 149, 166, 167, 171, 175, 177, 178, 180, 185, 189, 193, 207–10, 212, 227, 239, 240, 244, 251, 258–70, 274, 275, 288

Alcaldía: 10, 46, 260

Alday, Martín de: 68

Almagre (vermilion): 79–80, 83–84

Almazán, Alonso de: 262

Almazán, Doña Juana de: 262, 264

Almazán, Leonor: 262

Alonso, Fray Juan: 136

Alpuente, Fray Juan: 51, 54, 72, 74, 87, 95, 97, 129–31, 156, 165, 172–73, 185, 188, 197, 204, 205, 208, 209, 244, 245, 256, 264, 279

Alto de Cuma: 196

Alvarez, Fray Juan: 65, 68, 248

Anaya Almazán, Francisco de: 93, 174, 259, 266

Apache Indians: 19, 24, 28, 30–33, 38, 39, 43, 49, 54, 55, 58, 71, 126, 167, 174, 189, 196, 209, 210, 215, 226, 230, 247, 249, 260, 267, 271, 288, 292; *see also* Chilmo Apaches; Colorado River Apaches; Cuartelejo Apaches; Faraón Apaches; and Navajo Apaches

Arbizu, Fray José: 48, 50, 170–72, 177–79, 185, 200–201, 205, 210, 214, 215, 220, 223–24, 230–32, 243, 245, 247, 249, 258, 261, 263

Archuleta, Juan de: 259, 261, 267, 268

Audiencia, Royal, Mexico City: 9, 228, 242, 254

Avila, Spain: 140

Aviniz, Fray Miguel, Father Guardian of the Franciscan Convent at El Paso: 54, 246

Ayeta, Fray Francisco de: 32

Azevedo, Fray Antonio de: 156, 165, 204, 208, 253

Baamonde (Vahamonde), Fray Antonio: 41, 72

Barreda, Domingo de la: 151, 168, 190, 212, 240, 289

Barroso, Fray Cristóbal Alonso: 63, 67, 82, 83

Bartolito (Pueblo Indian): 267

Bartolo (Pueblo Indian): *see also* Ojeda, Bartolomé de

Benavides, Fray Alonso de: 15, 19–20; author of *Memorial,* 20

Bernalillo: 47, 49, 51, 55, 157, 176, 185, 192, 194, 198, 199, 204, 227, 230, 240, 251, 253, 255, 260, 261, 265, 267–69, 285, 287, 288, 291

Betanzos, Diego: 261

Blessed Virgin of Remedies: 96, 98

Bolsas, Antonio (Pueblo Indians): 34, 43, 44

Bolton, Herbert E.: 4

Burgos, Spain: 135, 140, 141

Cabeza de Vaca, Alvar Núñez: 4

Cabildo: 10, 11, 28, 43, 68, 73, 84, 112

Cabildo abierto: 42, 73

Cachina (Pueblo Indian): 266, 270

Cacique: 93, 270

Cádiz, Spain: 16

Canse Indians: 228

Carbonel, Fray Antonio: 50, 72, 74, 87, 94, 95, 109, 110, 117–18, 165, 183, 185, 197–98, 204, 205, 208, 211, 215, 219–23, 243, 245, 247, 249, 258, 261, 286

Casa de Contratación: 16

Casas Grandes: 140

Catalonia, Spain: 244

Catiti, Alonso (Pueblo Indian): 34, 36–38

Caudi: 33; *see* Pueblo Indian Revolt of 1680

Cazares, Juan de: 266

Celaya: 80

Chama River: 7

Charles II, King: 63, 64, 82

Chavarría, Fray Diego de: 176, 185, 195, 205, 253, 286, 287

Chávez, Fernando de: 51, 65, 239, 240, 258, 259, 265, 267–69

Chililí Pueblo: 18

Chilmo Apaches: 167

Chimayó: 48, 166, 171, 177, 178; Chimayó mountains, 272

Chimayó River: 171

Chumilla, Fray Julián: 135

Ciénaga of Cochití: 146
Cisneros, Antonio: 278
Cochití, La Cieneguilla de: 44, 45
Cochití Pueblo: 18, 24, 30, 37, 38, 51, 71, 75,
    84, 99, 100, 107, 108, 110, 112, 116–18,
    146, 148, 158, 170, 185, 199, 206, 211,
    212, 220, 234, 239, 251, 258–60, 263,
    267, 272–74, 286, 287, 291; Cochití moun-
    tains, 52
Colegio de Misioneros de Propaganda Fide de la
    Santa Cruz de Querétaro: *see* College of Santa
    Cruz de Querétaro
College of Santa Cruz de Querétaro: 16–17, 41,
    135, 234n.1, 250n.2, 285
Colorado River Apaches: 75
Commissary General of the Order of Saint
    Francis of New Spain: 16, 50, 53, 242, 288,
    292–94
Contreras, Fray Buenaventura de: 72, 74, 80,
    254
Contreras, José de: 263
Convent of Our Father Saint Francis, Santa Fe:
    246, 257, 291
Convent of Our Lady of Guadalupe, El Paso: 65,
    74
Convent of Santa Cruz de Querétaro: 16
Convent of Santiago de Querétaro: 243
Corbera, Fray Francisco: 39, 48, 50, 63, 64,
    66–68, 72, 74, 82, 87, 102, 103, 121–28,
    132, 158–59, 170n.2, 181–83, 185, 202,
    205, 210, 215, 243, 247, 249, 261, 264,
    286
Coronado, Francisco Vázquez de: 4, 5
Corral, Fray Juan Antonio del: 72, 74, 110,
    133–35, 253, 267
Cortés, Hernán: 4
Cortés, Juan: 262
Council of the Indies: 5, 9
Cristóbal (Pueblo Indian): 167
Cruz, Juan de la: 77
Cuartelejo Apaches: 54
Cuniju, Luis (Pueblo Indian): 34, 270
Custodian (*custodio*): *see* Holy Custody of the
    Conversion of Saint Paul of New Mexico
Custody (*custodia*): *see* Holy Custody of the Con-
    version of Saint Paul of New Mexico
Cuyamungué Pueblo: 75, 102, 116, 148, 180,
    188, 196, 261, 263, 277, 291

Damiana, Doña: 79
Daza, Fray Juan: 72, 74, 86, 156, 158, 179
Definidor: defined, 15; *definidores* of Custody of
    New Mexico, 156, 165, 185
Definitorio: defined, 15; see also *Definitorio* of the

Holy Custody of the Conversion of Saint Paul
    of New Mexico
Definitorio of the Holy Custody of the Conversion
    of Saint Paul of New Mexico: 15, 293; re-
    quests military protection for the missions,
    47, 155–56, 158; written petitions of, pre-
    sented to the governor, 163–65, 203–204
Diaguillo (Pueblo Indian): 247
Diez, Fray José: 41, 50, 72, 74, 87, 107,
    115–17, 163, 166, 174–76, 185, 188,
    196–97, 205, 211, 215, 234–36, 249, 285
Domingo (Pueblo Indian): 101, 107, 163, 166,
    174, 180, 260, 263, 270, 271, 275
Doñana: 66

El Alamo: 261, 262, 274
El Cacacha: 170–71, 177
El Jaca (Pueblo Indian): 34, 36
El Paso: 37, 39, 41, 48, 53, 58, 74, 78, 80, 84,
    101, 102, 106, 127, 136, 140, 144, 147,
    193, 232, 246, 248, 254, 255, 287, 293
El Paso del Río del Norte: 65, 68, 82, 83, 106,
    121, 246, 249, 255, 256, 261, 292, 293
El Paso district: 17, 32, 35, 37, 39, 40, 41, 55,
    58
El Tempano (Pueblo Indian): 260, 274
El Zepe (Pueblo Indian): 99, 100
Encomienda: 10, 12, 29
Epidemics: 19, 24, 53
Espeleta, Fray José de: 36
Estufa: see Kiva
Eulate, Juan de: 29–30

Faraón Apaches: 167
Farfán, Fray Francisco: 45, 80, 83, 84, 147, 254
Felipe, Don (Pueblo Indian): 259, 262, 266,
    270
Felipe: 247
Figueroa, Fray José de: 36
Fiscals: 93, 96, 98, 101, 103, 105, 116
Flanders: 126, 140, 239
Florida: 4
France: 140
Franciscan martyrs: 24, 30, 35–36, 50, 54, 55,
    243–44, 246–47, 249–50, 261–62
Franciscan personnel in New Mexico before
    1680: 5, 7, 18, 19, 24, 33
Francisco (Pueblo Indian): 261, 263

Galdámes, José Manuel de: 264
Galisteo Pueblo: 18, 42, 166, 171, 177
Gallegos, José: 65
Galve, Conde de, viceroy: 79, 80, 82, 147, 212,
    280

García de Noriega, Juan: 68
García Marín, Fray José: 41, 108, 135–41, 174, 185, 187, 201–202, 205, 209, 224–25, 253, 259
Gómez, Francisco: 71
Gonzales, Fray Miguel: 243
Gran Quivira: 263
Granillo, Luis: 166, 178, 185, 216, 272, 278
Griego, Juan (Pueblo Indian): 104, 275
Gualpi Pueblo: 67

Heresy: 14; heretics, 222
Herrera, Melchor de: 264
Hidalgo, Pedro: 83
Hinojosa, Fray Joaquín de: 82, 121
Holy Custody of the Conversion of Saint Paul of New Mexico: 14–16, 63, 65, 66, 74, 80, 82, 85, 86, 117, 157, 163, 283
Holy Office of the Inquisition: 15, 28, 30, 31, 86, 91, 107
Hopi (Moqui) Pueblos: 24, 25, 33, 38, 41, 43, 46, 48, 51, 52, 66, 67, 79, 82, 116, 122, 150, 159, 167, 174, 180, 226, 231, 232, 233, 239, 260, 265
Huerta, Toribio de la: 37

Inquisition: *see* Holy Office of the Inquisition
Isleta Pueblo: 18, 24, 30, 33, 37
Isleta del Paso del Río del Norte, Pueblo of: 84

Jacona Pueblo: 75, 102, 123, 127, 148, 180, 265, 291
Janos Indians: 167
Jémez pueblos: 19, 24, 30, 34, 35, 38, 39, 41, 44, 45, 49, 51, 52, 55, 71, 75, 77, 78, 80, 82, 91, 96–98, 110, 112, 144, 149, 157, 167, 170, 184, 185, 189, 192–94, 198, 212, 225–27, 233, 244, 247, 252, 257, 261, 265, 266, 270, 271, 285, 286, 288; San Diego del Monte, 19, 98, 148, 158, 170, 183–84, 186, 189, 193, 200, 206, 212, 243, 249, 252, 271, 285; San José de Jémez, 19, 158
Jesús, Fray Juan de: 35
Jesús María, Fray Domingo de: 41, 72, 74, 206, 209, 234
Jesús María Casañas, Fray Francisco de: 41, 50, 72, 74, 87, 99, 183–84, 186, 189, 193, 200, 206, 212, 228–30, 244, 245, 247, 250, 250n.2, 251, 252, 270
Jiménez de Cisneros, Fray Alfonso: 51, 173, 185, 198–99, 206, 211, 232–34, 239, 251, 253, 258, 287
Jironza Petriz de Cruzate, Diego: 37

Jongopavi Pueblo: 67
Jorge, Antonio: 65, 94, 100, 112

Keres pueblos: 19, 34, 36, 38, 44, 67, 78, 91, 94–97, 99, 100, 107, 110, 112, 144, 146, 148, 149, 157, 167, 189, 192, 193, 194, 211, 212, 225, 239, 247, 257, 258, 260, 265, 267, 269, 271, 272, 286
Kiva (*estufa*): 23, 33, 94, 134, 158, 181, 253, 264, 288

La Bajada: 42
La Ciénaga: 261, 262
La Cieneguilla: 113, 262
La Isleta Pueblo: 292; *see also* Isleta del Paso del Río del Norte
Lara, Miguel de: 267, 268, 271, 273
Ledesma, Fray Clemente de, Father Provincial: 54, 235, 246, 251
Llinás, Fray Antonio: 16
Lobato, Matías: 261
Lorenzo (servant): 247
Los Cerrillos: 261, 262
Lucero de Godoy, Francisco: 91, 93, 94
Lucero de Godoy, Juan de Dios: 65, 68

Madrid, Lorenzo: 216
Madrid, Roque: 51, 65, 167, 174, 177, 216, 220, 259, 260, 263, 264, 266, 272, 276
Madrid, Spain: 15
Malacate, Antonio (Pueblo Indian): 34
Maldonado, Fray Lucas: 35
Mandón, mandónes: 92
Manso, Juan: 25, 30–31
Manso Indians: 167, 247, 248, 251, 274
Matha, Fray Pedro de: 183, 185, 189, 193, 199, 206, 212, 227–28, 287
Mexicans: 205, 261
Mexico: 44, 45, 47, 53, 57, 80, 82, 188, 200, 262, 293
Mexico City: 4, 9, 25, 47, 53, 55, 212, 229, 243
Michoacán: 16, 234, 285
Missionary College of Santa Cruz de Querétaro: *see* College of Santa Cruz de Querétaro
Missioin-supply service: 19, 21, 25–27, 32, 33
Missions: 3, 17–24, 46–50, 55, 57; *see also* names of Indian pueblos
Missions system: 3, 17, 23–24; Benavides's description of daily life in, 20, 21–23; mission complexes, 20–21; churches, 21 (*see also* Religious art; Mission-supply service); trades and crafts in, 21; religious instruction in, 21–22, 23; administration of 22; religious processions in, 22; punishment of Indians in, 25

Mizquía, Lázaro de: 85, 278
Molina, Simón de: 261
Montenegro, Alonso de la Peña Rivas y: 8 n.8,
    72, 73, 227
Monzabál, Fray Manuel de: 242–43
Moqui pueblos: *see* Hopi pueblos
Morales, Francisco de: 242
Morales, Juan de: 295
Moreno, Fray Antonio: 50, 107, 243, 247, 249,
    262–64, 286
Moxonabi Pueblo: 67
Muñiz de Luna, Fray Miguel: 63, 82
Muñoz de Castro, Fray Juan: 46, 72, 74, 86,
    91, 101, 106, 107, 122; reports to Fray
    Francisco de Vargas, 142–46

Nambé Pueblo: 18, 71, 75, 77, 165, 166,
    170 n.2, 180, 183, 185, 187, 198, 205, 211,
    215, 220, 223, 243, 249, 262–64, 270,
    275, 277, 286, 291
Naranjo, Domingo (Pueblo Indian): 34 n.41
Naranjo, Lucas (Pueblo Indian): 51, 52, 103,
    270, 278 n.2, 278–79
Naranjo, Pedro (Pueblo Indian): 36
Narváez Balverde, Fray José: 72
Navajo Apaches: 140, 141
Navajo Indians: 55, 58, 75, 158, 210, 215
Navarro, Fray Blas: 41, 163, 173, 185, 196,
    205, 210, 245, 253, 261, 285, 287
Negroes: 11, 13, 24, 34 n.41
New Galicia: 41
New Mexico: as a mission field in the seven-
    teenth century, 3, 9, 11; Spanish society in,
    3, 11–14; Franciscans as the learned class in,
    13–14; agricultural innovations by Span-
    iards, 5, 7, 22–23; Spanish population of, 7,
    11, 33, 45, 47, 50, 58, 146, 257; Spanish
    government structure in, 9–11; racial com-
    position of area of Spanish settlement, 11, 13
New Spain, viceroyalty of: 4, 5, 9, 14–16, 24,
    27, 33, 37, 41, 79, 80, 82, 135, 147, 189,
    190, 229, 241, 285, 288, 289
New Vizcaya: 39, 41, 292, 295
Niza, Fray Marcos de: 4

Obregón, Fray Antonio de: 72, 74, 87, 104,
    105, 253, 263, 264
Ojeda, Bartolomé de (Pueblo Indian): 51,
    91–92, 96, 167, 239, 240 n.1, 240–41,
    247, 265, 267, 269–70
Olguín, Juan: 157, 167, 244, 247, 288
Oñate, Juan de: 5–9, 14, 18
Oraibi Pueblo: 36
Ortega y Montañés (viceroy): 241, 280, 292
Otermín, Antonio de: 32, 34, 37, 84

Páez Hurtado, Juan: 257
Paredes, Count of (viceroy): 84
Parral: 37, 41, 53, 84, 229
Patron saints of missions, names of: 94, 97, 98,
    115, 117, 136, 157, 158, 176, 180, 184,
    206, 219, 220, 223, 230, 234, 236
Pecos Pueblo: 19, 38, 41–44, 50–52, 71, 75,
    78, 91, 92, 132–33, 144, 166, 171, 174,
    175, 179, 180, 185, 188, 197, 206, 209,
    216–18, 233, 252, 253, 257, 259, 260,
    262–64, 266, 270, 272, 274–76, 279, 283,
    286–88, 291
Pecuchillo (Pueblo Indian): 172
Peña Blanca: 175
Peñalosa, Diego Dionisio de: 24, 31
Peralta, Pedro de: 7, 10, 17
Perea, Fray Estévan de: 15, 18–20; author of
    Verdadera relación, 20
Perea, Juan de: 259
Pérez, Antonio: 68
Peru: 15
Philip III: 9
Philip IV: 20
Picurís Pueblo: 19, 24, 34, 36, 41, 44–47, 49,
    52, 54, 55, 71, 75, 82, 112, 147, 148, 163,
    166, 170 n.2, 173, 185, 188, 193, 205, 210,
    230, 233, 257, 258, 261, 274, 275, 284,
    286, 287, 291
Piedra Blanca: 166
Pinjui (Pueblo Indian): 170; *El Cacacha,* 171,
    177
Pío, Fray Antonio Sánchez de: 217
Piros Indians: 178, 292
Poheyemo: 33; *see also* Pueblo Indian Revolt of
    1680
Pojoaque Pueblo: 55, 75, 102, 148, 223, 280,
    291
Popé (Pueblo Indian): 32–36, 38; *see* Pueblo In-
    dian Revolt of 1680
Presidio at Santa Fe: 10, 41, 187, 191, 215
Prieto, Fray Gerónimo: 41, 48, 72, 74, 87, 103,
    104, 118–21, 170 n.2, 179–80, 185, 187,
    202–203, 205, 209, 224, 234, 285
Principales: 209
Proverbs: 179, 200, 220, 239, 248, 248 n.3
Province of the Holy Gospel (Santo Evangelio):
    14, 15, 18–19, 54, 221, 235, 283, 292
Provincial of the Franciscan Province of the Holy
    Gospel: 293, 294
Puebla: 229
Pueblo Indian Revolt of 1680: 3, 17, 19,
    32–37, 44, 47, 58, 164, 168, 181, 182,
    202, 217, 218; underlying causes of, 3–4,
    24–25, 27–32, 33–34, 71; restored New
    Mexico to Pueblo Indian rule, 36–38

Pueblo Indian Revolt of 1696: advance warnings from Franciscans, 47–50, 58, 158–59, 163–65, 170–84, 195–203, 216–34; Franciscans plead for adequate military protection, 47–50, 163–234; reports of perilous situation at missions, 48, 49, 50, 170–234; governor places small military guard at missions, 49, 165–67, 186–89, 208–13; governor states that missionaries' fears are based on rumors and suppositions, 49, 186–90, 191, 216–34; most of the missionaries withdraw to Santa Fe, Santa Cruz, and Bernalillo, 49, 190–234; outbreak of the revolt, 50–51, 54, 55, 239–56, 258–70; continued hostilities, 51–53, 54–55, 270–80; factors in failure of the revolt, 53, 257–83; restoration of missions, 55, 57, 290–95; historical significance of suppression of the revolt, 57–58; peace restored, 292–93
Pueblo Indians: 3, 4, 5, 7; clash between Pueblo medicine men and Franciscan missionaries, 3–4, 13, 24, 25, 35–36, 48, 50–52, 78 (see also Pueblo Indian Revolt of 1680; Pueblo Indian Revolt of 1696); population of Christianized Indians, 9, 19, 19 n.21, 33, 39; exploitation of, 10, 28–30; population of, 11, 17, 33, 55, 58; see also names of pueblos and Pueblo tribes

Querétaro: 80

Rael de Aguilar, Alfonso: 64, 65, 68, 73, 80, 85, 91, 94–99, 102–13, 147, 151, 262
Ramírez, Fray Diego de: 176
Ramírez, Fray José: 185, 227
Real de minas: 148
Real de San Lorenzo: 292
Religious art: 21, 27, 27 n.33, 40, 40 n.48, 67, 85, 124, 264
Reneros de Posada, Pedro: 37
Requerimiento: 7, 220
Río Abajo: 10
Río Arriba: 10
Río del Norte: 140, 146, 251, 274, 275, 277; see also Río Grande
Río Grande: 7, 24, 45, 51; upper region of, 37, 47, 50; valley of the, 10, 11
Río Puerco: 241
Rodríguez, Fray Agustín: 5
Rosas, Luis de: 30
Royal Council of the Treasury, Mexico City: 9, 149
Royal Council of the Treasury and War, Mexico City: 82
Royal Junta, Mexico City: 149, 150, 290

Royal Office of Government and War, Mexico City: 212
Royal Ordinance of 1573: 5, 7; "just war," 7, 8, 8 n.8
Ruiz de Cáceres, Juan: 93, 100, 108, 112, 174, 179, 185, 275

San Antonio, Fray Salvador de: 44–45, 64, 71–74, 79–82, 86, 106, 122, 143; disagrees with Governor Vargas, 42, 44–45, 71–85
San Antonio River: 167
Sánchez, José: 262
Sánchez Chamuscado, Francisco: 5
San Cristóbal Pueblo: 48, 75, 100, 104, 148, 166, 170, 170 n.2, 171–73, 177–80, 185, 187, 197, 201, 205, 209, 210, 214, 217, 220, 223, 230–33, 243, 245, 249, 258, 260, 261, 263, 266, 284, 285, 291
Sandía Pueblo: 18, 75
San Felipe Pueblo: 18, 24, 30, 38, 41, 44, 50, 51, 75, 78, 91, 92, 94, 109, 110, 133–35, 148, 158, 170, 185, 239, 253, 255, 258, 259, 260, 265–67, 269, 283, 286, 287, 291; mesa of, 292
San Gabriel: 7
San Ildefonso Pueblo: 18, 44, 48, 49, 71, 75, 76, 79, 100, 102, 108, 121–28, 138, 143, 148, 159, 170 n.2, 174, 180–83, 185, 187, 205, 211, 214, 215, 218, 223, 230, 240, 243, 245, 249, 261, 263, 264, 280, 284, 286, 291
San Juan de Jémez: see Jémez pueblos
San Juan de los Caballeros: 7, 144, 148, 187, 209, 214, 259, 261, 291; see also San Juan Pueblo
San Juan Pueblo: 18, 32, 48, 49, 51, 71, 75, 92, 100, 103, 104, 108, 118–21, 129, 137, 146, 149, 167, 170 n.2, 180, 185, 193, 205, 209, 212, 214, 223, 233, 271, 275, 277, 284, 285
San Lázaro Pueblo: 18, 34, 71, 75, 104, 105, 108, 143, 148, 171, 174, 178, 180, 210, 214
Santa Ana Pueblo: 18, 36, 38, 41, 44, 50, 51, 75, 78, 92, 94, 129–31, 147, 148, 167, 212, 236, 239, 247, 251, 253, 255, 265, 267, 268, 283, 285–88, 292
Santa Clara Pueblo: 55, 75, 103, 107, 108, 135–41, 143, 146, 148, 170 n.2, 174, 177, 180, 181, 185, 187, 203, 205, 209, 214, 223, 225, 266, 270, 275, 277, 279, 285, 291, 292
Santa Cruz: 49–51, 54, 55, 58, 174, 177, 187, 192, 201, 202, 204, 206, 209–11, 214, 215, 224, 225, 253, 257–61, 263, 264,

Santa Cruz (*continued*)
  266, 267, 271, 272, 274–77, 279, 285,
  286, 290; population of, 47, 58
Santa Fe: 7, 10, 14, 18, 27, 30, 33–35, 39,
  41–43, 45–51, 54, 55, 58, 63, 66, 67,
  71–73, 75, 79–81, 83, 85, 87, 91, 92, 100,
  101, 105, 106, 110–12, 114, 122, 130,
  133, 136, 146, 147, 151, 155, 157, 165,
  168–70, 170n.2, 172–74, 176, 186, 187,
  190, 192, 194–97, 204, 207, 211, 215,
  216, 218, 224, 240, 248, 253, 255–57,
  259, 261, 262, 265, 267, 280, 283–87,
  291, 292, 294; population of, 13, 58
Santa María, Fray Agustín de: 36
Santo Domingo Pueblo: 17, 18, 34, 38, 44, 45,
  92, 99, 100, 107–109, 128–29, 146, 148,
  149, 158, 211, 212, 260, 262, 270, 273,
  286, 291
Sarmiento y Valladares, José, viceroy: 288, 294,
  295
Scholes, France V.: 20, 25, 27, 29
Senecú Pueblo: 37, 136, 292
Sierra, Fray Antonio de: 72, 74
Sierra Azul: 39
Silver mines: 148–59
Sinaloa: 39, 293, 295
Socorro Pueblo: 37, 292
Sombrerete: 58
Sonora: 39, 293, 295
Sotelo Osorio, Felipe: 30
Spain: 16, 82, 135, 140, 228
Suma Indians: 292

Tabardillo: 241
Tampico: 15
Tano pueblos: 19, 34, 38, 41, 42, 44, 45, 54,
  55, 64, 71, 75, 101, 106, 107, 111, 112,
  115, 144, 146, 148, 166, 174, 180, 182,
  193, 196, 207, 210, 213, 214, 216, 217,
  220, 223, 225, 230, 258, 260, 271, 274,
  275, 285, 286, 291
Taos Pueblo: 19, 24, 29, 30, 32, 33, 34, 36,
  38, 41, 44, 45, 46, 49, 52, 54, 71, 75, 82,
  147–49, 166, 167, 170n.2, 176, 185, 188,
  193, 195, 205, 210, 230, 249, 257, 258,
  261, 266, 274, 275, 284, 286, 287, 291
Tarahumara: 80
Tehuacán: 259
Tesuque Pueblo: 50, 51, 71, 74, 77, 101, 107,
  115–17, 146, 147, 163, 166, 170n.2, 180,
  185, 187, 196, 205, 211, 215, 219, 253,
  261, 263, 270, 272, 274–76, 279, 283–85,
  287, 291
Tewa pueblos: 19, 32, 38, 41, 42, 44, 45, 54,

  64, 71, 75, 76, 79, 100, 101, 106, 107,
  111, 112, 140, 144, 146–48, 166, 174,
  178, 180, 185, 193, 213, 225, 230, 259,
  266, 270–72, 274, 277, 286, 291
Texas: 4, 135, 228
Third Order of Saint Francis: 57n.89, 148,
  250n.2
Thuogue, Domingo (Pueblo Indian): 174, 175
Tilimi: 33; *see also* Pueblo Indian Revolt of 1680
Tiwa pueblos: 19, 31, 84, 128, 163, 231, 292
Tlascala: 80
Tlatole, tlatolero: 77, 165, 166, 180, 220, 229,
  230, 273
Tleume: 33; *see also* Pueblo Indian Revolt of
  1680
Tompiro Indians: 19, 31
Torre, Antonio de la: 259
Treviño, Juan Francisco de: 31, 32
Trizio, Fray Miguel de: 41, 109, 128–29, 185,
  189, 193, 198, 206, 212, 225–27, 252, 253
Trujillo, Augustín: 264, 265
Trujillo, Fray José: 36
Trujillo, Mateo: 262, 265
Tupatú, Don Luis, Pueblo Indian: 34, 36, 38

Ulibarri, Juan de: 151, 259, 261, 263, 264
Umbiro, Don Diego (Pueblo Indian): 266, 270
Urioste, Martín de: 168, 190, 275
Ute Indians: 38, 51, 58, 167, 174, 185, 189,
  209, 210, 214, 224, 239, 265

Val, Fray Juan de: 35
Valladolid, Spain: 241, 242
Valverde, Antonio de: 168, 179, 190, 258, 275
Vargas, Diego de, governor of New Mexico: 4,
  39, 57, 57n.89, 165–68, 186–90, 208–
  13, 239–40, 257–80, 284–89, 292–94;
  grants religious authority to Franciscans, 39,
  63–68; first expedition of into New Mexico,
  39–40; colonizing expedition of, 40–42; and
  battle of Santa Fe, 43–44; in continued hostilities, 44–46; installs Pueblo Indian officials
  at pueblos, 46, 93, 95–106, 110; and return
  to peaceful activities, 46–47, 86, 91–92;
  and reestablishment of missions, 46–47,
  86–87, 91–146; requests supplies and additional colonists, 50, 149–50, 190; frees
  Pueblo Indian hostages and slaves at Santa Fe,
  110–13; *see also* Pueblo Indian Revolt of 1696
Vargas, Fray Francisco de, custodian of Holy
  Custody of New Mexico: 46, 47, 53–55,
  57–58, 106–109, 113–15, 117, 129, 132,
  133, 146, 147, 155–56, 158, 163, 165,
  170, 184–84, 190–94, 203–208, 213–16,

232, 234–36, 240, 241, 243–57, 267, 283–84, 289–92, 294; obtains detailed reports from the missionaries, 46, 113–46, 158–59, 168–86, 190–203, 213–34; policy conflicts with the governor, 48–49, 54, 57–58, 244, 248, 254; *see also* Pueblo Indian Revolt of 1696
Velasco, Fray Fernando de: 71
Vera Cruz: 16
Villa de Santa Fe: *see* Santa Fe
Villalobos, Fray Enrique de: 225
Villa Nueva: *see* Santa Cruz
Villa Nueva de Españoles de Santa Cruz: *see* Santa Cruz
Villa Nueva de Santa Cruz: *see* Santa Cruz
Villa Neuva de Santa Cruz de Españoles Mexicanos: *see* Santa Cruz
Villa Nueva de Santa Cruz de Españoles Mexicanos del Rey Nuestro Señor Carlos Segundo: *see* Santa Cruz
Visita, definition of: 71 n.2

West Indies: 4

Xenome, Diego (Pueblo Indian): 270
Ximénez, Fray Lázaro: 9
Xongopavi Pueblo: 36

Ye, Juan de (Pueblo Indian): 41, 42, 71, 75, 76
Ye, Lorenzo de (Pueblo Indian): 93, 166
Yope Tete, Cristóbal (Pueblo Indian): 34, 105, 171, 172
Yunque: 7

Zacatecas: 58, 149, 257
Zavaleta, Fray Juan de: 72, 74, 165, 170 n.2, 172, 195, 204, 205, 208, 253, 287
Zeinos, Fray Diego: 72, 74, 81, 82, 85–87, 92, 132–33, 188
Zia Pueblo: 18, 37, 38, 41, 44, 48, 50, 71, 75, 78, 91, 92, 95, 97–99, 129–31, 149, 157–58, 167, 170, 181, 183, 185, 189, 193, 198, 206, 212, 227, 245, 247, 251, 253, 267–69, 271, 272, 283, 286–88, 292
Zuñi Pueblo: 24, 33, 38, 48, 51, 52, 66, 67, 79, 82, 83, 116, 122, 150, 167, 174, 180, 226–28, 232, 239, 261, 265, 271